AF538950

DEVELOPMENT OF JOURNALISM

DEVELOPMENT OF JOURNALISM

(For PG Diploma & Degree Courses in Journalism & Mass Media)

Seema Sharma

ANMOL PUBLICATIONS PVT. LTD.
NEW DELHI - 110 002 (INDIA)

ANMOL PUBLICATIONS PVT. LTD.
4374/4B, Ansari Road, Daryaganj
New Delhi - 110 002
Ph.: 23261597, 23278000
Visit us at: www.anmolpublications.com

Development of Journalism

First Published, 2005

ISBN 81-261-2342-7

PRINTED IN INDIA

Published by J.L. Kumar for Anmol Publications Pvt. Ltd., New Delhi - 110 002 and Printed at Mehra Offset Press, Delhi.

Contents

Preface

In Modern world, Journalism is one discipline, which attracts people like any thing, but, it is equally challenging and drastic in cases. Particularly, under the new world order and in current global scenario, its value has increased manifold.

Apart from being a glorious profession, Journalism, today is a full-fledged subject, mastery of which leads one to a successful career and an all powerful status in society.

As a discipline, Journalism requires proper training and a comprehensive course, if possible. Although, there is no defined qualification for appointment as a journalist, in any capacity, in any media organisation, yet it is always better to be properly qualified and well-equipped with all essential knowledge.

Of course, there are books on Journalism but not in a great number. And, if one goes selective, then only a few books would rest in hand, as there is still a dearth for exclusive and exhaustive books on several streams of Journalism.

This series of books on Journalism is an effort to fill the abovesaid vaccum only. Here are books on all subjects and topics, related to Journalism. The undersigned is confident enough that this humble endeavour would prove to be worthy on the basis of its merits and receive a warm acceptance by students of journalism, scholars and the working journalists, as well.

— Editor

1

Introduction

To, initiate it should be emphasised that despite being challenging and significant, there are many areas in the mass media of communications where research needs to be undertaken in earnest. Thus, for instance, while we have an entire range of studies showing the impact of mass media on psychological processes like attitudes and perception, there is not much range and depth in research focused on mass media's impact on institutions like family, polity, and economy. There have been efforts in these areas too but they are mostly in the form of small research papers or seminar presentations at the most, often necessitated by projects that sprung up at the instance of agencies every now and then, much like a fad. Novel experiments like SITE have remained buried in the bulging files of government departments, with the latter having no time to spare for follow-up.

It is strange to note that even while we survived with scant research, the media grew in leaps and bounds. The media growth was driven more by circumstances, increasing consumerism and literacy, than any conscious design on the part of the government. In fact, a large part of the onus for the deficiency in media research lies on the government, with the academia having made no concerted efforts to force the government for a re-thinking. No wonder, a couple of institutions that are devoted exclusively for 'so-called' media research are no more than mere training centres of budding bureaucrats and journalists, who pursue in their practice little of what they learn. As long as the coffers are full no one has the time or the inclination to care for the 'feedback', so essential to communications.

Political mobilisation is an important aspect in any country. It assumes different forms in different set-ups. A special distinction exists between political mobilisation in the West as compared to the developing countries. The bases of mobilisation in developing countries range from revocation of traditional authority to charisma to issues like national integration. Media plays an important role of agenda setting that is important for political socialisation and political option formation.

Political mobilisation is the collective and structured expression of commitment and support within society. It is a form of social mobilisation, which corresponds to a particular era and certain special needs. Mobilisation is a functional process for the attainment of the goal of national integration in developing societies.

Political participation is an important prerequisite for political mobilisation. It is the involvement of groups and individuals at various levels in the political system. Involvement expresses itself in various kinds of overt or manifest political activities. Political participation fosters stability and order by reinforcing the legitimacy of political authority for it is the principal means by which consent is granted or withdrawn in a democracy and rulers are made accountable to the ruled. Political participation denotes a series of voluntary activities, which have a bearing on the political process that involves issues like the selection of rulers and the various aspects of the formation of public policy. This is made possible by many factors including the press.

Besides aiding political participation, press helps in shaping public opinion. It helps us in the process of initiation and debate and to reach a recognisable collective decision on an issue. It helps establish public opinion, which is the collection of people's opinion on issues of public interests. We agree with social scientists who say that public opinion has a giant's strength and we may use it with frightful effects.

Gandhi was quite aware of the power of the press and used it as an effective instrument in mobilising people. He was constantly engaged with the production of newspapers and journals and wrote with the specific aim of educating the masses on issues concerning India's freedom. Besides, Gandhi would narrate the course of action to be taken during movements and elucidate on the methods of resistance and opposition to the British regime.

Gandhi was very well aware of the dynamics of media-society relationship. Considering the limitation of the use of media on a large scale for the illiterate class, Gandhi uniquely used signs and symbols, traditional and modern, for communicating his ideas. He made judicious use of both print and oral media besides resorting to symbols at appropriate times. Gandhi based his communication on concrete themes that added validity to the content of this communication, besides making it extremely effective.

Gandhi's system of formulating symbolic expression was rooted in the essential tradition of Indian philosophy. The channels of communication for the dissemination of his ideas were the traditional communication tools like *bhajans* (prayer meetings) as well as his speeches and writings. He reformulated the language in such a way that it converted his ideas into a concrete image, which sustained the imaginative perception of the audience; thousands listened to him and responded spontaneously. His words could feed back into the culture new forms of language (words like *Swadeshi* and *Harijan),* generating multiple meanings. This was the symbolic expression constituting Gandhi's mode of mass communication. Gandhi used multiple channels of communication. He also used a multi-pronged mobilisation strategy.

Gandhi was aware of the dynamics of mass participation too. He always believed in a carefully designed plan of action, especially when it was meant for people across the country. The press was a crucial partner in all his mobilisation efforts. Gandhi made elaborate use of the press during the non-cooperation and civil disobedience movements. The press, for him, was a tool for informing, educating and mobilising the masses. He used newspapers to educate masses about public causes for which he led mass movements. Gandhi's writings combined with his other communication techniques like speeches and *padyatras* (peace marches) bore fruits. Thus, press was an effective tool in political mobilisation in colonial India.

The press was also effective in political mobilisation in independent India, as apparent in the case of the JP movement.

Jayaprakash Narayan was an able communicator. A sincere student of political sociology, he took his time before plunging into activism. He made his impact as one of the most vibrant leaders of independent India. Well aware of press coverage, Jayaprakash Narayan would readily give interviews to the press and advocate his arguments during the famous JP Movement. He followed Gandhi in developing a judicious combination of oral communication and print media for the purposes of political education and mobilisation of millions of people, cutting across rural-urban and illiterate-literate barriers.

However, he was not a journalist in the true sense of the term. He did use the press to a great extent; had his own journal run by a group of professional journalists; even wrote occasionally to air his views. However, the intensity with which he used the press was perhaps less, especially when compared to Gandhi and his style of the use of press differed from Gandhi's. He was not editing his journal himself unlike Gandhi and his frequency of writing was far less than that of Gandhi. Besides, unlike Gandhi's journals, Jayaprakash Narayan's journals were not designed truly for mass consumption. It was targeted for a select group of politically sensitive audience who was of great consequence to him at the ideological level. The scale and intensity of his movement was far less than that of Gandhi's movement. This restricted his use of the press on a massive scale though he was well aware of the power of the press.

In a nutshell Jayaprakash Narayan did use the press, but it was not in the core of his design of political movements. He relied more on political debates and this is reflected in the number of pamphlets that he wrote. However, being a keen student of political science, his understanding of the political processes and especially mass action was unmatched. This is to be seen in the success with which he led the total revolution, relying a great deal on the power of the resurgent youth, a power that was recognised in the history of Indian movements after the epoch-making JP Movement.

Another factor that restrained Jayaprakash Narayan from using the press for political mobilisation with greater intensity was the fact that the mainstream and regional press, which had registered phenomenal growth since the times of Gandhi, were giving adequate coverage to JP Movement. He knew he did not require building the movement through the press. His journals, as a result, had become more of an ideological document for the literate and politically sensitive class. Gandhi's writings in the press, on the other hand, were staple diet of mass consumption—as Gandhi had branded his journals, bringing them out in many languages. This was necessary because the press, in Gandhi's time, was limited in its reach and literacy rates were lower then than in independent India.

2

Historical Background

Gandhi and Jayaprakash Narayan occupied the centrestage in two epoch-making periods of Indian history. While Gandhi moved millions during his struggle against the mighty British Empire, Jayaprakash Narayan stirred many souls in his campaign against the authoritative regime of Indira Gandhi. Gandhi in colonial times and Jayaprakash Narayan in independent India represent two of the most versatile and powerful mass leaders in the Indian tradition. Viewed superficially, however, they may represent two different models of leadership as well as ideologies. This is partly due to "the contexts in which they separated" and partly due to "their personal predilections and endowments."

In the beginning it is important to give an outline of the conceptual issues on which the following discussion is based.

Firstly, both Gandhi and Jayaprakash Narayan were communicators who well understood the basic processes of the mass media. They both had their own newspapers, and seemed to conform with the classical description of the way the press enables discrete individuals to join together in purposeful groups, as given by Tocqueville. "The effect of a newspaper is not only to suggest the same purpose to great number of persons, but also to furnish means for the execution of the designs which they may singly have conceived.... A newspaper then takes up the notion or the feeling that had occurred simultaneously, but singly, to each of them. All are then immediately guided toward the beacon; and these wandering minds, which had so long sought each other in darkness, at length meet and unite." This common action, believed the two great leaders, was made possible because of instrumental political participation, which is essentially directed towards the achievement of concrete goals. "

Though leading from the front in two different eras, both Gandhi and Jayaprakash Narayan relied heavily on public opinion. They agreed with Bailey who says that public opinion "has a giant's strength and we may use it with frightful effects". Like students of communication they saw the public as a semi-organised entity that in some way or another moves through stages of initiation and debate, and reaches a recognisable collective decision on an issue. To them the public was an organic entity linked together by means of mass communication.

Further, while Gandhi conducted his dialogue both with the 'mass public' and the 'attentive public,' a distinction suggested by Almond, JP communicated mostly with the 'attentive public'. The mass public informed by the mass media pays heed to the tone of discussion and issues and responds through moods of apprehension or complacency. The attentive public, a far smaller group, follows public issue in an analytical manner, is relatively well-informed and constitutes a critical audience for the discussion of public affairs. However, the size of the attentive public varies from time to time as new issues and problems arise. Again, at times, the attentive pubic may be large and quickly responsive to events and actions. At other times and on other questions, public discontent may be generated rather slowly. It may require years or decades for a public sentiment to develop. But whatever segment they may be targeting, both Gandhi and JP as communicators believed that an opinion has a bearing on groups of people and political mobilisation takes place on the basis of groups and associations.

Main Aspects

There are two main aspects to what occurs. On the one hand, there is the provision of a consistent picture of the social world, which may lead the audience to adopt this version of reality, a reality of facts and of norms, values and expectations. On the other hand, there is a continuing and selective interaction between self and the media, which plays a part in shaping the individual's own behaviour and self-concept. We learn about our social environment and respond to the knowledge that we acquire. In greater detail, we can expect the mass media to guide us about different kinds of social role and the accompanying expectations in the sphere of work, family life, political behaviour and so on. We can expect certain values to be selectively reinforced in these and other areas of social experience. We can also expect the mass media to give an order of importance and structure to the world they portray, whether fictionally or as actuality.

There are several reasons for the expectations listed above.

Firstly, there is a good amount of patterning and consistency in the media version of the world. Another is the wide range of experience, which is open to view and to vicarious involvement, compared to the narrow range of real-life experience available to most people. Third, there is the trust with which media are often held as a source of impressions about the world outside direct experience.

Gandhi and Jayaprakash Narayan were quite methodical when it came to the content of their journals. Their content broadly fell in Eisenstadt's three main classes of communication content: technical content, which provides instruction and information; general cognitive content, which covers news ranging from gossip to politics; and normative content, which defines what is proper behaviour and is oriented to the transmission and maintenance of social norms.

Besides, both strongly believed in the agenda-setting function of the media. This function was pointed out by Bernard C. Cohen who says that "the press may not be successful much of the time in telling people what to think, but it's stunningly successful is telling its readers what to think about." Political scientists too have been most alert to the process and McCombs and Shaw have given the term 'agenda-setting' to it.

What follows is a compartive study of Gandhi and Jayaprakash Narayan with regard to the style of leadership of the two, particularly on how they both made use of the press in political mobilisation. A large part of the analysis is based on interviews and content analysis.

The Communicators

Both Gandhi and Jayaprakash Narayan were great communicators. They knew the importance of getting their messages across to the people, that would in turn prompt them to action. "Both were masters of communcation."

Though rooted in a mix of saintly and traditional languages of Indian politics in their discourses, both Gandhi and Jayaprakash Narayan were operating in two different time periods, a fact that makes this comparative analysis quite interesting.

"Gandhi belonged to that generation when media was an instrument of articulation of public opinion." Even the authorities in the Gandhian era used to rely on the contents of the newspapers upto a large extent. This was possible because of two reasons, as pointed out by G.S. Bhargava. "A kind of moderation with which the complaints were aired, and the restraint shown by them." Gandhi was quite logical and sharp in his writings. Thus he wrote about a movement and the British response to it: "Every good movement passes through five stages: indifference, ridicule, abuse, repression, and respect. We had indifference for a few months. Then the viceroy graciously laughed at it. Abuse, including misrepresentation, has been the order of the day. The provincial Governors and the anti-non-cooperation press have heaped as much abuse upon the movement as they have been able to. Now comes repression, at present yet in its fairly mild form. Every movement that survives repression, mild or severe, invariably commands respect which is another name for success. This repression, if we are true, may be treated as a sure sign of the approaching victory. But, if we're true, we shall neither be cowed down nor angrily retaliate and be violent. Violence is suicide. Let us recognize that power dies hard, and that it is but natural for the Government to make a final effort for life even though it is through repression. Complete self-restraint at the present critical moment is the speediest way to success." On the other hand, Jayaprakash Narayan was operating at a time when the mass media were fairly well developed. Newspapers in different languages had proliferated and the increased literacy rates facilitated the wide reach of the media. No wonder, as both Ajit Bhattacharjee and G.S. Bhargava observe, his *Everyman's* had a specific focus of readership. "It was more for political readership than for mass consumption," observes Bhattacharjee. He further elaborates that unlike Gandhi's journals *Young India, Harijan* or *Navajivan,* the *Everyman's* "was conceived in a very specific setting and was primarily aimed at the educated class and policy makers and was not meant for the masses."

The journals of Gandhi were meant for a wide range of readership. The very fact that he brought out his journals in different languages drives home the point that Gandhi's publications were meant for mass readership.

Public Sphere

However, both Gandhi and Jayaprakash believed in the process of shaping public opinion through the use of the press. Both relied on the technique of conducting dialogue on various issues by creating a public sphere (as suggested by Habermas), for it. As communicators, both subscribed to the media-centred view of communication theories that focus on the means of communication as a force for change.

Thus apart from writing on issues that concerned their immediate agenda like non-cooperation and total revolution, Gandhi and Jayaprakash Narayan would also touch upon issues of wider relevance in their journals and other writings. Gandhi wrote on education in his weekly *Harijan* in the 8 May, 1937 issue: "I hold that true education of the intellect can only come through a proper exercise and training of the bodily organs e.g. hands, feet, eyes, ears, nose, etc. In other words an intelligent use of the bodily organs in a child provides the best and quickest way of developing his intellect. But unless the development of the mind and body goes hand in hand with a corresponding awakening of the soul, the former alone would prove to be a poor lop-sided affair. By spiritual training I mean education of the heart." According to him, a proper and all-round development of the mind, therefore, could take place only when it proceeded along with the education of the physical and spiritual faculties of the child. He continued, "They constitute an indivisible whole. According to this theory, therefore, it would be a gross fallacy to suppose that they can be developed piecemeal and independently of one another."

Similarly, Jayaprakash Narayan's weekly would highlight various social issues, despite being highly political in tone and tenor. In the thick of JP Movement, the April 12, 1975 issue of *Everyman's* carried an article 'Crimes against Harijans and Adivasis' written by Madhu Limaye. "Untouchability has no sanction of law," read the page seven story, "but it still rules the innermost recesses of the human heart. Unless men's hearts are purified, unless the pernicious principle of dividing people into higher and lower castes based on birth is abolished, unless the youth of the country are inspired by a burning hatred of this inequality, and unless a genuine sympathy for the lot of the oppressed is created, how could one expect a change in the mental outlook of the common people? Harijans and Adivasis constitute 21.53 per cent or more than one-fifth of India's total population. And they are the most oppressed of the citizens. Twenty seven years of freedom has neither altered their living standards nor their social status. There is an urgent need to transform the living conditions of these oppressed millions."

Thus, even in politically volatile times, Jayaprakash Narayan would not relegate social issues. Gandhi was, in fact, a step ahead of him in this regard. All the issues of his weekly newsletters would have some 'human interest' articles. Later on, Gandhi started *Harijan* solely for the purpose of propagating his campaign against untouchability.

It is also possible to argue against the contention that both the leaders used the press for conducting dialogues on various issues. According to a Gandhian journalist the element of dialogue was "missing in JP's approach, while it is more prominent in that of Gandhi's." He points out that "Gandhi had different target audience when he wrote in different languages." Thus for the English version of the *Young India* he had one kind of readership in mind and so on.

Gandhi even kept the sentiments of a particular section of readership in mind while bringing out various editions of his newspapers. In the Gujarati edition of the *Indian Opinion* of December 21, 1913, the following remarks were made, that substantiate the argument: "The Satyagraha campaign, as carried on this time and still continuing, has hardly a parallel in history. The real credit for this goes to the Hindi and Tamil speaking brothers and sisters living in this country. Their sacrifice has been the highest of all. Some of them have even lost their lives: killed by the bullets of the white soldiers. As a tribute to their memory, we have decided to give Hindi and Tamil news in this paper. Some years ago we used to bring out this paper in these two languages as well, but we had to discontinue the practice owing to some difficulties. Those difficulties are not yet over. And yet, we resume publication in these languages for the duration of the struggle, that being, in our judgement, the least we must do, even at some inconvenience to ourselves, in honour of communities whose members have made such sacrifices in a struggle of this kind." So sensitive Gandhi was to the sentiments of his readers!

Jayaprakash Narayan too cared about the sentiments of his readers. He too had due respect for his readership, but as pointed out by Ajit Bhattacharjee, his focus was limited largely to the politically active and educated class or the 'attentive public'.

In addition to considering newspapers as the "most powerful vehicle for transmitting pure ideas in a concise manner..." and making them a tool to educate public opinion, Gandhi had equal regard for opinions expressed by his readers. Jayaprakash Narayan came quite close to Gandhi in this respect. In fact a large part of page two of *Everyman's* was devoted to letters to the editor, that at times spilled over to page three also. And both of them gave proper display to letters representing dissent and the opposite point of view. Another quality of a great communicator.

Gandhi published a letter by CF. Andrews criticising 'The Growth of Intolerance' at the peak of the non-cooperation movement on the front page of *Young India* even at the risk of irking many: "I wish to make every allowance for mere boyish enthusiasm and for any juvenile ebullition of feeling; but these and other previous acts have gone far beyond this. They amount to persecution and cruel humiliation. I have watched, for a long time, with greatest pain, that in spite of all that Mahatma Gandhi has done to condemn the evil, it has increased, and it is not confined to one part of India only. As it is entirely opposed to the principle of non-violence, which attracted me so strongly to the Movement, and drew me out of the retirement of Shanti Niketan to take part in it, I feel that the time has come for me to declare publicly and openly my detestation of these practices."

Jayaprakash Narayan too provided space to his readers to air their opinions. One of the letters on page two of the 18 May, 1975 issue of *Everyman's* titled 'The Movement and the Men Behind' reads: "JP's Movement started with its main target being the elected representatives who have been constantly betraying the people who elected them. But how is it that these MLAs and MPs who are elected for a specific, brief period, are able to sit over the heads of the administrative and bureaucratic executives who are there to guard the system? What has happened to the sanity, morality and integrity of these people? JP relies too much on student power to achieve his goals. I feel that the students are generally not mature to be worthy of this faith. There may be a few individual students who think on the lines of JP, but as a force they cannot be relied upon. How can we depend upon our students to achieve higher ideas in the larger canvass of society when they tend to be corrupt in their small sphere? Can we expect a student, who claims copying in the examination hall to be his right, to turn out to be a worthy product? Students have generally impressed the common man as an irresponsible lot. The majority of our present day students are incapable of any useful service to the illiterate masses. The so-called education successfully makes them snobs, devoid of any human sympathy and stern moral attitude."

There was no editing even of the harsh criticism. This shows the high degree of professionalism adhered to by both Gandhi and Jayaprakash Narayan. In fact Gandhi went a step further and would reply to "almost all the letters personally", as pointed out by Bhargava. "He wrote endlessly and made his point very sharply." Gandhi is specially recognised for his letters. His letters, small or big, official or personal, were pure gems. These were worded appropriately and spoken from the heart. "Many are playful; some loving. Many administer a paternal rebuke; some with describable restraint, hit, and hit well; a few are intimates; scarcely any throbs with the impulse of an unguarded moment. The author adjusts the tone, the language and the perspective of every letter with uncanny precision so as to have the desired effect on the addressed. These letters have provided him with his greatest instrument of controlling the conscience and conduct of his friends and adherents. No man has wielded so great an influence through his letters; and few literary men have written theirs with such art."

Jayaprakash Narayan too wrote letters. But they used to be mostly political in nature. The available accounts do not indicate to his indulging in personal correspondence with the readers of his journal, as did Gandhi.

Commenting on the overall content of their journals, Ajit Bhattacharjee observes that while the content of the *Everyman's* was "basically political, criticising the politics and action of the government of the day, Gandhi covered broader national agenda as he had a much broader area to appeal to." He further points out that while Gandhi was fighting an alien government and anti-imperialist forces, the focus of Jayaprakash Narayan was much different. "He was fighting a native anti-democratic government, and hence the intensity differed." Rajiv Vora, in fact, goes a step further and sees very little role of the latter's journal in the Bihar Movement." It was primarily an organ informing the educated class about the various developments of JP movement," opines Vora.

Another factor that marks Gandhi as distinct from Jayaprakash Narayan is the fact that the former used to manage time to write even in the thick of movements. JP, on the other hand, did not write for mass consumption; however, "he did produce party documents and theses," informs G.S. Bhargava, who was an associate of Jayaprakash Narayan. On the other hand, even when the call for Quit India Movement had been given in 1942, Gandhi wrote a letter to his "American friends" in the August 9, 1942 issue of *Harijan*. "I invite you to read my formula of withdrawal or as it has been popularly called 'Quit India'. I claim to be a votary of truth from my childhood. It was the most natural thing to me. My prayerful search gave me the revealing maxim 'Truth is God' instead of the useful one 'God is Truth'. That maxim enables me to see God face to face as it were. I feel him pervade every fibre of being. With this Truth as witness between you and me, I assert that I would not have asked my country to invite Great Britain to withdraw her rule over India, irrespective of any demand to the contrary, if I had not seen at once that for the sake of Great Britain and the Allied causes it was necessary for Britain boldly to perform the duty of freeing India from bondage. Without this essential act of fair justice, Britain could not justify her position before the unmurmuring World Conscience, which is there nevertheless. Singapore, Malaya and Burma taught me that the disaster must not be repeated in India. You have made common cause with Great Britain. You cannot therefore disown responsibility for anything that her representatives do in India. You will do a grievous wrong to the Allied cause, if you do not sift the truth from the chaff whilst there is yet time. Just think of it. Is there anything wrong in the Congress demanding unconditional recognition of India's independence?"

Against Publicity

Another factor on which Gandhi and Jayaprakash seem to have been at par is their dislike for "any form of propaganda". "They would both make out their cases quite logically, convincingly and with great conviction even when there was scope of propaganda. They would never resort to cheap techniques of writing for mobilising the masses," says G.S. Bhargava.

Gandhi was guarded in his writings. Thus he wrote on Khilafat: "In my humble opinion attainment of Swaraj is the quickest method of righting the Khilafat wrong. Hence it is that for me the solution of the Khilafat question is attainment of Swaraj and vice-versa. The only way to help the afflicted Turks is for India to generate sufficient power to be able to assert herself. If she cannot develop that power there is no way out for India and she must resign herself to the inevitable. What can a paralytic do to stretch forth a helping hand to a neighbour but to try to cure himself of his paralysis? Mere ignorant, thoughtless and angry outburst of violence may give vent to pent-up rage but can bring no relief to Turkey. Nor can it increase the power of India to assert herself. And the measures taken to put down violence may well lessen the speed with which we are marching to our goal."

Jayaprakash Narayan was equally cautious and judicious in use of words. "It is interesting to note," he wrote in the November 16, 1974 issue of *Everyman's* "that the Prime Minister made a casual reference to the injuries inflicted on me by the police on November 4, saying that there was no intention to hit me and that I was injured in a stampede. There is however a crucial question involved concerning the role of law in the country including that of discrimination between two groups of citizens. The entire machinery of the state was deployed on November 4 and the days preceding it to forcibly prevent the people of Bihar from coming to their capital city for a peaceful demonstration and dharna... The constitution provides that there shall be no discrimination in the application of law. However, just a week after armed security forces did everything short of killing to prevent a peaceful demonstration, the CPI has not only been given permission to stage a rally in Patna but official agencies have gone out of the way to provide all possible facilities to help the CPI. The people do not want any facilities from the Government, but they certainly have the right not to be obstructed in activities of peaceful assembly and expression. What is a matter of great concern to all democrats is that if this is repeated then the people will have no chance to give expression to anything that goes against Government policies and actions however bad or evil such policies might be. If this policy continues during election time democracy would be destroyed in our country."

Similarly, Gandhi did not cross the limit while writing even against the harsh treatment of the South African administration against the Indians residing there. *Indian Opinion* was the spearhead of the struggle in South Africa. Gandhi continued to inspire and infuse a spirit of passive resistance through his writings, which were sharp, straight and effective. Thus Gandhi wrote: "Of the many accomplishments that passive resisters have to possess, tenacity is by no means the least important. . They cannot and must not lose faith in themselves or in their mission because they may be in a minority. Instead, all reform has been brought about by the action of minorities in all countries and under all climes. Majorities simply follow minorities." Then he wrote: "Brute force will avail against brute force only when it is proved that darkness can dispel darkness." And, "Death should cause no fear in us if we have .... done nothing in violation of the voice of our conscience. Then, indeed, is death but a change for the better, and therefore, a welcome change which need not evoke any sorrow. And resisters must learn not only not to fear death, but must be prepared to face it and welcome it when it comes to use in the performance of our duty.... I wish for no better end, and I am sure no other passive resister does." This reflects Gandhi's ability to put an event as emotive in a style that will not amount to propaganda.

No wonder a large section of the mainstream press relied heavily on Gandhi's journals, when it came to picking up issues. Almost all the issues discussed by Gandhi figured prominently in all the major newspapers of the day, informs Bhargava. However, the situation was a little different in Jayaprakash Narayan's case. In fact, he was already getting a good publicity through the wide coverage of his movement in the mainstream newspapers. And given the wide reach of the newspapers in the 1970s, as compared to the colonial decades, the impact was much greater. There were, however, cases when issues were picked up by the mainstream media from Jayaprakash Narayan's journal.

Despite this, both the communicators had to face the brunt of the respective regimes. While Gandhi's *Young India* was forced to close down during the Civil Disobedience Movement, Jayaprakash Narayan's *Everyman's* was gagged during the peak of emergency. Both the journals were perceived to be creating a great impact on people's mind and propagating the movements. Similarly, Gandhi's *Harijan* was closed down forcibly during the peak of the Quit India Movement. The British rulers had studied the penetration and power of Gandhi's journals. As has been said, the journals used to guide the masses about the various moves made by Gandhi and his workers. Similarly, Jayaprakash Narayan's journal, though meant primarily for the politically conscious educated class, was becoming a vehicle of ideological and moral debasement of Indira Gandhi's dictatorial regime. "There have been attacks on the freedom of press, the worst and most sustained occurring during the emergency when censorship was imposed and publications perceived to be hostile to the government were harassed legally and illegally."

Active Participation

Gandhi and Jayaprakash Narayan both made the press partners in their campaign and mobilisation efforts. They would not only inform their readers about the development of movements and ideological moorings behind them but also chalk out a programme for future action.

While talking about his stay in Musahari block in Bihar and his programme of *Gramdan*, Jayaprakash Narayan wrote: "I should make it clear that we are fully aware that the implementation of our present programme would certainly not mark the completion of our work here. In fact, it would be only the beginning: Gramdan will only prepare the necessary socio-psychological conditions for the direct democracy of the village to function properly. But much will still remain to be done to make the democracy work.

"The Gram Sabhas will have to develop the strength and moral resources to be able to resolve conflicts from being committed, and see that the Gram Kosh is collected regularly and utilized for the purposes laid down. The Sabhas will have to learn to prepare their own plans of development, to husband their own resources for their execution, and to obtain available help form Government agencies, credit institutions and other sources.... There are other future tasks too. The Gram Sabhas we are establishing are of an ad hoc nature, so they will have to be confirmed according to the provisions of the Gramdan Act. That is a tedious and time-consuming process. Then again, when Gram Sabhas have been set up in all, or at least in 80 per cent of the villages of the block, the next higher tier, or concentric circle as Gandhiji would have it, the Prakhand (Block) Sabha, will have to be organised. In that manner the structure of the communitarian policy of Sarvodaya will have to be raised tier by tier from the very grassroots of the primary community."

Again in the middle of this famous Bihar Movement, he wrote a signed letter titled 'Come with me to Parliament' in the March 2, 1975 issue of *Everyman's:* "I have made an appeal to the countrymen to hold at least a million-strong demonstration at the Parliament in support of the people of Bihar. The National People's Action Coordinating Committee has fixed March 6 for the demonstration."

Similarly Gandhi informed "How to Boycott Foreign Cloth" during the non-cooperation movement through his journal *Young India:* "The proposed boycott of foreign cloth is not a vindicative measure, but is as necessary for national existence as breath is for life.... It is of the highest importance to know how it can be brought about even before the first day of August next. To arrive at the boycott, it is necessary

1. For the mill-owners to regulate their profits and to manufacture principally for the Indian market.
2. For importers to cease to buy foreign goods. A beginning has already been made by three principal merchants.
3. For the consumers to refuse to buy any foreign cloth and to buy khadi wherever possible.
4. For the consumers to wear only Khadi cloth, mill cloth being retained for the poor who do not know the distinction between Swadeshi and Pardeshi.
5. For the consumers to use, till Swaraj is established and Khadi manufacture increased, Khadi just enough for covering the body."

Gandhi, in fact, was more elaborate in his writing about the steps, style and strategies of movements than Jayaprakash Narayan. The reason is pointed out by Ajit Bhattacharjee. He says that "while JP used the mainstream media during the Bihar movement, Gandhi had to rely mostly on his own journals for popularising his ideas." Ajit Bhattacharjee was the editor of *Everyman's* weekly for a large part of its life before it was shut down during the Emergency.

Additionally, Gandhi was multi-lingual (his journals were brought out in many languages) that enabled him to appeal to a much wider audience than Jayaprakash Narayan could. The latter could only write in Hindi and English, while Gandhi wrote prolifically in Hindi, English and Gujarati besides being conversant in languages like Sanskrit and Tamil.

A major difference between the two was the way they ran their newspapers. While Gandhi was directly involved in the production of all his journals and wrote for most of the issues, Jayaprakash Narayan appointed a group of journalists to run his journals: *Everyman's* in English and *Prajaniti* in Hindi.

Gandhi observed that during his association with the *Indian Opinion,* until 1914 "excepting the intervals of my enforced rest in prison, there was hardly an issue of Indian Opinion without an article from me."

Another contrast appears in the different role that the media played during the two time periods. The media played the role of mediator during the times of Gandhi; it changed its role to that of a messenger during the JP Movement in independent India. This was possible because literacy rates were significantly higher and the growth of press made it possible for a large number of people to access it in the later period. In Gandhian era it was a marginal motivator while during Jayaprakash Narayan's era it was playing the role of a monitor. It was a monitoring instrument for assessing the development of the JP Movement.

In the end, it can be said that both Gandhi and Jayaprakash Narayan, despite differences in their style of leadership and their ways of life, are likely to be seen more and more as belonging essentially to the same genre of leaders, who devoted their whole life to political activities and brought about major changes in politics without ever aspiring to hold state power in their own hands. And, in this endeavour, they used the press with dramatic results.

3

Gandhi's Legacy

Mahatma Gandhi used both written and oral media dexterously for political communication and mobilisation of the masses in colonial India. Before studying his style and use of strategies for the purpose, we shall briefly discuss the major events of his life.

Mahatma's Life Sketch

In a small, white-washed house in Porbandar, on the coast of Kathiawad in western India, Mohandas Gandhi was born on October 2, 1869. His parents were Karamchand Gandhi and Putlibai. He was small and dark, yet this was no ordinary child. He was to fight and overcome a great empire and, without taking to arms, set his country free. He was to be called the 'Mahatma' or the 'Great Soul'. Having led his people to freedom, he was to lay down his life for their sake.

As the age of seven he was sent to a primary school. He was shy and books were his sole companions. Mohandas was only 13 when he was told that he was soon to be married. His parents had already chosen his bride, Kasturba. After passing his high school examination, Mohandas was to go to England to study and become a lawyer. On September 4, 1888, Mohandas left Bombay for England. In London, young Gandhi found everything around him strange. His attempt to be an Englishman lasted only about three months; then he gave up the idea. He soon became a serious student, and concentrated very hard on his studies. On June 10, 1891, he was called to the bar. Gandhi was admitted as a lawyer and the next day he formally enrolled in the High Court. The following day, June 12, he sailed for India.

Gandhi, after returning to India, set up his practice as a lawyer in Rajkot. Soon, however, he was disgusted with the greed and the pettiness that he found among the lawyers. Gandhi realised that it was difficult for the poor and the humble to get away from such things. It was then that an offer came to him to go to South Africa on behalf of Dada, Abdulla & Co.

The opportunity to see a new country and a new people excited Gandhi, and he accepted the offer. In April 1893, he left Bombay for South Africa. Gandhi reached the port of Natal towards the end of May 1893. The first thing he noticed was that the Indians there were treated with very little respect. Gandhi spent three years in South Africa meeting the Indians and talking about social injustices. He was now a well known figure; everyone recognised his frockcoat and turban. His practice was going very well and he knew that the people there wanted him with them.

At this time, Gandhi was becoming more and more involved in public activities, and his way of life became simpler. It was in 1901, six years after Gandhi had brought his family to Durban, that he felt his future activity lay not in South Africa but in India. Upon his arrival in India, Gandhi went on a tour of the country. The annual meeting of the Indian National Congress was being held in Calcutta under the presidentship of Dinshaw Wacho. Gandhi attended the session. It was his first contact with the Congress which he was to lead so gloriously in the future.

Gandhi settled down in Bombay and started practice as a lawyer. He did well, much better than he had expected. In December 1902, however, a cable reached him from South Africa requesting him to return. Joseph Chamberlin, the Colonial Secretary, was arriving from London on a visit to Natal and the Natal Indian Congress wanted Gandhi to present their case to him.

Gandhi reached Natal in time to lead the Indian deputation, but the Colonial Secretary gave the deputation a cold reception. Gandhi now decided to stay in the Transvaal and fight the colour bar, which was becoming an ugly situation there. In August 1906, an ordinance was issued by the Transvaal Government requiring all Indian men, women and children to register themselves and obtain a personal certificate bearing name and thumb impressions. This card was to be carried by all individuals at all times and had to be shown on demand. Anyone failing to produce the certificate was liable to be fined or imprisoned.

Gandhi saw here the need for passive resistance or 'satyagraha'. To the people, he explained his concept of satyagraha. First, he said, they must be prepared to observe non-violence. The authorities would take all measures to put down the agitation. They might use violence, arrest people, and send them to jail, but all this must be faced without resistance.

A big bonfire was lit and more than two thousand certificates were burned. Many Indians openly crossed the border into the Transvaal, where their presence was illegal. Gandhi and many of his compatriots were imprisoned several times in the course of the agitation. When Gandhi was released from jail, the Indians held a meeting and decided to send a deputation to England to acquaint the British Government with the real situation in South Africa. Gandhi and Seth Haji Habib were asked to go to London and present the grievances of the Indians. Accordingly, they went, but the mission was a failure. They returned with grim determination to fight to the bitter end.

Gandhi found the government relentless in its actions against minorities. There seemed no solution in sight. He had to take further measures. In the October of 1913, Gandhi organised a march of over 6,000 Indian workers from the Natal mining area into the Transvaal, although crossing into the Transvaal without a permit was not allowed by law. Gandhi and many other Indians were imprisoned. The 'satyagrahis' were beaten and flogged to force them to go back to work, but without success. Gandhi had aroused in them the spirit of quiet, dignified resistance.

Soon the movement of passive resistance, or satyagraha, spread all through Natal and Transvaal. The Government did not know what to do, because none yielded to their cruel treatment. In December 1913, Gandhi was released, but he would not give up the struggle. Gandhi had been active in South Africa for 21 years and had contributed much to the welfare of the Indians of South Africa. Gandhi now felt that his mission in South Africa was over, and he wanted to return to India.

Gandhi was back in India after 12 long years. A great reception awaited him in Bombay. In May 1915, an 'aashram' was established in the village near Ahmedabad. Gandhi named the new institution 'Satyagraha Aashram'. A simple uniform style of clothing was worn by all who lived there. They took their food together in a common kitchen and strove to live as one family.

For two years, Gandhi travelled extensively and talked at different places. He then wanted to start some work connected with labour. His interest first centred on the problem of indentured labour, the system under which poor, ignorant labourers were enticed away from India to work in British colonies. With passive resistance, Gandhi started an agitation on this issue. He went to Bombay and consulted all the Indian leaders there. They fixed May 31, 1917 as the last date for the abolition of indentured labour. He then travelled throughout the country; meetings were held in all important places. Everywhere there was a great response. As a result of the agitation, the government announced that the system of indentured labour would be stopped before July 31, 1917.

Gandhi first conceived the idea of an all-India strike as the beginning of the satyagraha movement. The leaders at once took up the suggestion and gave much publicity to the forthcoming strike. The date was fixed for April 6, 1919. The people had received only a short notice for the strike, but it turned out to be most successful. That was the first great awakening of India in her struggle towards independence from the British. In Bombay, the strike was a huge success. The strike was observed all over India. Gandhi had asked the people again and again to be peaceful and not to be provoked to violence by the government's actions. In spite of this, violence broke out in many places. There were disturbances in Ahmedabad and also in Punjab, so he decided to go to these places to promote a non-violence struggle.

In Punjab the situation became very critical. The leaders were trying to keep the people peaceful, but the stern measures of repression taken by the authorities had few parallels in history. It was announced that a meeting was to be held in a garden called Jallianwala Bagh, to protest against the government's actions. General Dyer took no measures to prevent the meeting. He reached the place soon after the meeting began and he took with him armoured cars and troops. Without giving any warning he ordered, "Fire till the ammunition is exhausted." The garden was surrounded by walls and buildings and had only one exit. At the first shot, the exit was jammed and there was no hope of escape for the crowd. There were between 6,000 and 10,000 people there. The soldiers fired over 1,600 rounds at the unarmed mass of people. What was once a garden now became a scene of merciless massacre. Jallianwala Bagh' became a synonym of massacre.

The Influence

Gandhi's influence on the Indian people was steadily growing. The old leaders, many of them with liberal policies, were vanishing from Indian politics. By the close of 1920, Gandhi was the undisputed leader and head of the Indian National Congress.

In 1928, peasants in Bardoli in Gujarat were agitated by grievances and Gandhi advised them to resort to satyagraha and the non-payment of taxes. A new determination, to force the government to act, filled the minds of the people. Jawarharlal Nehru was elected President of the Congress at the insistence of Gandhi. India now demanded full independence. The whole country was excited. Everyone waited for the go-ahead from Gandhi. After two months of suspense, a salt satyagraha was announced by the leader. The salt tax was to be attacked and the salt laws were to be broken.

On March 12, 1930, at 6:30 in the morning, thousands of people watched as Gandhi started from his aashram with 78 volunteers on a march to Dandi, a village on the sea coast 241 miles away. For 24 days the eyes of India and the world followed Gandhi as he marched towards the sea. The government did not dare take the risk of arresting Gandhi. With each passing day, the campaign grew. Hundreds and thousands of people joined the procession. Men, women, and children lined the route, offering flowers and shouting slogans for the victory of the march.

The march ended on April 5 at Dandi. Gandhi and his selected followers went to the sea-shore and broke the salt law by picking up salt left on the shore by the sea. Gandhi then gave a signal to all Indians to manufacture salt illegally. He wanted the people to break the salt law openly and to prepare themselves for non-violent resistance to police action. All over India people swarmed to the nearest sea coast to break the salt law.

The government waited for some time before taking any action, and then the retaliation began. Gandhi was arrested. Gandhi's arrest had created a great sensation in India and abroad. Representatives were sent from all parts of the world to the British Prime Minister asking the government to release Gandhi and make peace with India. The government, under pressure, at last released Gandhi. As soon as Gandhi was out of prison he asked for an interview with the Viceroy, Lord Irwin. The interview was immediately granted. Gandhi and Irwin met, but the two men seemed to have come from two different worlds.

In August 1942, the All-India Congress Committee met in Bombay and was presided over by Maulana Abul Kalam Azad. Again, the demand to set up a provisional government was made. The 'Quit India' resolution was drawn up and passed by the meeting for presentation to the government. Nehru moved the resolution and Sardar Patel seconded it. The resolution also announced the starting of a mass struggle on the widest possible scale.

The government did not wait for the mass movement to begin. Gandhi was arrested overnight and so were many other leaders in various parts of India. Gandhi was confined to the Aga Khan's palace in Poona. With the leaders in jail, India did not remain idle. 'Do or die' was the slogan taken up by the people. There were mass movements everywhere, great outbursts of violence throughout the country. People began to destroy government buildings and whatever else they considered to be symbols of British imperialism.

All over India there were strikes and disorder. Lord Linlithgow, the Viceroy, attributed all this to Gandhi. Gandhi had incited violence, he claimed. In a long series of letters to Lord Linlithgow, Gandhi tried to persuade him to retract this charge against him. Failing in this, Gandhi decided to undertake a fast as "an appeal to the Highest Tribunal" against the unjust charges. Gandhi fasted for 21 days in February 1943. It was a great ordeal, but he survived.

A few weeks later Gandhi was taken seriously ill with malaria. The Indian people demanded his immediate release and the authorities, believing that he was nearing death, released him. Gandhi was slowly restored to health.

The demand for Indian independence had now grown into a world-wide question. Apart from India's own attitude, America and other countries pressed Britain to grant freedom to India. Two months later in May 1945, the Labour Party came into power in Britain and Attlee became the Prime Minister. A few months later, the British Government announced that they expected to grant self-government to India as soon as her internal problems could be solved.

This was a victory for India. It was victory for non-violence. Britain, defeated by the peaceful revolution, could not hold onto India any longer. Britian agreed to a planned withdrawal from India, without bitterness and in friendship.

All through his life Gandhi worked for unity between the Hindus and the Muslims. But he did not have much success. There was a large section of nationalist Muslims in the Congress, but the heads of the Muslim League were drifting farther away. Gandhi was not the man to give up hope, however, and he pursued his efforts to bring about a settlement. On the other hand, Jinnah, the leader of the Muslim League, was hostile to the idea of unity. He demanded a separate Muslim state before freedom was given to India. "We can settle the Indian problem in ten minutes if Mr. Gandhi agrees to the creation of Pakistan," said Jinnah. "Cut me in two," cried Gandhi, "but do not cut India in two."

In February 1946, the British Government sent a Cabinet Mission to India. The task of the Cabinet Mission was to study the situation and suggest what should be done. After careful consideration, the Cabinet Mission issued a statement proposing the withdrawl of British authority from India. They wanted a united India. On June 3, 1947, Attlee, the British Prime Minister, announced the plan for partition. The Congress and the Muslim League accepted it.

Thus on August 15, 1947, India's long struggle and suffering for freedom was over. A new nation was born.

Gandhi had never given his approval to partition, but when it was done he accepted it and did everything possible for Hindu-Muslim friendship. Yet the tension between Hindus and Muslims continued to increase. As a result of the partition, over 700,000 Hindus, Sikhs, and other non-Muslims in Pakistan, fearing the Muslims, left their homes and set out towards security in India. From India, about the same number of Muslims, fearing the Hindus, left their homes for Pakistan. The miseries of the mass migration, one of the greatest in history, were manifold. About 1,500,000 people on the move were exposed to starvation, disease, and massacre on the way.

Gandhi decided to do penance by fasting, which he thought would bring about change in the attitude of the Hindu fanatics. The fast began on January 13, 1948. There was gloom all over India at the news of Gandhi's fast. People thought that he would not be able to survive another fast. The whole world watched as Gandhi, 78 years old, fasted to save his country from destruction. On January 18, a peace committee, representing all communities, met and signed a pact pledging unity and the protection of life, property and faith to the Muslim minority. Gandhi was informed of the pledge and he broke his fast.

On January 30, after a midday nap, Gandhi woke up at 3:30 p.m. The whole day he had a stream of visitors. Gandhi left his room at 5 o'clock and went towards a prayer-meeting. He passed through a cordoned-off path, accompanied by Manu and Abha, his grand-daughters. As he was walking along, a youth named Nathuram Godsey came forward as if to seek his blessings. He stood in front of Gandhi and at point-blank range fired three shots in quick succession. All the bullets hit the great leader. Gandhi fell, uttering the prayer, 'Rama, Rama'. Gandhi was dead.

The assassination jolted the world, and all who learned of his death were shocked. Nehru told the country of Gandhi's death, his voice choked with emotion: "Friends and comrades, the light has gone out of our lives and there is darkness everywhere. I do not know what to tell you and how to say it. Our beloved leader, Bapu, as we called him, the Father of the Nation, is no more. Perhaps I am wrong to say that. Nevertheless, we will not see him again as we have seen him for these many years...."

"The light has gone out, I said, and yet I was wrong. For the light that shone in this country was no ordinary light. The light that has illuminated this country for these many years will illuminate this country for many more years, and a thousand years later that light will still be seen in this country, and the world will see it and it will give solace to innumberable hearts...."

Great Journalist

A year after Gandhi passed away, the *Harijan* wrote: "All work in whatsoever sphere was a means primarily of service in Gandhiji's eyes. Newspapers and journals can build up a fitting memorial to him in this matter by conforming or trying to conform to the unimpeachable standards of journalism practiced by our revered and beloved."

As a journalist, Gandhi wanted to educate the people so that they could understand not only the significance of independence—political, economic and social—but also participate actively in freeing humanity from the bondage it was in. Gandhi's motto as a journalist was service. He said once: "One of the objects of a newspaper is to understand the popular feeling and give expression to it; another is to arouse among the people certain desirable sentiments; and the third is fearlessly to expose popular defects."

Such was the conviction of Gandhi; and beginning in 1903 in South Africa, he constantly kept a companion for his writings and gave them expression through his journals and newspapers. That he used the press as a tool for political mobilisation is confirmed by the fact that he brought out four major journals: *Indian Opinion, Young India, Navajivan* and *Harijan,* all with the purpose of arousing "among the people certain desirable sentiments," besides a number of books producing a total of two million English wordage. "His instrument for creating social change was to create mass awareness. His tools were letters, articles and speeches."

Gandhi has been termed as the most influential writer and journalist that India has produced. Gandhi knew the power of the word, spoken and written, in inspiring people to action. He resembled a charismatic arbiter when airing grievances, be it in South Africa or India. His words were loaded with purpose. "No one who has used the words on a massive scale has been as passionately purposive as Gandhi. No one has used words with such intense longing to be down-to-earth on the one hand and, paradoxically, to reach for the stars on the other." Gandhi has plainly stated his objective in writing: "I write as the spirit moves me at the time of writing." He further says: "I write to propagate my ideas."

Gandhi's journey in journalism started quite early in his life, when he contributed nine articles on Indian diet, customs and festivals in a magazine *Vegetarian* in London. "When on arrival in London in September 1888, to study law, Gandhiji, at the age of 19, for the first time realised how actively he would be associated with the newspaper for the rest of his life." Gandhi consistently wrote for the next six decades. The press, for him, became a tool for informing, educating and mobilising the masses. "He used newspapers to educate masses about public causes for which he led mass movements."

The *Indian Opinion* was the first journalistic tool of Gandhi, that was unveiled on June 4, 1903 in South Africa. It was a weekly newspaper and was published in English, Gujarati, Tamil and Hindi for the benefit of Indians residing in South Africa. As Gandhi recalled later about the purpose for which the *Indian Opinion* was launched, "A struggle which chiefly relies upon internal strength cannot be wholly carried on without a newspaper we could not have educated the local Indian opinion, nor kept Indians all over the world in touch with the course of events in South Africa in any other way with the same ease and success as through *Indian Opinion*, which was a most useful and potent weapon in our struggle."

Next in Gandhi's armoury was *Navjivan*, a Gujarati monthly that was launched as a weekly on October 7, 1919 with Gandhi as the editor. And the magic of Gandhi's pen soon showed up. Writing the editorial for the first issue of *Young India*, which was also relaunched under Gandhi's editorship a day after *Navajivan*, Gandhi exulted: "The editing of *Navajivan* has been a perfect revelation to me. Whilst *Young India* has little more than 1,200 subscribers, *Navajivan* has 12,000. The number would leap to 20,000 if it would but get the printer to print that number. It shows that a vernacular newspaper is a felt want. I am proud to think that I have numerous readers among farmers and workers. They make India... the English journals touch but the fringe of the ocean of India's population."

Gandhi was aware of the readership while writing in different languages. A trilingual—he wrote in English, Gujarati and Hindustani, Gandhi's tone and tenor changed while writing in different languages, because he had the ability to empathise with the audience and understand their expectations and needs in a newspaper.

Gandhi said that he was editing the English journal *Young India*, which along with *Navajivan*, was priced at one anna each, mainly for the benefit of his friends in the Madras constituency. Still, however, "*Young India* sold more copies than the combined total of several newspapers in India. There was not only a new thought but a new language in newspaper writing, and what he wrote was finest in journalistic writing."

The last of Gandhi's journals, *Harijan*, also priced at one anna, started publication on February 11, 1933 from Poona. While the first Gandhi decade in India is often called the story of *Young India*, the decade of the thirties was dominated by *Harijan*, which was started to help Gandhi in his crusade against untouchability. Introducing the weekly to his readers, Gandhi wrote in the inaugural issue: "The English edition of the *Harijan* is being published by and for the Servants of Untouchables Society at my request. Ten thousand copies are being printed if you diligently study the *Harijan*.... it will give you an epitome of the week's doings in the various parts of India in connection with the campaign against untouchability."

In addition to the English version, *Harijan* was brought out in Hindi and Gujarati and it went by the names of *Harijan Sevak* and *Harijan Bandu* respectively. In later years the journal was also published in Urdu, Tamil, Oriya, Marathi and Kannada. Initially Gandhi wanted to keep politics out of *Harijan*, but soon the journal became the voice of Indian reaction. The message of 'Do or Die' rang from the meek looking pages of the *Harijan*. When Gandhi and his followers were locked up after the Quit India Resolution the government confiscated and destroyed every available copy including copies of the back issues. *Harijan* was revived in February 1946, survived Mahatam's death, only to peter out in 1956. Today, the crafts of Gandhi's journalistic charisma are repositories of vivid memories and scholarship. Adorning the thousands of libraries across the world, these journals reveal stories of India's emancipation from colonial rule; narrate the richness of India's heritage and culture, and provide innumberable leads to social scientists for pursuing research. The present work, which looks into the role of these journals in political mobilisation, is based on one such lead.

The vastness of Gandhi makes it extremely difficult to keep the focus of the topic intact. However, every attempt has been made, all precautions taken, to ensure that the focus remains.

Significant Journals

To explore the journalist hidden in Gandhi is no easy exercise, for he was versatile, meticulous and authentic in his writings as in his speeches and actions. No wonder he produced about two million English words alone, the estimate for Hindi and Gujarati being not known. Beginning in South Africa as a free-lance journalist, Gandhi went on to become one of the finest journalists, producing some of the best journals in the history of Indian journalism. *Indian Opinion, Young India, Harijan* and *Navajivan* were the major journals that were edited by Gandhi. Additionally, he was associated with a lot of other publications during the peak of India's freedom struggle.

This section attempts at profiling the above mentioned journals by Gandhi and evaluating them and their effectiveness in political mobilisation.

Indian Opinion : *Indian Opinion*, a fullscap-sized-three-column weekly journal, was launched at Durban on June 4, 1903 by two of Gandhi's close aides, Madanjit Vyavaharik and Manshukhlal Hiralal Nazar. The former looked after the press. The latter was a journalist from Bombay and held editorial charges till 1906. The *Indian Opinion* was started to vent the feelings of the Indians in South Africa and to improve their condition. It was a non-commercial venture. Intially, the journal was started in Hindi, Gujarati, Tamil and English languages. Later the Hindi and Tamil versions were withdrawn.

The journal was "a mirror" of an important part of Gandhi's life. "Week after week I poured out my soul in its columns and expounded the principles and practice of satyagraha." Starting from the first issue in which Gandhi wrote an editorial titled 'Ourselves', Gandhi continuously wrote for *Indian Opinion* till 1914, the year of his departure from South Africa. Gandhi's writings touched upon various aspects of exploitation of Indians in South Africa. Gandhi made the journal a potent weapon in his fight against the racial and discriminatory policies of the British Government. He declared at a later date: "Satyagraha would probably have been impossible without *Indian Opinion.*"

Gandhi outlined three objectives of the journal: first, to make Indian grievances known to the governments in South Africa and in Britain and to the people of India; second, to make the Indians in South Africa aware of their own shortcomings so that they could try to overcome them; and third, to eliminate the prevailing distinctions between Hindus and Muslims and among Gujaratis and Tamilians and others. Gandhi wrote in one of the initial issues of the journal, "The British rulers in India.... follow a different policy. They do not desire that we should come together and become united. Here in South Africa these groups are small in number. We are all confronted with the same disabilities we can easily essay an experiment in achieving unity."

The journal was quite interactive and readers were always invited to contribute their opinions and suggestions on crucial issues. In fact, the style of Gandhi's struggle—passive resistance—got an Indian name through a campaign in the *Indian Opinion.* Looking for an apt name for his technique of struggle, Gandhi invited suggestions from his readers. There was an overwhelming response and finally *'sadagraha'* was chosen which was modified as 'satyagraha' by Gandhi. This example reflects the wonderful ability of Gandhi in involving the masses constructively and instilling in them a sense of participation.

The files of *Indian Opinion* incorporate a series of growing images of the Gandhian spirit. In the early editorials only a mild protest against the racial segregation is seen. At the initial stage Gandhi had firm faith in the British Constitution which was gradually shattered. *Indian Opinion* continuously carried a vivid portrayal of the sufferings of the Indian community in South Africa. It successfully attempted to educate public opinion and indicated the line of duty that every Indian was required to follow in order to assert his or her basic human rights.

There existed a close link between the readers and the editorial office of *Indian Opinion.* Gandhi himself was in close touch with the readers through the regular correspondence column. The readership was not large enough, merely 1,100, but every issue had a group of eager readers making its reach to a much wider audience and furthering the cause of Gandhi's satyagraha.

The editorials and columns of letters apart, *Indian Opinion* carried several features of popular interest. It had contributors writing from abroad also. Gandhi kept Indians in South Africa informed about the progress of the freedom movement in India. He wrote in strong protest against the Bengal partition and encouraged the boycott of foreign goods by Indians in South Africa. He supported the adoption of the *Vande Mataram* as the Indian national anthem. Gandhi called it "a passionate prayer" and published it in Gujarati and Devanagari scripts in the *Indian Opinion.*

Young India : The success of *Indian Opinion* in educating and awakening the Indians in South Africa had been epoch-making and Gandhi knew it. He felt the need for a similar organ after he intensified his campaigns against the British rule in India, a couple of years after coming to his motherland in 1915. This need became more pronounced after Gandhi launched his satyagraha against the Rowlatt Act and the Jallianwallah Bagh massacre in 1919.

Gandhi assumed the editorship of *Young India,* which was published by the management of the *Bombay Chronicle,* in 1919. The objective of the *Indian Opinion,* as declared in the newspaper, was a "desire to promote harmony and goodwill between the different sections of one mighty empire." But by the time Gandhi became associated with the *Young India* and *Navajivan,* his hopes in the British justice had been shattered. He was becoming more and more conscious of the true nature of colonialism and was preparing the country to fight injustice through satyagraha, as practised in South Africa.

Gandhi thus spelt the policy of *Young India.* "Apart from its duty of drawing attention to injustices to individuals, it will devote its attention to constructive satyagraha as also sometimes cleansing satyagraha. Cleansing satyagraha is a civil resistance where resistance becomes a duty to remove a persistent and degrading injustice such as the Rowlatt Act." *Young India* in no time became a medium of aggressive campaign against the injustices of the British Government.

Gandhi poured out fire through his pen. He sincerely felt that the alien government had no right to govern. He wrote a number of fiery articles like 'Tampering with Loyalty' and 'The Puzzle and its Solution' in the pages of *Young India* to arouse the Indian masses. Besides, the journal was also used to educate the masses on various socio-political and economic issues of national and international importance. Gandhi used articles by renowned personalities of the freedom struggle on various issues. The journal was also used as a forum for intellectual debates, for example, the debates between Gandhi and Tagore on khadi and scope of education.

Navajivan : *Navajivan* was a regional journal in Gujarati, published alongwith *Young India* under the editorship of Gandhi. Outlining its purpose, Gandhi wrote in the March 12 issue of the *Young India* that it was published "for the sole purpose of educating the nation to win *Purna Swaraj* through truthful and non-violent means." Its fate ceased with that of the *Young India*.

Harijan : A couple of years after the *Young India* and *Navajivan* were silenced, Gandhi felt the need for another journal. But this time for a different reason: to help him in his crusade against untouchability. Born in 1933, the paper, *Harijan* initially carried items solely devoted to social issues. "It will be solely devoted to the Harijan cause," Gandhi wrote after being released from prison in May 1933, "and will scrupulously exclude all politics." So much so that there was a complete blackout of important political news of the day, there was no mention of the Congress session and the Government of India Act of 1935.

The *Harijan* became a mouthpiece for the Harijan movement and village industries. The paper published useful extracts from books on rural problems. However, the tide of surging nationalism in later years did not let *Harijan* maintain its focus. Increasingly, it started carrying the messages of the non-violent satyagraha of

Gandhi and became a chief messenger of the Quit India Movement. The slogan of 'do or die' given by Gandhi during the movement was conveyed to the masses through the *Harijan.* It became a fiery propaganda vehicle, so much so that soon after the arrest of Gandhi on 8 August 1942, the *Harijan* was closed down. However, even after that, Gandhi's message seemed to be echoing: "The *Harijan* may be suppressed, its message cannot be, so long as I live. Indeed the spirit will survive the dissolution of the body and somehow speak through the millions...." The millions did speak, and *Harijan* lived upto its cause.

***Hind Swaraj* :** One of Gandhi's seminal work is *Hind Swaraj* which was written in Gujarati and published in a book form in Gujarati in January 1910 by Gandhi's own International Printing Press. The English translation by Gandhi himself came out a few years later.

Hind Swaraj is written in the literary genre of dialogue: a dialogue between a newspaper editor and a reader. It was addressed to a mixed audience: the expatriate Indians who were attracted to terrorism and political violence, the extremists and moderates of the Indian National Congress, the Indian nation and the English. As to why he wrote the book, he said there was first of all the consequent urge to communicate. Secondly, he wanted to clarify the meaning of Swaraj. Thirdly, he felt it necessary to respond specifically to the ideology of political terrorism adopted by the expatriates. Fourthly, Gandhi was anxious to teach the Indians that modern civilisation posed a greater threat to them than did colonialism. Fifthly, he wanted to contribute towards the reconciliation of Indians and Britons. Finally, Gandhi believed that through *Hind Swaraj* he would be able to give Indians a practical philosophy, an updated conception of *Dharma,* that would fit them for life in the modern world.

Hind Swaraj was the seed from which the tree of Gandhian thought has grown to its full stature. No wonder that it has been called "a very basic document for the study of Gandhi's thought," his "confession of faith", a "proclamation of ideological independence", and the nearest he came to producing a sustained work of political theory.

Two Marches

The Dandi March (Salt Satyaraha) was a meticulously planned event. To understand its dynamics and use as a communication tool, we have to examine how Gandhi visualised the event, why he chose salt, why he decided to march and why he selected Dandi as the destination.

After the Lahore Congress of 1929 had authorised the Working Committee to launch a programme of civil disobedience, the latter invested Gandhi with full powers to launch the movement at a time and place of his choice. Gandhi was already desperately in search of an effective formula for the movement. By the end of February, the formula began to surface as Gandhi started talking about salt: "There is no article like salt outside water by taxing which the state can reach even the starving millions, the sick, the maimed and the utterly helpless. The taxes constitute therefore the most inhuman toll tax the ingenuity of man can devise."

The plan for the launch of the civil disobedience movement by breaking the salt law was brilliantly conceived. "Gandhi along with a band of 78 members of the Sabarmati Ashram, among whom were men belonging to almost every region and religion of India, was to march from his headquarters in Ahmedabad through the villages of Gujarat for 240 miles. On reaching the coast at Dandi, he would break the salt law by collecting salt from the beach. This deceptively innocuous move was to prove devastatingly effective."

Salt had a great significance and by choosing it for the civil disobedience movement Gandhi "in one stroke fulfilled all the criteria he had set himself." As a substance of common use salt cut across all the differences—religious, caste and class. It provided Hindus and Muslims a platform for a joint struggle on an economic issue; it was a symbol of exploitation of the poor; for the rich, a struggle against salt laws gave an opportunity for symbolic identification with mass suffering. Additionally, salt had great emotional appeal. In the West too, there was a long tradition of opposition to the salt tax. "But it was the cultural appeal of salt which was Gandhi's trump card. In both Indian and Western tradition, salt is the symbol of all that is vital to human life." Thus salt lent itself to linguistic and metaphoric use by Gandhi.

Despite its appeal Gandhi knew that he needed to introduce salt in an effective way to attract maximum appeal. So he decided for a march. "A march would give him the opportunity to arouse the people in the countryside through which he passed." It would enact a live drama, thought Gandhi, and would evoke great interest in national and international press.

Like salt, the march too has a place of significance in Indian tradition. Pilgrimages to holy places are made on foot and viewed as penance and such pilgrims are revered in India. In Western and Indian mythology, marches are associated with determination, righteousness and sacrifice for a good cause. The *Bible* describes Moses leading his people to the Promised Land, Jesus leading his followers to Jerusalem, Rama leaving home to honour his father's pledge, and Gautama renouncing his home in the quest for enlightenment. "Gandhi used this association to great effect."

The desire to choose Dandi as the destination to break the salt law was taken after much deliberation. It was felt that the itinerary of the march should give an opportunity to rally the public in entire Gujarat and give time for the impact to spread to the rest of the country.

The Salt Satyagraha was planned in less than a month's time. It was conceived in mid-February and conducted in mid-March, and the final act performed on April 6. The massive mobilisation, which the event achieved, was possible not only because of the issues it addressed but also due to the support of a network of trained workers. This network did not develop overnight but over years of grassroot constructive work. Now at the time of crisis, students and teachers of the national schools and colleges researched the salt laws, the Khadi workers and Gandhian *aashram* inmates wrote articles explaining the issues and practical instructions on salt manufacture, and the village workers explained the nature of the struggle to the rural masses and later courageously produced under-ground newspapers. Along with political training, these workers, many of whom were women, were trained to develop their communication skills. They were taught to use prayer meetings for the politicisation of the masses. After devotional activities, articles from the journals, *Young India* and *Navajivan* were read out and explained to prepare the audience for the coming struggle. They were taught *bhajans* and songs, which would be useful for raising consciousness.

The print medium too was well developed before the march began. Gandhi had taken over the editorship of *Young India* and *Navajivan* after coming back from South Africa. He was simultaneously developing the network of workers for distribution. When the time for Satyagraha came, these weeklies with their established readership were made to carry the message of salt. Gandhi also consciously maintained contact with the world press. In the days before the march, despite hectic preparations, he spared time for foreign journalists. They were the only channels through which the struggle could be publicised abroad. He was very conscious of the power that the press possessed and was particular about being quoted accurately. "He used to insist as a pre-condition that his messages and statements should be published without the slightest alteration." The three elements of salt satyagraha—salt, march and Dandi—with their historic, symbolic, metaphoric and linguistic associations were used to great effect by Gandhi to propagate his vision of Swaraj among his Indian audience and to gain the sympathy of his audience abroad.

Gandhi included in his co-workers people from all parts of the country, giving the group a truly all-India character. By selecting Abbas Tyabji and Sarojini Naidu to replace him as leader in the event of his arrest, he symbolically conveyed his regard for Muslims and women. Thus Gandhi used the structure of the march itself to communicate the idea of a united India that he envisaged.

During the 25 days of March, Gandhi made great use of speeches. During his tour he visited 40 villages and at each village he gave a speech, reaching an estimated five lakh people. In these speeches he presented salt as the epitome of British exploitation and attempted to exhort people to break the law. Gandhi used the speeches as an occasion to attract women to the movement. He used examples from mythology referring to the courage of Sita and Draupadi.

The symbolic imagery related to salt, march and Dandi was infectious. It was echoed in the writings of foreign journalists who compared Gandhi to Moses and Jesus and in the articles by Mahadev Desai who drew parallels between Dandi march and Buddha's *mahabhinishkraman.* Songs were another way of stirring people. The importance of these media can be gauged by the fact that the British tried to counter the Satyagraha by systematically choking the means of communication. Ordinances were promulgated to ban the press to curb the growing influence of Gandhian newspapers. The British arrested Gandhi as his speeches were making a great impact. Congress leaders and village level workers were also arrested. "Letters and telegrams were of course censored but the British police relentlessly pursued the editors of the underground newspapers which replaced the outlawed nationalist press."

Civil disobedience movement thus reflected how Gandhi used traditional symbols along with the print media for effective mobilisation.

It is relevant here to mention the core of Gandhian strategy of the use of media of communication for political mobilisation. Gandhi used to maintain multiple levels of communication. Firstly, he used oral tradition of communication where he relied on techniques like *prarthna sabha,* speeches and one-to-one meeting. This helped him understand the masses well. This, in turn, led to concept formation for Gandhi—concepts about people's perceptions, attitudes, needs and aspirations. Having established a rapport with the masses through oral communication, Gandhi proceeded to strike a rapport with the social and political elites of the society. Here he relied on the print medium. The essence of his writings, though intended for the masses, were grasped first by the literate elite class or the 'attentive public' and then filtered down to the masses which ultimately helped in shaping public opinion and political mobilisation. Thus along with multiple levels of communication, Gandhi used a multi-pronged mobilisation strategy.

A Long Journey

Gandhi's sojourn with journalism started with his first paper, *Indian Opinion* which was launched in South Africa. In order to ventilate the grievances of Indians and mobilise public opinion in their favour, Gandhi started writing in and giving interviews to newspapers. He maintained a list of friendly papers which gave him wholehearted support. He focussed on open letters and letters to the editor, but soon realised that occasional writings and the hospitality of newspapers were inadequate for the political campaign he had launched.

Gandhi had all the qualities of a good journalist. Gandhi made known the ideals he had set before himself as a journalist in his autobiography. He wrote, "The sole aim of journalism should be service." He further stated that reference to the abuses in the states is undoubtedly necessary part of journalism and it is a means of creating public opinion. I have taken up journalism not for its sake but merely as aid to what I have conceived to be my mission in life." Defining the objects of a newspaper, Gandhi said that a purpose is "to understand the popular feeling and give expression to it; another is to arouse among the people certain desirable sentiments; and the third is fearlessly to expose popular defects."

The genesis of Gandhi's reliance on mass media and his usage of newspapers/journals to generate public opinion and political mobilisation can be traced back to his struggle in South Africa.

The Indian labourers who had gone to South Africa and the merchants who followed them were denied the right to vote. They had to register and pay toll tax. They could not reside except in prescribed locations which were dirty and congested. Gandhi soon became the leader of the struggle against these conditions and during 1893-94 was engaged in a heroic though unequal struggle against the racist authorities of South Africa. It was during this long struggle, lasting nearly two decades, that Gandhi evolved the technique of Satyagraha based on truth and non-violence.

As early as 1896 the roots of the Satyagraha took shape in Gandhi's mind. In the 'Green Pamphlet' he pointed out that his method in South Africa was to conquer "hatred by love." In 1899, Gandhi held out the hope: "...victory must be ours, for our case has been universally regarded as just, our methods moderate and without reproach." And to achieve this victory Gandhi resorted to Satyagraha.

When the Satyagraha struggle commenced, Gandhi became involved in the publication of the weekly journal *Indian Opinion,* published in English and Gujarati. It made a significant contribution in educating Indians and instilling in them courage to resist injustice. Satyagraha in South Africa would probably have been impossible without it. According to Gandhi, through the "medium of this paper we could very well disseminate the news of the week among the community. The English section kept those Indians informed about the movement who did not know Gujarati and for Englishmen in India, England and South Africa *Indian Opinion* served the purpose of a weekly newsletter." Gandhi considered *Indian Opinion* as an effective instrument for mass mobilisation.

Gandhi also regularly wrote for the local white press to clarify the Indian stand and expose the partisan and anti-Indian policies of the South African Government. In a letter published in *Rand Daily Main* on 6th August, 1910, Gandhi wrote: "Will you permit me to correct some statements made in your leading article on Lord Ampthills' action in the House of Lords on the passive resistance struggle?.... May I remind you that passive resistance commenced in 1907 when the question of priests, doctors and lawyers had not come up for public discussion, and when it did arise, it simply arose in order to forcibly illustrate the injustice that had been done by the Government in not conceding the demands of the community." In the same letter, he wrote, "Passive resisters who are not criminals in the ordinary sense of the term have been sent to a penal settlement, like Diepkloof, where the ordinary privileges of prisoners are withheld." In his opinion, this was undoubtedly a glaring instance of mistreatment. This reflects Gandhi's concern for highlighting issues through the press.

In fact, the files of *Indian Opinion* reflect the gradual growth of the Gandhian spirit. The early issues carried petitions and prayers. There was appeal- to reason and expostulation. The great bulk of editorials of *Indian Opinion* contained a mild protest against racial segregation. For, at this stage, Gandhi had "firm faith in the British Constitution." However, with the passage of time, as he realised the harshness of the Empire, Gandhi had to change his stand. "Is this monstrous injustice to be really done?" he asked, in regard to the anti-Indian regulations which were steadily growing in number. "Even at the eleventh hour..... we cannot abandon hope that the better nature, the truer self,, of our white brokers will yet assert itself." He kept on repeating this hope in numerous editorials until at last exasperated, he said, "Perhaps in the Transvaal, people are living in the Middle Ages."

He had already alerted every Indian in South Africa to be ready for self-sacrifice for the sake of the whole community whose fate was hanging in the balance. He appealed, "Individual differences must be sunk in the face of common danger. The slightest deviation would bring us down the precipice, because the opposition set up against us is overwhelming."

After moving its office and printing press to Phoenix, *Indian Opinion* continuously carried a vivid portrayal of the sufferings of the Indian community in South Africa. It attempted to educate public opinion and simultaneously indicated the line of duty that every Indian must follow in order to win his elementary human rights. Close communion linked the editorial office with the readers of the journal. The correspondence columns were a good training ground for Gandhi himself. It was as though the entire community of the Indians thought audibly with him through the piles of letters the mails brought. *Indian Opinion* hardly ever had more than 1,100 subscribers but each copy had a group of eager readers and passed from hand to hand. In fact, Gandhi adopted this style in all his future journalistic endeavours.

Gandhi returned to India in 1915 at the age of 46. He was keen to serve his country and his people. He first decided to study Indian conditions before deciding the field of his work. He found the ground ready for action in 1919 that was a watershed year in Indian history. Discontentment was brewing all over the country for several reasons. The Rowlatt Act, the Jallianwala Bagh massacre and martial law in Punjab had belied all the generous wartime promises of the British. The Montagu-Chelmsford Reforms that were announced towards the end of 1919, with their ill-considered scheme of dyarchy, satisfied few. The Indian Muslims too were angry when they discovered that their loyalty had been purchased during the war by assurances of generous treatment of Turkey after the war—a promise British statesman had no intention of fulfilling.

Gandhi was in close touch with the Khilafat leaders for quite some time. He was sympathetic to the Khilafat cause because he felt that the British had committed a breach of faith by making promises which it had no intention of keeping. In February 1920, Gandhiji suggested to the Khilafat Committee to adopt a programme of non-violent non-cooperation to protest the government's behaviour. On June 9, 1920, the Khilafat Committee at Allahabad unanimously accepted the suggestion of non-cooperation and asked Gandhiji to lead the movement. Prior to this in May 1920, the All India Congress Committee in a meeting decided to convene a special session in September to enable the Congress to decide on its course of action.

Meanwhile, the non-cooperation movement was launched formally on August 1, 1920, after the expiry of the notice that Gandhiji had sent to the Vicerory in his letter of 22 June in which he had asserted the right recognised "from time immemorial of the subject to refuse to assist a ruler who misrules."

The Congress accepted non-cooperation as its own programme of action in its special session of September. The Non-Cooperation programme proposed by Gandhi consisted of surrendering of titles and honours, refusal to attend government functions, boycott of government-affiliated schools and colleges, gradual boycott of courts, refusal of military to serve in Mesopotamia, a complete boycott of the reformed council and boycott of foreign goods, besides others. Gandhi promised that if the programme was fully implemented, Swaraj would be ushered- in within a year.

The Nagpur session of the Congress in December 1920, where the non-cooperation resolution was passed, thus committed the Congress to a programme of extra-constitutional mass action. Many revolutionary terrorist groups also pledged support to the movement. In order for the Congress to fulfill its new commitment, significant changes were introduced in its creed and its organisational structure. The goal of the Congress was changed from the attainment of self-government by constitutional and legal means to the attainment of Swaraj by peaceful and legitimate means. The new Constitution of the Congress, the handiwork of Gandhiji, introduced other major changes, among them, the working committee was reconstituted with 15 members; Provincial Congress Committees were to be organised on a linguistic basis; membership was reduced to four annas per year.

The adoption of the Non-Cooperation Movement by the Congress, which was initiated earlier by the Khilafat Conference, gave it a new energy and from January 1921, it began to register considerable success all over the country.

After having conceived the programme of non-cooperation, Gandhi took a whirlwind tour of the country to popularise his ideas of non-cooperation. He addressed hundreds of meetings and met a large number of political workers. Along with this he strategically used the press to add impetus to the movement. He had also taken over the editorship of the journals, *Young India* and *Navajivan* by then. Introducing the two journals to his readers, Gandhi wrote: "with much striving I have formulated some principles for my life and put them into practice.... it is my sincere aspiration to place these principles before India and share my happiness with her. A newspaper is one means to that end...." He further wrote, "The agitation against the Rowlatt Act was an object lesson in Satyagraha. Hence *Navajivan* will keep it alive before the public."

In these journals Gandhi freely ventilated his views and also used them to educate the public on Satyagraha.

Gandhi used these journals to inform the masses on many aspects during the non-cooperation movement. For instance, in an article 'The Doctrine of the Sword' in the *Young India,* Gandhi wrote: "Non-violence is the law of our species as violence is law of the brute.... I have therefore returned to place before India the ancient law of self-sacrifice. For Satyagraha and its offshoots, non-cooperation and civil resistance are nothing but new names for the law of suffering."

In speech after speech and in editorial after editorial, Gandhi explained ceaselessly and untiringly the nature of this movement. "The movement of non-cooperation is nothing but an attempt to isolate the brute force of the British from all the trappings under which it is hidden and to show that brute force by itself cannot for one single moment hold India."

Thus Gandhi adopted various techniques for mobilising the masses such as extensive tours and *padyatra,* speeches at public meetings, effective journalism, prayers and *bhajans,* fasts, *brahmcharya* and *swadeshi,* and fighting for the rights of minorities and especially untouchables. "Gandhi touched every heart and every aspect of Indian life. He mobilized the masses and directed their struggle for complete freedom and reconstruction of the society."

Gandhi's writings were quite forceful and were written with conviction. They left a deep impression on his readers. Thus he wrote once in the context of non-cooperation in the *Young India:* 'Our non-cooperation is neither with the English nor with the West. Our non-cooperation is with the system the English have established, with the material civilisation and its attendant greed and exploitation of the weak. Our non-cooperation is refusal to cooperate with the English administrators on their own terms." He asked the English: "Come and cooperate with us on our terms, and it will be well for us, for you and the world."

However, Gandhi was aware of the mood of the masses and

the sentiments that prevailed. He was quick to warn his countrymen about any form of violence through his journal. "Violent resistance," Gandhi wrote, "is itself non-cooperation and it is immoral because of its violence. It becomes moral when it is non-violent. Non-cooperation with evil is a sacred duty." Gandhi advocated non-cooperation based on nonviolence. "The active state of *ahimsa* requires you to resist the wrong doer."

Gandhi was quick to respond to the different forms of participation by different sections of the society during the peak of the non-cooperation movement. The 19th January, 1921 issue of *Young India,* for instance, had the following item as a flier (the top news): "Students strike in Calcutta. The latest information to hand about the great students' strike of Calcutta is that nearly 8,000 college students are on strike. The following colleges are affected—some wholly, others partially: (1) Bangabasi (2) Ripon...." This was not only a great morale booster for the students' struggle in Bengal but also inspired students' groups in other parts of the country.

This caption was followed by a long letter titled 'To Young Bengal' written by Gandhi himself that was carried over in the second page. Gandhi wrote, "I have just read an account of your response to the nation's calls.... I had expected no less: I certainly expect still more. You have taken the step. You will not recede."

Gandhi exhorted the youth in the same letter, "We cannot get *Swaraj* if not one class in the country is prepared to work and sacrifice for it. The Government will yield not to the logic of words. It knows no logic but that of brave and true deals.... You dare not go back without hurting yourselves and the case." Though the letter was addressed to the students, it had a message for all sections of the society and touched upon socio-political and economic aspects. Thus Gandhi had something to convey, as a mature editor would do in times of crisis, to those inclined towards violence: "Intolerance is a species of violence and therefore against our creed. Non-violent non-cooperation is an object lesson in democracy. The moment we are able to ensure non-violence, even under circumstances the most provoking, that moment we have achieved our end, because that is the moment when we can offer complete non-cooperation."

The next issue of the *Young India* had a one and a quarter column report titled 'The Student Movement in Calcutta' on the front page. It was basically a news report and contained all the facts and figures about the protest movement, besides explaining the style and method of the students' struggle. This was certain to inspire and train other such movements in other parts of the country.

As the non-cooperation movement progressed, cases of assault on people increased. Gandhi would immediately know the importance of publishing something like brutalities of the British administrators on the freedom fighters. Thus the January 12, 1922 issue of *Young India* had an item titled 'Summary of Reports of Repression'. Besides the news of 'Cases of assault at Secunderabad' on volunteers, brave tales of 'two wives' of the secretary of Sitapur District Congress Committee, and beating up of two reputed 'Zamindars' of Hajipur in Bihar, the summary contained details like number of workers sent to jails from Chittagong. "It has sent 355 workers to jail up to now, including one Congress President and two secretaries. The third secretary is on trial. The fourth is now holding office. Number of arrests and imprisonment: October 31; November 18; December upto 10th-12th. Of the industrial prisoners one is a Mohamedan gentleman aged about 80, the president of the Khilafat Committee."

During the non-cooperation movement Gandhi vehemently propagated the need for restoring the local economy by resorting to activities like home spinning that would reduce the dependence on foreign cloth. In an article 'The Duty of Spinning' in *Young India,* Gandhi wrote: "Just as we cannot live without breathing and without eating, so is it impossible for us to attain economic independence and banish pauperism from this ancient land without reviving home spinning. I hold the spinning wheel to be as much a necessity in every household as the hearth. No other scheme that can be devised will ever solve the problem of the deepening poverty of the people."

Gandhi advocated the boycott of foreign cloth. The boycott, as Gandhi conveyed to his readers through his journals, was "as necessary for national existence as breath is for life." Equally powerful were Gandhi's views on subjects like untouchability and Hindu-Muslim unity and other socio-political issues. "The removal of untouchability means the abolition of the fifth caste. There should therefore be no objection to a *Panchama* boy drawing water from the common well of a village and to his attending its common school. He should freely exercise all the rights of a non-Brahmin," wrote Gandhi. He also appeared anguished at the atrocities against them. In an article in *Navajivan,* his Gujarati journal, Gandhi wrote that cruelties to the untouchables constituted "an outrage grosser than that in the Punjab against which we have been protesting." "We ... segregate them... drive them to live on the outskirts of the village, (are) not concerned whether they live or die... give them food left over by others."

Thus Gandhi touched upon a whole range of issues in his journals. Combined with his other communication strategies, Gandhi's journals greatly helped in mobilising the people. The massive participation of a wide section of people in the movement confirms the success of Gandhi's strategies.

4

The Stalwarts

B.G. Horniman

The battle for freedom was fought as much with the pen as with the weapon of *Satyagraha.* Editors of Indian newspapers used their pens like sharp swords to harass the alien government and to make deep thrusts at their vulnerable points to expose their oppression and exploitation. They inspired and encouraged freedom fighters and gathered support for them. They were patriots and their patriotism bordered on fanaticism. They were crusaders in the fight for independence and they made sacrifices and suffered privations (including imprisonment) unheard of in the annals of journalism of any country in the world. There were giants among them who have found a place in the roll of honour of India's freedom. There were two foreigners in their ranks, one an Englishman who made India his home and was called a traitor by his countrymen, and the other an Irishman who edited a British owned nawspaper and proved a great embarrassment to the British rulers. One of them, B.G. Horniman is the subject of this chapter.

Horniman came to India in the early years of this century as an assistant editor of the *Statesman.* He was the son of a former paymaster-in-chief of the British navy and the brother of a rear-admiral and a famous actor. He was a staunch advocate of Indian independence and was soon disgusted with the uncongenial atmosphere of Chowringhee (Calcutta) where the *Statesman* was printed. He resigned his job in 1912. Recommending him to Sir Pherozeshah Mehta who was in search of an editor for his newly started *Bombay Chronicle,* Surendranath Bannerjee wrote: "I may assure you that Horniman is as good an Indian as myself. During the days of the partition of Bengal he used to walk with us barefooted through the streets of Calcutta with a shawl on his broad white shoulders."

Before Horniman arrived in Bombay and took charge of the *Bombay Chronicle* in 1913, vigorous, dynamic public life was unknown. What public activity there was centred round the chambers of Mehta and Sir Chimanlal Setalvad. One commentator says: "Bombay got inspiration, advice and drive from the new editor who wrested for her a permanent position in Indian politics." An Englishman as editor of an Indian newspaper necessarily had to work under great strain but Horniman had the advantage of professionalism which made him an expert. There had been British champions of the Indian cause before and after Horniman but none as eminent for personal identification with the causes he took up and for the vigour with which he pursued them. To his qualities as a trained journalist he added emotional involvement in the fight for Indian freedom. He was an indefatigable worker active in public life and in movements for relief to the people. By his incessant attacks on the British owned press he shook the *Times of India* (which virtually enjoyed a monopoly until the arrival of the *Chronicle)* out of its smugness and exposed its anti-Indian views and race prejudice. It soon became a habit for the citizens of Bombay to read the *Chronicle* the first thing in the morning. As one writer remarked: "It supplied them their war cry. The fascination lay in the editor's nationality. A radical outlook, a consciousness and feeling born of right and a ruthless exposure of evil were the dominant features of Homiman's writings." An European bureaucrat said of him: "I hate Horniman though I can't help admiring his articles which are a tonic." The officials branded him a traitor to his motherland.

Referring to this, Horniman said: "They (his enemies) read every line I write. They read between the lines and above them, underneath them and in all sorts of positions but they couldn't catch me." Horniman, as president of the Bombay Journalists Association led a deputation to the viceroy early in 1916 to protest against the misuse of the Press Act of 1910. Other members of the deputation included C.Y. Chintamani, S.N. Bannerjee and Pandit Malviya. The viceroy's reply was not satisfactory but the deputation had the satisfaction of utilising the occasion to give wide publicity to the misdeeds of the government (central and provincial). Horniman's relations with the Board of Directors of the *Chronicle* were not happy and he was in frequent conflict with it. It was dominated by Moderates but as long as Mehta was alive, things went on smoothly; with his passing away, Horniman began to feel the strain much more. Although he protested again and again against the interference of the Board with editorial policy, he was unable to make his voice felt. Annie Besant wrote to him that it was wrong to allow his independence of expression to be curtailed by a "stupid Board of Directors". "In your place", she said, "I would tell them frankly that either I edit as I like or I resign." Horniman had close relations with Besant and when she was interned in 1917 he went to Madras to edit her paper, *New India,* until P.K. Telang, acting editor took over. The Board of Directors of which Sir Chimanlal Setalvad was the chairman did not approve of his support for the Home Rule Movement started by Besant.

When Edwin Montagu, Secretary of state for India, visited India in 1917 in connection with constitutional reforms, the Viceroy, Lord Chelmsford, had made arrangements to accommodate his party in tents on the grounds of the Viceregal Lodge in old Delhi instead of offering rooms in the Lodge itself. Horniman protested in the columns of the *Chronicle* against what he called "this snobbery" of an English aristocrat who, Horniman said, thought it below his dignity to put up in his house a commoner who happened to be a Jew, Homiman's protest was taken up by other papers throughout India. Chelmsford offered an apology and said that no insult was meant. He said owing to lack of accommodation in the Viceregal Lodge and for Montagu's own convenience, he had decided to give him separate quarters. Horniman refused to be convinced by this explanation and did not abate his criticism of the viceroy. Later, when Horniman met Montagu in the presence of Chelmsford, Montagu defended Chelmsford and chided Horniman for taking up the cudgels on his behalf. Horniman replied: "I admire your extreme courtesy to your not very cordial host, but I still I maintain that respecting the traditions of India, he had better given you, even at some personal inconvenience, accommodation in the Viceregal Lodge."

In 1919, Horniman wrote almost daily on the Punjab atrocities under Martial Law and exposed the abuse of power and the humiliation imposed on the people. As one observer of the scene remarked: "His articles struck terror in the hearts of bureaucrats as they read them morning after morning. One reader described the *Chronicle* as an appetiser to a hearty meal for the public and a paper which destroyed the appetite of the government and its sycophants. It was inspiring in its candid criticism of both the government and the Moderates. Every time they read the *Chronicle* they could not help jumping in their chairs." Horniman's tussle with the Board became acute and one day it reached the crisis point. The board tried to dictate to Horniman what he should write and what he should not. Horniman refused to be dictated to and resigned. He announced the resignation in the paper itself. His resignation created a commotion among his readers and angry crowds invaded the *Chronicle* office and demanded the recall of Homiman. The Board asked N.M. Samath, a leading Moderate, to reorganise the paper and he called in Pathan Joseph, a talented writer who had earlier served as assistant editor in a number of papers, to take charge. The circulation of the paper began to fall rapidly and the Board resigned. Setalvad relinquished control of the paper and a new Board was formed with M.A. Jinnah as chairman. Horniman was recalled. Pothan Joseph remained as assistant editor and Syed Abdullah Brelvi, who was a sub-editor, was made an assistant editor. Horniman was, however not to be in the *Chronicle* for long. The Bombay Government was out to take action against him for his articles on the Punjab. In his own words: "Lord Lloyd (government) and his secretariat gang pored and pored over every *Chronicle* file until DORA (Defence of the Realm Act) came to their rescue and I was bundled off." Horniman was deported in April 3919. He was then recovering from an operation. He was removed to a ship in the harbour and sent back home.

Gandhi presided over a protest meeting of Bombay citizens in June, 1919, which urged the government to revoke the deportation order. Gandhi said: "Mr. Horniman is a very brave and generous Englishman. He has given us the *mantram-Liberty*. He has fearlessly exposed the wrong wherever he has seen it and thus has been an ornament to the race to which he belongs and rendered it a great service. Every Indian knows his services to India. The continuance of the *Chronicle* without Mr. Horniman would be like an attempt to sustain the body when the soul has departed. The national cause will certainly feel hurt to find that one who presented it with a daily draught of Liberty is no more in its midst." Gandhi said he did not agree on many occasions with that Horniman wrote and said, he thought the language used by him was more suited to a Western than an Eastern country. But the question was one of liberty of the press and liberty of public speech and it was for this reason that they wanted the deportation order to be revoked.

Defending the action against Horniman Montagu said in the House of Commons: "We have been very patient with Homiman. In no case has there been a better example of our relutance to interfere with mere eccentricities of political belief. But when this gentleman began to use his paper in the middle of the riots resulting in loss of life to spread and fan the flames and opened his columns to an accusation that British troops had been using soft-nosed bullets in the streets of Delhi and when his paper was being distributed free to British troops in Bombay in the hope of inciting disaffection and insubordination, why, then, I say, it was high time he left India." He added: "An Englishman, upon whom far greater responsibility certainly rests, cannot be tolerated in India if he is responsible for the occurrences which we associate with Mr. Homiman."

Horniman defeated himself through the çolumns of the *Manchester Guardian.* He wrote: "Though the government was strongly criticised as it deserved and the strongest protest was made in my paper regarding the public flogging of people in streets, the dropping of bombs on unarmed crowds, machine gunning of demonstrators without adequate provocation, the whole of my personal influence and that of my paper— neither of which is inconsiderable—were used in support of restoration of order and the inculcation of the doctrine and practice of *Satyagraha*—the very negation of violence—both before and during the disturbances that occurred." In a letter to the *Chronicle* in September, 1919, he related the circumstances under which he was deported. He was ill, he said, and under doctor's orders after an operation not to leave the house, when the police came and asked him to pack up. He was carried from his house to an ambulance and placed on board the ship. Horniman returned to India early in 1926, defying a government order, by way of Colombo and according to one writer: "His journey from Dhanushkodi to Bombay was a triumphal march." He became the editor of the *Sentinel,* a sister evening daily of the *Chronicle.* He also wrote a column in the *Chronicle* under the pseudonym, Atropos, which he used to attack the government and the Moderates. He called the *Times of India* "the Old Woman of Bori Bunder" which became famous. As editor of the *Sentinel* he became the *bete noire* of the police for his exposures of gambling in the city. He was trapped in a police raid while investigating and was hauled up before a magistrate like an ordinary felon. The chief Presidency magistrate acquitted him and took the police to task for their treatment of him. Even the *Times of India* was forced to condemn the police action and demand an enquiry. In 12 articles after his acquittal, titled, "I accuse the police", Horniman charged the police with deliberately staging the raid and organising mass arrests merely to trap him and parade him before the public as a gambler. He had an amazing knowledge of the law and of "lawless laws" and this helped him to keep out of trouble. He always appeared in court without a lawyer and conducted his own defence. His articles in the *Chronicle* and the *Indian Daily Mail* during the *Satyagraha* movement in 1932 resulted in security being demanded from these papers by the government. "Horniman has done the work of 100 leaders", said a prominent Congressman. His sense of news was disconcerting to his opponents, in the profession. He was the *guru* of over a dozen journalists who have made good in Indian journalism. He was temperamental and this created several crises in his career. In the words of a writer: "He became at once the proud master and pitiless slave of his temperament. It also invested him with a uniqueness of strength unknown to the majority of men." K. Rama Rao, who was one of his disciples, wrote: "He was a great chief. In a few words he would give instructions that illumined the sub-editor's or the reporter's path. Sitting in his room he gathered Bombay's political strings in his hands and knew all that was happening politically, noble as well as ignoble."

"I shall not set down my pen, he said on the occasion of the golden jubilee of his entry into the profession, until the freedom of India is achieved." "He was a school of journalism himself; taught many aspirants and saw several of them seated in editorial chairs. Stem and unbending were his political convictions, whatever his weakness otherwise. He had a genius to make history, not merely record it, whether he was participating in the Bengal anti-partition demonstrations in the early decades of the century or throwing out a reactionary Board of Directors and replacing them by men of his choice; whether he was being deported from his sick bed or was returning to India to a hero's welcome; whether he was founding, editing or killing newspapers or defying the tin gods of bureaucracy; whether he was defying the High Court needling a home member. He had a positive genius for lampooning the government and its overzealous minions and yet circumventing the law cleverly. He was justly proud of his sound judgment which the gods give only to their favourites. He was a lovable, adorable person and his colleagues called him, 'Governor'. He could rifle our pockets at leisure and we his. He ate no salt and only beetroot sugar for the sake of his throat. He argued his own cases and once expounded in court the startling doctrine that he had a right to travel first class on trains because no accommodation was available in the second. He dressed like a peacock, whoever paid the bills. He occasionally wore the *dhoti*. He spoke brilliantly on the platform and he wrote like an angel but could not, unlike some of us smaller fry, dictate an article. He invariably wrote it out. He spent money faster than he earned it and innumerable were the pirates and parasites around him."

After Horniman was deported in 1919, the *Bombay Chronicle* was placed under official censorship. The directors asked Gandhi to take over the conduct of the paper but before he could do so, the paper suspended publication following the forfeiture of the security of Rs. 10,000 deposited when the pre-censorship was imposed. When the paper resumed publication, S.A. Brelvi was appointed editor. The *Chronicle* went through a financial crisis which was aggravated when a libel suit was filed against the company which owned the paper and heavy damages were awarded. The company went into liquidation. The paper was purchased by Belgaumwala who sold it to N.M. Cama who formed the Associated Paper Company. Brelvi brought a measure of stability to the paper and it played a notable part in the freedom movement. Both *the Chronicle* and *Sentinel* closed down in 1959.

Arthur Moore

Arthur Moore belonged to that rare species of editors who have a mind of their own and do not care what others think about it. Moore enjoyed in letting people in high positions in government or in politics know what he thought, and what he thought and wrote was not always palatable to the parties for whom it was intended. He was an unconventional editor and the Statesman which he adorned for 10 years from the editorial chair was not always happy with him. K.P.S. Menon, the veteran diplomat, said: "Arthur Moore was no respector of persons. Some VIPs disliked him and he reciprocated their sentiments cordially. On the whole, he was regarded by the Establishment as a difficult person to deal with."

Moore succeeded Alfred Watson as editor of the *Statesman* in 1932. Watson was the target of terrorist attack twice and he was injured in the second attempt when he was shot at by a young terrorist. The attacks were a sequel to some articles published in the *Statesman* and according to Muggeridge who had just then joined the paper, as an assistant editor, they had been written by Moore. Watson resigned his job and returned home. "Moore's mercurial temperament", Muggeridge wrote, "look him from the out and out imperialist position which might have cost Watson his life and did cost him his job, to one of close affinity with the Swarajists. He was a gifted, unstable, northern Irishman fated to make a mess of his career, not through being too rigid—which is one way of doing it—but through being flexible— which is another."

Muggeridge found that Moore "disliked the view I expressed in my leaders no less than Wordsworth (who acted as editor in Moore's absence) did. So it was axelief to all the three of us when it was decided, that I should go to Simla and represent the paper during the summer months when the Government of India functioned there." Before he came to India, Moore had worked as a reporter on the *Times* of London and was considered an authority on Balkan and Persian affairs. He served as the *Times'* correspondent in Persia (Iran) for some years. He came to India in 1924 and joined the *Statesman* as an assistant editor.

His most famous brush with authority was during the viceroyalty of Lord Linlithgow to whom he was like a red rag to a bull. In 1937 there was a constitutional deadlock in the provinces where the Congress had been returned in a majority in the elections to the Legislative Assembly. The Congress refused to accept office unless assurances were given that the governors would not use their reserve powers under the Constitution. The viceroy supported by the Home Government was unwilling to give any such assurance. It was at this time that an article appeared in the

Statesman with the heading, "Indian impasse deplored—Unofficial anxiety. Viceroy's silence unhelpful." The article said that the House of Commons was critical of the government's attitude to the deadlock, that the viceroy's advisers in India were unwilling to help the Congress extricate itself from the impasse and that considerations of prestige on both sides could not be overlooked. The article said the viceroy's prolonged silence was increasingly noticed and regarded as unhelpful. Parliamentary opinion, it said, was most impatient of this attitude and held that unless the legislatures in the Congress provinces were summoned, officialdom would incur some share of the responsibility for any further deterioration in the situation. The dispatch was purported to have come from Reuter's news agency but Reuter denied it. The viceroy found that the evidence suggested that the Message was sent from the *Statesman's* London office and inspired by the editor, Arthur Moore.

Linlithgow had met Moore from time to time and he had considered him to be an impulsive Irishman but read his editorials with particular care. He thought him markedly short of ability and extremely slapdash and impetuous in his methods. The article in the *Statesman*, he told Lord Zetland, secretary of state, might have very embarrassing reactions. If it really had been sent by Moore, he said, it would justify strong pressure on the Board of Directors of the *Statesman* in London to bring him under control. Zetland confirmed to Linlithgow that Moore was indeed the author of the dispatch. He said he had met Moore before his departure for India and "found it difficult to understand his mind." Moore told Zetland that he believed that with tactful handling, Jawaharlal Nehru could be led into the cooperation fold. Zetland hoped for the support of Lord Cato, chairman of the *Statesman's* Board of Directors, in dealing with Moore.

The *Statesman* again fell foul of the viceroy when in a leading article it said that there were many in the British Government who were to be profoundly mistrusted; they would be capable of Petain's conduct in comparable circumstances and they had their British counterparts in India. "We do not speak entirely without knowledge," the editorial said. Linlithgow was wild with rage. He wrote to L.S. Amerly, secretary of state, that "this gross and damaging libel came as a climax to a long series of damaging indiscretions". He said he had little doubt that the editorial was written by Moore "whose removal alone could correct the situation". But Moore did not go until 1942 by which time, according to the Establishment, he had done more damage to British prestige and authority.

On August 10,1942, Moore wrote an editorial, after the arrest and detention of Gandhi and other Congress leaders, criticising the government's action in terms which were considered by the government as "demoralising and defeatist". Members of the Viceroy's Executive Council were angry and wanted that action should be taken against the paper and the writer. However, to the great relief of Linlithgow, the Board of Directors decided to relieve Moore of his post and appointed Ian Stephens to replace him. On the eve of Linlithgow's departure from India, the *Statesman,* while remembering the occasions on which it had criticised him, expressed in a generous leader its gratitude for his "courageous services" to India. Ian Stephens wrote in his memoirs that for two years after he became editor in August, 1942, "I suffered much embarrassment from his (Moore's) activities. He kept on revisiting our offices in Calcutta, Delhi or London or making speeches or issuing press statements and writing articles several of which by implication affected my shaping of the paper's policy.... His conduct then seemed inconsiderate."

Maulana-Abul Kalam Azad, the Congress leader, mentions in his autobiography, that when Gandhi went on a fast unto death in Delhi in 1947, following communal disturbances, Moore who was staying in the Imperial Hotel, also began a fast. The Hindu-Muslim riots had moved him deeply. He told Azad that if the disturbances did not end he would also fast unto death. He had been in India for many years and had adopted it as his home. As an Indian he regarded it as his duty to put a stop to the human misery and degradation that were taking place. Death, he said, was preferable to "this terrible tragedy" that had overtaken India.

Azad sent him a message after Gandhi broke his fast and requested that he should do the same.

Moore served as a member of the Legislative Assembly in Delhi for a term as a member of the European Group and his presence and frequent interjections made the proceedings lively. At one time he crossed swords with the President, Vithalbhai Patel, and was admonished. He was a fearless critic and did not spare anyone, friend or foe if he thought he was in the wrong. Although a supporter of the nationalist cause, the Congress and especially Gandhi, had been at the receiving end in many of his by-lined editorials. He was a brilliant writer and commanded a simple style which at the same time was forceful and effective. He served India and her oppressed people in his own way and made Indian journalism the richer by his contribution to its vitality and strength.

S. Sadanand

In the history of Indian journalism S. Sadanand has an important place as an able editor, an innovator and a fearless patriot. Born in Tamil Nadu, he made Bombay his headquarters for his multifarious ventures in journalism. That was where he held sway during the *Salt Satyagraha* of 1930-33 when his newspaper, *Free Press Journal,* was a rage and eclipsed all other nationalist papers. He was a pioneer of popular journalism in English, who sold his papers at six piece a copy, an unheard of thing in those days when the minimum price of a newspaper was one anna (6 paise). He created a mass base for himself by espousing popular causes and airing public grievances in a big, spectacular way which caught the imagination of the educated masses. He, more than any other journalist, strove to instil pride and devotion among the people for their country and for the epic battle for freedom waged by the Congress under the leadership of Gandhi. He was a powerful, wholehearted supporter of the Congress movement and the *Free Press Journal* paid the penalty for it when the alien government persecuted it by demanding securities and forfeiting them and demanding fresh deposits. Sadanand did not flinch and survived the ordeal even after paying Rs 70,000 in one year alone. He revolutionised editorial writing. Instead of the long and meandering editorials, very often going above the head of the ordinary reader, which were a feature of the nationalist newspapers then, Sadanand introduced the sharp, telling and pungent editorial paragraphs which, with their mythical *oxPuranic* allusions and anecdotes, went straight to the heart of the readers and enabled him to grasp with ease what was being conveyed to him. The reader became emotionally involved in whatever was suggested and his cooperation was assured. And that was how the Congress gained its supremacy in Bombay. His right-hand man on the *F.P.J.* was "Stalin" Srinivasan who was an able and experienced journalist. The sobriquet, "Stalin", was given to him by his colleagues in the profession because of his moustache which closely resembled that of the Russian dictator.

Sadanand started his career as a journalist in Burma in the 1920s when it was part of India. He worked on the staff of a Rangoon newspaper and later came to India. He purchased the *Indian Express* from Dr. P. Varadarajulu Naidu in 1932 who had started it a year earlier. Sadanand ran it for some months and soon got tired of it for all his concentration was on the *E.PJ.* in Bombay. He went to C. Rajagopalachari in April, 1932, and urged him to take over the *Indian Express.* Rajaji told him that the man who could help him was K. Santhanam, who had just been released from prison where he had undergone imprisonment as a *Satyagrahi.* Santhanam had lost his wife while in prison and had declined the offer of the authorities to release him. When he came out of prison he had decided to renounce politics but fate willed it otherwise. Rajaji advised him to take over the *Indian Express* as its editor. For Santhanam, Rajaji's words were a command and he started a new life as a journalist.For him editing and running the *Indian Express* was a national service and a mission. The *Indian Express* became a morning paper and spokesman for the Congress. It was sold at half an anna in line with Sadanand's innovative seal. Very soon a sister Tamil daily was added and the *Dinamani* in a short time outstripped its rivals. The *Indian Express,* however, fell into a financial crisis and it finally passed into the hands of Ramnath Goenka who later became a newspaper baron and the owner of the largest chain of newspapers.

Sadanand was a man of great ambition. He wanted to start a paper in every province of India. As a nationalist he felt that was the only way to promote the integration of the country. In 1932, he started an evening newspaper, *Free Press Bulletin,* in Bombay and Gujarati daily, *Nav Bharat.* As we have seen, he bought the *Indian Express* in Madras in 1932, and started the Tamil daily, *Dinamani,* in 1934. He also started a Marathi daily in Bombay, *Navasakti. Free India,* an English daily which he began in Calcutta, had a very short life. In anticipation of establishing newspapers in other major cities, he purchased machinery and appointed editors but unfortunately he was not successful in his efforts. According to a close associate of his, hundreds of linotype machines which he had bought for the proposed newspapers lay idle in the godowns. "He was too ambitious", one of his friends said, "and he aimed at too much."

Sadanand's notable failure was the Free Press News Agency which he formed in 1927 as a rival to the Associated Press of India (A.P.I) which was a subsidiary of Reuter's Agency and enjoyed the patronage of the Government of India. Sadanand's objective was to survey news from a nationalist angle and to cover areas neglected by the semi-official news agency and also to provide Indian commercial news. He also had an ambition of appointing correspondents abroad to supply international news of interest to nationalist opinion in India. He was backed by big industrialists like Sir P. Thakurdas, G.D. Birla, Walchand Hirachand and M.R. Jayakar. But the nationalist news agency failed to evoke the sympathy and support of the Indian-owned press from the beginning and this was a great disappointment to Sadanand. For over three years he made brave efforts to stabilise the news agency but the reluctance of the established Indian newspapers to subscribe to its service and the sustained pressure of the rival and more influential news agency to kill it proved too overwhelming and the Free Press News Agency steadily lost ground. Also, Sadanand had to fight against official censorship both at the distribution and receiving ends. The agency's speciality was supply of news about *Satyagraha,* of police firings and beatings of volunteers and these could not be carried by the newspapers as they were afraid of retaliatory action by the Government. Pressure from the Government forced the resignation of four directors of the agency in 1926 and the fifth in 1931. The government came down heavily on newspapers which published news from the agency and the Press Ordinance of 1930 signed its death warrant. Most of its clients shied away. It was stated that the A.P.I. also applied pressure by insisting that its services would not be available to newspapers which subscribed to a rival news agency. Adding to Sadanand's troubles, his financiers withdrew support and the most grievous blow was his failure to win the support of influential Congress leaders. Sadanand's dream was to establish a world news agency. He had a talented correspondent in London who collected the important dispatches of foreign news agencies, selected the choicest among them and they were cabled to India and often Reuter was left standing. But the agency's scoops were of no avail. The Free Press News Agency died in 1935, unsung and unwept.

Sadanand was a builder of newspapers. His forte was management and improvisation. He was a competent news getter but it was always difficult for him to resist the temptation to transform news into brash publicity and propaganda. His news agency suffered from this foible of his and lacked credibility. One of his admirers called him "a man with a giant's energy." He had the capacity to get more out of man and machine than most others. He could produce a newspaper single-handed. It was nothing for him to sit before a linotype machine and compose copy or to sit at a news desk and edit telegrams. Once when there was stoppage of news supply owing to arrears of payment, he made up the pages with news he had written in his own hand. He could write a dispatch as lobby correspondent sitting in his chair in Madras about what took place in the Central Legislative Assembly in Delhi. He was a workaholic with a restless mind. He did not have patience with lazy people. He commanded the absolute loyalty of his workers. And when creditors pressed him for payment he would tell them: "I am doing a national service. Give me credit for that." He looked upon journalism as a sacred calling which combined the highest ideals of nationalism and of public service. His motto and that of his papers was "Free and Fearless." In the words of a writer: "He had a rugged individuality, an embarrassing independence and a fierce possessiveness. He made lasting friends in the profession but his colleagues were overwhelmed by his exacting demands and his haunting suspicions. He combined a strange predilection for adventures on the side with an almost fanatical dedication to journalism."

A colleague who worked with Sadanand in the *F.PJ.* has written: "The honours of the freedom fight of 1930-33 went equally to Sadanand and the *F.P.J.* on the press front. The paper was waging an epic fight against the Government. In fact, it was the head and front of the journalistic onslaught. Sadanand was in high mettle and in more affluence too then. The *F.P.J.* was the dauntless bark he sailed and he was the pilot who weathered a myriad storms. The bark was often near going down but he somehow held it on course. He has left behind him a legendary fragrant reputation for a gallant courage and enterprise, and undying tradition of editorial audacity and several institutions firmly established and exceedingly useful to the country. He started life with a broken typewriter and died in a blaze of glory."

K. Rama Rao who joined the *F.PJ.* in 1932 wrote: "The combination of two mercurial minds and two devil-may-care spirits like us lasted long enough to cause surprise in friendly as well as in unfriendly quarters. We all appreciated Sadanand's superb courage, his capacity to plan like a genius and to execute like a giant. Made of tempered steel, he did not have an atom of fear in him. He was courageous to the point of being reckless, resourceful to- the point of being inventive and original to the point of being unpredictable. Security after security was forfeited for defiance of law, blow after blow fell, but he did not bat an eyelid; he did not budge an inch from the firing line. With head bloody but unbowed, he went on attacking. No risk was too big, no adventure too reckless. He revelled in crises, some self-created. A soldier in every inch of him, how he fought and won; now he fought and lost; but he never ran away from danger or difficulty. His faith in his stars was unassailable."

Sadanand, who passed away in 1933, was a fighting editor, a great organiser, a powerful writer and a gentleman of extraordinary calibre.

Frank Moraes

The story is told that when Frank Moraes was a student at Bombay's St. Xavier's College in the 1920s, he was bored by the droning voice of a lecturer. As he slowly started sliding on his bench towards the door, the lecturer noticed it and shouted: "Moraes, what does that slow movement to the right indicate?" "Departure, Sir," said the nonchalant Moraes as he left his seat and made for the exit. True or not, it exemplifies Moraes' spirit of independence and his ready wit and humour. He was a journalist who did not suffer fools gladly and called a spade a spade. Long training and apprenticeship in a British-owned and edited newspaper had given him a discipline and keen sense of what was right and what was wrong, and integrity and clear thinking, so that when he came to assume positions of responsibility in a newspaper he commanded great respect and authority.

He asked himself once: "What did England give me?" and provided the answer: "Primarily, I think, a sense of tolerance combined with a habit of evaluation which while enabling one to listen to the other man's point of view did not necessarily imply that one necessarily accepted it. I suppose this attitude of mind really adds up to democracy. England also laught me to recognise the importance of standards in human relationship and individual conduct which in a way spells civilisation. I think the most valuable gift England gave me was a sense of proportion." It is this sense of proportion which marked his editorship of the *Times of India* and later of the *Indian Express*. He occupied the editorial chair of India's two leading newspapers at a time when the country was facing enormous problems of reconstruction and survival. He was a constructive critic whose writings were valued in the highest quarters of Government and paid the greatest attention. A close associate described him as "one of the most straightforward journalists and a gentleman." He was of a reserved nature and a man of few words. He had the advantage of moving with the leaders of government on an equal footing which developed intimacy and trust and he established high level contacts in all spheres of public life. His close friendship with Jawaharlal Nehru and Indira Gandhi was a great asset. His involvement with, and appreciation of, Nehru were such that he became his biographer.

Son of an Indian government servant, Moraes was born in Bombay in 1907. He graduated from St. Xavier's College, Bombay, and later took a degree from Oxford. He was also a barrister of Lincoln's Inn, and practised law for some time before he entered journalism in 1934. He worked first on the *Times of India* as a junior assistant editor. Of this period Moraes writes: "*The Times of India* then on the eve of its centenary was a British newspaper whose senior editorial and production staff were exclusively British and I was at the time the only Indian assistant editor. The editor, Sir Francis Low, was a competent Scotsman who had worked his way up through various departments of the paper. Outwardly he appeared to be reticent and diffident but he was not easily overawed or taken in."

The *Times of India* then was a firm supporter of the government since it was British-owned. "Its political policy, though more liberal than that of the Raj, moved broadly in step with it," Moraes wrote. "Its antennae were sensitive to New Delhi but less sensitive to London which failing led it occasionally to trip on British foreign policy, most noticeably as the war drew nearer. It approved the Italian invasion of Ethiopia only to make a quick about turn when Whitehall's reaction came over the wires. Its thinking was perhaps too overcast by the colonial smong." Moraes said the system suffered "from a few imperial hangovers". He was, for instance, not invited to use the senior staff canteen which was exclusively British. "Nor was I profferred a key to their exclusive lavatory." He was also excluded from the daily morning conference which the other assistant editors, all British, attended. "In accordance with government office routine and the practice of European commercial establishments, the senior staff worked by the clock and only very rarely round it. Our daily office hours were from 10 a.m. to 5.30 p.m. with an hour and a half for lunch and in my 19 years on the *Times of India* I do not believe I came more than a dozen times to the office at night."

It was common in those days to think that every Indian who worked on the staff of a British-owned newspaper was anti-nationalist. "For an Indian to work as a senior member of the staff of any one of these (British-owned) newspapers was to be tarred with a semi-official brush," Moraes said. "Yet like most Indian officials who were part of the British bureaucratic machine, the majority of Indian journalists even on British newspapers were nationalistic in outlook. From my own experience, there is no denying that this conflict produced something of a split personality." Writing about the Indian press under British rule, Moraes said: "The Indian press could not be described as a free press in British days for though British-owned papers like the *Statesman* and *Times of India* rarely drew official frowns and a certain latitude of expression was permitted even to Indian-owned newspapers the Raj could, and did, descend heavily on the latter."

Moraes was not anti-British. He was conscious of the benefits of British rule. "Fairness compels the admission," he once wrote, "that whatever Britain's sins of commission and omission might have been in India, the credit side of the ledger overweighs the debit. Britain, opened for India new windows on the West. In a sense she helped India also to rediscover herself for until the researches of European scholars little or nothing was known of the pre-Islamic period nor of Hindu culture and civilisation. The British association made Indians familiar with the marvels of Western science and technology and with concepts like democracy and Parliamentary Government."

Moraes went out as a war correspondent to Burma in 1943 and his dispatches were prominently displayed in the *Times of*

India. They were exhaustive and Moraes was able to meet all the top brass and wrote with authority and precision on allied strategy and of the victories and defeats. He particularly dwelt on the heroism of the Indian troops and their commanders. Moraes later went to China to cover the war on that front. After the war he took over as editor of the *Times of Ceylon* in 1946 and remained in that post for two years. The *Times of India* changed hands at the end of the war and its new owner was Ramakrishna Dalmia. Moraes was appointed editor of the *Times of India* in 1950. It was the high watermark of his career and during the seven years he adorned the editorial chair he brought it much prestige and influence. His term as editor was marked by a brush with Bombay's Chief Minister, Morarji Desai, and he was hauled before the State Legislative Assembly on a charge of contempt of the legislature.

An editorial comment on certain proceedings in the Assembly during question hour had provoked Chief Minister Morarji Desai. The question and answer which led to the comment related to prohibition and involved issue of permits to judges. In his editorial Moraes pointed out the impropriety of the Assembly questioning the conduct of the chief justice of a High Court or the chief justice of the Supreme Court or his colleagues which could be done only by Parliament. The Assembly appointed a committee to decide if Moraes had committed contempt of the Legislature. The chairman of the committee after some hearings advised him to apologise, which he refused. He was then arraigned before the House. Moraes read out a statement justifying his comment. The Assembly decided to withdraw the press cards of the paper's Parliamentary correspondent. Moraes thereupon issued instructions that the *Times of India* should use only the slender agency reports of the proceedings of the Assembly. "In less than three months", Moraes wrote, " an emissary approached me with a plea to forget, I forgot. So did the State Assembly. The press cards of our Parliamentary correspondent were returned." On another occasion, Morarji Desai, angry over an editorial of Moraes, withdrew all government advertisements to the *Times of India.* "Had we been a small provincial journal his action could have brought us to our knees," Moraes said, "but we were sufficiently affluent to continue defying him and his policies. In time the advertisements were restored."

Moraes became the editor-in-chief of the *Indian Express* in 1957. He scored many triumphs and his editorials carried great weight and influence both with government and the people. At times of national bereavement or disaster or when problems of great magnitude confronted the nation, Moraes wrote his editorial on the front page to focus attention and to convey the importance and seriousness of what was being written. He was a fearless critic of the government regardless of the personalities involved and his criticism was unbiased and free from taint of vindictiveness. He was a responsible journalist who weighed his words and did not criticise for the sake of criticism. He was an intellectual who was also author of many books, including an autobiography and a biography of his favourite Indian leader, Jawaharlal Nehru. Moraes believed in a free press as an essential corollary of a vibrant democracy. "In a colonial country", he said, "there can be no independent press but in an independent country dedicated to socialism and democracy a free press is a natural concomitant." He said Jawaharlal Nehru, always "conscious of democracy in democratic socialism scrupulously respected the freedom of the press;... So did his successor, Lai Bahadur Shastri."

Moraes thought that the political columnist or commentator had still to come into his own in India "where the newspaper reader more often than not takes opinions from the editorials which are perhaps more widely read and discussed in our country than in any other land. It does not follow from this that the average Indian reader's opinions are automatically moulded by his newspaper for most educated or even literate Indians tend to have definite political views even if these are sharper and more defined at local or state levels than at the national level."

K. Rama Rao

C.P. Scott, the great editor of the *Manchester Guardian*, said this of journalism: "What a work it is! How multifarious, how responsive to every need and incident of life! What illimitable possibilities of achievement and excellence!" Kotamaraju Rama Rao, a giant Indian journalist, drank deep the nectar of journalism, jumping from one flower to another, never satiated, ever humming and searching for more drops of honey. His was a restless spirit which sought adventure and excitement and did not mind the cost. He was in revolt not only against the British rules but also against the system which they perpetuated, the injustice and exploitation and sycophancy which they generated. He was a fierce patriot who used his pen like a sword and he made no bones about it. His words were meant to kill, to destroy the opponent if words could do so. He did not believe in soft language, in expostulations and arguments, in legalistic terminology and quibbling. Not for him what was said of another great editor, A. Rangaswami Iyengar, the quality of moderation and use of sober language which marked his editorials. Mild language, however, direct or uncompromising in import, was with him a betrayal of timidity. He was blunt and outspoken and he used his pen with vitriolic effect. He was not happy with the proprietors whom he served for he kept them in perpetual fear of penal action against the paper. He moved from one paper to another, almost all of them espousing the national cause but his ebullient aggressive spirit could not be contained and the proprietors who believed in the stability and safety of the newspapers, although appreciating his patriotic fervour, were chary of entrusting him with the fortunes of their papers. He worked on the staff of more than 25 papers (including two weeklies) and was sent away in three places. It was said that Rama Rao, who hailed from Andhra Pradesh, always worked with a resignation letter in his pocket.

Rama Rao had his early training as a reporter under T.L, Vasvani of *New Times*, Hyderabad (Sind) like his brother, K. Punniah, who was editor of the *Sind Observer*, did much to promote the nationalist cause. Rama Rao later came to Bombay and joined the staff of the *Times of India.* After some years he left that paper to seek new pastures. When the editor asked him the reason for his resignation he said: "I have been long enough here and have learnt my work pretty well. I have my own ambitions. Can I ever be the editor of the *Times of India?"*

Then began Rama Rao's adventurous journey in journalism.

He joined, as we have seen, Sadanand in the *Free Press Journal* during the crucial years of 1932-34 when the paper was a frequent victim of the rulers' persecution and fury, then moved on to T. Prakasam's *Swarajya* in Madras where he spent 100 days struggling to inject vigour and stamina into a paper which was dying for lack of resources. He was with the *National Call* in 1934 and with the *Hindustan Times* for a brief period of six months in 1938. He became the editor of the *National Herald*. Lucknow, the same year and spent there the longest period he had served any newspaper. The founder of the paper, Jawaharlal Nehru, liked him although he was not always in agreement with his writings and language and style. The two, one a great national leader and considered as a leftist by the alien rulers and the other a firebrand who believed in fire and brimstone in the attack on colonialism in the press, easily established a rapport and friendship which was to transcend the boundaries of journalism.

Rama Rao was a crusading editor. Day after day he wrote with passion and zeal and his writings played a great part in rousing the masses to follow the leadership of Gandhi in the freedom struggle. The *National Herald* under him became a symbol of the nation's fight against tyramny and exploitation and against repression and denial of human rights. It was in the vanguard of the freedom struggle and became a propaganda forum for the leaders of the movement. Rama Rao was defiant and fearless of authority and he slashed the opponents of freedom, be it British officialdom or the sycophantic moderates who flourished under the favours bestowed on them by the alien regime, with his pen which he used like a sword. He exposed abuse of power, and police brutality in language which made the blood boil in Indian hearts as it made the rulers sit up and vow vengeance. The officials involved him in a defamation case when the jailor of a prison where *Satyagrahi* prisoners were kept sued him for libel for an editorial on the treatment of political prisoners. Rama Rao was convicted and sentenced to six months' imprisonment. The *Herald* stopped editorials from 1940 as a protest against the pre-censorship and other restrictions on the press. In August, 1942, Rama Rao saw the police raid of the office and press of the *Herald* and seizure of machinery which resulted in the closure of the paper. Rama Rao returned to his desk after the paper was revived in 1946 but left it shortly afterwards. He was a freelancer for some time and worked at Gandhi's headquarters. He took over as editor of *Searchlight* of Patna in 1948. His services were terminated in 1950. He saw service with some other newspapers and ended up as a legislator when he was nominated to the Rajya Sabha. His end was tragic when he was killed in a train accident in Uttar Pradesh.

Gandhi called him a "fighting editor". Nehru described him as "an outstanding figure in Indian journalism". For C. Rajagopalachari, he was a "dear dreadnought". The list of newspapers with which he was associated is pretty long and besides the papers we have already mentioned it includes *the Pioneer, Leader, Bombay Chronicle, Indian Daily Mail, Advocate of India* and *India News Chronicle.*

Rama Rao said: "Journalism is the destroyer of rust, a foe of pessimism and an amplifier of the areas of life and work", was a rebel who questioned many things accepted as gospel truth. When talking about the freedom of the press, he posed the question: "Freedom for whom? Freedom for the proprietor or freedom of expression in the public interest?" He said: "While the proprietor-editor has all the power and no responsibility and who reserves to himself the right to dictate policies with an eye to his several other interests, the editor *de facto* as distinguished from the editor *de jure* has all the responsibility and no power." Rama Rao recalled that journalism of the 1930s was of a very high standard. "Discussions were kept at a high level, if only because the traditional standards of this country demanded excellence in things pertaining to the spirit and the intellect, notwithstanding the vicissitudes of kingdoms and empires and the lapses and degradations of social life. The newspaper was a lengthened shadow of its crusading owner-editor. Today, the Fourth Estate is, for good or evil, totally different in aim, purpose and content." He said: "From the point of effective service, moral values and social usefulness, the press in India can boast of a record as good as that of any other in the world. It has treated its work as a trust, sacred and vital. By and large, it has been loyal to the doctrine that facts are sacred but comment is free and it has been national in more senses than one."

"What was the lure of journalism in the days when I started," Rama Rao asked and answered the question: "It was the nearest route of attack on an empire which we ail hated and wanted to overthrow and the best avenue of service in the cause of purposeful patriotism. We thought we could be Annie Besants or Homimans, Tilaks or Motilal Ghoshs. It was the quickest way to fame which is certainly not the least nor the last infirmity of noble minds and is definitely an honourable ambition, an energising aspiration. I have enjoyed the thrills of the hourly chase, the sensations of the daily adventure. I have savoured the pleasures of success and suffered the pangs of defeat. The profession was a rough but challenging pathway to national service and incidentally to a good name."

Rama Rao believed that journalists should be trained and taught in schools of journalism. He said that a school of journalism could teach the beginner the essentials which could not be learnt by working in a newspaper for over five years. He himself trained many journalists who later came to occupy high positions in Indian journalism. He fought for the rights and protection of working journalists and helped in the formation of the Federation of Working Journalists in Delhi in 1950. He was a member of the Standing Committee of the All-India Newspapers Editors Conference for many years. He waged a relentless war against monopoly control of the press.

N. Raghunathan

Not many outside the world of journalism would have heard of N. Raghunathan, the celebrated senior assistant editor of *The Hindu* who virtually functioned as the *de facto* editor for over 20 years. He prided in his anonymity and allowed his writings which were marked by scholarly approach and erudition to speak for him. His mastery of the language was incredible and his arguments were irrefutable. His great weapon was a capacity to marshal facts and point to the unerring conclusions which destroyed the opponent's strenuously built up case. Not for him the sword or aggressive language which attracted the spotlight and popular applause. He relied on cold logic and telling arguments helped by a prodigious memory, which was elephantine in character, which unearthed precedents and situations to demolish the points made by constitutional experts and politicians of the ruling race. He was a great constitutional foe of the colonial rulers from whom he commanded a measure of respect and also fear. The leaders of the national movement found in him a stout champion and adviser in their fight against the alien rulers on the constitutional plane. He tore to pieces and ridiculed the futile arguments of British spokesmen, from the secretary of state downwards to the viceroy and his minions, to deny India freedom and dignity. He digested white papers and reports on constitutional reforms with relish and he was unsurpassed in his analysis and exposure of their weak points and unacceptable postures. It was nothing for him to dash off three two-column editorials in one day and once when his colleagues played a prank on him, he wrote all the editorials, sometimes extending four to five columns, for a week.

His friends and admirers thought Raghunathan would have been a fairly prosperous lawyer (he had a law degree), a fairly successful teacher or even a fairly good administrator. Raghunathan said he escaped being an administrator by "malice prepense". As for lawyering or teaching "I wonder whether I could have stood the hungry backchat of the bar room or the bland superciliousness of the common room for a day. Indeed, the more I think of it, the more I doubt whether I could have secured and kept any other respectable employment. By a strange quirk of fate I seem to have slid almost without knowing it into that odd shaped hole in a million which seemed to have been made for this oddly constructed individual. That I have stuck there bespeaks therefore, no special virtue. I could not have got out had I tried.... I do not know whether the millions of words I have written ever influenced a single soul. It would be a relief to know that even if they did no good they did no evil. No man is good enough to tell another what to think. Aesop's fly on the wheel might have done far more harm if he could have put a spoke in it."

Raghunathan came to *The Hindu* in 1926 from a morning newspaper, the *Daily Express,* in Madras of which he had been editor for some years. He was a discovery of V.S. Srinivasa Sastri who was a close friend of Kasturi Srinivasan. Raghunathan had rejected *The Hindu's* offer the previous year since he loved the freedom as editor, which he enjoyed. He, however, reluctantly accepted the offer when it was renewed the following year and thus began a historic and rewarding association with India's leading nationalist newspaper. He very soon established an intimate relationship with Kasturi Srinivasan and the two became inseparable associates in running the paper. They had similar views on most subjects and the points of disagreement were far too few to break their intimacy. N.R., as he was popularly known, shaped the policy of the paper with Srinivasan in total agreement and together they made *The Hindu* the most powerful and influential paper in the country. So much was his confidence and trust in N.R. that when he wanted to retire in 1948, Srinivasan, who refused to let him go, said: "A memo from me will never go to N.R," N.R. did not retire till 1957 when Srinivasan reluctantly agreed.

N.R. was a master craftsman who sanctified everything that he handled. He was an outstanding sub-editor who could edit copy, especially *mofussil* copy (which had to be wholly rewritten) with an instinctive feel for mistakes in grammar, faulty style and expression. He wrote his editorials by hand with a sharpened pencil in bold letter which for all their hugeness in size were all the same mostly illegible and only the practised eye of the linotype operator (what he wrote went straight to the press and was not typed) could decipher them. He wrote less than a dozen sentences on a sheet of paper and the matter was set up and the proof sent to him as fast as he wrote them. During the 30 years he served *The Hindu,* his dedication to the paper was total and he had no other interest in life. He spurned invitations to go abroad and isolated himself from the outside world. Although he wrote about all the big leaders and personalities of India and the world, he never came in contact with any of them nor did he want to. He was not a crusader like a Horniman or a Rama Rao. His writing lacked passion and anger and the vibrant quality which roused the feelings of all those who read it. His strong point was argument and cold logic presented in a style which was majestic and powerful in its onslaught. He was an orthodox Hindu who fully believed in the tenets and rituals of his religion and in the wisdom of his ancestors. He was opposed to Gandhi's reform movement and asked to be excused from writing on it. A notable achievement of his was the *Literary Supplement* which he edited for *The Hindu* for over 25 years. It gained national and international reputation and it had a circulation independent of *The Hindu.*

It was not only as the *de facto* editor of *The Hindu* that N.R. was famous, but also as a columnist under the pseudonym, Vigneshwara. He was permitted by Srinivasan in 1946 to contribute a column to *Swatantra* and then to *Swarajya,* a weekly, edited by Khasa Subba Rao, which was titled *Sotto Voce.* Explaining his role as a columnist N.R. said: "I thought that it might be rewarding to examine current ideas and developments in the light of those basic purposes and abiding values that one who cares to look behind the superficialities of modern life may discern in the age-long culture and way of life of the Indian people. As regards his pen name he said: "The adoption of a pen name was due partly to a self-imposed rule of anonymity which I observed all through my working life as a journalist and partly to a desire to prevent facile— and wrong—inferences being drawn as they might be if the writer of this column were known to be one who was closely associated with the political comment of a daily newspaper."

A staunch believer in the freedom of the press, N.R. advocated an independent press unattached to any party, ideology or group. "The press has a duty to expose and denounce force, fraud and chicanery by whomsoever employed. But it has no need to enter into a partnership with the state for this purpose. In fact, freedom from any commitments of any sort to anybody except its own conscience is a condition of its efficiency." To a press that knows its own mind, no man is a god, no power is infallible. It will refuse to be overawed by authority or smothered under the blanket of respectability. And it will avoid like the plague the bovine contentment of "forty head of cattle feeding like one."

N.R. was pessimistic about the future of the honest newspaperman. "The honest newspaperman," he wrote, "becomes less and less sure with the years of the rationale of the enterprise he is engaged in. He does not know for whom he writes and in serving up the day's news he engages in a process of selection and emphasis which is as irresponsibly hazardous as divination. He is exhorted to remember that he must give his unknown and unknowable reader what he wants. And he finds it a safe rule in the circumstances to give just what the paymaster, whom he knows only too well, thinks is good for that mythical being, the average reader. The one thing that seems to be fairly clear about the great public is that its understanding of the newspapers it consumes is in inverse ratio to its enjoyment."

N.R. thought aloud more on the "mythical average reader" "Your average man is a myth", he wrote. "The writer for the press who directs his daily fussilade of advice, remonstrance or exhortation at this phantom is really shooting his bolt in the dark. He has not the time, even if he had the capacity, for that candid self-questioning by which he may hope to understand something of our common human condition. Meanwhile, the 'people' are hot on his heels, gobbling up, like the ostrich, whatever they see in print. The balance is not redressed by the handful of cynics who refuse to believe anything they see in print. The fusillades are so many, so furious and so contrary, the reader clings so desperately to his spar of private hopes and fears in a chopping sea of universal uncertainty and there is such an intermittent squall of irrelevant news blowing that the confused din of opinion seems to matter no more than the crackling of thorns. In the multitude of counsel there is an alibi for the muddled reader. But a newspaperless world is not necessarily a better world."

Noticing a lowering of standards in journalism, N.R. warned: "It was said of C.P. Scott that he made righteousness readable. The ambition may strike many of our smart newspapermen as amusingly old fashioned. But while by giving the public plenty of crime stories, spicy gossip and sports chatter, the journalistic cheap Jack may reap rich dividends, he is already steadily undermining in the safety of the realm. For he debases standards and renders the doped public incapable of rational judgement. No Government which works for the emergence of an instructed democracy can afford to look on unconcerned. If it actually helps in the demoralisation, though doubtless without intending it, where shall we look for succour? The influence of a newspaper is ultimately a matter of character. The personality that an established newspaper has built up over long years is, like the coral reef, the work of innumerable hands. It is subdued to a design implicit in the social situation. The reader moulds his paper at least as much as the paper colours his thoughts. Such a paper evolves a style of its own, a way of doing things, which is the right way for it Bungling interference by authority which might have the effect of forcing its individuality into a strait-jacket would be a public misfortune."

N.R. was not happy with the radical policies of free India's government. "In their anxiety to make up for lost time, they shut their eyes to the realities of our national life. They resolved that radical changes involving wholesale adoption of the goals that the West had set itself as well as methods it had forged must be forced through. What they failed to see was that large-scale industrialisation and modem technology, though they had powerfully aided, were not solely or even primarily responsible for the Western nations having in varying degree opted for a secularist society and a planned socialism. These had evolved from certain specific and distinctive qualities of the European mind. The character, temperament and outlook of the Indian people have been moulded by a different spiritual tradition. Gandhiji saw this clearly enough but not his successors who thought that on the old stock a new and in many ways alien tradition could be successfully grafted."

The born leader writer that he was N.R. noted with regret that the leading articles were on the way out in many countries. "The leading article was pronounced dead ages ago," he wrote, "and one or two papers have shown the world that they have the courage of conviction by actually dropping it. But others seem to be in no hurry to follow. On their broad pages, the fount of home-brewed wisdom has thinned to a trickle perhaps but has not dried up altogether. And in the place of one anonymous leader writer, there has sprung up a whole host of columnists and specialists whose names are household words in four continents."

In a tribute to N.R. as a columnist, K.R. Srinivasa Iyengar, the educationist, said: "The purveyor of serious political comment in a daily paper of national vogue became the miscellaneous columnist of an individualist weekly paper and the columnist presently revealed himself as the perfect humanist and the flawless literary craftsman. A lifetime of training in the exacting discipline of expression in a difficult foreign language now yielded results. Week after week the essay appeared— with somewhat quiet assurance and look of effortless ease—and as the weeks gathered into months and years, the *Sotto Voce* feature became almost the sole standard bearer of traditional values and robust sanity in world of rattle and glare and slogans and screams. Raghunathan's is often the conservative, unpopular, diehard views; his assent in the tradition is apt to assume the tone of dissent with current notions of propriety and progress; and yet his views cannot be dismissed as of no consequence for these undertones of assent and dissent come with an accent of authority that compels attention if not acquiescence."

N.R. passed away in 1982 at a ripe old age, but for him there was no retirement He produced two monumental works, translations of the *Bhagavatham* and the *Ramayana* besides minor literary works in the closing years of his life. They were masterpieces and perfect examples of his scholarship and mastery of both English and Sanskrit. He was the inimitable journalist to the last

M. Chalapati Rau

Among India's great editors M. Chalapati Rau stands out as the champion of the working journalist for whom he strove to secure basic rights as a worker and a decent wage, and as the uncompromising fighter for a free and independent press. He fought against pressures on the newspaper internally from the owner or externally from vested interests. He had a sharp wit and a keen sense of the absurd and ridiculous and used his powerful pen to deflate the egos of power crazy politicians and bureaucrats. The high point in his career was the close rapport he established with Jawaharlal Nehru and the vigour and clarity with which he expounded his ideals and philosophy. It was a "concordat of minds." It was a very special relationship between the man who founded the *National Herald* and the man who edited it during its great years.

Chalapati Rau or M.C. as he was known among his friends, joined the *National Herald* in 1938 as number 13 in the staff. Within two years he became number two. It was a phenomenal rise due to sheer merit. When the paper closed down in 1942, he spent some time working in the *Hindustan Times* and rejoined the *Herald* when it was revived in 1945. He was appointed editor in 1946 and held that post for 30 years which must be quite a record. His command of the language was the envy of his collegues in the profession and according to one of them there were not then a dozen in India who had that mastery. In the words of one admirer: "He wrote in a heavy, granite-like style untouched by poetic feeling and imagery. He wrote with vigour and precision when putting forth his view or rebutting an opposite one. He could be delightfully allusive drawing liberally from the wells of literature and history. He owed this to wide and purposeful reading all through his life. He did occasionally dip his pen in vitriol to make sleeping statements and pass forth harsh judgments." He once wrote of Indian writers in English: "The Indo-Anglian writer is typical of our intellectual wastefulness."

"Our Fleet Street is a street of ink", Chalapati Rau wrote, "a street of adventure but also a street of perils. Indian journalism has been one of many vigorous forms of the expressiveness of Indian nationalism. To Kristodas Pal, Motilal Ghosh, Subramania Aiyer, and Chintamani, Fleet Street was not their spiritual home, though the last one absorbed most of the traditions without being burdened by techniques. They were great journalists. They built up traditions which have made journalism what it is today or what it was till yesterday. Our society is still amorphous, weighed down by the millstone of an English-educated middle class and it seems difficult for journalism to recover its sociological functions. For one sad feature of our journalism is the lack of social vision which includes political vision."

"The editors of those days," according to one writer, "drawn from the learned professions, combined a fine public acumen, a flexibility of outlook that was well above the reproach of opportunism, a determination to keep the flag flying in the face of repression and press laws and find best way of doing well by themselves as much as by the country. There can be no questioning the quality of service they rendered to the country, their skill in that kind of tight-rope walking or skating on thin ice which was required to escape the attention of the new minister and at the same time adhere to the standards of courageous support of the national cause." Chalapati Rau must have had these editors in mind when he wrote about the Indian Fleet Street

M.C. was an expert in foreign politics. "His knowledge of foreign politics would suffice half a dozen chancelleries", says an admirer. His Sunday articles reviewing the progress of World War II were acclaimed as outstanding. He had that "inestimable virtue of a diplomat—he can be as silent and as enigmatic as the sphinx. Tickle him, he will not laugh; prick him, he will not bleed. His reserves are more intriguing than his revelations. He does not believe in going out to meet humanity at large; he is like a famous editor who said that humanity might as well meet him by appointment. He has a soft and warm heart which he hides effectively behind an austere and aloof pose." He spent almost his entire career as a journalist in one newspaper the *National Herald,* which although it did not have a big circulation, was a powerful voice of the national movement, the voice of its most enlightened section, under the stewardship of Chalapati Rau. His dedication to the paper was overwhelming. Of the *National Herald's*, contribution he said: "In the process of Constitution-making, the integration of the country, in free India's contribution, to the fight for freedom in other parts of the world, in the shaping of India's plans and the ceaseless task of nation building, in the political, social and economic integration of the people—the *National Herald* has written stout-heartedly and freely as a critic and as a friend with the ideals of service for which it was started kept constantly in view. The *National Herald* wrote without fear but without malice."

The philosophy which guided him and to which he was deeply committed was the philosophy of Jawaharlal Nehru. "M.C. was the best and the most lucid exponent of Nehruism apart from Nehru himself," says a writes. "At the same time it was the freedom that Nehru always insisted that a journalist should be assured that enabled Chalapti Rau to rise to great heights as a distinguished editor whose views commanded wide respect. The relationship between the two stands out indeed as a model of how a political leader and a journalist of integrity should interact in a democracy where the masses have to be informed so that they are equipped adequately to elect those who are to wield power. Not only did Chalapati Rau understand the significance of this relationship but this understanding became the basis of his monumental endeavour to popularise Jawaharlal Nehru as the architect of Indian democracy." Indira Gandhi once described Chalapati Rau "as the conscience keeper of my father." It was said of him that reading his editorials in those days one felt that virtually every word in them had been tested and weighed against the quality of understanding and judgement that informed Jawaharlal Nehru's own approach to men and matters and policies. In the words of an admirer: "His finest hour, there is little doubt, coincided and was coterminous with Jawaharlal Nehru's stewardship of Indian affairs. He belonged to and represented what was the best in the Nehru phase to Indian journalism. He survived... to see another age begin... but he was not of it and it was hard at times altogether to avoid the impression that he was ill at ease in it and even seemed something of a forlorn, if distinguished alien in it."

Chalapati Rau had the remarkable capacity to absorb all that was happening around him and to react and convey his impressions of what they signified. There was no major event in his life-time on which he had not made weighty comments in his editorials. To the last he was uncompromising in his integrity and in his principles. An admirer wrote: "Himself living a life of an ascetic, he commanded a moral stature which acted as a living indictment of all those in the press who would for personal gains, make peace with inequity and injustice. He never forgave those in the journalist profession who would sacrifice their integrity for a comfortable life-style. Chalapati Rau could never suffer cant and hypocrisy in the community of pressmen as he stood for a cleaner public life."

He believed in a free press and for him it did not mean merely a press free from legal restrictions. The press must be free from both internal and external pressures, he said. "An independent press is not. merely a press independent of the Government but independent of vested interests," he declared. "Internal pressures arise within the newspaper from the owner or from the manager on behalf of the owner. Editorial freedom and independence means not only the editor's freedom and independence but the freedom and independence which the editor's staff share with him.... Internal pressures are multiplied by the growth of what are known as chains, groups and multiple units.... There are pressures from advertisers also.":

Working journalists will remember Chalapati Rau for the dedication with which he worked to gain them recognition and a decent wage. As a member of the first Press Commission he was greatly instrumental in focusing attention on the conditions of the working journalists and to suggest measures to bring cheer and hope into their lives. "He was no ivory tower editor," says a writer, "nor a fat salaried scribed insensitive to the lot of others in his profession. He was undoubtedly the builder of the working journalists' movement in the country. Under his constant care and guidance, this movement has grown into a pivotal organisation in the world of the Indian press. Chalapati Rau looked upon the working journalists' movement not merely as a platform to protect the working conditions of the Indian journalists but as an organ to defend the freedom of the Indian press from pollution by proprietorial and other vested interests as also from executive pressures and blandishments." He founded the Federation of Working Journalists in 1950 and was its president for three terms. He commanded the respect and affection of his colleagues and peers in the profession. "Journalism is not a matter of wages and benefits," he said, "It is a matter of craft and craftsmanship and journalists are expected to possess not only professional skill but professional pride. It is a free and equal profession. The competition is open. Anyone can rise by enterprise. There is a sense of fellowship between the editor and machine man, between the sub-editor and the proof-reader. The newspaper is one entity. Every member of the staff should stand or fall by it.

Chalapati Rau passed away in 1983. He was apparently killed in a road accident and his body was found on the road-side. In a tribute to him, one of his admirers wrote: "Chalapati Rau as a personality of outstanding calibre stood out in the national life of India. Behind this massive figure was a person of shy and gentle nature. With his abundance of wit and irrepressible humour, was not attracted by the glamour of social life; by temperament he was lonely—almost a lone wolf. But he was by no means unapproachable. Particularly to those younger to him, he had always something to impart out of his vast erudition and professional experience. He was a teacher *par excellence* -but only to those who could break through the outer crust of his strange aloofness. Even when he was irritated he bore no rancour. And he left this world as unobstrusively as he lived. All those who knew him could sense that a giant had departed, the like of whom is not to be found in the intellectual world of the India of today."

5

Major Players

Amrita Bazar Patrika

There are today in India five English dailies which have crossed the century mark. Three of them, the *Amrita Bazar Patrika, The Hindu* and the *Tribune,* are Indian owned and Indian edited and the other two, the *Times of India* and the *Statesman* were British-owned and British-edited and progressively changed into Indian hands after India became free. AH these newspapers have played a major role in the evolution and growth of Indian journalism and the Indian-owned dailies made a striking contribution to creating and nurturing Indian nationalism and to the freedom struggle.

The *Amrita Bazar Patrika* is the oldest Indian-owned daily and in 1920, Lenin described it as "the best nationalist paper in India". It was born as a weekly in Bengali in February, 1868, in the village of Amrita Bazar in Jessore district (now in Bangladesh). It was started by four brothers to fight the cause of peasants who were being exploited by indigo planters. Sisir Kumar, the more famous among the brothers, was the editor and the story of *Patrika* was the story of Sisir Kumar's relentless fight against the alien rulers who were determined to suppress this mouthpiece of the poor and downtrodden Indians. The *Patrika* moved to Calcutta in 1871 and functioned as a bi-lingual weekly, publishing news and views in English along with Bengali. Its anti-government views and its influence among the people provoked the Government of Lord Lytton to take action against the language press. But before the Vernacular Press Act of 1878 (said to be mainly directed towards the *Patrika)* When Tilak was promulgated, the *Patrika* overnight became an English weekly and so escaped the clutches of the law. With increased circulation and greater influence with the people, the *Patrika* continued to remain a thorn in the side of the administration. Every effort was made to buy the *Patrika* by temptations but Sisir Kumar refused to be tempted. The *Patrika* became a daily in February, 1891, and plunged into the nationalist movement which had received a fillip with the formation of the Indian National Congress in 1885. The *Patrika* created history during the term of Lord Landsdowne as viceroy when it published a confidential document of the Foreign Office concerning Kashmir. It created a sensation among official circles and a law was passed to prevent disclosure of official documents and background material without prior permission. Sisir Kumar fought for the rights of Indians and demanded for them increased representation in the administration and in the professions. He launched vigorous campaigns against restrictions on civil liberties and economic exploitation. He pleaded for the establishment of representative institutions for Indians to have a say in the administration. He contributed much to arouse the political consciousness of the people and he founded the Indian League in 1875, which probably was the first political association in India. Sisir Kumar and his brother Motilal Ghosh were deeply attached to Bal Gangadhar Tilak. When Tilak was prosecuted for sedition in 1897, they raised funds in Calcutta for his defence. When Tilak was again tried for sedition for articles in the *Kesari* and sentenced to six years' imprisonment by an Indian judge, Motilal Ghosh, who succeeded his brother as editor pointed out "the absurdity of a homeless Parsi judge (Justice Dawar) unfit to tie the shoelaces of Tilak, indulging in wanton insult to the distinguished accused and presuming to teach true patriotism to a proved and Unparalleled patriot."

The *Patrika* had many brushes with Lord Curzon, viceroy, who partitioned Bengal and roused the people to a paroxysm of fury. The partition saw the birth of the *Swadeshi* movement which spread like wildfire throughout the country. On one occasion, the overbearing and arrogant viceroy in an address to the Calcutta University said Indians were lacking in veracity. The *Patrika* replied to this sweeping denunciation with an equally scathing retort. It quoted passages from Curzon's book on the Far East which described the falsification of age and other particulars in his interview with the president of the Korean Foreign Office. It was unwise, it told the viceroy, for one who lived in a glass house to throw stones at others. When Curzon resigned in 1905, the *Patrika* wrote: "Young and a little foppish and without previous training but invested with unlimited powers, Lord Curzon, a superior' purzon' rose like a rocket and fell like a stick." The *Patrika* was one of the victims of the Press Act of 1910. When in 1913 a security of Rs.5,000 was demanded from it. Motilal Ghosh was charged with contempt of court in one case. He fought bravely in court and the case was dismissed. When Subhash Bose and other students were expelled from the Calcutta Presidency College for nationalist activities, the *Patrika* took up their case and succeeded in having them re-admitted. Motilal, who was an extremist in politics, often clashed with his Moderate counterpart, Surendranath Bannerjee, through the columns of their newspapers.

When for the first time an Indian member of the Imperial Legislative Council stood up to criticise the government's budget as Gokhale did in 1902, the *Patrika* wrote: "We had entertained the ambition of seeing some Indian member openly and fearlessly criticising the financial statement of the government. But this ambition was never satisfied. When members had ability they had not the requisite courage: when they had the requisite courage they had not the ability. For the first time in the annals of British rule in India, a native of India has not only succeeded in exposing the fallacies which underlie the Government statements but has ventured to do it in an uncompromising manner. Mr Gokhale has demonstrated that the members of the council have their duties towards their country and in performing them must not think of self."

A leading role was played by Motilal to bring about a compromise between Gokhale the Moderate leader, and Tilak, who were bitter political opponents. Motilal, who was a friend of both, advised them to end their feud and forge a united Congress. He wrote to Gokhale in November, 1914: "My heart weeps for the motherland.... I am anxious that you and Tilak should shake hands and embrace each other as brothers. I know you bear no malice or ill-will to him. I further know that even if you have any cause for offence, you are generous enough to forgive and forget, especially at the present critical moment. As you are in a more favourable position, it would be a graceful act for you to make an advance. If he rejects, the people will blame him and bless you. Bui I believe he will appreciate your motive. The so-called Bengali leaders are now fossils. It is a Mahratta intellect and patriotism which must save the country. If you and Tilak make up, there is yet hope for India."

Motilal Ghosh has been described as a man "thin and erect with his mass of grey hair surmounting a face in which pathos, humour and subtlety were mingled." His occasional exuberant professions of loyalty to the British Crown could have shamed the most sentimental royalist in England. Writing in the *Patrika* in 1887, on the Madras Congress, he said it had drawn the hearts of the people towards the governor as their own real ruler. In short, the European community in general at Madras seemed to sympathise with the movement like true and genuine Britons. He added: "An institution like the National Congress implies, in fact, requires the permanent existence of British rule in India." His loyalty however, did not prevent him from directing the guns of the *Patrika* at the viceroy, the governor of Bengal, and other officials to the great delight of his readers and the great annoyance of his victims.

After the Surat Congress fiasco when the Moderates charged Tilak with being the villain of the piece, Motilal Ghosh persuaded Tilak to appease his opponents in writing what amounted to a letter of regret and waiving his opposition to the election of Rash Bihari Ghosh as president. He invoked he spirit of forgive and forget and offered his cooperation to preserve the unity of the Congress. Motilal himself took the letter to the Moderates but was, in his own words, "simply bowled out by the Moderate leaders headed by Pherozeshah Mehta."

When Motilal died in September, 1922, the *Statesman* wrote: "The death of Babu Motilal Ghosh removes perhaps the most remarkable personality in Bengal. For more than half a century he carried on through his paper what was neither more nor less than a journalistic vendetta against the British Government and against the English race. No incident was too trivial to be pressed into the service of his propaganda or to be twisted into some real or fancied grievance. Yet Motilal Ghosh had a warm corner in his heart for individual Britons even while he insisted on regarding the majority of their countrymen as vampires. He was in many ways a genial soul, which if it had not been warped by a fanatical hatred of everything British, might have done a great deal to promote a mutual understanding between the two races."

The *Patrika* contributed its share to the success of the freedom movement under the leadership of Gandhi and suffered for its views and actions at the hands of the British rulers. Its security of Rs. 5,000 deposited in 1913 was forfeited in 1919 and a hesh security of Rs. 10,000 was demanded. The *Patrika* wrote: "We shall go on doing our duty as usual so long as life and freedom are preserved for us." The *Patrika* forfeited its security for a second time in 1932 during the Salt *Satyagraha* and it had to furnish a fresh security of Rs. 6,000. There years later its editor, Tushar Kanti Ghosh (son of Sisir Kumar) was hauled up in court on a defamation charge and sentenced to imprisonment.

The *Patrika* espoused the cause of communal harmony during the darkest periods of communal frenzy which disfigured Calcutta and other parts of the country. During the great Calcutta killing in 1946, the *Patrika* in anger and sorrow left its editorial columns blank for three days. When freedom dawned on August 15,1947, the *Patrika* wrote: "It is dawn, cloudy though it is. Presently, sunshine will break." In the words of an admirer of the *Patrika*: "In its 117th year, the *Patrika* continues to serve the public as a living example of responsible journalism, upholding the ideals of independence, democracy and secularism and holding its head high against all forms of communalism and parochialism."

The Hindu

Six young men, all in their twenties, founded *The Hindu* in Madras on September 20, 1878. Two of them. G. Subramania Aiyer and M. Veeraraghavacharier, stayed on later to become joint proprietors of the paper which started as a weekly and became a daily in 1889. They all belonged to a society called the Triplicane Literary Society which was a forum for discussion of political and social topics and attracted the elite of Madras. The immediate reason for starting the paper was the criticism by British-owned newspapers of the appointment of T. (later Sir T.) Muthuswami Aiyer as judge of the Madras High Court. In the words of Subramania Aiyer: "Unable to stand this unfairness, six of us joined together and started *The Hindu*. When we started the newspaper we had no idea of the responsibility which its publication would involve, of how to conduct it, of the expenditure to be incurred, etc. Since we had no money with us, we borrowed one rupee and three-quarters and printed and published 80 copies."

In its first editorial *The Hindu* wrote: "We are inclined to be conservative as much as it is consistent with the national progress of the natives. The principles that we proposed to be guided by are simply those of fairness and justice. It will always be our aim to promote harmony and union among our fellow countrymen and to interpret correctly the feelings of the natives and to create mutual confidence between the governed and the governors." At the time *The Hindu* appeared, public opinion in Madras Presidency was stagnant and there were very few recognised forums to voice the feelings and grievances of the Indian population. It filled a vacuum and was instantly popular. Bipin Chandra Pal, who was at one time its Calcutta correspondent, said of *The Hindu* in 1881 "I found *The Hindu* had already become a great power and an influence for good in Madras Presidency." He said that the emphasis of English educated Indians was not on our respective provincialities, but almost exclusively on India's national unity. This helped *The Hindu* to be accepted from its very birth as an all-India paper even though it could not claim any large all-India circulation."

From its inception *The Hindu* clashed with officialdom and exposed its misdeeds and abuse of power. In line with the thinking of the nationalist leaders of the time it was a firm believer in British rule and its quarrel was with the bureaucracy, with the way it functioned in India. *The Hindu* and its editor, Subramania Aiyer, were from the beginning closely associated and the Congress and Subramania Aiyer had the distinction of moving the first resolution in the first Congress session in Bombay in 1885. This close association was to continue even after independence. Subramania Aiyer, who started life as a college lecturer, was a great social reformer and he used the columns of *The Hindu* to propagate his views. He was much ahead of his time and his vigorous campaigns led to a fall in circulation and he had to part company with the paper in 1898. C.Y. Chintamani said of him: "He was the greatest journalist of his generation. He was not only great in Indian journalism but also a great social reformer whose revolutionary ideas were almost a century ahead of his times." *The Hindu* described him as the "maker of Indian journalism in Madras Presidency."

The Hindu changed hands in 1905 when S. Kasturiranga Iyengar, a lawyer, bought it and became its editor. He was a man of tremendous energy and capacity. Within a year he reorganised the paper, improved its get-up and news service and made it a commercial proposition. He had in his nephew, S. Rangaswami, a versatile writer, whose editorials were charged with power and emotion and were read with avidity. He hit hard at opponents and his main target was the Moderates whom he described as "lost leaders" who left tfieir comrades for a "handful of gold or riband." His strong editorials on the Punjab atrocities in 1919 led to a demand from the government for a security of Rs. 2,000 under the Press Act. *The Hindu's* entry was banned in Britain in 1918 even while its editor was in that country as a member of the editor's delegation which visited the war fronts, on the grounds that it carried news and views prejudicial to the conduct of the war. The Nizam of Hyderabad also had the distinction of banning *The Hindu* in 1923 because he did not like some articles on Hyderabad published in the paper.

A. Rangaswami Iyengar became the editor in 1928 and he performed the duties of both an editor and a Congressman. He was secretary of the Indian National Congress for many years and also a leading member of the party in the Central Legislative Assembly. *The Hindu* had many distinguished correspondents abroad, among them Subhas Bose in Vienna and V.K. Krishna Menon elsewhere in Europe. After the death of Rangaswami Iyengar, Kasturi Srinivasan, son of Kasturiranga Iyengar, took over as Managing editor of the paper in 1934 and remained in that post till his death in 1959. Srinivasan's stewardship was the golden era of the paper when it forged ahead and established its reputation and fame not only in India but also abroad. Although Srinivasan did not actively participate in politics, he acted as a wise counsellor and guide to Congress leaders and sometimes as an intermediary for them with the government. During the great confrontation between the Indian press and the alien government he was, as we have noted in an earlier chapter, the champion of the rights of the press and did not hesitate to non-cooperate with the government when it became necessary. He saw *The Hindu's* page one become a news page in 1958 when it abandoned its policy of over 80 years of carrying only advertisements on that page. His brother's sons, G. Narasimham and G. Kasturi took over after Srinivasan's death.

The Hindu has many firsts to its credit. It was the first Indian newspaper to have its own plane service for distribution of the paper to its far-flung readers. This was done in 1963, and in 1969, *The Hindu* achieved another first when it launched its facsimile editions in Coimbatore and later extended it to Bangalore,

Hyderabad and Madurai. Again it was the first to introduce phototype setting for printing the paper. In 1978, *The Hindu* brought out a sports weekly, *Sportstar.* Its predecessor, *Sports and Pastime* which made its mark in sports journalism, had to be closed down in 1968 owing to labour trouble. In 1984 the *Frontline,* a fortnightly news magazine, made its appearance with news pictures as its strong point.

The Hindu has been praised as one of the world's best newspapers by the London, *Times* and western journalists and authors. It was the recipient of the World Press Achievement Award for 1968 from the American Newspaper Publishers' Association Foundation. When G. Narasimham passed away in 1977, the post of managing editor was abolished and G. Kasturi took over full control of the paper as editor, '*The Hindu* has had the good fortune to be served by a dedicated team of journalists during its long career who have made it an institution whose watchwords have been accuracy, reliability and credibility. Most notable among these men was N. Raghunathan, seniormost assistant editor, who retired in 1957 after 30 years of devoted service. We shall note his career in another chapter.

The Hindu in an editorial in 1967, wrote what can be termed as its testament: "We must make it clear", it said, "that we are an independent, non-party newspaper, wedded to the national interest as we see it. We are not the mouthpiece of any party. We have been more often critical of the ruling party perhaps than singing its praises. We have always made a distinction between programmes and measures on the one side and personalities and parties on the other. Our criticism have been primarily concerned with the nonwisdom or inappropriateness of certain policies or decisions and whatever governments may come to power we shall continue to judge them not by their professions but by their performance." *The Hindu* has postulated three basic principles to make freedom of the press real. The first is that the press must keep its own house clean and exercise resonable restraint on its functioning. Freedom should not be allowed to degenerate into licence which would open the door to government interference. The second is the response of authority to the smooth functioning of the press by removing physical restraints and to enable it to reach as wide a readership as it would wish. The third and the most important is the attitude of society as a whole, which besides the public, includes politicians, trade unions, advertisers, etc. The press has been subjected to pressure from one or another of these sources and the less viable among the press have found it difficult to withstand it. "Press freedom can come to prevail only when all sections of the body politic resolve to make to prevail by removing all impediments in the way", *The Hindu* has said.

The Statesman

Jawaharlal Nehru, it is said, read the *Statesman* every morning during the days of the freedom struggle when he was out of prison and its was one of the newspapers supplied to him when he was in prison which happened frequently. In 1928, when the nationalists organised a boycott of the Simon commission which came to enquire into constitutional reforms, the *Statesman* applied to them to cooperate with the commission and this led to a campaign to boycott the paper and copies of the paper were burnt. But it did not deter a prominent nationalist-leader from reading the paper's editorials. Asked about it he said: "We may not agree with them but we must concede that they talk sense. And look at the brilliant way they have put forward their arguments. What wonderful language, what style! No, no, we mustn't burn a paper like this." "The *Statesman* is singularly free from prejudice," *The Hindu* wrote in 1895, "and its sincere advocacy of the Indian cause is well and widely known. The pro-Indian attitude of our contemporary enhances the value of its opinion." Nirad C. Chaudhuri said that the Statesman had replaced Macaulay among the Bengalis in their worship of fine English. "If you want to write good English, read the *Statesman*, our elders and teachers admonished us."

Robert Knight, who founded the *Statesman* in 1875 (as we have noted in an earlier chapter) was one of the early British journalists, who like Silk Buckingham, encouraged critical review of the government's actions and policies which set him apart from other British-owned papers which while supporting the government steadfastly also indulged in denunciation of Indians and specially the nationalists. Knight welcomed the formation of the Indian National Congress in 1885. "The Congress needs no other justification than the truism that if the people of India are ever to enter upon a course of real progress, it can only be by their learning to govern themselves," he wrote. "No people can make any solid or enduring progress under any system of government which does not devolve upon them more or less completely the responsibility for their own advancement. In India, we have, unwittingly and unfortunately, set up what is perhaps the very worst form of government that the civilised world has yet seen.,.. But the time for reform has come and while India will, we hope and believe, escape the sufferings and sacrifices by which the American colonists achieved their freedom, it is the primary duty of her educated sons—a duty to Englishmen as well as to themselves—that they should use every means in their power to awaken their rulers to the fact that no people can ever make solid or lasting progress under a system of government such as that exists in India.... It is not revolution that the Congress asks for but reforms that is as urgently needed in our own interests as theirs. Knight passed away in 1890."

The *Statesman*, which was described as the *Manchester Guardian* of the East, has had a long line of able and dedicated editors who have left their mark deep on it. There were many occasions when it got into trouble with the government. On one such occasion, Gokhale had to use his influence to rescue its editor, Samuel Ratcliffe, from government displeasure. This happened during the viceroyalty of Lord Minto. The paper had published a secret minute of Lord Curzon on the partition of Bengal and the Home Department withdrew from it government advertisements and other privileges as a punishment. Gokhale spoke to Dunlop Smith, private secretary to the viceroy, who helped to arrange an interview for Ratcliffe with the Home Member, Arundel. The *Statesman* published an apology and the government withdrew the ban.

During the turbulent days of 1930 and later when the freedom struggle was at its height, the *Statesman* came under fire from the nationalists. Describing the situation, James Cowley wrote: "An attempt on the life of the editor, Sir Alfred Watson, was made. They were turbulent times. The *Swadeshi* campaign was rapidly gathering momentum, bullets flew, and home-made bombs exploded, disturbingly often with lethal effect and the toll of heads broken by the ubiquitous iron-shod *lathi* was beyond count. The *Statesman* had incurred the activists' ire partly because of its allegedly unhelpful attitude to nationalist aspirations and partly because in those days that paper was British-owned which made its stance doubly offensive to many people."

The *Statesman* in the twenties represented what we now call the rightist point of view. It was both conservative and liberal; conservative in the sense that it wanted the country and people to conserve their best traditions and liberal in the sense that it reflected an attitude free from dogmas and prejudices. To the nationalists and fighters for freedom, however, it was the mouthpiece of British imperialism and of the British community in India. Even so, there were few nationalists and freedom fighters who did not read it daily. Its editorials were scrutinised and analysed by people holding diverse political views.

Malcolm Muggeridge came to India as an assistant editor of the *Statesman* during this period and he was not happy. "I should never have come," he wrote. "I am obsessed with the feeling that I am on the wrong side... and though I know what the Indian nationalist movement amounts to, it pricks my conscience sometimes to read Congress newspapers." He lived in a flat above the *Statesman* office with Wordsworth who was acting editor. Wordsworth, who claimed to be a descendant of the great poet and had gravitated from the Indian Educational Service to journalism, was a "short, plump, pasty man who had all the correct liberal views and attitudes of mind believing that it would be possible through constitutional changes to transform the British Raj peacefully into a Westminster style self-governing democracy,...His soft persistence in upholding such views led me to go out of my way to pour scorn and ridicule on them.,.." Muggeridge was convinced that there could be only one outcome in India—the British would have to go. "And yet they themselves, in their clubs and offices, on their polo grounds and tennis courts, were serenely convinced that with some adjustments here and there, the Raj, in one form or another, would go on for centuries yet. A favourite saying among them was that if the British left within six months, the Indians would be down on their knees begging them to come back." Muggeridge was posted to Simla as special correspondent and he was introduced to the Viceroy, Lord Willingdon, at one of his parties. The viceroy told Muggeridge: "People were inclined to think that India was difficult to govern, but I have found it almost ridiculously easy. You just have to be nice with these fellers and they respond. That, at least, had been my experience. 1 doubt if there is in all the world an easier country to govern than India."

This was Muggeridge's description of how correspondents functioned in Simla, headquarters of the Government of India: "Journalists follow authority as sharks do a liner hoping to feed off the waste it discharges with perhaps someone occasionally falling overboard to make a meal and once in a way the whole ship going down and providing a positive feast. There was a little band of us swimming along in the wake of the Government of India.... Public relations as we know it today, was in its infancy but already the Government of India had its spokesman whom we constantly pursued for handouts and leakages and to arrange interviews. Among other useful services, we made a point of mastering the first names of Indians who were going to be knighted.... I doubt if any government had ever existed so cut off from the governed as the Government of India nestling among the Himalayas in Simla."

Wordsworth under whom Muggeridge served was notorious for his absent mindedness. On one occasion the news editor was surprised by his enquiry whether he worked there. The news editor said he had been news editor for some years. "I doubt it," Wordsworth said but did not say why. On another occasion, he summoned the news editor to his room and handed him a newspaper with his markings in red pencil and comments like "disgraceful", "criminal grammar", etc. The news editor told him that the newspaper which had provoked his comments was not the *Statesman* but a rival paper. "God bless my soul," Wordsworth said, "don't take any note of all that" Muggeridge's stay in India was very brief.

There were two great editors of the *Statesman*, Arthur Moore and Ian Stephens, who earned the admiration and gratitude of the Indian people by their sympathy and support for their political aspirations and for highlighting their legitimate grievances. We shall write about Moore Separately for he deserves a chapter to himself. Ian Stephens who succeeded Moore in 1942, was an unconventional editor. He cycled to his office in khaki shorts, singlet and chappals followed on another cycle by his bodyguard with a change of clothing.

Stephens' greatest achievement was to expose the horrors of the Bengal famine in 1946 through revealing pictures and gruesome stories day after day in the *Statesman* which made him unpopular in government circles in Simla. He did all a man could do to assuage human suffering on a massive scale and certainly brought the Government of India to its senses. The story is told that once when seeking an interview in the capital he wrote his name on the back of a particularly revolting famine picture and sent it in as his visiting card. In 1950, Stephens was in fear of assassination for some weeks and was guarded day and night by plainclothes police. "It was an occupational hazard for a *Statesman* editor," he said.

For many years the *Statesman* published on the edit page an article by a Muslim contributor under the pseudonym Shahed. The identity of Shahed was kept a closely guarded secret Stephens did not know who he was even five years after he joined the paper and for several weeks after he became editor. "He was as much a mystery man to me as to the public," he said, "I then only discovered his identity by accident and thereafter had strong reason for secrecy." The mysterious contributor was Altaf Hussain, who was then in the service of the Government of India and who later became editor of the *Dawn*, the organ of the Muslim League. His articles in the *Statesman* provoked great controversy and were responsible for creating bitter feelings towards the paper among the nationalists.

On August 15, 1947, the *Statesman* wrote; "Now is the appointed day. Now is the day of salvation. If we start right, we can continue right. On everyone of us who live in India, be it in the Indian Union or Pakistan, there is a personal responsibility to start this day with our thoughts right.... It is the fitting climax of the intertwined story of Britain and India, the fulfilment of Britain's mission, a mission carried out under God's blessing with many failures to sense its greatness, with some inevitable personal yieldings to the lure of pomp and circumstance of pride and glory of the world and the love of money, but for all that a mission writ in the stars of the East and West and discharged from the British throne and the High Court of Parliament downwards with a large and steady faithfulness, through ever rarer good report and ever increasing ill-report. Now the day has come and what was British India is resolved into two states. Let us waste no tears on that. The essential thing is to preserve and foster the unity of systems and of outlook that exists." Stephens, as we have noted already, resigned in 1951 as he disagreed with the Kashmir policy of the Government of India. The *Statesman* progressively changed into Indian hands and today it is a fully Indian-owned and Indian-edited newspaper.

When the *Statesman* celebrated its centenary in 1975, it wrote: "The *Statesman* has seen every development towards Indian independence, the Minto-Morley reforms, the Montagu-Chelmsford ones, the movements of Tilak, Gandhi, Subhas Bose and others. Its opinions have not always been popular though it was the first paper which Nehru used to read in the morning. But it has almost always been respected. Us technical standards have been high: for many years, for instance, either the Calcutta or the Delhi edition annually carried off the president's award for printing; several of its features, including the correspondence columns, have been rated by many competent judges as the finest in the country."

The *Statesman* was one of the papers which suffered during the Emergency for its anti-government postures. Today, it is a vigorous independent paper, fearlessly voicing its views on all questions affecting the common man and some of its investigative stories have achieved national prominence.

The Times of India

The Times of India is the oldest English daily in India and it is also a great newspaper which has played an important role in the development of journalism in this country. Before the advent of freedom and especially in the closing years of the last century and the beginning of this century, it had been a controversial newspapers which had stood as a bulwark of colonial rule and had nothing but contempt for Indians and their aspirations to freedom. It belonged to the class of British-owned newspapers which was described by one historian as those newspapers which were not "a model of sobriety and good manners. Their slighting and supercilious tone towards educated Indians wounded and alienated sensitive people." *The Hindu* wrote in 1900: "The *Englishman,* the *Pioneer* and the *Times of India* are three well-known organs of Anglo-Indian opinion which most violently oppose the advancement of the Indian people. Much of the harsh treatment which of late we have received from our rulers is due to their incitement and in the future Indian reforms, we apprehend much trouble from these and other champions of the dominant class." It wrote again in 1909: "Most of the Anglo-Indian papers seem to consider themselves the watchdogs of the British Government in this country. They always take a high and mighty tone with the alleged delinquencies of Indians and think it their special mission to egg on the government to take this action or that."

In a vituperative attack on Indians in 1900, the *Times of India* wrote: "Mr Ranade's (Mahadev Govind Ranade, judge of the Bombay High Court) experience as a judge must have convinced him long ago that the people of this country set no value upon truth for its own sake. Indeed, the average Hindu lies by preference. Sentiments, however lofty and ennobling are thrown away upon people who are dead to the rudiments of virtue. Widow re-marriage, *sati,* polygamy, child marriage, all these are surface blemishes, symptoms and signs of the profoundly deep-seated canker at the heart, of Indian life—its hopeless want of honesty, its unexplained mendacity. The mass of the people are brought up in an atmosphere of lies. From the cradle to the grave, they are shadowed by the habits of lying and servility."

We have already seen in an earlier chapter how Robert Knight became editor of the *Bombay Times* and how by merging in it two other newspapers, renamed it *Times of India* in 1861. The first issue of the *Bombay Times*, a bi-weekly, appeared on November 3, 1838. Its editor was J.E, Brennan, a retired Irish doctor who was also secretary of the Bombay Chamber of Commerce. He wrote in the first issue on the need for education of the people of India "whose capacity for improvement is inferior to that of no one elsewhere", but who he thought were "spell-bound victims of ignorance and delusion." A later editor, George Buist, roused Indian sentiment by inciting other newspapers to demand reprisals against the Indians after the Mutiny in 1857. The government did nothing to restrain him but when a Parsi shareholder, Nowroji Furdonji, objected, Buist was eventually dismissed. The *Bombay Times* had many Indian shareholders from 1850 to 1859 when Knight bought them. Under the editorship of Thomas J. Bennett, who later became the sole proprietor of the *Times of India*, the paper maintained close relations with Indians many of whom contributed to its columns. Bennett vastly improved the paper by bringing talented people from England among whom was a master printer, F.M. Coleman, who had wide experience of daily newspaper production.

With its high class printing and news service (it was the earliest newspaper in India to subscribe to Reuter's news service) the *Times of India* made rapid progress and in 1890 it printed daily 3000 copies. Indian subscribers were small in number because free public libraries served their needs. According to one writer, two circulating libraries between themselves took up one-third of the daily output of the paper at reduced rates. The copies were distributed to one class of subscribers at 6 a.m.: They were taken from them at 9 a.m. and passed on to a second group and then to a third group at noon. They were collected for a fourth time and "after ironing the well thumped copies were posted to upcountry places." The *Times of India* in 1870 asked its readers to contribute items of interest and regular contributors were rewarded with a free copy of the paper. One observer of the period wrote: "The newspapers were never dull. When nothing outside deserved notice, editors started quarrelling among themselves which they pursued with rigour and diligence." Bennett and Coleman combined and formed a company called Bennett-Coleman Company which continues even today although it has changed into Indian hands. Bennett brought experienced journalists from England to edit the paper and they included Lovat Fraser and Sir Stanley Reed. Pat Lovett wrote in 1883, when he joined the paper, that it consisted of an editor, an assistant editor, a sub-editor, a chief reporter (all brought from England) and four reporters recruited locally, two of them Parsis.

In the wake of the partition of Bengal there was a spurt of violence and the British-owned press screamed for strong government action. It set itself to be a defender of the government and its technique was to snipe at Indians, both extremists and moderates. The government was in a mood to ignore their lapses from good taste and journalistic ethics. When the *Times of India* was hauled up for contempt of court during the trial of Tilak for sedition in 1897, it was let off with a warning. Commenting on the articles in the British-owned press, Gokhale wrote: "The terms of race arrogance and contempt in which some of these newspapers constantly speak of Indians and specially of educated Indians cut into the mind more than the lash can into the flesh.... I would like to see the official who would dare to arrest and march to the police *thana* the editor of an Anglo-Indian newspaper. But so far as Indian editors are concerned, there are, I fear, officers in this country who would not be sorry to march whole battalions of them to the police *thana*"

The *Times of India* suffered serious loss of face in 1905 when an editorial writer or some imp of mischief played a dirty trick on it. A newspaper reprinted an article which it said had appeared in the *Times of India* and it was a condemnation of Lord Curzon, the viceroy. It began: "One might well wish that Lord Curzon had not returned to Indie for the second time for he could not have chosen a more effective way of wrecking his reputation than he has done." The article was reprinted by more and more newspapers and the *Times of India* which had always considered Curzon as its hero, was embarrassed. It issued a contradiction but even then the article continued to be reprinted, both in India and England. At the Surat session of the Congress in 1907, which ended in confusion, a representative of the *Times of India,* Pears, who covered the proceedings for his paper, was manhandled and suffered injuries. When the president of the session, Rash Behari Ghosh was in physical danger, it was Pears who escorted him back to the pavilion.

The *Times of India* was favourite target in the early years of the century was Sir Pherozeshah Mehta, the Congress leader in Bombay. In 1901, during a debate on a land revenue bill in the Bombay Legislative Council Mehta, Gokhale and others staged a walk-out which caused surprise because it was considered strange for Moderates to indulge in that kind of protest. The *Times of India,* in an editorial written by Lovat Fraser (Mehua's bitter enemy) made fun of Mehta and his friends. It wrote: "It is difficult to contemplate seriously the spectacle of Mehta striding towards the door in order to emphasise the novel theory that the duty of the true patriot is to run away while the gentlemen who rather sheepishly stole after him only excites feelings of compassionate amusement. Mr Meath does not often make tactical mistakes but he blundered rather badly in his pre-arranged exit from the council hall. Meant to be dramatic, his performance was merely comic... He forgot too, that little scenes of this description should at least convey the idea of spontaneity; whereas a good many people knew beforehand what was going to happen. It is a risky experiment for public men to take to histrionics towards the end of their careers." In an earlier editorial, the paper complimented Mehta and his associates on their proficiency in the English language. Commenting on the speeches made at a meeting addressed by Mehta and others, it said at least two or three of the speakers "displayed knowledge of the English language in its more subtle aspects which is gratifying to those of us who believe that there is a great intellectual future before the leading Indian races. Indeed, three of the creators on the occasion, Messrs Telang, Badruddin and Mehta, showed themselves to possess as great a mastery of our somewhat difficult Cicero ever did as of the Greek, accomplishment on which the foremost Roman orator rather prided himself."

K. Rama Rao who served as a sub-editor of the *Times of India* in the 1920s wrote that "subject to the natural limitations of a European-owned institution, there was freedom from race prejudice, certainly on the editorial side." Once, he recalled, "a European official walked into the sub-editors' room with a communique announcing the release of Gandhi. He was so much surprised at the presence of so many Indians that the next day he confronted the editor in his club and in the presence of others called the *Times of India* a " Black man's show". The editor complained to the governor and the official had to apologise. On another occasion, Sir Stanley Reed, editor, wrote that every Englishman in India was ashamed of the deeds of General Dyer at Amritsar (General Dyer was responsible for the Jallianwala Bagh massacre). A section of the Europeans in Bombay was offended and it was reported there was a plan to give a "sound thrashing to the impudent journalist who had let down his country." A timely hint enabled Reed to keep out of the club until tempers cooled down.

It was a complete paper, Rama Rao wrote, "carrying the highest prestige in particular for its sports and commercial coverage. It carried more Indian news than many Indian papers." The two basic principles which governed the *Times of India*, according to Rama Rao, were that the King's Government must be carried on and the political susceptibilities of the Indian people must be respected. Among the editors, S.T. Sheppard was one who was kind to the staff and stood up for their rights. During the editorship of Sir Francis Low, which saw a climax in the battle for freedom and a confrontation between the press and the government, the *Times of India* touched heights it had not reached before and according to Rama Rao it outstripped other papers in point of circulation and volume of news printed. Frank Moraes became the first Indian editor when freedom came. The *Times of India* passed into Indian hands in 1946. Its sister journal, the *Illustrated Weekly of India*, started in 1888 is today one of the major weeklies and a host of other journals in Marathi, Hindi and English have been added to the group including the *Economic Times* (1916) which was the first daily dealing with financial and economic news to be published in India. The *Times of India* today occupies a premier position and it has the second largest circulation among English dailies, according *to Press in India,* 1984.

The Tribune

Gandhi said in 1932: "The *Tribune* is the best viewspaper......Its editor's readings and analysis of events are unsurpassed." He said of its great editor, Kalintth Ray: "Long live Kalinath Ray! His articles nowadays on the communal problem and on joint electorates for Harijans bear witness to his deep knowledge and wide experience." Kalinath Ray was to the *Tribune* what G. Subramania Aiyer and Kasturiranga lyengar were to *The Hindu* and Motilal Ghosh to the *Amrita Bazar Patrika.* He was a Bengali who had worked on Surendranath Bannerjee's *Bengalee* Calcutta before he came to Lahore in 1917 to take over editorship of the *Tribune.* He was a fearless writer who bravely faced the risks involved in fighting the strongly entrenched alien government. His fierce attacks on the Punjab Government and on General Dyer, hero of Jailianwaia Bagh in 1919 led to his being arrested and sentenced to two years' imprisonment. On appeal, however, it was reduced to three months. Ray had his differences with Gandhi. He did not believe in non-violence and the methods adopted by Gandhi to achieve freedom but he was a good Congressman and took an active part in the freedom struggle. He told Mulk Raj Anand, the novelist: "We Bengalis do not agree with Gandhi that India can win freedom with non-violence. We can embarrass the government with non-cooperation. But they will not go with our *dharnas.* Some of our young students have turned terrorists.... You know one of the men who threw the bomb at Lord Hardinge in 1911 was a Bengali called Rash Behari.... He escaped to Japan afterwards. And one of our writers, Sarat Chandra, has written a novel lauding the gospel of tit for tat." Mulk Raj Anand said he had heard that Rabindranath Tagore did not approve of Gandhi's non-violence. Ray said: "Yes, he says that the illiterate people in a non-violent *dharna* may not remain non-violent. The natural thing men do is to defend themselves. Only the Jains are supine and Gandhi is from Gujarat where Jainism is still practised." Ray added after some thought: "I wish I had the courage to do something more than write editorials."

Amolok Ram, a former editor, has said that Ray who edited the *Tribune* for 28 years was known for his uprightness, integrity, sobriety and independence. He did not allow his judgement to be influenced by personal or sectarian considerations. Nor did he brook any interference, internal or external in the conduct of the paper. "Intensely patriotic as he was, he wrote with passion and vehemence but his views were based on reason and fairness," Amolok Ram said. "It was a treat to read his analytical editorials particularly at a time when the British bureaucracy was out to suppress all patriotic aspirations." Kali Babu, as he was affectionately called by his admirers, was generally disinclined to meet any V.I .P. He rarely attended any social function. He had a deep insight into the affairs of state and the working of various political organisations. He differed from Gandhi on certain aspects of the non-cooperation programme and expressed his opinion candidly and freely. But he had a high regard for those with whom he happened to differ. In spite of his differences, he gave unrelenting support to Gandhi in the long and arduous fight for freedom. Although the *Tribune* was an uncompromising critic of British rule, Ray commanded great respect even among the British bureaucrats of the day. He maintained the highest journalist standards. He did not indulge in character assassination, nor in hitting below the belt. J.N. Sahni who served under him says that Ray was the *Tribune.* He wrote the entire editorial page and sometimes his writing overflowed into another page. "Whatever he wrote was logical, scintillating and convincing." A.C. Bali, special representative of the *Tribune*, told a story about Jawaharlal Nehru and Ray. Nehru had come to Lahore once in the course of a tour of the Punjab. He asked Bali why the *Tribune* took particular care to call him Mr. Nehru or Pandit Nehru. Why could it not call him just Jawaharlal Nehru as in the case of Stalin or Churchill? Ray's reply when he was told about this was that Nehru had not yet attained the heights which Stalin or Churchill had in the international sphere.

Ray emerged with chronic asthma from prison and never recovered. He passed away in 1943 and the *Tribune* passed through many ups and downs until the final calamity in 1947 when, on the eve of independence, two of its staff members were stabbed and the publication of the paper in Lahore was suspended.

The *Tribune* was started as a weekly in Lahore in 1881 by Sardar Dayal Singh Majithia who was a great admirer of Raja Ram Mohun Roy and the Brahmo Samaj. He was helped by Surendranath Bannerjee to buy a printing press and chose as its first editor, Sital Kanta Chatterjee of Dacca. The *Tribune,* which became a daily in 1906 had a number of Bengalis as its editors in its early career, including Kalinath Ray. Bipin Chandra Pal was its editor for some time in the early years. A great philanthropist and prominent nationalist of northern India, Sardar Dayal Singh established a trust for the *Tribune* which continues to function till today. In its first issue on February 2,1881, the *Tribune* said: 'The aim of the *Tribune* will be, as its name imparts, fairly and temperately to advance the cause of the mute masses.... We shall strive as much as lies in the compass of our humble abilities to create and educate such opinion." The progress of the *Tribune* was intertwined with the country's political and social history and especially of the north-western region which at one time extended from Peshawar to Delhi and from Quetta to Karachi. It wielded great influence in the region comprising the North West Frontier Province, the pre-partition of Punjab, Sind and Delhi. From its inception, it succeeded in making itself a recognised organ of public opinion. It often clashed with the British rulers who were determined to suppress the freedom movement but it stood like a rock in the performance of its duty to educate the people and inculcate in them the spirit of patriotism and resistance to oppression and tyranny. It earned the reputation of being a fearless champion of the cause of the people and of freedom.

On the eve of independence when Punjab was partitioned, riots rocked Lahore and a mob attacked the office of the *Tribune.* Two members of the staff were killed, the printing machinery building and land were lost. The paper suspended publication.

In a telegram to Vallabhbhai Patel, home minister, the manager of the paper, said: "*Tribune* Lahore has lost, property, cash, machinery, newsprint etc., worth Rs. 25 lakhs. Newsprint worth Rs. 2 lakhs removed under orders of the West Punjab Government to government printing press, Lahore. Our van and six typewriters have also been given over to *Pakistan Times.* Our press and office have been sealed by the government. I learn that our press and building are being given to *Pakistan Times*" Patel asked the Rehabilitation Minister, K.C, Neogy to give all facilities to the *Tribune* to resume publication from Indian soil. The *Tribune* had opposed partition but when it became a *fait accompli,* its trustees decided to continue to publish it from Lahore and its editor wrote an editorial supporting Jinnah's views. Jinnah appreciated the *Tribune's* stand but the chaos and anarchy that followed partition left no option for the paper and it moved to Simla and later to Ambala in May, 1948. The paper's rehabilitation was unexpectedly rapid and the support it received from the people was phenomenal, said Amolok Ram, its editor.

The *Tribune* moved to its present home in Chandigarh in 1969. The paper, whose editor then was Madhavan Nair, got into trouble with the Government of India during the Emergenc in 1975. It was one of the three papers blacklisted by the government and denied advertisements and other facilities. Two sister papers, one in Pubjabi and the other in Hindi *(Punjabi Tribune and Dainik Tribune)* were started in 1978 and were an instant success. In the words of Sahni: "Apart from the high standard of integrity shown by its editors ever since the paper was founded, the *Tribune* has built up a rare tradition for fairplay, restraint and courageous pursuit of truth. This has been possible to a considerable extent also because of a succession of able managers (who resisted pressures from the advertisers' lobby) and the understanding shown by the trustees....The present Editor-in-Chief, Prem Bhatia, has not only preserved but also enhanced the reputation of the paper as a fearless exponent of public opinion and an understanding critic of the government."

6

March to New India

The British-owned *Pioneer* of Allahabad was an early instance of Indianization of newspaper ownership. Under the editorship of F.W Wilson, an able and vivacious journalist the *Pioneer* made good progress in circulation. But he was a thorn in the side of the bureaucracy and the management terminated his services. After this the newspaper's fortunes declined and in the early 1930's the proprietors sold the paper to some Indian landlords and businessmen of the United Provinces.

The process of Indianization was stimulated by the negotiations for the transfer of power that began as the war drew to a close. Like the owners of many plantations and industrial units, the British proprietors of newspapers decided to sell their interests and repatriate the proceeds; they feared that restrictions might be imposed by the government of a free India on the remittance of foreign exchange. Bennett Coleman sold the *Times of India* to Seth Ramakrishna Dalmia, a leading industrialist who had interests in banking and airlines. The Madras *Mail* also changed hands. The *Statesman* too eventually came under Indian management after independence.

Freedom and Holocaust

Partition was the other, and gruesome, side of the medal of independence. The Hindu-Muslim riots set off by the Muslim League's 'direct action' on 16th August 1946 made it impossible for many Hindu-owned newspapers to function in Pakistan; and for *Dawn to* continue publication in Delhi. Prominent among newspaper counterparts of the refugees who fled to India from West Pakistan were the, *Tribune* of Lahore which shifted first to Ambala and subsequently, to Chandigarh; and the Urdu *Pratap* and *Milap* which moved from Lahore to Delhi.

More far-reaching than these physical displacements were the psychic effects of partition. The scenario in post-partition India was that though the eligible voters among Muslims had voted almost to a man for the Muslim League and its two nation theory in the 194546 elections, most of them stayed back in every Indian province except Punjab. Gandhiji and Nehru wanted that the millions of Muslims who chose to remain in India after the creation of Pakistan should be able to live in safety and dignity, irrespective of how Hindus were treated in Pakistan. This was a high morality of unilateral right doing, far above the ordinary human morality of reciprocal obligation. Not many could rise to that height.

A curious feature of the newspaper scene in the post partition years was that several Hindu-owned Urdu newspapers campaigned against, Urdu, and for Hindi. Urdu was perceived as a symbol of the Muslim domination of India prior to British rule, and of the re-establishment of Muslim rule in the western and eastern wings of the sub-continent in 1947 as the result of partition. Many Muslims for their part, and for Iong, had looked upon Urdu in the same way as a symbol of Muslim supremacy. When the government of the United Provinces passed an order on 8th April 1900 to the effect, that law courts and government offices should entertain petitions written not only in Urdu but in Hindi in Devanagari script, many Muslim politicians objected and held protest meetings. They said it would lower the status and prestige of Urdu.

If the post-partition campaign against Urdu in a section of the Indian Press betrayed pique, Urdu was soon to attract much solicitude from politicians, both Muslim and non-Muslim, many of whom are moved not by genuine concern for Muslims and for the language which they regard as theirs, but by calculations of the number of Muslim votes they could gain by espousing Urdu as 'the language of the minority'.

Another psychological effect of the vivisection of India in order to create an Islamic State was the feeling generated among some Hindus that what remained of India should, logically, be a Hindu State. A prominent exponent of this view was Seth Ramakrishna Dalmia, who urged that India should be proclaimed a liberal religious State. He said in the course of a statement in July 1950, published prominently by the Times of *India:* "The only right course for saving the country from economic collapse, ending refuge distress, establishing cordial relations with Pakistan and assuring complete protection to the Muslims in India is to declare India a liberal religious State, which is beyond doubt the wish of an overwhelming majority of India's citizens." He expressed regret that "though the country had not recovered from the shock of the tremendous human tragedy created by the influx of East Bengal refugees, the outbreak of the Korean war has diverted the attention of Government to international politics. Neglecting the country's most urgent domestic problems, all are busy speculating about the possibilities of a third world war."

The suggestion that India should be a religious State, even if a liberal one, was directly opposed to the thinking of Jawaharlal Nehru, educated in England and nurtured in rationalism and Marxism. He had been unhappy with Gandhiji's description of the ideal State as Ram Rajya because of its evocation of India's Hindu heritage. Nehru must have been irked also by the dig at his propensity to interest himself at least as much in the problems of the world as of India. The Prime Minister's aversion to Seth Dalmia was to be a factor in the formation of India's first Press Commission and in the framing of its terms of reference.

Liberty of Press

There were two aspects of the operations of Reuters in India as a limb of the British empire. One was its total control of the flow of news from and to India, and the other was its dominant role in news gathering and distribution within India.

An early instance of bias in reports of world events supplied by Reuters to Indian newspapers related to the Russian revolution of 1917 and subsequent events in the Soviet Union. In an article that Jawaharlal Nehru wrote for the *Hindu* (3rd April 1928) on his return from a visit to Russia the previous year, he said: "It is right that India should be eager to learn more about Russia. So, further information has been largely derived from subsidised news agencies inimical to Russia, and the most fantastic stories about her have been circulated. The question most frequently asked me has been about the alleged nationalisation of women!" Nehru went on to pour ridicule on the fictitious 'Riga correspondents' who sat in London or Paris and concocted stories denigrating the infant Soviet State.

News sent out from India by Reuters to the rest of the world tended to be governed by Britain's imperial interests. The viewpoint of the Muslim League, after it became separatist and implacably hostile to the Indian National Congress, was enthusiastically projected abroad, as will be seen from the following instance.

When the Congress Working Committee met at Bardoli during December 1941, C. Rajagopalachari persuaded the Committee to revive the offer made by it earlier, in July 1940, to support the war effort if the British government agreed to recognise India's independence at the end of the war and to form immediately a provisional national government. At this point the British Viceroy, Lord Linlithgow, decided to use reuters to publicise abroad the Muslim League's objections to the Congress proposal. The historian S. Gopal writes: "The Viceroy, having no wish to cooperate with the Congress, disliked the Bardoli resolution. He therefore saw to it that Reuters cabled the full text of Jinnah's statement criticising the resolution, and urged Amery to give the statement the fullest weight in Britain and use it in the United States. 'If, under pressure from liberal quarters in the U.K., Rajaji and his friends were able to stifle me in their close embrace, I feel quite sure that the Mahatma would emerge once again upon the stage to give the *coup de grace* to British influence in India'.

Then, in the spring of 1942, there was, a, gaffe about the supposed death of Subhas Chandra Bose in an aeroplane accident. Bose had effected a dramatic escape from house detention in January 1941, and made his Way to Germany to canvass aid for India's freedom struggle in the belief not shared by Mahatma Gandhi, Jawaharlal Nehru and the great majority of the nationalist leadership that imperialist Britain's enemies should be regarded as India's friends. The whole country was shaken with grief. The Congress president and Gandhiji sent telegrams of condolence to the aged mother of Bose. When the allegedly dead Indian leader broadcast a talk from Radio Berlin, Reuters tried to disclaim responsibility for the report.

More grave was the failure of Reuters to make known abroad the firm opposition of the Congress leadership to the plans of Subhas Bose to liberate India with German and Japanese assistance. Mahatma Gandhi wrote in *Harijan* of 26th April 1942: "It is folly to suppose that aggressors can ever be benefactors. The Japanese may free India from the British yoke, but only to put in their own instead. I have always maintained that we should not seek any other power's help to free India from the British." Again, Viceroy Linlithgow cabled to Secretary of State Amery a summary of a report, intercepted by Intelligence, of an interview with Gandhiji on 15th May 1942 of a group of Bombay Congressman led by the former Chief Minister, B.G. Kher. The report, sent by Sharaf Athar Ali, a Communist, to P.C. Joshi, then secretary of the Communist Party of India, quoted Gandhiji as telling Kher (who had asked whether civil disobedience at that point would not mean help to the Japanese): "Oh, no. We are driving the British (out). We do not invite the Japanese. I disagree with those who think them liberators. Chinese history points that out. In fact I believe that Subhas Bose will have to be resisted by us. Subhas

has risked much for us; but if he means to set up a government in India under the Japanese, he will be resisted by US."

The Viceroy, who had got Reuters to cable Jinnah's anti Congress statement, did not organise similar publicity for these anti-Axis views of Mahatma, Gandhi. The Viceroy apart, if Reuters had performed properly its duty as a world news agency, the British Press and public opinion would not have been as grossly misinformed as they were: "In the London Press, libellous propaganda was made by publishing on the front page of certain newspapers a huge headline, 'GANDHI'S INDIA-JAP PEACE PLAN EXPOSED!' The 5th August 1942 issue of the London *Daily Sketch carried* a photograph of Miss Slade (Mira Behn) with the caption, 'ENGLISH WOMAN GANDHI'S JAP PEACE ENVOY!' Punch cartoons were unspeakable. The London *Daily Herald, too was* clotted by the contagion."

Reuters' monopoly of news flow from and to India was a matter of concern to many members of the Indian and Eastern Newspaper Society. Reuters responded to this in its own fashion. At a meeting of the Society in New Delhi on 15th February 1943, F.R. Jones of the Reuters' office in Bombay suggested that "if members desired an additional service they might as well get it from the Associated Press of America through Messrs Reuters Ltd. for an additional fee." Objection was raised on the ground that it would merely be a new Reuters service specially charged. Amritlal Seth *of Janmabhoomi* urged that a competitive service to Reuters was necessary in the interest of newspapers.

The end of Reuters' dominant role in the gathering and distribution of news within the country became inevitable with the British decision, after World War II, to withdraw from India.

Transfer of proprietorship of the Associated Press of India to Indian newspapers had been urged by Arthur Moore of the *Statesman* during the four years of his presidentship of the Indian & Eastern Newspaper Society from its inception in 1939. A liberal who believed in unimpeded flow of information, he also pressed for the abolition of the monopoly clause in Reuters' contract with Indian newspapers which bound them not to utilise any competing world news agency, and for a reduction in the Reuters subscription rate in consonance with the lowered Press cable rate.

Arthur Moore questioned the stand taken by Reuters that the issue of the transfer of API's ownership to Indian newspapers should await the end of the hostilities. Referring to the change in ownership of Reuters in October 1941 when publishers of the London newspapers, organised in the Newspaper Proprietors Association, came in and held an equal number of shares with the Press Association comprising publishers of the provincial newspapers of Britain, Moore said: "If it could be possible for the main body of Reuters to change hands in wartime, it should not be impracticable to effect a change of ownership of the Associated Press under the same conditions."

With the pressure mounting, over the years, for transfer of control of domestic news to Indian newspapers, Reuters thought of a way to ensure at least the continuance of its exclusive distribution of foreign news in India. The expedient thought of was to make the Indian successor to API a partner in Reuters. The new approach was embodied in a draft resolution that was presented at the 21st general meeting of IENS held in Bombay in mid-December 1943: "The Society is of the opinion that the time has arrived for a further and direct discussion of the question of Indian newspapers securing representation in Reuters' central organisation and assuming the management of their Indian concern (Eastern News Agency, which distributed foreign news) and of the API. With a view to the formulation of definite proposals thereon, the Society suggests: (a) the deputation of two representatives of the Society to visit London, if necessary, for such discussion; and (b) pending the final fulfilment of these objectives, the establishment of closer association between Reuters and API."

The terms that Reuters initially offered to Indian newspapers would have retained the cream of the profits, as well as control, for Reuters. These terms were acceptable to the British-owned newspapers represented in IENS. Unlike the All India Newspaper

Editors' Conference in which the editors of both Indian and British owned newspapers took a common stand as professional journalists against restrictions on publication of news ever since they first met in November 1940, IENS was an association of newspaper publishers and a divergence in approach was not surprising. The story of Reuters' one-sided formula has been told by A.S. Bharatan, who became the first general manager of Press Trust of India which eventually took over API:

> "Reuters' attitude in the early stages was based on the belief that they could part with the minimum and hold on to the maximum. After prolonged discussions a scheme emerged under which Reuters were to retain full control of the foreign news service and transfer the internal news agency, API, to the new Indian company. The annual income of these two agencies was in the proportion of two-to-one... This amounted to transferring a deficit-making agency to the Indian company and keeping the profit-making part in Reuters' own hands."

Even the Indian newspaper publishers among the members of IENS were divided in their approach to the question. Eventually the following resolution was adopted: "The IENS is indebted to Mr. Sadanand and Mr. Goenka for the proposals put forward by them for organising a news service owned by newspapers in the country. The Society has in the past strongly expressed the view that steps should be taken by the newspapers in India to acquire complete control of the API and an interest in the Reuters services in the country, with a view to reorganising them on cooperative lines. To put forward concrete proposals to this end, the Society hereby appoints the following subcommittee: the president (H.W. Smith of the Times of *India)*, *K.* Srinivasan, S. Sadanand, and Ramnath Goenka."

The name Press Trust of India for the new agency emerged during discussion at a meeting of this Press Agency Sub Committee held at Madras in February 1946. The company was incorporated at Madras on 27th August 1947, within two weeks of Independence Day. The salient features of PTI's constitution as amended from time to time are:

(i) No distribution of profits to shareholders. Any profits are to be applied entirely to expanding the range and improving the quality of PTI's services to its media and non-media subscribers.

(ii) Membership is restricted to owners of newspapers published in India and subscribing to one or more of the agency's services.

(iii) To ensure the integrity, independence and freedom from bias of PTI's news service, no person can hold more than 1,000 shares of the company, and no member is entitled to more than five votes in all.

(iv) In order to guard and promote the wider public interest, there is provision for the appointment of up to, four Directors unconnected with the newspaper business.

Meanwhile, rapid political developments in the subcontinent made Reuters give up its old approach of dictating terms to IENS. It agreed to a total transfer of its operations in India, and invited an Indian newspaper delegation to visit England and negotiate an agreement under which PTI would become a shareholder in the main Reuters organisation. The members of the IENS delegation-K. Srinivasan, Devadas Gandhi, Sadanand, Goenka and C.R. Srinivasan-assembled on 20th May 1948 in London for the negotiations, which dragged on for thirty days.

In the meanwhile, Prime Minister Nehru made a critical reference to Reuters in the Indian parliament on 12th March, 1948. He said in reply to a question that the news agency had not fully and correctly covered the speeches of Indian representatives in the United Nations Organisation. He also said that the Government were aware that Reuters gave different versions of the news relating to Kashmir, in India and Pakistan. The Prime Minister finally announced that the Government had decided to discontinue, after due notice, the arrangement for the supply of

Reuters news, on payment, to government offices in India and for use in the broadcasts of All India Radio. Yet it was a favourable nod from the Indian Government in mid-1948 that eventually resulted in the acceptance by IENS of the draft agreement with Reuters that the delegation led by K. Srinivasan brought from London. Did the Nehru government hope that PTI, by entering into partnership, could reform Reuters from within?

Different Experiences

Kasturi Srinivasan's biographer writes: "The delegation was a divided house right from the beginning. Sadanand and Goenka were both strongly antagonistic to Reuters and preferred an arrangement with an American news agency instead. Devadas Gandhi, who was not particularly opposed to Reuters, was still of the view that prior commitments had been made with the Associated Press of America and it would have been much better if an agreement had been arrived at with that agency. C.R. Srinivasan was the only member of the delegation who stood by Kasturi Srinivasan all the time.

"The main points for negotiation were the terms for the transfer of API to Indian ownership, and the basis on which Reuters should supply world news to PTI. In regard' to the latter, two alternatives had been suggested: one, bulk purchase of news from Reuters on a seller-buyer basis without PTI becoming a partner of Reuters; and the other, a partnership in Reuters on terms similar to those that had been obtained by the Australian and New Zealand Associated Presses. But the Reuters sub-committee throughout pressed only for the conclusion of a partnership arrangement and consequently no other proposition was canvassed during the negotiations." Sadanand and Goenka, however, preferred bulk purchase of news by PTI from Reuters, without entering into partnership. The Indian delegation's mandate was that four signatures were necessary for it to conclude any agreement. Since this majority was not forthcoming, the delegation returned with a draft agreement. Its main features were as follows:

> On taking up 12,500 shares, PTI would nominate one Director and one Trustee of Reuters.. Apart from the share capital, PTI would bear its portion of the running costs of the organisation. The day PTI took its shares, API would be transferred to PTI for a value to be agreed to by the auditors of both parties.

PTI would operate as a national news agency in India and would be responsible for providing Indian news to Reuters, transmitting news outside India at Reuters' cost. Reuters might, send correspondents to India on special occasions in consultation with PTI, and while in India these would be under the discipline of PTLPTI would set up an Indian Desk in London and its Chief Representative there would be responsible for the contents of the world news service sent to India by Reuters. He would advise Reuters' Managing Editor on this, as well as on the use of incoming Indian news, and be under the discipline of Reuters. The Indian Desk would take over from Reuters the despatch of news services to Ceylon, Burma, Pakistan, Malaya and also certain Far Easter countries. The PTI Director on Reuters would have special responsibility for the contents of the service to these countries.

The area from Cairo in the west to a point eastwards to be fixed in consultation with the Australian Associated Press would be called the Indian Zone. Subject to the general responsibility of Reuters' Board, the primary responsibility of collecting news and supervising the work of correspondents in the zone would vest in PTI. A number of correspondents nominated by PTI would be added to the Reuter set-up in the zone. Reuters would introduce Indian journalists at the executive level into their world news organisation. A PTI man would be appointed in New York to cover the United Nations, and another would be appointed in Washington.

PTI would have exclusive use of Reuters news in India for the Press as well as the radio. PTI could sell its own news anywhere outside and should consult Reuters if it intended to sell the service to a competing world agency.

The scene shifted to India. At a four-day general body meeting of IENS in Bombay which began on 21st July 1948, the president of the Society, Tushar Kanti Ghosh, read out a letter received by him from Sardar Patel. In the course of this letter the Home Minister, who also held charge of. Information & Broadcasting, said that "having regard to the totality of the circumstances and taking a broad view of the agreement, I feel it is demonstrably in the interests of India and should be accepted." The agreement was endorsed by the Society and formally announced on 21st September 1948.

PTI had to raise funds quickly for buying the shares of Reuters. It issued 10,000 debentures of Rs. 100 each, carrying interest at 4 1/2 per cent. Sardar Patel, with whom Bharatan had good rapport, helped by persuading the ruler of Baroda to buy a large portion of the debentures. PTI remitted the money, and became a partner of Reuters with effect from 1st February 1949. Reuters' Agreement of Trust was suitably amended. The PTI Board appointed C.R. Srinivasan as its Trustee and Devadas Gandhi as Director of Reuters. Ramnath Goenka was appointed as alternate Director. PTI took over the operations of API on lst February 1949.

What nullified the potential of the partnership agreement for PTI emerging as a major player on the world news scene was PTI's lack of resources to deploy correspondents to cover adequately the zone of operations allotted to it. The newspaper publishers who owned PTI were interested in securing the staple of news at the cheapest possible rate, supplementing it with their own correspondents in some of the world capitals. Even these few correspondents posted abroad sent home as many of them continue to do news letters rather than spot news. The publishers did not share the vision that had impelled Jawaharlal Nehru to say at the Allahabad session of the All India Newspaper Editors' Conference on 16th February 1946: "I should like the owners of all newspapers present here to think of starting your own foreign news. service. A number of newspapers could combine for the purpose and appoint their agents. I would particularly like them to go to places which are not sufficiently covered by other agencies-in South East Asia, the Middle East and the rest of the world."

PTI was without a correspondent in Moscow till 1963, and except for a two-month visit in 1949 by M. Sivaram, there was none in Peking till November 1980. It had, a maximum of only five correspondents at any time in the whole Indian zone, making do with, stringers at other places. The tenuous presence of PTI men was compounded by PTI's misjudgement in making Bombay-which did not have direct communication links with the capitals in the Indian zone-the controlling centre. It would have been more appropriate to give operational control of the Indian zone to the Chief Representative in London.

To direct the Indian Desk at the headquarters of Reuters in London, the PTI Board chose as its Chief Representative G Parthasarathi, who had been assistant editor of the *Hindu* since 1936. K. Gopalan, a senior member of the staff from the API days, was assigned to assist him. They found on arrival, in April 1949, that the 'Eastern desk' which was supposed to select and edit the news file of the world service that would go out to India and to a large number of other Asian countries consisted of six men who, except for one person, were professionally mediocre: "Five had no knowledge of Indian conditions and even Indian geography. The sixth had a distant acquaintance with India by virtue of his having been a sub editor on the Statesman of Calcutta about twenty years ago. But he was long past the age of retirement." It was only after a personal discussion in Bombay, during a visit to India by Parthasarathi that PTI's management was persuaded to strengthen the Indian desk by replacing three of the Englishmen by Indians.

Meanwhile the Englishmen on the Indian desk presented problems not only of ignorance of the region they were expected to serve but of political prejudice imbibed over years of work in Reuters. When dealing with despatches from the United Nations the English sub-editor, Gopalan says, tended to apply as before "the British news agency treatment of five hundred words to the British delegate, hundred to the American and twenty words to say that 'the Iraqi, Pakistani, Egyptian and Indian delegates also supported the motion' or some such thing." In, addition to its work of processing for the Indian zone the Reuters world service which was "eighty per cent British in concept and content " the Indian desk contributed to coverage from the Indian and Asian viewpoint of international events in London like the conferences of Commonwealth Prime Ministers. The posting of D.P. Wagle at New York led to better coverage of United Nations proceedings. From Indonesia, N. Rajamani who had close links with Dr. Soekamo and other nationalist leaders did some fine reportage. When talks opened at the Hague on the political future of Indonesia, Reuters initially relied entirely on the ANP news agency of Holland. The Indian desk sent a special correspondent, on PTI account, to the Hague to ensure that justice was done also to the Indonesian nationalist viewpoint in Reuters despatches.

These limited gains were more than offset by another factor which militated against the partnership arrangement from the start, namely the conflict between India and Pakistan which were the two most important countries-at any rate at that time-of the zone allotted to PTI. Indo-Pakistan hostilities were in full swing when the PTI-Reuters agreement was being negotiated, a ceasefire coming into effect only, at the end of December 1948. Altaf Hussain, president of the Pakistan Newspaper Editors' Conference, stated in Karachi on 8th March 1950 that Pakistan "has never accepted and will never accept" the position of being treated as a part of the Indian zone mentioned in Reuters' agreement with PTI. When there was a massive exodus that year of members of the minority Hindu community from the eastern wing of Pakistan (now Bangladesh) to India, PTI sent two correspondents to Dacca. Both were arrested by Pakistan authorities. Reuters, instead of helping to find a practical solution to the problem of news blackout in a situation of widespread human distress, sent its general manager to conduct negotiations with the Eastern News Trust of Pakistan for the operation of a separate Pakistani beam by Reuters. This new beam would additionally cover several countries which were already included in the Indian zone under the agreement with PTI which had come into force only the previous year.

Another irritant for the Indian partners of Reuters was the posting of a British correspondent in New Delhi on a regular basis, whereas the partnership agreement had visualised that "Reuters may send correspondents from headquarters to India on special occasions in consultation and in cooperation with the PTI." When the four-year partnership agreement expired at the end of 1952, it was not renewed. Instead, PTI entered into a contractual relationship with Reuters as between buyer and seller for the supply of the Reuters news and commercial service to PTI and for the supply of the PTI service to Reuters. This was what Sadanand and Goenka had urged from the beginning.

With the ending of the unequal partnership in Reuters, PTI became free to augment its sources of foreign news, including pictorial coverage, through arrangements with other international news agencies besides Reuters.

Kasturi Srinivasan had told his colleagues of the All India Newspaper Editors' Conference in October 1942 that the Indian Press could not be fully free till the country became free. But it soon turned out that, in certain respects, each State is like every other, whether it be alien and autocratic or native and democratic, capitalist or socialist. None of them will tolerate attempts at subversion through sedition and violence, or the disclosure of State secrets.

Sadanand's *Free Press journal* learnt this to its cost. When Indian ratings of the Royal Indian Navy mutinied in Bombay in February 1946 against racial discrimination, "*FPJ* stood foursquare behind the R.I.N. boys of 'Talwar' and other ships and establishments and allowed them the full use of *FPJ* columns to air their grievances, even though the R.I.N. mutiny came at a time when the Congress had started negotiations with the British Cabinet Mission and frowned on the mutiny. *FPJ* went a step further. It employed two of the R.I.N. boys sacked by the Navy and pilloried the authorities editorially. This was something Sardar Patel could never forgive."

As the war ended and it become clear that India's independence could not be long delayed, Sadanand made plans for starting an Indian international news agency with the same during-do that he had shown in organising the Free. Press of

India news agency in the late 1920's. He visited Cairo, London and New York during 1945-46 and entered into agreements with American and other news agencies and individual journalists to launch the Free Press of India World Service. The project ended in smoke when the *Free Press Journal* disclosed in September 1947 that Indian naval and land forces were being moved towards Junagadh. The Muslim ruler of that overwhelmingly Hindu majority State on the Gujarat coast had acceded to Pakistan; and while the people demonstrated in protest, the Nawab was preparing to bring in outside armed support.

The story of the movement of Indian forces was broken by B.C. Dutt, who was working on the FPJ and the afternoon *Free Press Bulletin*. He recalls: "Through the grapevine I still maintained with the navy, I heard a startling piece of news. Ships and some army units were heading for Junagadh by sea and land. Natarajan (the editor) could not doubt the authenticity of the news, as I had managed to smuggle out a carbon copy of the movement order." The story was banner-headlined in the *Free Press Bulletin* on a Saturday and the news agencies sent it on teleprinter for the Sunday papers which carried it on the front page. On Monday morning the editor, S. Natarajan, called B.C. Dutt and told him how angry Sardar Patel, Home Minister, who was also in charge of Information & Broadcasting, was: "He is furious that we published news about the armed forces without official clearance. The phone almost burnt up by the time he hung up on Sadanand last night."

The Indian government denied to Sadanand the lease of teleprinter lines and other facilities he needed, though he had placed a large order for teleprinters. This was the beginning of his financial decline and serious ill-health. He died in 1953, a heroic and tragic figure in the history of Indian journalism.

7

Freedom at Last

The long and arduous battle for independence came to an end on August 15,1947, when India after partition became free from alien rule. As the country rejoiced and celebrated the historic event, a jubilant press joined its countrymen in hailing the advent of freedom for which it had fought shoulder to shoulder with the nationalist forces and made enormous sacrifices in men and material, braving the cruel persecution of the colonial rulers. In a striking editorial, *The Hindu* described the ship of freedom which had reached port thus: "After a century of storm and stress, the ship of Indian freedom has come into port. Battered heavily by wind and sea, scarred and seamed in many a fierce encounter with embattled hosts, she has suffered grievous losses and has had to jettison much precious cargo. She is not spic and span as we had pictured her in the morning time of our hopes, it is on the whole a sad home coming. There are treacherous shoals about and the pilot is more than a little weary. But she is a brave little ship for all that, for she carries the high hopes and ambitions of 400 million. On her proud mast-head there broods, like the spirit of peace, the white soul of India....India embarks on the endless adventure of freedom, crippled and maimed in the sight of the world. She is, however, a great believer in the healing touch of time and in the magic of natural affinities."

In the first flush of freedom, the press rode with the current and was sympathetic and cooperative with the new national government which was faced with a deluge of problems plunging the country into strife and bloodshed and instability. A section, however had not got over the hangover of colonial rule and indulged in fanning communal passions and hatred and in scurrilous writing. Sensational journalism became a fashion with some and the country's interests ceased to be paramount. A Bengali editor is quoted by a writer as having confessed that he adopted a communal policy "because playing down riots and disturbances curbed his sales." "Even the news boys", the editor is quoted as having said, "refuse to touch my paper if my rivals report a larger number of deaths than I do." The leaders who were running the government and who had established complete rapport with the press during the freedom struggle were now saddened that the press as a whole was not with them in meeting the challenges faced by the new-born government. They seemed to behave, the leaders thought, as an opposition force as they did during the British regime when the need was to play a constructive and cooperative role.

Frank Moraes, editor of the *Times of India,* referred to the attitude of Indian editors in the early years of Independence and said: "In the early years of independence, Indian editors had to make up their minds on what attitude they should adopt vis-a-vis Nehru's newly established government.... I decided after some reflection and consultation that since Nehru was faced virtually with no opposition in Parliament and since a democratic government could not effectively express itself in the absence of an opposition, the press should take it upon itself to function as an unofficial opposition outside Parliament, exercising that role with responsibility and circumspection."

Writing on the same subject *The Hindu* felt that even barely a year after freedom was achieved the suspicion and distrust which clouded the relations between the alien government and the nationalist press "continued in a very perceptible manner under the Free India Government." The Hindu said in the new circumstances the "Press may be expected to take a more detached as also a more responsible view of its obligations on the one hand to the government of the day, and on the other to the people as a whole, opposing official policy when it must, supporting it when it can and at all times bringing instructive opinion to bear from different angles on all important issues so that the people may decide with full knowledge."

Jawaharlal Nehru was one of the earliest in the government to voice his displeasure against the press. He had a dig at editors when addressing the All-India Newspapers Editors Conference in 1952, he said: "Of course, it is hardly proper to use the word 'wise' in connection with newspapers. There is no reason why newspapers should not have at least some small bit of leisured thinking and wisdom hidden away in a corner if not in the leading article always." Nehru asked: "For whom do we want press freedom—for the writer or for the owner to coerce his employee to write against his conscience?" Seven years later, in 1959, in speeches in Chandigarh and Bombay, Nehru again attacked the press, questioning the bonafides of the editors. He said it had been taken for granted that editors of Indian newspapers could not be expected to realise or speak the truth when discussing certain aspects of state policy. He recalled Stanley Baldwin's (British prime minister) remark about newspapers that they enjoyed power without responsibility and said there were no great editorial personalities in India who could stand up to newspaper owners and to advertisers. In another speech in Delhi Nehru described the press as both the product and symbol of private enterprise and editors as its champions against state control and regulation.

N. Raghunathan, well-known journalist, made this comment on Nehru's fulminations against the press: " Mr Nehru has got into a habit of coming down with a heavy hand on the bad boys of the press. But though he is never consciously unfair, the cumulative effect of these periodical fulminations is definitely unfortunate. According to their personal predilections, people may conclude that he is inclined to be intolerant of all criticism or that the press of this country is dominated by the bad boys."

Touch of Irony

There was a touch of irony in Nehru's disparaging remarks for he was the darling of the Indian press both before and after independence. He occupied quite a considerable space in the columns of newspapers. When he was not making speeches, which were reported at length and verbatim in some papers, he was issuing statements about the party, Government and international affairs and these were treated as news of great importance. When he was not speaking or making statements, he wrote articles which were distributed to the national dailies which published them prominently. *The Hindu* wrote: "It is clear that the prime minister looks upon the press more or less as a kind of permanent opposition. He has evidently been surprised by the range and volume of criticism made newspapers of domestic policies initiated by his government and he has brought himself to think that these have been inspired by self-interest. This is pure delusion."

Sardar Vallabhbhai Patel, the strong man of the Congress and number two in the National Government, was also not happy with the status of the press after freedom. In a letter to Nehru in June 1949, he wrote: "There is an absence of understanding both in the press and in the legislature in regard to some of our foremost problems of the day. Yet there can be no stopping their writing on these subjects or making public references."

When the *Times of India* wrote an editorial critical of the government in connection with the escape from house arrest of Mir Laik Ali,ex-prime minister of Hyderabad, in March, 1950,Patel's secretary, Shanker, wrote to K. Gopalaswami, acting editor of the paper: "I saw editorial on Laik Ali's escape. I hope in calmer moments you have realised that you have rushed into print far too soon. That particular news about his keeping a beard is entirely unfounded. He did keep his moustache untrimmed but that you will agree is unlikely to be particularly noticed. I would have liked the press and Parliament to suspend judgement until there was some material to go upon. As it is, both have reacted on sheer speculation even to the extent of involving the I.G. of Police without realising that he is not in a position to defend himself. What is worse, when statements are contradicted or proved untrue, there is no retraction or regret either on the part of the press or on the part of members of Parliament. After all, it is common prudence to allocate responsibility only after the facts have been ascertained."

In another letter on the same incident, Shanker wrote; 'The whole press seems to have reacted to it as if a great national calamity has happened. Escapes of criminals from jails where guards and rules were much more strict, are not uncommon."

C. Rajagopalachari, another great leader and the last governor-general of India, did not have a good opinion of the Indian press. Campbell Johnson, press attached to Lord Mountbatten, writes in his book, *Mission with Mountbatten* that C.R. told him "that the Indian press had a long way to go before it could achieve its full freedom. Asked what influence it had on Indian politics he said: Very little. The Congress had dominated the political scene and the press instead of providing informed criticism was nothing more than a body of political propagandists. If there was to be a change in the balance of power all that the press would do would be to follow suit and one lot of propagandists would succeed another.' He said he had told an old journalist friend of his in Madras that the essential thing for the Indian press to do was to concentrate first of all on administrative matters rather than on political formulae. Once they began dealing with things which affected the daily lives of the people they would begin to exert a genuine influence. He said he agreed with the view that Indian journalism was much nearer the American in its tendency to outspokenness and overstatement."

C.R. who as home minister, introduced the first press control bill after freedom became the victim of a controversy in the press when his candidature was canvassed for the Presidentship of the Indian Republic in 1950. The press disclosed that besides C.R.., Rajendra Prasad, president of the Constituent Assembly, was also a candidate for the prestigious post. The *Lokvani*, a Hindi weekly of Jaipur in Rajasthan, published pictures of C.R. and Rajendra Prasad side by side on the front page along with a story on who was likely to be chosen president Sending a cutting of this report to C.R., a Congressman told him that Hiralal Shastri, prominent Congress leader who later became chief minister, and his followers were canvassing in favour of Prasad and against him.

Sending the letter and cutting to Patel, C.R., who was then governor-general, wrote that he did not want that the Presidency should become the subject matter of "title page propaganda". He added: "If it is true that the *Lokvani* belongs to one of Shastri's group perhaps he may be told that the picture is objectionable so that he may not repeat such stuff." Patel in his reply said that Hiralal Shastri had told him that the editor had taken the idea from the Statesman and there was no intention whatsoever to raise any controversy. C.R. sent him another press cutting, this time from the Bombay weekly, *Blitz*, with the remark: "This cutting seems to be too bad to be ignored." He asked. "Do you think we could induce Rajen Babu to do something to prevent this kind of gossip? The *Blitz* report had said that members of the Constituent Assembly from the south who were "anxious to keep Rajaji away from Madras politics are canvassing in his favour for the Presidency while a large number of members from the north, who dislike C.R. for being too clever and crafty for an average Congressman, prefer Rajendra Prasad." The report added: "A cold and calculating politician that Rajaji is, he is in the meantime quietly consolidating his position. While pretending that he has only four trunks to pack to quit Government House, he is nevertheless spreading his roots all over the place."

In another letter, C.R. unburdened himself: "It seems as if one cannot have peace as long as one lives. Who wants this governor-generalship or presidentship or deputy prime ministership or anything else? It will not do to be depressed. Otherwise, there is plenty of cause for being thoroughly disgusted with our semi-educated folk."

Patel replying to C.R. said: "With our notions of civil liberties and freedom of the press and many impediments in the way of corrective action, I am afraid it is impossible to reform *Blitz*." Rajendra Prasad, who was approached to contradict the *Blitz* report wrote to Patel that there was nothing for him in the report to contradict "There is no allegation against me." He, however, issued a statement saying: "There is and there can be no question of any rivalry between Rajaji and myself for any post or honour. I would, therefore, warn the public not to be misled by any propaganda of this nature and request all not to indulge in it."

In a letter to Patel in September, 1949, Nehru said there was a deliberate move to keep Rajaji out of the Presidency. He mentioned the name of a newspaper owner and said he was "one of the most active agents in this business." In his reply, Patel said that a large majority seemed opposed to Rajaji. He agreed with Nehru that the newspaper owner mentioned by him was involved in it "I do not know," Patel wrote, "when our people, particularly the press lords and the press will learn to behave with a sense of responsibility and to maintain the dignity of at least the higher offices. Instead, it seems that no person or position is sacred to them."

The Controversy

The whole controversy took an entirely different turn when Rajendra Prasad and Nehru fell out over the issue of presidentship and the former accused the latter of "ignoring him" and condemning him and "all that I have stood for and done during all these years in association with you (Nehru)". Nehru had suggested that Prasad should withdraw in favour of Rajaji. Upset by the tenor of Prasad's letter, Nehru asked Patel to deal with him. Patel wrote to Prasad pacifying him and Prasad apologised to Nehru and the incident was closed. In the event, Rajaji lost the battle and it was Prasad who won.

A speech by Dr. B.R. Ambedkar, law minister, reported in the National Herald in April, 1948, caused concern to Nehru and Patel. According to the report, Ambedkar attacked the Congress Government and particularly Nehru and Patel. Nehru in a letter to Patel drew attention to passages in the speech "which seem very odd to me as coming from a Cabinet minister." Ambedkar in his reply to Nehru and Patel called the press report "perverted" and that "no fair-minded man could have any objection to anything I said in Lucknow." He said his speech was devoted to answering criticism from his followers on (1) why he had been silent ever since the departure of the Cabinet Mission; (2) why he joined the Congress Government; and (3) what he proposed Congress and there was no reference to any member of the government. "The press has never been kind to me. It has always done its best to twist facts and phrases, take them out of their context and pervert the sense of anything I have said. I fear this is what has happened to my speech in Lucknow." Referring to the report in the *National herald,* he said the correspondent could not have distorted his speech in a manner worse than he had done. "I delivered my speech in Hindustani", he said, "which is not my mother tongue. It is, therefore, possible for misreporting and misrepresenting the intention of the speaker. Added to this the press in India has had its knife in me for the last 25 years. Consequently, deliberate perversion of my speeches by the press have occurred many a time."

There was one British journalist in India whose admiration for Patel bordered on hero worship. He was Ian Stephens, editor of the *Statesman,* who guided the destinies of the British-owned newspaper at a crucial period on the eve of India's independence and after. Campbell Johnson mentions in his book that the viceroy directed that Gandhi should be referred to in court circulars as "Mahatma Gandhi" instead of the usual "Mr Gandhi" after a representation by Stephens. Stephens quit his post as he did not approve of the government's acceptance of the accession of Kashmir to India and as he would have to attack the government on this ground. He believed that Kashmir should have gone to Pakistan and he moved over to Pakistan. He detested Nehru and admired Patel. "It is my belief", he wrote that Patel would have made a better prime minister. He and Rajagopalachari were the Congress party leaders I most admired Both understood the nature of the Muslim problem in India better than Nehru did." Had Patel been chosen, Stephens said, he "would have stayed on contentedly in India longer than I did" because of the policies he believed Patel would have pursued. "Patel was a realist", Stephens said, "with down to earth understanding of how the masses felt. He wasn't half mesmerised by them as Nehru during his brilliant speeches seemed to be." Stephens said: "It's my belief that for his own earthy Hindu reasons Patel wouldn't—had he been prime minister in October, 1947—have seized Kashmir or anyhow in Nehru's or Mountbatten's way. He knew I admired him."

Stephens carried a special dispatch on Patel and his picture on his birthday in October, 1948 in the *Statesman* and also sent him a very affectionate message of greeting. "You are a great man on your public achievements alone", he said, "but also one who in my case at any rate, as I have ventured to mention more than once, inspires—whatever political differences there may be and some will doubtless recur—an unusual glow of personal affection. Prolonged good health and happiness to you."

Thanking him for the greetings and the dispatch in the paper about him, Patel wrote to Stephens: "During all our contacts I have appreciated your frankness as much as you did mine and that is largely responsible for the personal regard which both of us entertain for each other despite political differences which at times divide us. I need hardly assure you, therefore, that I have been deeply touched by the kindness and warmth of the reference about me both in your letter and the *Statesman's* dispatch." Stephens was overwhelmed by the prompt reply and sentiments in it and he wrote back: "Nowhere but in India, I think, do busy ministers and other leading men spare so much time and trouble for outside individuals. You should not have done it. But it was quite remarkably nice of you and I am grateful."

Patel was alert in taking action on disclosure made by the press regarding administration in the states. In December, 1947, the *Indian Nation* of Patna featured a report on its front page with banner headlines that the Governor of Bihar, Jairamdas Daulatram, had resigned because "he refuses to be a silent spectator of the Congress Ministry's misdeeds." The report said that the reason for his decision was that "under his very nose, His Excellency finds widespread corruption, favouritism and muddles and he finds that owing to the Congress Ministry's attitude refusing the governor to have his say, he has to be silent spectator of all misdeeds and bunglings of the ministry."

The chief secretary to the Bihar Government in frantic telegrams to the prime minister and home minister said the government did not know the governor had resigned and for the reasons mentioned in the press report. He added: "Now as a version damaging the reputation of the Ministry has appeared in the press it is very necessary that the government here should know if it is a fact that he has resigned and that too for reasons mentioned in the report." Although Patel in his reply to the chief secretary said there was no truth in the press report regarding the governor's resignation and the reasons given, in a letter to Patel on December 23, the governor did request to be relieved early. Patel assured him that there would be no delay in relieving him.

Earlier in October in the same year there was another report about the Bihar Ministryin the *Free Press Journal* of Bombay. It alleged corruption and profiteering in regard to purchases of molasses under government permits: It said that molasses was bought at a cheap price and sold at 20 to 30 times more than the control price. In a letter to the Bihar Chief Minister, Sri Krishna Sinha, Patel said: "It is amazing that such a thing should have happened in such an unseemly fashion. If the evil is as extensive and as high placed your government could have dealt with the matter drastically before it became public."

Enquiry Committee

Almost the first thing the National Government did after assuming office was to set up a Press Laws Enquiry Committee which submitted its report in May, 1948. It favoured the abolition of laws specially concerning the press and the incorporation of their major provisions in the ordinary laws of the land. It supported the provisions in the Telegraph Act, Post Office Act and Sea Customs Act which provided for interception of messages and literature. It recommended the retention of th: Official Secrets Act and the three sections of the Indian Penal Code, 124-A, 153-A, and 505 dealing with disaffection, communal hatred and tampering with the loyalty of the armed forces. The government brought in the Press (Objectionable Matters) Bill in 1951 to give effect to some of the recommendations of the committee. The Bill repealed the four Acts relating to the press suggested by the committee. It gave power to the government to demand and forfeit security from a newspaper or printing press after a judicial decision. It was provided that a complaint against a paper or printing press had to be made to the'sessions judge who could, after a judicial enquiry with the help of a jury, demand security from the keeper of the press. On failure to deposit the security, the declaration under the Press and Registration of Books Act, 1867, was to be deemed to be cancelled. What distinguished the Bill from the previous press laws was that the judiciary and not the executive was to decide on the necessity for action and the nature of action to be taken. It was explained that the Bill was intended to stop encouragement of violence and sabotage and certain other "grave offences" as also publication of matters of a scurrilous nature. Rajagopalachari, who as home minister, introduced the Bill in Parliament said: "I wish to leave behind me a law that should comprise the essential donts for printed stuff. We cannot afford to let people's minds be poisoned." He hoped that the press would frame its own code of professional ethics and discipline and ask the government for statutory powers to execute its decisions.

N. Raghunathan made this bitter comment on the Bill: "The Britisher at his worst did not dream of consigning the press perpetually to the status of a prisoner on parole. It was left to the Mahatma's understudy to turn Rousseau's dictum upside down and say that the press was everywhere bom in chains and in

India it must continue to wear a good few of them for its own good. The luxury of a free press is not for us. Everyone of the home minister's specious pleas for muzzling the press was in an earlier day denounced by him and his fellow paladins as an affront to common sense and a sin against the light. The sabotage that the August patriots so easily reconciled with their non-violent consciences owed nothing to the instigation of the press; still it did help them to climb to power. And is if not the most natural thing in the world to kick the ladder by which you rose?" The Bill which became law was allowed to lapse in 1956.

Press Commission

A Press Commission was appointed in September, 1952 under the chairmanship of Justice Rajadhyaksha. Its terms of reference included the state of the press, working conditions, of journalists' freedom of the press and machinery for ensuring high standards of journalism. The commission, which submitted its report in 1954, recommended the establishment of a Press Council whose objects should be :

(1) to safeguard the freedom of the press and help the press to maintain its independence;

(2) to censure objectionable types of journalistic conduct and by all other possible means to build up a code in accordance with the highest professional standards;

(3) to keep under review any development likely to restrict the supply and dissemination of news of public interest and importance;

(4) to encourage the growth of a sense of responsibility and of public service among those engaged in the profession of journalism;

(5) to study the development in the press which may tend towards concentration or monopoly and, if necessary, to suggest remedies therefore;

(6) to publish reports, at least once a year, recording its work

and reviewing the performance of the press, its development and the factors affecting them;

(7) to improve methods of recruitment, education and training for the profession by the creation of suitable agencies for the purpose such as a Press Institute.

The commission recommended the appointment of a press registrar who would keep a close watch on the circulation of newspapers and if he came to the conclusion that in a particular area or language, a monopoly had developed he was to bring it to the notice of the Press Council who would conduct an investigation into the existence of a monopoly and what measures were necessary, if any, to meet the situation. It suggested the fixing of minimum basic wages for working joumalists, introduction of price page schedule for newspapers and the diffusion of ownership. The commission found a considerable degree of concentration in the ownership of newspapers and warned of the danger that the tendency might develop in the future. The commission stated that outside the British-owned press, which had passed mostly into Indian hands, there were no hard and fast demarcations, no allocation of set duties. Most of the staff had been taken as sub-editors or reporters. Somewhere between editorial staff and the press, there were proof-readers. There was an editor and there were assistant editors. Affluence was rare for newspapers. It was remarkable, said the commission, that so many good men joined the profession, more remarkable that they stayed on showing considerable adaptability. However, the transformation of the newspaper into a business enterprise had begun and the new proprietors were businessmen who did much to straighten out finances. The commission noted the declining status of the editor in the daily newspapers and said that the "growing importance of the economics of production had also contributed to bring about the gradual eclipse of the editor by the manager." To reverse the trend it suggested that the editor be vested with administrative control over his staff, that appointments in the editorial department be made in consultation with him and that all members of the staff be made to realise that they were working "towards a common goal under the leadership of the editor."

The Press Council was established by an Act of Parliament in 1965. Its first president was Justice N. Rajagopala Iyengar, who said the council had a close likeness of the reconstituted British Press Council. It was, however, unique in having statutory authority. Its power to summon and enforce attendance of persons and examine them on oath; to require the discovery and production of documents; to receive evidence on affidavits; and to issue commission for the examination of witnesses or documents were valuable aids in the conduct of investigations. Every inquiry held by the council was deemed to be a judicial proceeding and no suit or other legal proceedings lay against the council or its members in respect of anything done in good faith. The inclusion of members of Parliament on the council, said Rajagopala Iyengar, was a novel feature. The council had 28 members out of whom 20 were nominated by the various newspaper organisations.

The working Journalists Act of 1955 recognised working journalists as industrial workers as recommended by the Press Commission and empowered the government to set up a wage board to fix the minimum wage for journalists. A wage board presided over by H. V. Divatia was appointed and its recommendations were published in May, 1957. The Supreme Court, however, in March, 1958 held the recommendations invalid as they were not based on consideration of capacity to pay. An ordinance was issued in June, 1958, setting up a committee of officials to remove the defects pointed out by the Supreme Court. The committee's report, published in December, 1958, was accepted by the government and its recommendations were passed into law. A press registrar was also appointed. The Newspaper (price and page) Act of 1956 which was passed in accordance with the press commission recommendations and whose object was to regulate prices charged for newspapers in relation to their maximum or minimum number of pages and for the space allotted for advertising matter in relation to their matters was held invalid by the Supreme Court. The court said imposing strictions on the business aspect of a newspaper would amount to an infringement of the freedom of the press.

The Press Council Act was repealed in January, 1976, during the Emergency and the council was re-established under the Press Council Act of 1978. Some important changes were made in the new Act. A second Press Commission was set up in May 1978, under the chairmanship of Justice P.C. Goswami but Justice Goswami and his colleagues on the commission resigned in January, 1980, with the formation of a new government. The commission was reconstituted in April 1980 under the chairmanship of Justice K.K. Mathew. Its terms of reference included:

(1) the role of the press in a developing and democratic society;

(2) the present constitutional guarantee with regard to freedom of speech and expression; whether this is adequate to ensure freedom of the press, adequacy and efficacy of the laws, rules and regulations for maintaining this freedom;

(3) means of safeguarding the independence of the press against economic and political pressures from proprietors and management;

(4) role of the press and the responsibilities it should assume in developmental policies;

(5) ownership patterns, management practices and financial structures of the press; their relation to growth, editorial independence and professional integrity;

(6) chain newspapers; links with industry, their effect on competition and on the readers' right to objective news and free comments;

(7) economics of the newspaper industry.

The commission, in its report submitted in 1982, said: 'The role of the press in a developing and democratic society should neither be that of an adversary nor an ally of government. To be a mindless adversary or an unquestioning ally would be to abdicate judgment. A free press should be, in our view, a constructive critic." The commission felt that the editors should insist "on their right to have the final say in the acceptance or rejection of advertisements, specially those which border on or cross the line between decency and obscenity, legitimate claims for a product or service and the profferring of magical remedies." The editors authority, it said, should extend, not only to the contents of the advertisements but also to the proportion of space devoted to them. It wanted the discontinuance of astrological predictions in newspapers and magazines. It said that the positive role of the press of "bringing together the diverse elements in the nation's life by emphasising those aspects which tend towards unifying the communities is as important as avoidance of objectionable communal or casteist writing. This calls for a sustained campaign to promote the concept of human brotherhood." The commission said that while the press should bring to light and extend support to genuine public grievances, it should oppose unconstitutional methods of agitation. It welcomed the trend towards investigative reporting in so far as it was oriented to social and economic issues. "But the investigative reporter should not give occasion for the criticism of lack of follow-up which is a widespread failing in the Indian Press."

The commission said that a newspaper was essentially a public utility and whatever be the precise form of ownership of newspapers, the exercise of ownership rights had to be subject to some measure of restraint and regulation. Public interest was the criterion that should regulate this activity. The commission said: "The press has a social responsibility and accountability to the public. The theory that the freedom of press knows no restraints is gone." It said in the changed situation, the freedom of the issuer of news alone is not sufficient; the freedom of the consumer must also be protected. It warned that the press should be able to resist not only external pressure but also "inducements which would undermine its independence from within. Journalists should be on guard against the temptation to enjoy favours, whether from government authorities, employers, advertisers or others."

The commission declared that the Press Council, which had functioned for 15 years had "within limits set by the legislation done useful work" and it recommended that the institution should continue. It said the council should be given powers to deny facilities of accreditation for a specified period to those editors or journalists who had been held by the council thrice to have violated the accepted principles of journalistic ethics. Also, that a newspaper would invite "sanction if it comes to the adverse notice of the council thrice, whether by way of disapproval, warning, admonition or censure." The commission said: "We are of the view that it would not be desirable to draw up a code of ethics for newspapers. Such a code could be built up case by case over a period of time."

The commission said: "The Indian press is free, but does not have a wide enough reach and it has an urban and middle class base which limits its contribution towards making the development process more widely participatory." The commission recommended enactment of legislation to curb the influence of foreign money on the press. Under the law, it proposed newspapers would be required to submit their annual accounts to the Press Council giving details of the revenue obtained from advertisements and from foreign sources and names of the top 100 shareholders with their nationality and address. It recommended the amendment of the Press Council Act of 1978 to enable the council to review the quality and adequacy of training facilities for journalists and monitoring of the performance of newspapers by the council in respect of important issues.

Emergency

The declaration of Emergency in June, 1975, by the government of Indira Gandhi came as a shocking blow to the Indian press which was its greatest victim. There was a raging controversy (and it has continued even to this day) whether Indira Gandhi was justified in imposing the Emergency but there was universal condemnation of the muzzling of the press and the drastic action taken against some newspapers. In a letter to a foreign friend in

March, 1971, Indira Gandhi had this to say about the Indian press: "Our own press has done everything possible to mislead the public about me personally and about my aims and objectives. Even though everything they had said about my father earlier and then about me in being proved wrong all the time, the columnists continue with their supercilious analyses. The real trouble is that they have no depth or values themselves and do not care to have contact with the people. Their judgment is circumscribed by their own limited experience, so they try to fit people into preconceived and prejudiced forms. Neither my father nor I can fit into any of these."

Describing Indira Gandhi's attitude to the press, her former Press Adviser, B.G. Verghese said: "She is very shy of the press. At the beginning, I persuaded her to hold a press conference every month. But she gave up this practice after I left. She treats the press conferences as a necessary evil. Instead of using the press as a forum, she is very evasive in her answers and tries to disclose as little as possible. In the game of journalistic hide and seek, Indira Gandhi is usually the winner. Over the years she perfected a technique which enabled her to ward off inquisitive newsmen. She was always on guard with the press and unlike her father rarely allowed herself to be provoked into emotional outbursts. In the early years of prime ministership she was wont to lose her temper and lash out at pressmen who persisted in asking awkward questions. Since then her style had matured and she fielded questions with calm and good humoured self-confidence, silencing interrogators with humorous and cryptic retorts and sometimes turning inconvenient questions back at them.

"The Indian press and especially those controlled by the Opposition had been critical and even abusive about her. But while supporting suggestions that the newspaper industry should be separated from big business, she consistently rejected proposals for nationalising the press. She believed in a free press though she is not much influenced by it. Press criticism might annoy her temporarily but she soon cooled down."

The worst form of pre-censorship was imposed on the press during the Emergency and a paper of the standing of *The Hindu* had to scrap an editorial on the proclamation of the Emergency as the censor refused to permit editorials on the Emergency. The do's and dont's of unimaginative and authoritarian censorship made it almost impossible for the press to function and even factual news and innocuous comments came under the axe. J.N. Sahni wrote: "In the absence of news, the newspapers filled their columns with such vital topics" as the origin of the Ramayana and Mahabharata, the discovery of skull fossils of the ape man and the relative antiquity of Harappa and Mohenjo Daro."

Defending pre-censorship Indira Gandhi told an interviewer: "To have had to impose regulations on newspapers does not make me happy. But some journals had shed all objectivity and independence and allied themselves totally with the opposition front and done everything to spread doom and defeatism. The press was very much against us even before. Our newspapers are very much class oriented....In today's world, it is absolutely essential to eradicate poverty to the greatest possible extent in order just to keep harmony. It can't be done immediately. It can't be done totally and it should be done as much as possible and yet as soon as we bend ourselves to this task and people see we are serious, the full weight of money, economic power, the press, industry, local and foreign combines. They don't say they are against the policy. Everybody says poverty is bad, nevertheless they want to obstruct our going ahead with programmes to eradicate it. Some of the press-here and abroad-are highlighting baseless charges of corruption. We have always looked into such matters and shall deal them strictly."

The pre-censorship was imposed under Rule 48 of the Defence of India Rules "in order to maintain public order." It prohibited all categories of news, comment and rumour relating to the Emergency, to arrests and detentions unless pre-authorised in writing by an "authorised officer" from the Public Information Bureau in Delhi or by the director of information of a state government. Guidelines for the press which were issued said that "in the manner in which information is printed, published or disseminated, there can be an accretion of enormous strength to those who are posing a threat to internal security." The press was called upon for help "in the fulfilment of the primary taks of ridding the nation of the causes of the Emergency; by suppressing news themselves through moderation, particularly in illustration and headlines; by publishing nothing to excite disaffection towards government established by law in India; nothing to promote feelings of enmity between different classes of persons in India or likely to cause the cessation or slowing down of work in any place, not anything objectionable already published in a foreign newspaper, nothing containing false allegations against leaders or denigrating the institution of prime minister; nothing to subvert the functioning of democratic institutions and nothing relating to agitations."

On July 26, 1975 editors received even more detailed instructions according to which "news was not to be published which contributes to the scare and demoralisation about the general situation or public interest in all respects as determined by the Central Government nothing which will contribute even in a remote way to affect or worsen the law and order situation; nothing which is likely to convey the impression of protest or disapproval of governmental measures." These embargoes were extended to cartoons, letters to the editor and captions.

On December 8, 1975, three ordinances were issued banning the publication of "objectionable matter", abolishing the Press Council, and removing the freedom of the press to report proceedings of Parliament. The ordinance relating to publication of objectionable matter was made into a law on January 28, 1976. Among other things it prohibited "inciting any individual or class to disaffection disharmony or ill-will or causing fear or alarm to any section of the public whereby any person may be induced to commit an offence against the state of public tranquillity." They included anything defamatory (whether by word or sign) of the president, vice-president, Speaker of the Lok Sabha, slate governors, the prime minister and all members of the

Cabinet of Central and state governments or deemed to be so by them. The law gave wide powers of search and seizure to the police and other petty officials. It provided for the forfeiture of securities of press deposits as safeguard against "objectionable writing". The Press Council was abolished, it was stated, because it had "failed to curb tendentious and provocative writing."

How did the press react to these draconian laws? According to Sahni: "The year 1976 will be specially remembered for a progressive voluntary blackout by the press and a weakened submission by many editors to proprietors and to the establishment in a conspiracy of suppression. What was painful was that the readers did not show lack of interest in the stuff they read and were least concerned about the adulterated food they were being provided with. While a lot will need to be written to explain the voluntary collapse, one may say that all along money has won and the conscience of the pen has lost Reporters see things but the pen does not see. Editors know things but look ignorant. One cannot remember such transition in the behaviour and attitude of the press anywhere, at any time, so willingly and voluntarily achieved.... There have been in the past repression, suppression and brain washing but never a voluntary collapse of the mind, the desire to do more to suppress or eliminate than even demanded, the refusal to stretch censorship even to the end of the permitted teacher. In the long run, people will say, as of the daily meteorological forecasts, what the press publishes is not in accord with what happens." Sahni was bitter that "today most editors are loyal to the establishment as also to the tycoons who control the purse strings. So what we get as a result is a synthetic form of 'popular' opinion, an amalgam of conformism mixed with self-interest of the controlling tycoons."

However, there was at least one newspaper which fought grimly and with determination the assault on the press and became the special target of persecution, and vindictiveness. The *Indian Express*, with its proprietor Ramnath Goenka and editor, V.K. Narasimham wrote a glorious chapter in the battle for the freedom of the press and when the nightmare ended and the press became free again, they were hailed as heroes. All the restrictions on the press were removed when the Janata Government came to power in 1977 and the Indian press once again breathed freedom, never again to lose it. In the words of Justice Grover, president of the Press Council, "The Indian press today is as free as in any other free country in the world".

The freedom of the press is guaranteed in Article 19 (1) of the Constitution which protects freedom of speech and expression. Although the guarantee is not in the same language as in the First Amendment to the Constitution of the United States where press freedom is specifically mentioned, the Supreme Court of India has held that the freedom of the press is included in the concept of freedom of speech and expression. In 1951, the Constitution Act (First Amendment) Provided for reasonable restrictions being imposed on the exercise of press freedom in the interest of the security of the state, friendly relations with foreign states, public order, decency or morality or in relation to contempt of court, defamation or incitement to an offence. By the Constitution Act of 1963 (16th Amendment), the words "sovereignty and integrity of India" were inserted before the words "security of the state."

In the case *Express* Newspapers Vs Union of India the Supreme Court held that freedom of the press was an essential part of the right of freedom of speech and expression. The court also observed in that case that the fundamental right to freedom of speech and expression enshrined in Article 19 (1) (a) of the Constitution was based on the provisions of the First Amendment to the Constitution of the U.S.A. In another case, Romesh Thapar Vs the State of Madras, the Supreme Court held that the freedom of speech and expression included freedom of propagation of ideas and that freedom was ensured by the freedom of circulation. In Brij Bhushan Vs the State of Delhi the court said that the imposition of pre-censorship on a journal was a restriction on the liberty of the press which was an essential part of the right to freedom of speech and expression declared by Article 19 (1) (a).

The Press Commission said the expression "freedom of the press" carried different meanings to different people. Some people stressed the freedom of the editor to decide what should be published in the paper. Some others emphasised the right of the owners to market their publications. The commission said; "The press as a medium of communication is a modern phenomenon. It has immense power to advance or thwart the progress of civilisation. Its freedom can be used to create a brave new world or to bring about universal catastrophe." The commission pointed out that a citizen was entirely dependent on the press for the quality, proportion and extent of the news supply. In such a situation, the exclusive and continuous advocacy of one point of view through the medium of a newspaper which held a monopolistic position was not conducive to the formation of healthy public opinion. "The assumption in a democratic set up is", the commission said, "that the freedom of the press will produce a sufficiently diverse press not only to satisfy the public interest by throwing up a broad spectrum of views but also to fulfil the individual interest by enabling virtually everyone with a distinctive opinion to find some place to express it."

The commission noted that with the revolution in communication technology on the one hand and the newspapers' development of an antipathy to ideas which were opposed to their commercial interest on the other, the operation of a market place of ideas had ceased to exit. "The constitutional issue generally is whether the expression already uttered should be given the shelter of Article 19 (1) (a)."

Revolution in Communication

But what of those ideas which are unacceptable to the media and which do not find access therein? The usual answer is that Article 19 (1) (a) "guarantees freedom of the owner to do as he chooses with his media. This answer stressed the view that a newspaper is emphatically the private property of the owner who sells a manufactured product at his risk; a newspaper owes nothing to the public which grants it no franchise. Thus, the constitutional imperative of free expression becomes the very instrument for repressing competitive ideas. The freedom guaranteed by Article 19(1) (a) must be reviewed in this light." The commission said a realistic view of Article 19 (1) (a) "has to recognise that the right to expression is somewhat thin if it can be exercised only at the sufferance of the managers of mass communication." "Self-censorship by the press," it said, "is practically as great a menace to the freedom of expression as government censorship. The whole point of a free press is that ideas deserving public hearing and the decision as to which ideas deserve that hearing shall not rest solely within the editors and owners.... The widest possible dissemination of information from as many diverse and antagonistic sources, as could be ensured, alone will secure public welfare and the constitutional guarantee of freedom of speech and expression rests on this postulate. Article 19 (1) (a) does not sanction repression of that freedom by private interests including the press."

8

Post-Independence India

India's experience over the post-independence years has demonstrated the need, if a free Press is to flourish, not only for a constitutional guarantee of Press freedom but, equally, for those in authority to honour the spirit of the Constitution and not merely go by its letter. The importance of the second requirement is illustrated by the difference in the fortunes of the Press during the prime ministership of Jawaharlal Nehru and of some of his successors.

Golden Period

Though the Indian Constitution does not expressly guarantee freedom of the Press, the Supreme Court has held in successive judgements that freedom of the Press is covered by, and is an essential part of, freedom of expression which is guaranteed by Article 19. This occurs in Part III of the Constitution which enumerates the citizens' Fundamental Rights that are enforceable by appeal to the High Courts and the Supreme Court. A controversial amendment of this Article, relating to freedom of expression, was effected by the first amendment of the Constitution, in 1951, in Jawaharlal Nehru's time.

The provisions relating to freedom of expression had initially read as follows in the Constitution of republican India that came into force on 26th January 1950: It initially read as follows:

"19. (1) All citizens shall have the right

(a) to freedom of speech and expression;

(2) Nothing in sub-clause (a) of clause (1) shall affect the operation of any existing law in so far as it relates to, or prevent the State from making any law relating to libel, slander, defamation, contempt of court or any matter which offends against decency or morality or which undermines the security of, or tends to overthrow, the State."

In the light of this, several laws which sought to abridge the right to freedom of the Press in the interests of public order came to be challenged before various High Courts. In one such case a special bench of the Patna High Court held by a majority that "if a person were to 90 on inciting to murder or other cognizable offences either through the Press or by word of mouth, he would be free to do so with impunity". The possible consequences of this court decision were so serious that the government thought it necessary to amend Article 19 (2). But the actual amendment went beyond providing for the protection of public order. The clause as amended by parliament in 1951 read:

> "(2) Nothing in sub-clause (a) of clause (1) shall affect the operation of any existing law, or prevent the State from making any law, in so far as such law imposes reasonable restrictions on the exercise of the right conferred by the said sub-clause in the interests of the securlty of the State, friendly relations with foreign States, public order, decency or morality, or in relation to contempt of court, defamation or incitement to an offence."

It will be seen that three grounds were added: public order, incitement to an offence, and friendly relations with foreign States on the other hand, the requirement that restrictions imposed should be 'reasonable' made any restrictive laws justiciable.

Of the three additional grounds, the one relating to friendly relations with foreign States was patently questionable. For instance, under a law made in terms of the amended Article 19 (2), could criticism of American policy in Korea, or of totalitarian dictatorship in the Soviet Union, or of the ill treatment of the Hindu minority in Pakistan become punishable? Prime Minister Nehru said in the course of the parliamentary debate on the constitution amendment that the amended 19 (2) was only an enabling clause which empowered parliament to frame legislation in case the need arose. He gave an assurance that it was not the intention of the government to prevent criticism of its foreign policy. While there has been no legislation in this respect so far as the Press is concerned, the Cinematograph Act does empower the government to deny or withdraw certification of a film for exhibition on the grounds enumerated in Article 19 (2) as amended. The Press Information Bureau of the Government of India announced in a release on 20th July 1981 that the censor certificate issued to the English film 'Midnight Express' had been withdrawn. A notification issued in this connection said that the film contained scenes of brutality and debased human values and showed the government, the people and the judicial system of Turkey in an unfavourable and tendentiously adverse light. According to the notification, the exhibition of the film was likely to affect "our friendly relations with Turkey" and thus contravened the provisions of the Cinematograph Act.

Liberty of Press

After the constitution amendment, as before, there was no lack of criticism of Jawaharlal Nehru's foreign policy in a section of the Press. Kashmir was the first issue on which he was faulted, particularly for his reference of the matter to the United Nations. Among the critics was Khasa Subba Rau (1896-1961) publisher and editor of the English weekly *Swatantra* of Madras, who was as fearless as a journalist as he had been as a freedom fighter. His column 'Sidelights' and 'Sotto Voce' by Vighneswara (pen name of N. Raghunatha Iyer, for long years chief leader writer of the *Hindu)* were looked forward to week after week.

Khasa wrote in *Swatantra* of 10th September 1949: "The folly of the rash rush to the United Nations over the Kashmir issue will be apparent if it is studied in the light of the entirely different attitude adopted by the Government of India over the Hyderabad Issue. The Government of India never swerved from the view that the settlement of the Hyderabad dispute was their own domestic concern in which outside powers would not be allowed to interfere... Pandit Nehru is now surprised at the letter to himself and the Premier of Pakistan written about Kashmir by President Truman and Mr. Attlee, which he has rightly characterised as intervention. But what is surprising is that he should be so surprised. Pandit Nehru invited the intervention which he now resents."

The weekly *Thought* of Delhi was prominent among critics of Jawaharlal Nehru's China policy, as of his policy towards the Soviet Union. India was among the first countries to recognise Communist China following the 1949 revolution, though its leaders called Nehru and his colleagues 'running dogs of imperialism' Nehru was unhappy when Chinese troops invaded Tibet (though he was to recognise Tibet as 'a region of China' in April 1954). During the crisis touched off by the war between North and South Korea, India voted in favour of United Nations action against North Korea but resisted the condemnation of China as an aggressor by the General Assembly of the United Nations, in order not to enlarge the area of hostilities. It is in this context that the verbal exchange between *Thought* and Jawaharlal Nehru during 1951, narrated below, has to be viewed.

Press Trust of India, after consulting the Indian government, decided in November 1949 not to put out a report received from its correspondent M. Sivaram, who had visited Communist China, about the massive preparations under way for Chinese entry into the Korean war. With a tight censorship in force on the Communist-controlled mainland, Sivaram had necessarily to cable his story from Hongkong. Following, are extracts from Sivaram's message:

Hongkong, November 19,1949: This is the first uncensored despatch out of Communist China from Sivaram , PTI staff correspondent who returned to Hongkong tonight after a two-month assignment in Peking Communist China has completed preparations to throw half a million crack troops into the battle for Korea 'even at the risk of a major war, PTI learned on reliable authority in Peking. The leaders of the Chinese People's Republic, according to this authority, intervened in Korea deliberately and fully prepared to face the consequences and after having secured, so it is understood, pledges from the Soviets of assistance in the event of reverses in the campaign to roll the United Nations forces down the Korean peninsula this winter.

This authority added that a secret Chinese-Soviet deal to halt 'imperialist aggression' was concluded last month before the Chinese People's Liberation Army 'volunteers' crossed into Korea.

From all parts of China today the finest units of the Chinese Communist Army and the best available military equipment are being rushed to Manchuria, while the entire nation is being geared for war through an intensive propaganda campaign...

The official Chinese Press is filled with lists of university students and professional men, model workers and combat heroes who have volunteered to fight in Korea...

Communist China, observers believed, was gambling on two possibilities- persuading the United Nations and the world that there was no official Chinese military intervention in Korea or, alternatively, depending on the reluctance of the United Nations and of the powers fighting in Korea to expand the sphere of hostilities and thus probably precipitating a major war involving Soviet Russia as well."

A year and a half later, the above report of Sivaram's was discovered and published by *Thought.* It said in an editorial note: "The Press Trust of India, losing their nerve at an Indian journalist's daring to paint a picture different from that officially prescribed by Mr. Nehru, referred the message, before releasing it, to the Foreign Affairs Subcommittee of the Cabinet. Mr. Nehru and Mr. N.G. Ayyangar, it is believed, favoured suppressing it;

Sardar Vallabhbhai Patel and Mr. Rajagopalachari considered that it should not be Concealed from the Indian public and the world's press. The dissenting views were conveyed to the Press Trust of India, who decided on suppression. Reuters abided by this suppression, and a message sent by an Indian journalist to the Indian public was released for publication only in Australia, where it had little effect. Where Chinese Communist censorship failed, Mr. Nehru's censorship temporarily succeeded."

On the matter being raised in the Lok Sabha by the leader of the opposition, Dr. Syama Prasad Mookerjee, Prime Minister Nehru denied that the Foreign Affairs Committee of the Cabinet had discussed the report sent by the PTI correspondent, but in effect confirmed that PTI suppressed the message on official advice. Nehru said: "In regard to this message. I enquired today and the Secretary General sent a note to me. What happened was this: that a representative of the, PTI went over some time to our foreign office and consulted the Secretary General there about it. I shall use his own words (it is absurd to talk of censorship): 'On receipt of this message Mr. so and so of the PTI saw me and sought my advice as to whether or not it would be helpful. I told him that I did not think it would, and he went away. It was for him to decide to publish it or not.' Then so and so advised his General Manager accordingly. He decided not to publish it. I did not know anything about this message at all. But a number of messages appeared round about this time, a little before and a little after, in the Press from the PTI correspondent about conditions in China. Some of the messages seemed to me not to be quite balanced judgment... It seemed to me particularly unfortunate that anything that the correspondent wrote should have been written not from China itself but after coming to a place like Hongkong which is a very peculiar place today, a hotbed of the opponents and enemies of the Chinese Government. Hon. Members may remember, long ago there was a place on the Russian border--Riga--from which all kinds of messages came." (*Parliamentary Debates,* I June 1951, Vol. 12, Part 11).

Thought said in a concluding comment (8th June 1951) on the

Prime Minister's statement in parliament: "If Mr. Bajpai (the Secretary General) acted entirely on his own initiative, as the Prime Minister at one point of his speech suggested, then he was wrong in taking so grave a step without authority. But if he was carrying out the policy of the Prime Minister and the Government, he was only doing his duty, and the Prime Minister and the Government were wrong to have framed such a policy."

V.K. Krishna Menon, close friend of Jawaharlal Nehru, was Defence Minister at the time that India's relations with China changed from the euphoria of the 'Hindi-Cheeni Bhai Bhai' slogan popularised by the Indian government in the early 1950's. The acerbic Defence Minister was a target of sustained criticism by a section of the Press which regarded him as a crypto-Communist. Prominent among political leaders who felt that Krishna Menon was unduly soft in relation to the two Communist powers was Acharya J.B. Kripalani. He said in the course of a Foreword written in December 1959 to a compilation of writings in *Thought* about China: "The nation has to congratulate itself that, at long last, it is recognized that Red China is red in tooth and claw and its aggression is a challenge to the nation. Yet it was ominous that the Defence Minister in his speech said that it was difficult to define aggression, which even the UNO had not been able to do for years. It may be difficult to define aggression even as it is difficult to define pain. But surely the man who suffers from pain does not fail to feel it simply because he cannot define it. It would appear that our Defence Minister does not feel the pain of foreign aggression as do the overwhelming majority of his countrymen... Anyway, it is all to the good that the Prime Minister, in spite of the doubts of his Defence Minister, considers Red China's excursions in our territory as aggression and as such a challenge to the nation."

Following the humiliating reverses suffered by the Indian army, ordered by the political leadership into a war along the Himalayan border for which it was wholly unprepared, Jawaharlal Nehru was constrained to drop Krishna Menon from the Cabinet. This was after an initial downgrading of Menon, from Defence to Defence Production, failed to satisfy angry critics within the Congress parliamentary party. During this time, Jawaharlal Nehru's critics, in the Press and in political parties including his own could have been muzzled through censorship, or physically jailed, by invoking Emergency powers. But such measures were foreign to his nature.

Checks and Restrictions

In contrast, the Press was to be brought under rigid censorship, and the country's news agencies subjected to extralegal arm-twisting, under the emergency rule of Prime Minister Indira Gandhi during 1975-76.

Jawaharlal Nehru had entertained high hopes for his daughter and did his best to train her, beginning with the correspondence course he conducted in order to afford her and a wider reading public, glimpses of world history. The process of grooming culminated in her being chosen as Congress president in 1958. After Nehru's death in 1964, Indira Gandhi joined the Union Cabinet as Minister of Information & Broadcasting. Following the sudden death of Prime Minister Lal Bahadur Shastri at Tashkent, she was elected as leader of the Congress parliamentary party and became Prime Minister in January 1966.

After a hesitant start during which she found that her decision to devalue the rupee, though inescapable on economic grounds, was politically unpopular, she decided to chart her course as a radical dedicated to the removal of mass poverty. She shook herself free of the provincial Congress barons, known as the Syndicate, and cultivated the Left within and outside the Congress. Communists supported her programme of bank nationalization and abolition of the princes' privy purses. With this support she got elected as President of India an Independent candidate, V.V. Giri, defeating the Congress nominee Sanjiva Reddy whose candidature had been sponsored earlier by Indira Gandhi herself among others. The split in the Congress that ensued had profound consequences for the Indian Press.

Several newspapers with a large circulation, some of them

owned by entrepreneurs who had interests in other branches of industry and trade, opposed bank nationalization . Big newspapers therefore came to be regarded as 'bad', with the corollary that small newspapers, many of which looked to advertising and other support from the governments at Delhi and in the States were 'good'.

The initial mood of elation in the Leftist Press at the triumph of Indira Gandhi as well as its subsequent doubts are brought out in the following extract from an article by Aruna Asaf Ali, publisher of the *Link* magazine (from 1958) and the daily Patriot (from 1963) till January 1993: "I was thrilled when I came to know that Indira had made up her mind to challenge the conservative forces in the Congress. I went to her and said that her decision to oppose the Syndicate's bid for the Presidency was a historic step which would lead to far-reaching changes in the party and in the country... Indira Gandhi became the heroine of Link House, and so she remained through the stirring years of bank nationalization, abolition of the princes' privy purses, and the liberation of Bangladesh.

"Indira Gandhi's initiatives of the early 1970's antagonized the Rightist, communal and disruptive forces. Lawless agitations were fomented by a motley combination of political groups, encouraged by hostile foreign forces intent on -toppling her and destabilizing India. To arrest this dangerous trend, Indira Gandhi proclaimed a state of internal emergency. This step was supported in the initial stages by me and my colleagues of the Left. But there emerged a few months later some distortions of the emergency regulations. Well-meaning but unimaginative and harsh measures were adopted, to promote family planning and carry out slum clearance for instance, which alienated large sections of the people."

In the wake of an adverse verdict in June 1975 by a single-member bench of the Allahabad High Court, which held Prime Minister Indira Gandhi guilty of electoral malpractice in the 1971 elections to the Lok Sabha, Indira Gandhi persuaded the then President, Fakhruddin Ali Ahmed, to proclaim a state of internal emergency. The action was strictly in accord with the letter, though it was not in the spirit, of the Constitution. Article 352 read at that time as follows:

> "352 (1) If the President is satisfied that a grave emergency exists whereby the security of India or of any part of the territory thereof is threatened, whether by war or external aggression or internal disturbance, he may, by Proclamation, make a declaration to that effect.
>
> (3) A Proclamation of Emergency declaring that the security of India or of any part of the territory thereof is threatened by war or by, external aggression or by internal disturbance may be, made, before the actual occurrence of war or of any such aggression or disturbance if the President is satisfied that there is imminent danger thereof."

In the words of Arun Shourie, "Democratic constitutions are framed on the premise that citizens and politicians will abide by their spirit. The determined usurper thus has no difficulty in finding articles, clauses-the letter--to stab the spirit. The morning after the Reichstag fire Hitler goes to the aging Hindenburg and gives him a highly coloured account and persuades him to issue an Emergency Decree. The Emergency Decree is issued under Article 48 of the Weimar Constitution ."

With the Fundamental Rights suspended for the duration of the emergency and the judiciary thus put out of action, the executive ran amuck in relation to the Press. Electric supply to newspaper establishments on Bahadur Shah Zafar Marg, where most of the capital's dailies are located, was cut off during the night of June 25-26,1975, so that they could not report truthfully or comment freely on the events culminating in the proclamation of emergency.

The Emergency : From 1st February 1949 when the Reuters' subsidiary API began to function as the Indian Owned Press Trust of India, it had the stimulus of competition to supplement the self-motivation of its employees. But the United Press of India, closed down in 1958 because it was financially unviable.

Soon, however, a number of newspapers came together to sponsor a new agency, the United News of India. It started operations on -21st March 1961. Observers have pointed to a number of factors that might have impelled the sponsoring newspapers to take this initiative. One is the desirability, in the words of the First Press Commission in its report (1954), of there being "at least two news agencies, each competing with the other and also acting as a corrective to the other". Another was, as an analyst put it, "the desire of the larger newspapers to have a second competing agency on which they could fall back in the event of PTI, where working journalists had begun to unionise themselves, becoming strike-bound." A third factor that has been cited is the anxiety of the then Chief Minister of West Bengal, Dr. B.C. Roy, and others to find alternative employment for the hundreds of employees who were thrown out of work when the Calcutta based UPI closed down.

The emergence of UNI in 1961 meant the revival of competition after a three-year interval during which PTI was the only English-language wire news agency in the country. The desirability of competition as a stimulus to keen journalistic effort Was demonstrated by each agency on a number of occasions. The last occasion, however, was a few hours before an event which made competition in news gathering irrelevant, namely the clamping of censorship on the Press on 25th June 1975. Tarun Basu describes- UNI's scope in these words:

> "Staffers made a beeline for the police stations. Their efforts did not go unrewarded. Amid signs of frenetic activity at the Parliament Street police station at 2 a.m., a black Ambassador drew up with an occupant that was all too familiar. As tough-looking guards tried to shield the frail figure of Jayaprakash Narayan, we made a dash for the car. *Vinashakale Viparita Buddhi* (madness takes hold as the end nears):, these historic words of J.P. were to be on the front pages of every newspaper which managed to come out next morning.

What was done in the name of an emergency, in the 28th year of India's freedom, exceeded in coarseness anything done to the Press by alien rulers during the colonial period: from governor-general Wellesley's Regulations of 1799 and the Vernacular Press Act of 1878 to the restrictions imposed during World War II. With suspension of the constitutional guarantee of Fundamental Rights, the brute force of the State (ultima ratio regum, title of an anti-Fascist poem by Stephen Spender) took over.

Muzzled Press : The Defence and Internal Security of India Rules were invoked to clamp a censorship more rigorous than what the British rulers enforced during World War II. Truthful reporting even of the proceedings of Parliament, and of the highest courts of the land, became impossible. M.A. Jinnah, in his early phase as a liberal and a nationalist, condemned in 1936 the action taken by the British authorities, under the Indian Press (Emergency Powers) Act of 1931 against *Abhyudaya* of Aflahabad-founded in the 1920's by Pandit Madan Mohan Malaviya for publishing a speech of Pandit K.K. Malaviya in the Central Legislative Assembly. Jinnah said: "It is the privilege of the newspaper to have the proceedings published, and so long as they are true, fair and faithful faithful it is not liable to action." Of the same liberal view as the early Jinnah was Feroze Gandhi who, as a Congress back-bencher, in the Lok Sabha, was a Leftist and an advocate of nationalization much before his wife Indira was to assume that role. He introduced as a non official Bill, and got enacted by Parliament in 1956, a law to protect newspapers from legal action on grounds of libel etc. for the publication of truthful accounts of parliamentary proceedings.

Press Legislation : Among, three Press laws, which Prime Minister Indira Gandhi got enacted during the emergency, through Presidential ordinances issued on 8th December 1975 which were subsequently endorsed by parliament during January-February 1976, was one repealing the Feroze Gandhi Act. During the debate on this Bill the proceedings were blacked out at the time and were made public only in 1977, Hiren Mukherjee of the C.P.I. said in the

Lok Sabha on 27th January 1976: 'We all know that it is not normal to oppose government legislation at the introduction stage, but on this occasion I am constrained to do so because this is a Bill we shall oppose from A to Z. The reason is that, quite gratuitously, government has cope forward with,, legislation which strikes at the roots of parliament functioning in an efficient manner and responsively to the needs of the country... We do not want a captive parliament. The people of our country have a right to know what is being done inside parliament.' The next day Hiren Mukherjee went on to twit the, Indira Gandhi Regime about its patronage of pliant capitalists: "They are coming to term with them, people like K.K. Birla, who are coming to control not only their own papers but the *Indian* Express group also. They are treated as socially conscious capitalists with whom they are beginning to join hands. They are punishing decent, honest, independent reporting by putting up here a censorship apparatus."

P.G. Mavalankar (Independent) said: "Unfortunately, radio and television are departments of the Government of India. Therefore, only the Press remains As a free agency... I would suggest to the Minister and to all others, that a free Press is inevitably an extension of a free Parliament. If you take away the free Press, the Parliament does not remain a free Parliament... The record (of parliamentary proceedings) may have everything for the future historians, but people of the present generation will not know what is taking place in Parliament."

Bhupesh Gupta, C.P.I. member, said in the Rajya Sabha on 3rd February 1976: "It pains me that today... the Feroze Gandhi Act is sought to be assassinated by the very people who used to be his friends... Twenty years have passed since that law was enacted. Would there be any Vivian Bose Enquiry Committee report published, even if ;it had been laid on the Table of the House, if there had been no Feroze Gandhi Act? It would not have been possible because Dalmia had enough money to threaten defamatory action and prevent publication. What would have happened to the Mundhra case which led to the appointment of the Chagla Commission, the report of which was again published?

Sir, many of the disclosures made courageously by Feroze Gandhi himself in the Lok Sabha in 1957 and in later years would not have seen the light of day, as far as the public is concerned, had there been no protection given by the Act he had conceived and piloted, and got passed. Sir, this is a shameful Bill."

A second repealing legislation enacted-during the emergency abolished the Press Council of India that had been established in 1966. The actual and proximate reason for this action was that the Press Council seemed likely to pronounce against K.K. Birla, proprietor of the *Hindustan Times* and a supporter of the emergency regime, in a case concerning his treatment, of the editor, B.G. Verghese. The ostensible reason given in the 'statement of objects and reasons, was that, the Press Council had not been able to frame a code of conduct for the Press, Erastmo de Sequeira (Bharatiya Lok Dal) said in the Lok Sabha on 28th January 1976: 'In 26th years we have not been able in this House to codify our own privileges... I say that if the Press Council has not been able to draft a code a conduct for the Press, it probably 'faced' precisely the same difficulties as we find with reference to the codification of our privileges, and these are difficulties which we should, more than anybody else, understand. This Bill is one in a series of measures which can end up only in one direction, towards the destruction of democracy."

P.G. Mavalankar probed the reason for the repeal: "Is it because the Press Council did not toe the line of the Government since it declared the 'internal emergency? Is it because the Press Council did not want to go all the way with the Government and approve of what it has done with regard to suppression of freedom of the Press through censors and all kinds of other controls? Did the Minister want the Press Council to say that they were good?"

In the Rajya Sabha, Dr. K. Mathew Kurian (CPI-M) asked "whether it is not a fact that the B.G. Verghese case was very much in the mind of the Government when this Bill was drafted." Dr. T.N. Singh (Congress-Organisation) said: "I often wonder whether we have not already reached a stage where India is not a democracy but a dictatorship."

In addition to repealing the Feroze Gandhi Act and the Press Council Act, the emergency regime got legislation enacted for 'Prevention of Publication of Objectionable Matter'. The Act would have placed censorship on a permanent footing unless, of course, struck down by the higher judiciary after the end of the emergency and the restoration of Fundamental Rights. (The Act was repealed by the new parliament that emerged from the elections held in March 1977 in which the Congress party led by Indira Gandhi, and she herself, were defeated. The Press Council and protection of publication of parliamentary proceedings were also restored.)

Section 5 of the 1976 Press Act empowered a District Magistrate to direct that any matter relating to a particular subject or class of subjects may not be published for a period of two months. Krishna Kant, opposing the Bill in the Rajya Sabha, said on 4th February 1976: "Apparently there is no bar on continuing the censorship for successive two-month periods by issuing fresh orders. This is a provision which puts precensorship on a permanent basis on the statute book of India."

The definition of objectionable matter covered defamatory writing or visible representation relating to the President-of India, the Vice President and the Prime Minister. Though listed last according to formal protocol, it was the Prime Minister who was principally sought to be protected. As Dr. Mathew Kurian of the C.P.I (M) put it: "This Bill has the primary objective of protecting the Prime Minister from public criticism." He referred to the threat to trade union activity implied in the Bill's prohibition of incitement "to interfere with production, supply and distribution of food and other essential commodities or with essential services" and urged members of the C.P.I. to get rid of their 'confusion' that 'progressives' were occupying "the pinnacles of power in the ruling party"

T.N. Singh said that "if Gandhiji were to be reborn, he would be put behind the bars and his *Harijan* would not be allowed to be published." Umashankar Joshi, renowned poet, warned that terror "breeds cowards on one side and sycophants on the other". Referring to the effect of the legislation on artists, writers, cartoonists and musicians, he said, "Future historians would say that British rule ended up in, releasing the creative energies of the people of our country even under conditions of political subjugation and economic exploitation, but that free India found it necessary to choke these energies." Krishna Kant quoted a Nigerian journalist who had said in London: "African newspapers which were vigorously in the vanguard of the nationalist struggle for independence now have relatively less freedom to publish under the indigenous African governments they helped to found than they did under White colonialists." Krishna Kant asked: "Is it not an irony that India, the citadel of parliamentary democracy in the midst of the growing darkness of dictatorship in Asia and Africa, is now following these countries instead of giving them a lead?"

In the Lok Sabha, Saroj Mukherjee (C.P.I.M) compared the provisions of the 1951 Press Act framed by Rajaji as Union Home Minister, following the amendment of Article 19, to establish that the 1976 legislation was worse. Whereas under the Rajaji Act it was for a sessions judge to decide on imposition of security on a press, etc., such powers were now given to district magistrates. More than one speaker referred with nostalgia to Jawaharlal Nehru's democratic temper. Satyendra Narayan Sinha (Congress-Organisation) recalled Nehru's ringing words while addressing the A.I.N.E.C. on 3rd December 1950 in New Delhi: "I have no doubt that even if the government dislikes the liberties taken by the *Press* and considers them dangerous, it is wrong to interfere with the freedom of the Press. By imposing restrictions you do not change anything; you merely suppress the public, manifestation of certain things, thereby causing the idea and thought underlying them to spread further. Therefore, I would rather have a completely free press with all the dangers involved in the, wrong use of that freedom than a suppressed or a regulated press."

New Commissions

Jawaharlal Nehru had strong likes and dislikes, and could be impulsive in utterance. As will be seen presently, both these traits were in evidence in connection with the formation of India's first Press Commission in 1952. This Commission made certain proposals that were well-intentioned but could have proved damaging to the growth and liberty of the Indian Press. Nehru refrained from pushing them through.

Nehru was allergic to Seth Ramakrishna Dalmia, the new proprietor of the Times of India because Dalmia was a capitalist and an advocate of a religious State and of cow protection. Another irritant was that Dalmia had four, wives. Polygamy was legal at that time for Hindus, as it continues to be for Indian *Muslims*. Dalmia did not justify or advocate polygamy; an obituary carried by the Statesman on 27th September 1978, on Dalmia's death at the age of 85, said that he "once expressed a desire to write a book on the evils of polygamy."

Dalmia extended the range of the Bonibay-based Times of India as a carrier of his views by launching an edition in India's capital in January 1950. The Statesman of Calcutta had opened a Delhi edition in 1930. *National Herald* of Lucknow wished to do so too (though the ambition was to be realised only in March 1968). Uma Shankar Dikshit (managing director of National *Herald* from 1957 to 1971) writes: "With the emergence of free India in 1947, Pandit Jawaharlal Nehru decided that the National *Herald* should be published from Delhi. He thought that the national government needed a powerful organ for promoting its policy of Five Year Plans building up a strong and growing public sector and the other progressive policies of socialism and secularism in a democratic set-up." Dikshit adds: "Pandit Nehru did not want his name as Prime Minister to be associated directly or indirectly with the job of raising funds for establishing and running the National *Herald,* (in Delhi). He depended on his colleagues and associates to acquire the needed finances, and Rafi Ahmed Kidwai did act the role in good measure."

It would thus appear that Nehru's objection was not to multiple editions of newspapers, or to money as such, but to the kind of ideas which money power enabled Dalmia to -propagate. The Prime Minister said in the course of his speech at the annual meeting of the All India Newspaper Editors' Conference on 17th September 1952 in New Delhi: "What exactly is the Press? Whatever it may be, the money involved, the owner and proprietor of that money, are major factors. Does the freedom of the Press ultimately mean freedom of the rich man to do what he likes with his money through the Press? Normally speaking-and I speak with all deference-high standards and high intelligence are not allied with large quantities of money. A person with a large amount of money need not necessarily have high cultural standards or high literary standards or any high standards at all, though, he may have the knack of making money. Therefore, the freedom of the Press may come to mean the freedom of persons who have a knack of making money and that, after all, is not such a noble thing." M. Chalapathi Rau, who was for long years editor of National *Herald* during and after the Nehru era, recalls: "There was a minor sensation when the National *Herald* was to restart publication (November 1945). 'Nehru received through intermediaries the offer of a crore of rupees from Seth Ram. Krishna Dalmia to start a chain of newspapers. Nehru rejected it outright... Later Nehru was to describe him as that 'ugly man with an ugly, face, ugly mind and ugly ears'. The appointment of a Press Commission was announced by the government on 23rd September 1952, a week after the Prime Minister's address to the A.I.N.E.C.

If Dalmia's ownership of the *Times of India* and the advent of its Delhi edition was the main internal factor that spurred the establishment of a Press Commission in India, an external stimulus was the formation in 1947 of Britain's first Press Commission by the post-war Labour Government. There is an unmistakable resonance between the terms of the British and the Indian commissions, though the state of the industry in India, with newspapers having pitifully small circulations, was far different from conditions in industrially advanced countries like Britain.

The Ross Commission in Britain (194749) was required "to inquire into the factors affecting the maintenance of the independence, diversity and editorial standards of newspapers and periodicals, and the public's freedom of choice of newspapers and periodicals, nationally, regionally and locally, with particular reference to:

(a) the economics of newspaper and periodical publishing and distribution;

(b) the interaction of the newspaper and periodical interests held by the companies concerned with their other interests and holdings, within and outside the communications industry;

(c) management and labour practices and relations in the newspaper and periodical industry;

(d) conditions and security of employment in the newspaper and periodical industry;

(e) the distribution and concentration of ownership of the newspaper and periodical industry, and the adequacy of existing law in relation thereto; and

(f) the responsibilities, constitution and functioning of the Press Council."

The mandate for the Indian body was: "The Press Commission shall enquire into the state of the Press in India, its present and future lines of development and shall in particular examine:

(i) the control, management and ownership and financial structure of newspapers, large and small, the periodical press and news agencies and feature syndicates;

(ii) the working of monopolies and chains and their effect on the presentation of accurate news and fair views;

(iii) the effect of holding companies, the distribution of advertisements and such other forms of external influence as may have a bearing on the development of healthy journalism;

(iv) the method of recruitment, training, scales of remuneration, benefits and other conditions of employment of working journalists settlement of disputes affecting them and factors which influence the establishment and maintenance of high professional standards;

(v) the adequacy of newsprint supplies and their distribution among all classes of newspapers and the possibilities of promoting indigenous manufacture of (a) newsprint and (b) printing and composing machinery;

(vi) machinery for (a) ensuring high standards of journalism and (b) liaison between Government and the Press; the functioning of Press Advisory Committees and organisations of editors and working journalists.; and

(vii) freedom of the Press and repeal or amendment of laws not in consonance with it."

A demand from journalists' trade unions was a common factor accounting for the formation of the Press Commissions in Britain and India. The Ross Commission said in its report, in an introductory section: Me demand for a Royal Commission was initiated by the National Union of journalists. It came before the House of Commons on 29th October 1946, when two Members, both journalists, moved the following motion:

> 'That, having regard to the increasing public concern at the growth of monopolistic tendencies in the control of the Press and with the object of furthering the free expression of opinion through the Press and the greatest practicable accuracy in the presentation of news, this House considers that a Royal Commission should be appointed to inquire into the finance, control, management and ownership of the Press.'

> "The opponents of the motion, among whom also were several journalists, argued that its supporters had failed to make a prima facie case. It was suggested that they were actuated by political prejudice and by a desire to limit the freedom of the Press, or of that part of it which opposed the Government. There was nothing approaching a monopoly in the ownership of newspapers... A Royal Commission could, produce no important information about the ownership of newspapers that was not already available; if it found

> inaccuracy or distortion, it could do nothing about them; if it suggested legislation, it would open the way to government control; whatever' it did, its mere existence would throw unjustified doubt on the integrity of the Press. The House divided, and on a free vote the, motion was carried by 270 votes to 157."

In contrast to the division of opinion in Britain, both among journalists and the public, in India the climate of opinion at that time among the English-educated intelligentsia was strongly influenced by Prime Minister Jawaharlal Nehru's commendation of socialism understood as public ownership in key areas and government regulation of private enterprise. The Press Commission was headed by a former Judge of the Supreme Court and its members included a distinguished economist, journalists, and public men covering the political spectrum from liberal to socialist. It included :

> Justice G.S. Rajadhyaksha (Chairman), Dr. C.P. Ramaswami Aiyer, Acharya Narendra Deva, Dr. Zakir Hussain, Dr. V.K.R.V. Rao, P.H. Patwardhan, T.N. Singh, Jaipal Singh, J. Natarajan, A.R. Bhat, M. Chalapathi Rau.

These disparate personalities recommended with one voice governmental intervention in the economics of newspaper publishing in order purportedly to facilitate the expression of diverse viewpoints, while they turned a blind eye to the total monopoly exercised by the party in power at the centre over the news and views broadcast by All India Radio.

This can be understood only in the context of the belief then prevalent that State ownership and governmental regulation would conduce to promotion of the public good. There was little fear of the manipulative use of state power by the political party and its leaders for the time being in power. It wag later that the Indian scene began to resemble the situation that obtained in Britain in the early decades of the 20th century, about which G.K. Chesterton wrote: "The mere proposal to set the politician to watch the capitalist has been disturbed by the rather disconcerting discovery that they are both the same man. We are past the point, where being a capitalist is the only way of becoming a politician, and we are dangerously near the point where being a politician is much the quickest way of becoming a capitalist." Over the four decades since the First Press Commission reported India has learnt the hard way that managers of publicly owned undertakings can be as venal as those of private enterprises, and that politicians in power are not immune from the temptation to misuse public office for personal profit.

Janata Days : A second Press Commission was formed after the fall of the Indira Gandhi government in March 1977 as the result of the sixth elections to the Lok Sabha, and the restoration of Fundamental Rights. The new government headed by Morarji Desai announced in May 1978 the formation of a Commission comprising: Justice P.K. Goswami (retired judge of the Supreme Court); Abu Abraham; Prem Bhatia; S.N. Dwivedi; Moinuddin Harris; Ravi J. Mathai; Yashodhar N. Mehta; V.K. Narasimhan; F.S. Nariman; Arun Shourie (on whose resignation Nikhil Chakravarty was appointed); and S.H. Vatsyayan. Their terms of reference reflected concern about safeguarding the freedom of the Press:

> "The Press Commission shall enquire into the growth and status of the Indian Press since the last Press Commission reported, and suggest how best it should develop in future. It shall, in particular, examine:
>
> (i) The present constitutional guarantee with regard to the freedom of speech and expression, whether this is adequate to ensure freedom of the Press, and the adequacy and efficacy of the laws, rule's and regulations relating to and affecting the Press;
>
> (ii) Means of safeguarding the freedom and independence of the Press against pressures of all kinds from Government, proprietors, advertising, commercial, trade union, political or other sources, in a plural and democratic society;
>
> (iii) Ownership patterns and the financial structure of organs

of the Press with a view to ensuring editorial independence and professional integrity and the readers' right to objective news and views and comments freely expressed;

(iv) The relationship that should exist between the Government and the Press, especially with regard to access to information, accreditation, official patronage or subsidies;

(v) The structure and functioning of the existing news and feature agencies and measures necessary for their growth as strong and viable organisations that can cover news, monitoring at every level right down to the grassroots and also world news;

(vi) Relations that should subsist between different elements of the Press, viz., publishers, managers, editors and other professional journalists, etc.;

(vii) Measures necessary to raise and maintain high standards of journalism and to inculcate among journalists and newspapers a due sense of public and social responsibility corresponding to the power of the Press, its role in national reconstruction and its obligation to the readers;

(viii) Ways and means to promote the growth and development of the language and regional Press as also the periodical Press, specialised journals and syndicated services;

(ix) The economics of the newspaper industry, including ways and means of rectifying deficiencies and evolving the basis for a fair price for newspapers keeping in view legal and constitutional requirements; and

(x) The adequacy of training in communications journalism, adequacy newspaper management, printing technology and newspaper design and graphics as also the desirability and feasibility of higher learning in journalism and mass communications."

Return of Mrs. Gandhi : Following the fall of the Government headed by Morarji Desai, the Goswami Commission submitted its resignation on 30th July 1979, stating that "as a matter of propriety it is desirable for a Commission to tender its resignation on a change of government. This enables the new government to view afresh the subject of continuance of the Commission in all its aspects." The Information Minister, Purushottam Kaushik, in the new government headed by Charan Singh, replied to the Chairman of the Commission: "Government appreciate the sentiments which have prompted you to write this letter. They have considered the matter and would like you and the members of the Press Commission to continue with the work."

When, following the fall of the Charan Singh government and the elections held in January 1980, the Congress party led by Indira Gandhi returned to power, the Goswami Commission once again offered its resignation. This time it was accepted. Vasant Sathe as Information Minister in the Indira Gandhi government wrote to justice Goswami: "I am happy to note that during the course of the short period the Commission has been in existence, it has done valuable work by going round to different centres in the country, interviewing a large number of witnesses and collecting a mass of data and information. The new Government would like to continue the Commission based on a more comprehensive set of terms of reference. This, you will kindly appreciate, will be possible only if the Commission is reconstituted. It is in this context that the Government has regretfully decided to accept your resignation as well as the resignation; of your colleagues."

The terms of reference of the Commission, reconstituted with justice K.K. Mathew as Chairman, were announced on 24th July 1980:

> "The Press Commission shall inquire re into the growth and status of the Press since the first Press Commission reported and suggest how best it should develop in future. It shall, in particular, examine and make recommendations on:

1. The role of the Press in a developing and democratic society;
2. The present constitutional guarantee with regard to the

freedom of speech and expression, whether this is adequate to ensure freedom of the Press; adequacy and efficacy of the laws, rules and regulations for maintaining this freedom;

3. Constitutional and legal safeguards to protect the citizen's right to privacy;
4. Means of safeguarding the independence of the Press against economic and political pressures and Pressures from proprietors and management;
5. Role of the Press and the responsibilities it should assume in developmental policies;
6. The Press as an industry, a social institution and a forum for informed discussion of public affairs;
7. Ownership patterns, management practices and financial structures of the Press; their relation to growth, editorial independence and professional integrity;
8. Chain newspapers; links with industry, their effect on competition and on the readers' right to objective news and free comments;
9. Economics of the newspaper industry, newsprint, printing machinery and other inputs for newspapers;
10. Advertising-government and private, educational and commercial;
11. Government-Press relations and the role of official agencies;
12. Relations that should subsist between-different elements of the Press, namely publishers, managers, editors and professional journalists and others;
13. Growth of small and medium papers and of the language Press;.
14. Development of the periodical Press and specialised journals;
15. News coverage and news values; structure and functioning

of news agencies and feature agencies; flow of news to and from, India;

16. Training of professional manpower; steps to improve professional standards and performance; research in, journalism and mass communication;

17. Journalism as a means of better mutual understanding in the context of proposals for a new international information order; and

18. Perspective of newspaper development."

The final composition of the reconstituted Commission was: justice K.K. Mathew, retired Judge of the Supreme Court (Chairman); justice Sisir Kumar Mukherjee, retired Judge of the Calcutta High Court; P.V. Gadgil, author and journalist; Ishrat Ali Siddiqui, Editor, *Qaumi Awaz,* Lucknow; Rajendra Mathur, Chief Editor, *Nai Duniya,* Indore; Girilal Jain, Editor, *Times of India,* Bombay; K.R. Ganesh, former Union Minister of State; H.K. Paranjape, economist and former member,. Monopolies and Restrictive Trade Practices Commission; Ranbir Singh, Editor, *Milap,* Delhi; Prem Chand Verma, President of the All India Small and Medium Newspapers' Association and former member of the Lok Sabha; and Justice A.N. Mulla, retired Judge of the Allahabad High Court And former member of the Lok Sabha and the Rajya Sabha.

There was a sharp cleavage of views as between the Chairman and six members of the Commission, on the one hand, and four other members, namely S.K. Mukherjea, Rajendra Mathur, Girilal Jain and H.K. Paranjape. The majority of seven, broadly speaking, favoured governmental regulation of newspaper ownership and management, while the minority of four were opposed to it. The report of the Mathew Commission is remarkable for the lengthy joint minute of dissent, which is virtually a separate minority report, rejoinder thereto, reply to rejoinder, and other comments.

Regulated v. Free Press : Surveyed in this section are, the proposals made by the First Press Commission, several of which were endorsed and further elaborated by the majority of the Second

Press Commission but opposed by the minority, for regulation of newspaper ownership and management. (Proposals similar to these were considered and commented on also by one or more of the three Press Commissions of the U.K.) The various views on each proposal, and the response of successive Indian governments, are reviewed below.

Newspaper Ownership : The Rajadhyaksha Commission, conceded (pp. 271-272) that the defects of newspapers are not invariably linked to the form of ownership: "We agree that the shortcomings to which we have drawn attention are not peculiar to any particular form of ownership... There has been evidence about newspapers whose ownership was vested in a political party, where the profit motive was not the dominant one, which indulged in misrepresentation of political opponents. There have been cases of small newspapers, owned by individuals or groups or partnerships, indulging in scurrilous and offensive publications... There has also been evidence about a newspaper, whose ownership is kept within a family, which has set up high traditions of stability and objectivity in journalism... There may also be cases where trustees of newspapers become tyrants, or cooperative ownership may become coercive, particularly if those in control do not have a proper sense of values. Whatever the forms of ownership, the character of a newspaper will depend on the character of the editor and the proprietors and not on the form of ownership."

Despite this, the first Press Commission went on to commend voluntary transfer of the control of a newspaper by its owners to a public trust: "A proposal was put before us that all newspapers, big and small, should be compelled by legislation to come under the Trust form of ownership or control. While we do not recommend any compulsion of the type suggested, we do regard the Trust form of ownership as the most desirable... We would welcome in India this trend which the Royal Commission on the Press in the United Kingdom has described as one of the most interesting developments of the last 25 years." The Ross Commission had said in its report of 1949: "A trust does not necessarily convert a newspaper from a commercial to a non-commercial concern, or give it quality which it did not previously possess. For these reasons we do not consider that it would be effective or appropriate to put any pressure on proprietors by fiscal inducements or otherwise to adopt either trust ownership or any of the arrangements whose purposes are similar. A trust can be, however, a valuable means, of preserving qua quality where quality already exists. We accordingly welcome the action of public spirited proprietors who have taken such steps as lie in their power to safeguard the character and independence of their papers; and we hope that the number of papers so protected will grow."

Though the First Press Commission did not recommend compulsory delinking of newspaper ownership from other business interests, it gave sufficient arguments in favour of delinking to encourage the government in the post-Nehru years to initiate legislation for the purpose. "It would be ideal", the Rajadhyaksha Commission had said, "if the proprietor of a newspaper has no other interests." (page 273 of Report). The Commission also gave numerous suggestions for diffusing widely the ownership and control of newspapers. These ideas of delinking, and diffusion came to be discussed widely in the wake of the Congress split of 1969 and the nationalisation of banks by the Indira Gandhi government which lost its majority but ruled with Communist support. When Indira Gandhi emerged strong from the mid-term elections to the Lok Sabha in 1971 and formed a new government, a Bill was drafted for amending the Companies Act so as to incorporate provisions for delinking newspaper companies from other business interests.

Another approach to securing the same end, of emasculating the most influential section of the Press, was embodied in a draft Bill prepared in July 1974 following discussions between the then Minister of information & Broadcasting and the Law Minister. Its aim was to interpose by law a Board of Control between the proprietors and the editorial staff in order in the words of a note prepared in the Ministry of I & B" to ensure editorial freedom and the newspaper's social responsibility". The draft Bill required every big newspaper company, in general meeting, to specify succinctly its editorial policy. The functions of the proposed Board of Control included the following:

> "The Board of Control shall, if it is of opinion that the editorial board is not giving proper effect to the editorial policy, or that the views expressed in the big newspaper per by the editorial board are in conflict with the editorial Policy or are prejudicial to the interests of the big newspaper company or are against the public interest, advise the editorial board...
>
> If the editorial board omits or refuses to act in accordance with the advice tendered by the Board of Control, that Board may advise the big newspaper company to so reconstitute the editorial board as to ensure that due effect is given by it to the editorial policy.
>
> Notwithstanding anything contained in any contract or in any law (other than this Act) in force for the time being, a big newspaper company may, if advised by the Board of Control so to do, terminate the contract of service of the Editor-in-Chief or any other member of the editorial board."

Though the Bills of 1971 and 1974 were not proceeded, with, the threat of legislation on such lines continued to hang over the head of the Press like the legendary sword of Damocles.. Then came the emergency and censorship in mid-1975 which knocked the Press down flat. It remained supine till the emergency regime was voted out in the March 1977 elections.

The majority of members of the Second Press Commission, formed by Indira Gandhi following her return to power in January 1980, were moved by an even deeper distrust of private enterprise and correspondingly greater faith in State regulation than the members of the first. The majority report said: "It is precisely because the business men owning or controlling big newspapers have not acted on the advice of the First Press Commission, of creating trusts for their management, that we are obliged to seriously consider the question once again and seek other remedies... We think that in the interest of the public it is necessary to insulate the Press from the dominating influence of other business interests. We propose the enactment of a law making it mandatory for persons carrying on the business of publishing a newspaper to sever their connections with other businesses to the extent indicated hereinafter... In the first instance it should be enforced in the case of all persons who are in a position of controlling the publication of one or more daily newspapers, with the same or different titles, in one or more languages, the circulation of which, taken singly or cumulatively, exceeds one lakh copies per day... If the shares of a newspaper company are not readily purchased by eligible persons from the open market, such shares should be acquired and held by an autonomous body or agency to be specified by the legislation till they are purchased by eligible persons."

This amounted to a recommendation for the nationalisation of big newspapers if their capitalist owners do not succeed in offloading their shares to their employees or to other 'eligible persons'. (The Rajadhyaksha Commission had recommended nationalisation only in the case of the Press Trust of India news agency. Though the Mathew Commission in the majority report affirmed that "the legislature is competent to enact the proposed law under Article 19 of the Constitution", the Congress (Indira) Government headed by Rajiv Gandhi was apparently not sure on this point. An 'action taken' report on the recommendations of the Second Press Commission, laid on the table of parliament on 14th May 1986, said: "The Government appreciates the recommendation made by the Commission but feels that in view of the legal, constitutional and other complexities involved, the matter may be referred to an expert committee for examination and report."

Events since 1982 have served to underline the skepticism voiced by the minority of the Second Press Commission about State regulation of the newspaper industry: "The majority seem to think that mercantile winds are blowing over the Press more furiously than they do elsewhere. Is it true that the democratic managers of our political system are trustees unaffected by industrial and mercantile conditions? All the ills to which the press is allegedly heir have a more virulent counterpart in the political system. Not all our politicians are delinked from money-bags, nor are they delinked from votes because of which they have to pander to the aspirations as well as the bigotry and parochial interests of the electorate... Of course, this parallel does not absolve the Press; the parallel has been drawn only to point out that there are no panaceas." (Page 227, Report of Second Press Commission.)

Limit on Advertising Space : The Rajadhyaksha Commission recommended that the total space allotted to advertisements in daily newspapers should not exceed 40 per cent of the printed area. "We expect", they said, "that when newspapers are forced either to reduce the number of pages or to increase the price of each copy, there would be a strong temptation to condense news and editorial matter so as to accommodate all the advertisements that they have booked. As a consequence, the ratio of advertisement space to reading matter would increase. We are of the opinion that it should be kept within the definite limit that we have prescribed."

On the subject of revenue from advertisements, the Ross Commission in the U.K. had said in its report (1949): "As long as newspapers are sold to the public for less than they cost to produce, they will need a supplementary source of income. Of the various possible sources of income, the sale of their space to advertisers seems to us to be one of the least harmful. The income to be feared is that which comes from a concealed source and can be earned only by the sale of the editorial columns... The publication of advertisements should not be regarded, moreover, as a departure, under pressure of economic necessity, from the proper function of a newspaper. It is an essential part of the service which the newspaper renders to the community, valuable alike to commerce and industry and to the general public."

On the proposal for a news-to-advertisement ratio and or a tax on newspaper revenue from advertising, the Ross Commission said: "During the war some national advertising was diverted from the mass-circulation papers, by the contraction of their space, into the provincial papers; and it has been suggested to us that if this state of affairs could be preserved, the small papers would be assisted both directly by increases in their own revenue and indirectly by a reduction of the revenue, and consequently of the competitive advantages, of the large national papers. It has therefore been proposed that a limit should be set either to the amount of advertising a newspaper of a given size may carry, or to the amount of advertising revenue it may earn. We do not think that these proposals would necessarily achieve their ostensible object; in normal circumstances their effect might merely be to drive advertisers to use other media than the Press... The limitation of revenue might necessitate either an increase in the price of newspapers or a reduction of the amount spent on producing them, and possibly of the quality of the service given to the public." The 2nd (Shawcross) Commission also rejected the proposals for a statutory limit on the proportion of space devoted to advertising, or a levy on the advertisement revenue of newspapers graded according to the size of their circulation, or a duty on the advertising revenue of newspapers with over $2 million of such revenue.

In India, however, the Second Press Commission endorsed the proposal made by the Rajadhyaksha Commission for a law to regulate advertising space. On the ground that newspapers with a small circulation needed to carry a larger proportion of advertising on account of their lower advertisement tariff and fewer number of pages, the Mathew Commission recommended that the news-to-advertisement ratio should be fixed at 60-40 for big, 50:50 for medium and 40:60 for small newspapers.

Price-Page Schedule : Another major recommendation of the First Press Commission was legislation to fix a minimum price of newspapers depending on the number of pages offered to the reader. "A paper with a large circulation" it was argued, "because of its lower cost of production per copy enjoys certain advantages over other papers with smaller circulation. Similarly, a paper with large capital resources behind it is free from certain handicaps which affect another paper with limited capital. Papers of long standing, which have been able to build up a large and stable volume of advertisement revenue, are in a very advantageous position as compared to others who have just entered the field. It is true that such economic advantages and handicaps exist in a number of industries but their presence in the newspaper industry is not, in our opinion, conducive to the even and healthy development of the press. Newspapers serve as media for the free exchange of information and of ideas. The proper functioning of democracy requires that every individual should have equal opportunity, in so far as this can be achieved, to put forward his opinions. We feel that to fix a minimum price at which papers of a particular size can be sold would be the most effective measure to bring about this end."

An attempt was made during Jawaharlal Nehru's prime ministership to give effect, through legislation, to the Rajadhyaksha Commission's recommendations for enforcing a price-page schedule and a new news-to-advertisement ratio. Parliament enacted the Newspaper (Price and Page) Act in 1956. The Daily Newspapers (Price and Page) Order was issued in 1960, under the Act, fixing the number of pages that could be published by a newspaper according to the price charged. However, both the Act and the Order were struck down by the Supreme Court in *Sakal Newspapers v. Union* in 1962 as being violative of Article 19.

The Nehru Government left the matter at that. The Prime Minister did not think of amending the Constitution in order to get over the Supreme Court's judgement. An amendment of the Constitution is precisely what the majority of the Second Press Commission suggested in 1982. Though only one out of the seven members constituting the majority--namely the Chairman himself-had a judicial background, they opined that the. *Sakal* case had been incorrectly decided by the Supreme Court and merited a review. The majority of the Mathew Commission said:

"Even if an amendment of the Constitution is required to give effect to our proposals regarding price page schedule and news-to-advertisement ratio, We are of the view that such an amendment will not destroy or damage the basic structure of the Constitution. No doubt Article 19 (1) (a) has been held to be a basic structure of the Constitution; but a law prescribing a, price-page schedule or news-to-advertisement ratio is not a measure which will destroy or damage, that freedom; on the contrary, its object being promotion of competition and prevention of monopoly, the law will advance freedom of speech and expression. Shri Girilal Jain, Rajendra Mathur, S.K. Mukherjea and HK Paranjape are opposed to the prescription of price-page schedule and news-to-advertisement ratio."

It is noteworthy that at two places the majority of the Mathew Commission give the game away. They say (p.156 of the Report): "While arriving at this view (prescription of a price-page schedule with a news-to-advertisement ratio) we have not been oblivious of the fact that those papers which are today attracting a disproportionately large, amount of advertisement revenue are utilizing it to a certain extent for improving their quality and subsidising the selling price for the benefit of the readers." Again, "We are conscious that the newspapers which will come within the ambit of the proposed legislation are all quality newspapers rendering good service to the community."

The 'action report' tabled in parliament by the Rajiv Gandhi government said: "'The observations made by the' Press Commission and the arguments given in support of the constitutionality of the recommendations made by them are noted. In view of the decision of the Supreme Court and the present legal position, an expert committee may be set up to go into the question of working out a price-page schedule and news-to-advertisement ratio." This was in May 1986. There the matter stands.

Internal Relations in the Press : The majority of the Mathew Commission were so fearful of proprietorial interference with editorial autonomy, even after the compulsory delinking of big newspapers from big industry, that they proposed the interposition of trustees to protect the editor from rough advances by the proprietor or the management. One of the members remarked in the course of discussion of this proposal that, it was as quixotic as the notion of interposing a trustee between husband and wife; it is a different matter that this member, as a loyal supporter of the Congress (1), eventually voted with the majority. The view of justice Mathew and his colleagues of the majority was as follows: "To provide an effective safeguard against proprietorial or managerial interference in editorial independence, there should be legislation for interposition of a board of trustees between the management of a large daily newspaper and its editor. The legislation should be applicable in the first instance only to daily newspapers with a circulation of over one lakh copies. The policy of every such newspaper should be clearly laid down in writing. The function of the boards of trustees would be to ensure that full effect is given to the policy of the newspaper and to act as umpire in disputes between the editor and the management of the newspaper... They (trustees) should be appointed by the managements of the newspapers themselves in consultation with and with the approval of the Chairman of the Press Council and the Chief justice of the High Court or the Chief justice of India, as the case may be, depending upon the area of circulation of the newspaper concerned. In the event of a difference of opinion between the Chairman of the Press Council and the Chief justice on the choice of the members submitted to them by the management of a newspaper, the view of the Chief Justice should prevail."

This recommendation seemed to the Rajiv Gandhi government to go too far. The action report tabled in parliament in May 1986 said: "It is not clear what responsibility would be cast on such a board (of trustees) in the running of the newspapers and how the proposal could be implemented in a practicable manner. It is also noted that even organisations on which, among others, editors were represented had expressed themselves against the proposal. The recommendation is not, therefore, accepted."

Right to Information : On the citizens' right to information, which was one of the terms of reference, the Mathew Commission recommended repeal of Section 5 of the Official Secrets Act of 1923 and its replacement by provisions suited to reconciling the vital interests of the State with the right of the people to know the affairs of the State affecting them. This recommendation was rejected by the Rajiv Gandhi government. The 'action taken' report said tersely: "Not considered necessary as the existing provisions in law seem to be adequate."

Worth pondering in this connection are the comments of two American writers Edgar and Schmidt in the course of writings by them, in the 1970's, on 'The Espionage Statutes and Publication of Defense Information':

> "Statutes aimed at protecting defense secrets from disclosure must deal with cloak-and-dagger spying, with the fidelity of government employees to executive policies of secrecy and, most troublesome of all, with the rights and duties of journalists and the rest of us to engage in or refrain from discussing matters that may be critical to informed democratic policy choices... The press rarely tested the limits of its right to publish; secrets were kept because people in and out of government with access to military and diplomatic secrets shared basic assumptions about national aims. The Vietnam war changed all that. The radical perspective of I.F. Stone ('Every government is run by liars and nothing they say should be believed') became an accepted premise in reporting about the war. The Pentagon Papers dispute symbolized the passing of an era in which journalists could be counted on to work within understood limits of discretion in handling secret information."

The writers cited, in support of their plea for greater freedom to publish, the view of President Kennedy expressed retrospectively that the *New York Times* should have, in the public interest, published the information it had gained about the American 'Bay of Pigs' plan for the invasion of Cuba.

Defamation Bill : It is noteworthy that, perhaps due to the chastening effect of the March 1977 electoral verdict following the period of emergency and censorship, the Press .was left free of legislative intervention for more than eight years from January 1980 when Indira Gandhi returned to power. There was once again a confrontation when the Rajiv Gandhi government introduced in parliament in August 1988 a Defamation Bill.

It placed the onus on the person accused of having made a defamatory statement to prove the truth of the statement and to establish also that the statement was made for the public good. Section 13 created a new class of offence called criminal imputation, which the Minister piloting the Bill described as "ark aggravated form of defamation calling for punishment": Punishment was provided also for aggravated those printing or engraving and selling defamatory matter.

The Defamation Bill was brought forward after disclosures and allegations in the Press about kick-backs received by or on behalf of Prime Minister Rajiv Gandhi and/or the Congress (1) from Nobel Industries of Sweden in a contract for the purchase of the Bofors gun for the Indian Army. This scandal was to cost Rajiv Gandhi dearly: as leader of the Congress (1) he could secure for his party less than 40 per cent of the popular vote in the elections held for the Lok Sabha in November 1989, as against the unprecedented share of' about a half of the votes that the party received when he led it in the December 1984 elections within Weeks of his succeeding his assassinated mother as Prime Minister. The difference was due to absence of the sympathy factor that had been at work in 1984, as well as to the adverse impression created by the Bofors scandal.

The Defamation Bill was hurriedly introduced by the Rajiv Gandhi government in the Lok Sabha on 29th August 1988 and was passed the next day. In a remarkable display of unity, newspaper employees, who had been looking to the government for securing improved wages and working conditions, joined hands with their employers in demonstrations all over the country against the Defamation Bill as an attack on Press freedom. The rallies-were climaxed by a march in the capital along Raj Path to Parliament House in which newspaper publishers marched alongside representatives of the All India Newspapers Employees Federation, the Indian Federation of Working Journalists, National Union of journalists and the Editors' Guild.

Doubtless recalling the ruling party's experience in 1977, when the voters' verdict was in part against the emergency regime of Press censorship, Prime Minister Rajiv Gandhi thought it wise to drop the Defamation Bill. It was not proceeded with in the Rajya Sabha. When all manner of allegations were made against persons prominent in public life during the securities scandal of 1993 involving banks and commercial undertakings, in the public sector and the private, many in the ruling party must have recollected the Defamation Bill with nostalgia and wished that it had been enacted and brought into force.

Another Bill pertaining to the Press that was initiated during Rajiv Gandhi's tenure as prime minister, but was abandoned, was an amendment of the Press and Registration of Books Act. Introduced in December 1988, the Bill sought to empower district magistrates to carry out inspection checks of newspaper establishments to verify circulation claims, and to increase the amount of fine that could be levied on newspapers for violation of the Act from Rs. 500 to Rs. 5,000. The amending legislation would also have permitted cancellation of the concessional rate of postage for newspapers if they consisted mainly of advertisements.

After decades since the coming into force of India's republican Constitution, guaranteeing freedom of expression subject to certain limitations, have thus witnessed, as it were, a swing of the pendulum between the spirit and the letter of Article 19.

Freedom at Last

The long and arduous battle for independence came to an end on August 15,1947, when India after partition became free from alien rule. As the country rejoiced and celebrated the historic event, a jubilant press joined its countrymen in hailing the advent of freedom for which it had fought shoulder to shoulder with the nationalist forces and made enormous sacrifices in men and material, braving the cruel persecution of the colonial rulers. In a striking editorial, *The Hindu* described the ship of freedom which had reached port thus: "After a century of storm and stress, the ship of Indian freedom has come into port. Battered heavily by wind and sea, scarred and seamed in many a fierce encounter with embattled hosts, she has suffered grievous losses and has had to jettison much precious cargo. She is not spic and span as we had pictured her in the morning time of our hopes, it is on the whole a sad home coming. There are treacherous shoals about and the pilot is more than a little weary. But she is a brave little ship for all that, for she carries the high hopes and ambitions of 400 million. On her proud mast-head there broods, like the spirit of peace, the white soul of India....India embarks on the endless adventure of freedom, crippled and maimed in the sight of the world. She is, however, a great believer in the healing touch of time and in the magic of natural affinities."

In the first flush of freedom, the press rode with the current and was sympathetic and cooperative with the new national government which was faced with a deluge of problems plunging the country into strife and bloodshed and instability. A section, however had not got over the hangover of colonial rule and indulged in fanning communal passions and hatred and in scurrilous writing. Sensational journalism became a fashion with some and the country's interests ceased to be paramount. A Bengali editor is quoted by a writer as having confessed that he adopted a communal policy "because playing down riots and disturbances curbed his sales." "Even the news boys", the editor is quoted as having said, "refuse to touch my paper if my rivals report a larger number of deaths than I do." The leaders who were running the government and who had established complete rapport with the press during the freedom struggle were now saddened that the press as a whole was not with them in meeting the challenges faced by the new-born government. They seemed to behave, the leaders thought, as an opposition force as they did during the

British regime when the need was to play a constructive and cooperative role.

Frank Moraes, editor of the *Times of India,* referred to the attitude of Indian editors in the early years of Independence and said: "In the early years of independence, Indian editors had to make up their minds on what attitude they should adopt vis-a-vis Nehru's newly established government.... I decided after some reflection and consultation that since Nehru was faced virtually with no opposition in Parliament and since a democratic government could not effectively express itself in the absence of an opposition, the press should take it upon itself to function as an unofficial opposition outside Parliament, exercising that role with responsibility and circumspection."

Writing on the same subject *The Hindu* felt that even barely a year after freedom was achieved the suspicion and distrust which clouded the relations between the alien government and the nationalist press "continued in a very perceptible manner under the Free India Government." The Hindu said in the new circumstances the "Press may be expected to take a more detached as also a more responsible view of its obligations on the one hand to the government of the day, and on the other to the people as a whole, opposing official policy when it must, supporting it when it can and at all times bringing instructive opinion to bear from different angles on all important issues so that the people may decide with full knowledge."

Jawaharlal Nehru was one of the earliest in the government to voice his displeasure against the press. He had a dig at editors when addressing the All-India Newspapers Editors Conference in 1952, he said: "Of course, it is hardly proper to use the word 'wise' in connection with newspapers. There is no reason why newspapers should not have at least some small bit of leisured thinking and wisdom hidden away in a corner if not in the leading article always." Nehru asked: "For whom do we want press freedom—for the writer or for the owner to coerce his employee to write against his conscience?" Seven years later, in 1959, in speeches in Chandigarh and Bombay, Nehru again attacked the press, questioning the bonafides of the editors. He said it had been taken for granted that editors of Indian newspapers could not be expected to realise or speak the truth when discussing certain aspects of state policy. He recalled Stanley Baldwin's (British prime minister) remark about newspapers that they enjoyed power without responsibility and said there were no great editorial personalities in India who could stand up to newspaper owners and to advertisers. In another speech in Delhi Nehru described the press as both the product and symbol of private enterprise and editors as its champions against state control and regulation.

N. Raghunathan, well-known journalist, made this comment on Nehru's fulminations against the press: " Mr Nehru has got into a habit of coming down with a heavy hand on the bad boys of the press. But though he is never consciously unfair, the cumulative effect of these periodical fulminations is definitely unfortunate. According to their personal predilections, people may conclude that he is inclined to be intolerant of all criticism or that the press of this country is dominated by the bad boys."

Touch of Irony

There was a touch of irony in Nehru's disparaging remarks for he was the darling of the Indian press both before and after independence. He occupied quite a considerable space in the columns of newspapers. When he was not making speeches, which were reported at length and verbatim in some papers, he was issuing statements about the party, Government and international affairs and these were treated as news of great importance. When he was not speaking or making statements, he wrote articles which were distributed to the national dailies which published them prominently. *The Hindu* wrote: "It is clear that the prime minister looks upon the press more or less as a kind of permanent opposition. He has evidently been surprised by the range and volume of criticism made newspapers of domestic policies initiated by his government and he has brought himself to think that these have been inspired by self-interest. This is pure delusion."

Sardar Vallabhbhai Patel, the strong man of the Congress and number two in the National Government, was also not happy with the status of the press after freedom. In a letter to Nehru in June 1949, he wrote: "There is an absence of understanding both in the press and in the legislature in regard to some of our foremost problems of the day. Yet there can be no stopping their writing on these subjects or making public references."

When the *Times of India* wrote an editorial critical of the government in connection with the escape from house arrest of Mir Laik Ali,ex-prime minister of Hyderabad, in March, 1950,Patel's secretary, Shanker, wrote to K. Gopalaswami, acting editor of the paper: "I saw editorial on Laik Ali's escape. I hope in calmer moments you have realised that you have rushed into print far too soon. That particular news about his keeping a beard is entirely unfounded. He did keep his moustache untrimmed but that you will agree is unlikely to be particularly noticed. I would have liked the press and Parliament to suspend judgement until there was some material to go upon. As it is, both have reacted on sheer speculation even to the extent of involving the I.G. of Police without realising that he is not in a position to defend himself. What is worse, when statements are contradicted or proved untrue, there is no retraction or regret either on the part of the press or on the part of members of Parliament. After all, it is common prudence to allocate responsibility only after the facts have been ascertained."

In another letter on the same incident, Shanker wrote; 'The whole press seems to have reacted to it as if a great national calamity has happened. Escapes of criminals from jails where guards and rules were much more strict,.are not uncommon."

C. Rajagopalachari, another great leader and the last governor-general of India, did not have a good opinion of the Indian press. Campbell Johnson, press attached to Lord Mountbatten, writes in his book, *Mission with Mountbatten* that C.R. told him "that the Indian press had a long way to go before it could achieve its full freedom. Asked what influence it had on Indian politics he said: Very little. The Congress had dominated the political scene and the press instead of providing informed criticism was nothing more than a body of political propagandists. If there was to be a change in the balance of power all that the press would do would be to follow suit and one lot of propagandists would succeed another.' He said he had told an old journalist friend of his in Madras that the essential thing for the Indian press to do was to concentrate first of all on administrative matters rather than on political formulae. Once they began dealing with things which affected the daily lives of the people they would begin to exert a genuine influence. He said he agreed with the view that Indian journalism was much nearer the American in its tendency to outspokenness and overstatement."

C.R. who as home minister, introduced the first press control bill after freedom became the victim of a controversy in the press when his candidature was canvassed for the presidentship of the Indian Republic in 1950. The press disclosed that besides C.R.., Rajendra Prasad, president of the Constituent Assembly, was also a candidate for the prestigious post. The *Lokvani*, a Hindi weekly of Jaipur in Rajasthan, published pictures of C.R. and Rajendra Prasad side by side on the front page along with a story on who was likely to be chosen president Sending a cutting of this report to C.R., a Congressman told him that Hiralal Shastri, prominent Congress leader who later became chief minister, and his followers were canvassing in favour of Prasad and against him.

Sending the letter and cutting to Patel, C.R., who was then governor-general, wrote that he did not want that the Presidency should become the subject matter of "title page propaganda". He added: "If it is true that the *Lokvani* belongs to one of Shastri's group perhaps he may be told that the picture is objectionable so that he may not repeat such stuff." Patel in his reply said that Hiralal Shastri had told him that the editor had taken the idea from the Statesman and there was no intention whatsoever to raise any controversy. C.R. sent him another press cutting, this time from the Bombay weekly, *Blitz*, with the remark: "This cutting seems to be too bad to be ignored." He asked. "Do you think we could induce Rajen Babu to do something to prevent this kind of gossip? The *Blitz* report had said that members of the Constituent

Assembly from the south who were "anxious to keep Rajaji away from Madras politics are canvassing in his favour for the Presidency while a large number of members from the north, who dislike C.R. for being too clever and crafty for an average Congressman, prefer Rajendra Prasad." The report added: "A cold and calculating politician that Rajaji is, he is in the meantime quietly consolidating his position. While pretending that he has only four trunks to pack to quit Government House, he is nevertheless spreading his roots all over the place."

In another letter, C.R. unburdened himself: "It seems as if one cannot have peace as long as one lives. Who wants this governor-generalship or presidentship or deputy prime ministership or anything else? It will not do to be depressed. Otherwise, there is plenty of cause for being thoroughly disgusted with our semi-educated folk."

Patel replying to C.R. said: "With our notions of civil liberties and freedom of the press and many impediments in the way of corrective action, I am afraid it is impossible to reform *Blitz*." Rajendra Prasad, who was approached to contradict the *Blitz* report wrote to Patel that there was nothing for him in the report to contradict "There is no allegation against me." He, however, issued a statement saying: "There is and there can be no question of any rivalry between Rajaji and myself for any post or honour. I would, therefore, warn the public not to be misled by any propaganda of this nature and request all not to indulge in it."

In a letter to Patel in September, 1949, Nehru said there was a deliberate move to keep Rajaji out of the Presidency. He mentioned the name of a newspaper owner and said he was "one of the most active agents in this business." In his reply, Patel said that a large majority seemed opposed to Rajaji. He agreed with Nehru that the newspaper owner mentioned by him was involved in it "I do not know," Patel wrote, "when our people, particularly the press lords and the press will learn to behave with a sense of responsibility and to maintain the dignity of at least the higher offices. Instead, it seems that no person or position is sacred to them."

The Controversy

The whole controversy took an entirely different turn when Rajendra Prasad and Nehru fell out over the issue of presidentship and the former accused the latter of "ignoring him" and condemning him and "all that I have stood for and done during all these years in association with you (Nehru)". Nehru had suggested that Prasad should withdraw in favour of Rajaji. Upset by the tenor of Prasad's letter, Nehru asked Patel to deal with him. Patel wrote to Prasad pacifying him and Prasad apologised to Nehru and the incident was closed. In the event, Rajaji lost the battle and it was Prasad who won.

A speech by Dr. B.R. Ambedkar, law minister, reported in the National Herald in April, 1948, caused concern to Nehru and Patel. According to the report, Ambedkar attacked the Congress Government and particularly Nehru and Patel. Nehru in a letter to Patel drew attention to passages in the speech "which seem very odd to me as coming from a Cabinet minister." Ambedkar in his reply to Nehru and Patel called the press report "perverted" and that "no fair-minded man could have any objection to anything I said in Lucknow." He said his speech was devoted to answering criticism from his followers on (1) why he had been silent ever since the departure of the Cabinet Mission; (2) why he joined the Congress Government; and (3) what he proposed Congress and there was no reference to any member of the government. "The press has never been kind to me. It has always done its best to twist facts and phrases, take them out of their context and pervert the sense of anything I have said. I fear this is what has happened to my speech in Lucknow." Referring to the report in the *National herald,* he said the correspondent could not have distorted his speech in a manner worse than he had done. "I delivered my speech in Hindustani", he said, "which is not my mother tongue. It is, therefore, possible for misreporting and misrepresenting the intention of the speaker. Added to this the press in India has had its knife in me for the last 25 years. Consequently, deliberate perversion of my speeches by the press have occurred many a time."

There was one British journalist in India whose admiration

for Patel bordered on hero worship. He was Ian Stephens, editor of the *Statesman,* who guided the destinies of the British-owned newspaper at a crucial period on the eve of India's independence and after. Campbell Johnson mentions in his book that the viceroy directed that Gandhi should be referred to in court circulars as "Mahatma Gandhi" instead of the usual "Mr Gandhi" after a representation by Stephens. Stephens quit his post as he did not approve of the government's acceptance of the accession of Kashmir to India and as he would have to attack the government on this ground. He believed that Kashmir should have gone to Pakistan and he moved over to Pakistan. He detested Nehru and admired Patel. "It is my belief", he wrote that Patel would have made a better prime minister. He and Rajagopalachari were the Congress party leaders I most admired Both understood the nature of the Muslim problem in India better than Nehru did." Had Patel been chosen, Stephens said, he "would have stayed on contentedly in India longer than I did" because of the policies he believed Patel would have pursued. "Patel was a realist", Stephens said, "with down to earth understanding of how the masses felt. He wasn't half mesmerised by them as Nehru during his brilliant speeches seemed to be." Stephens said: "It's my belief that for his own earthy Hindu reasons Patel wouldn't—had he been prime minister in October, 1947—have seized Kashmir or anyhow in Nehru's or Mountbatten's way. He knew I admired him."

Stephens carried a special dispatch on Patel and his picture on his birthday in October, 1948 in the *Statesman* and also sent him a very affectionate message of greeting. "You are a great man on your public achievements alone", he said, "but also one who in my case at any rate, as I have ventured to mention more than once, inspires—whatever political differences there may be and some will doubtless recur—an unusual glow of personal affection. Prolonged good health and happiness to you."

Thanking him for the greetings and the dispatch in the paper about him, Patel wrote to Stephens: "During all our contacts I have appreciated your frankness as much as you did mine and that is largely responsible for the personal regard which both of us entertain for each other despite political differences which at times divide us. I need hardly assure you, therefore, that I have been deeply touched by the kindness and warmth of the reference about me both in your letter and the *Statesman's* dispatch." Stephens was overwhelmed by the prompt reply and sentiments in it and he wrote back: "Nowhere but in India, I think, do busy ministers and other leading men spare so much time and trouble for outside individuals. You should not have done it. But it was quite remarkably nice of you and I am grateful."

Patel was alert in taking action on disclosure made by the press regarding administration in the states. In December, 1947, the *Indian Nation* of Patna featured a report on its front page with banner headlines that the Governor of Bihar, Jairamdas Daulatram, had resigned because "he refuses to be a silent spectator of the Congress Ministry's misdeeds." The report said that the reason for his decision was that "under his very nose, His Excellency finds widespread corruption, favouritism and muddles and he finds that owing to the Congress Ministry's attitude refusing the governor to have his say, he has to be silent spectator of all misdeeds and bunglings of the ministry."

The chief secretary to the Bihar Government in frantic telegrams to the prime minister and home minister said the government did not know the governor had resigned and for the reasons mentioned in the press report. He added: "Now as a version damaging the reputation of the Ministry has appeared in the press it is very necessary that the government here should know if it is a fact that he has resigned and that too for reasons mentioned in the report." Although Patel in his reply to the chief secretary said there was no truth in the press report regarding the governor's resignation and the reasons given, in a letter to Patel on December 23, the governor did request to be relieved early. Patel assured him that there would be no delay in relieving him.

Earlier in October in the same year there was another report about the Bihar Ministryin the *Free Press Journal* of Bombay. It alleged corruption and profiteering in regard to purchases of molasses under government permits: It said that molasses was bought at a cheap price and sold at 20 to 30 times more than the control price. In a letter to the Bihar Chief Minister, Sri Krishna Sinha, Patel said: "It is amazing that such a thing should have happened in such an unseemly fashion. If the evil is as extensive and as high placed your government could have dealt with the matter drastically before it became public."

Enquiry Committee

Almost the first thing the National Government did after assuming office was to set up a Press Laws Enquiry Committee which submitted its report in May, 1948. It favoured the abolition of laws specially concerning the press and the incorporation of their major provisions in the ordinary laws of the land. It supported the provisions in the Telegraph Act, Post Office Act and Sea Customs Act which provided for interception of messages and literature. It recommended the retention of th: Official Secrets Act and the three sections of the Indian Penal Code, 124-A, 153-A, and 505 dealing with disaffection, communal hatred and tampering with the loyalty of the armed forces. The government brought in the Press (Objectionable Matters) Bill in 1951 to give effect to some of the recommendations of the committee. The Bill repealed the four Acts relating to the press suggested by the committee. It gave power to the government to demand and forfeit security from a newspaper or printing press after a judicial decision. It was provided that a complaint against a paper or printing press had to be made to the'sessions judge who could, after a judicial enquiry with the help of a jury, demand security from the keeper of the press. On failure to deposit the security, the declaration under the Press and Registration of Books Act, 1867, was to be deemed to be cancelled. What distinguished the Bill from the previous press laws was that the judiciary and not the executive was to decide on the necessity for action and the nature of action to be taken. It was explained that the Bill was intended to stop encouragement of violence and sabotage and certain other "grave offences" as also publication of matters of a scurrilous nature. Rajagopalachari, who as home minister, introduced the Bill in Parliament said: "I wish to leave behind me a law that should comprise the essential donts for printed stuff. We cannot afford to let people's minds be poisoned." He hoped that the press would frame its own code of professional ethics and discipline and ask the government for statutory powers to execute its decisions.

N. Raghunathan made this bitter comment on the Bill: "The Britisher at his worst did not dream of consigning the press perpetually to the status of a prisoner on parole. It was left to the Mahatma's understudy to turn Rousseau's dictum upside down and say that the press was everywhere bom in chains and in India it must continue to wear a good few of them for its own good. The luxury of a free press is not for us. Everyone of the home minister's specious pleas for muzzling the press was in an earlier day denounced by him and his fellow paladins as an affront to common sense and a sin against the light. The sabotage that the August patriots so easily reconciled with their non-violent consciences owed nothing to the instigation of the press; still it did help them to climb to power. And is if not the most natural thing in the world to kick the ladder by which you rose?" The Bill which became law was allowed to lapse in 1956.

Press Commission

A Press Commission was appointed in September, 1952 under the chairmanship of Justice Rajadhyaksha. Its terms of reference included the state of the press, working conditions, of journalists' freedom of the press and machinery for ensuring high standards of journalism. The commission, which submitted its report in 1954, recommended the establishment of a Press Council whose objects should be (1) to safeguard the freedom of the press and help the press to maintain its independence; (2) to censure objectionable types of journalistic conduct and by all other possible means to build up a code in accordance with the highest professional standards; (3) to keep under review any development likely to restrict the supply and dissemination of news of public interest and importance; (4) to encourage the growth of a sense of responsibility and of public service among those engaged in the profession of journalism; (5) to study the development in the press which may tend towards concentration or monopoly and, if necessary, to suggest remedies therefore; (6) to publish reports, at least once a year, recording its work and reviewing the performance of the press, its development and the factors affecting them; (7) to improve methods of recruitment, education and training for the profession by the creation of suitable agencies for the purpose such as a Press Institute.

The commission recommended the appointment of a press registrar who would keep a close watch on the circulation of newspapers and if he came to the conclusion that in a particular area or language, a monopoly had developed he was to bring it to the notice of the Press Council who would conduct an investigation into the existence of a monopoly and what measures were necessary, if any, to meet the situation. It suggested the fixing of minimum basic wages for working joumalists, introduction of price page schedule for newspapers and the diffusion of ownership. The commission found a considerable degree of concentration in the ownership of newspapers and warned of the danger that the tendency might develop in the future. The commission stated that outside the British-owned press, which had passed mostly into Indian hands, there were no hard and fast demarcations, no allocation of set duties. Most of the staff had been taken as sub-editors or reporters. Somewhere between editorial staff and the press, there were proof-readers. There was an editor and there were assistant editors. Affluence was rare for newspapers. It was remarkable, said the commission, that so many good men joined the profession, more remarkable that they stayed on showing considerable adaptability. However, the transformation of the newspaper into a business enterprise had begun and the new proprietors were businessmen who did much to straighten out finances. The commission noted the declining status of the editor in the daily newspapers and said that the "growing importance of the economics of production had also contributed to bring about the gradual eclipse of the editor by the manager." To reverse the trend it suggested that the editor be vested with administrative control over his staff, that appointments in the editorial department be made in consultation with him and that all members of the staff be made to realise that they were working "towards a common goal under the leadership of the editor."

The Press Council was established by an Act of Parliament in 1965. Its first president was Justice N. Rajagopala Iyengar, who said the council had a close likeness of the reconstituted British Press Council. It was, however, unique in having statutory authority. Its power to summon and enforce attendance of persons and examine them on oath; to require the discovery and production of documents; to receive evidence on affidavits; and to issue commission for the examination of witnesses or documents were valuable aids in the conduct of investigations. Every inquiry held by the council was deemed to be a judicial proceeding and no suit or other legal proceedings lay against the council or its members in respect of anything done in good faith. The inclusion of members of Parliament on the council, said Rajagopala Iyengar, was a novel feature. The council had 28 members out of whom 20 were nominated by the various newspaper organisations.

The working Journalists Act of 1955 recognised working journalists as industrial workers as recommended by the Press Commission and empowered the government to set up a wage board to fix the minimum wage for journalists. A wage board presided over by H. V. Divatia was appointed and its recommendations were published in May, 1957. The Supreme Court, however, in March, 1958 held the recommendations invalid as they were not based on consideration of capacity to pay. An ordinance was issued in June, 1958, setting up a committee of officials to remove the defects pointed out by the Supreme Court. The committee's report, published in December, 1958, was accepted by the government and its recommendations were passed into law. A press registrar was also appointed. The Newspaper (price and page) Act of 1956 which was passed in accordance with the press commission recommendations and whose object was to regulate prices charged for newspapers in relation to their maximum or minimum number of pages and for the space allotted for advertising matter in relation to their matters was held invalid by the Supreme Court. The court said imposing strictions on the business aspect of a newspaper would amount to an infringement of the freedom of the press.

The Press Council Act was repealed in January, 1976, during

the Emergency and the council was re-established under the Press Council Act of 1978. Some important changes were made in the new Act. A second Press Commission was set up in May 1978, under the chairmanship of Justice P.C. Goswami but Justice Goswami and his colleagues on the commission resigned in January, 1980, with the formation of a new government. The commission was reconstituted in April 1980 under the chairmanship of Justice K.K. Mathew. Its terms of reference included: (1) the role of the press in a developing and democratic society; (2) the present constitutional guarantee with regard to freedom of speech and expression; whether this is adequate to ensure freedom of the press, adequacy and efficacy of the laws, rules and regulations for maintaining this freedom; (3) means of safeguarding the independence of the press against economic and political pressures from proprietors and management; (4) role of the press and the responsibilities it should assume in developmental policies; (5) ownership patterns, management practices and financial structures of the press; their relation to growth, editorial independence and professional integrity; (6) chain newspapers; links with industry, their effect on competition and on the readers' right to objective news and free comments; (7) economics of the newspaper industry.

The commission, in its report submitted in 1982, said: 'The role of the press in a developing and democratic society should neither be that of an adversary nor an ally of government. To be a mindless adversary or an unquestioning ally would be to abdicate judgment. A free press should be, in our view, a constructive critic." The commission felt that the editors should insist "on their right to have the final say in the acceptance or rejection of advertisements, specially those which border on or cross the line between decency and obscenity, legitimate claims for a product or service and the profferring of magical remedies." The editors authority, it said, should extend, not only to the contents of the advertisements but also to the proportion of space devoted to them. It wanted the discontinuance of astrological predictions in newspapers and magazines. It said that the positive role of the press of "bringing together the diverse elements in the nation's life by emphasising those aspects which tend towards unifying the communities is as important as avoidance of objectionable communal or casteist writing. This calls for a sustained campaign to promote the concept of human brotherhood." The commission said that while the press should bring to light and extend support to genuine public grievances, it should oppose unconstitutional methods of agitation. It welcomed the trend towards investigative reporting in so far as it was oriented to social and economic issues. "But the investigative reporter should not give occasion for the criticism of lack of follow-up which is a widespread failing in the Indian Press."

The commission said that a newspaper was essentially a public utility and whatever be the precise form of ownership of newspapers, the exercise of ownership rights had to be subject to some measure of restraint and regulation. Public interest was the criterion that should regulate this activity. The commission said: "The press has a social responsibility and accountability to the public. The theory that the freedom of press knows no restraints is gone." It said in the changed situation, the freedom of the issuer of news alone is not sufficient; the freedom of the consumer must also be protected. It warned that the press should be able to resist not only external pressure but also "inducements which would undermine its independence from within. Journalists should be on guard against the temptation to enjoy favours, whether from government authorities, employers, advertisers or others."

The commission declared that the Press Council, which had functioned for 15 years had "within limits set by the legislation done useful work" and it recommended that the institution should continue. It said the council should be given powers to deny facilities of accreditation for a specified period to those editors or journalists who had been held by the council thrice to have violated the accepted principles of journalistic ethics. Also, that a newspaper would invite "sanction if it comes to the adverse notice of the council thrice, whether by way of disapproval, warning, admonition or censure." The commission said: "We are of the view that it would not be desirable to draw up a code of ethics for newspapers. Such a code could be built up case by case over a period of time."

The commission said: "The Indian press is free, but does not have a wide enough reach and it has an urban and middle class base which limits its contribution towards making the development process more widely participatory." The commission recommended enactment of legislation to curb the influence of foreign money on the press. Under the law, it proposed newspapers would be required to submit their annual accounts to the Press Council giving details of the revenue obtained from advertisements and from foreign sources and names of the top 100 shareholders with their nationality and address. It recommended the amendment of the Press Council Act of 1978 to enable the council to review the quality and adequacy of training facilities for journalists and monitoring of the performance of newspapers by the council in respect of important issues.

Emergency

The declaration of Emergency in June, 1975, by the government of Indira Gandhi came as a shocking blow to the Indian press which was its greatest victim. There was a raging controversy (and it has continued even to this day) whether Indira Gandhi was justified in imposing the Emergency but there was universal condemnation of the muzzling of the press and the drastic action taken against some newspapers. In a letter to a foreign friend in March, 1971, Indira Gandhi had this to say about the Indian press: "Our own press has done everything possible to mislead the public about me personally and about my aims and objectives. Even though everything they had said about my father earlier and then about me in being proved wrong all the time, the columnists continue with their supercilious analyses. The real trouble is that they have no depth or values themselves and do not care to have contact with the people. Their judgment is circumscribed by their own limited experience, so they try to fit people into preconceived and prejudiced forms. Neither my father nor I can fit into any of these."

Describing Indira Gandhi's attitude to the press, her former

Press Adviser, B.G. Verghese said: "She is very shy of the press. At the beginning, I persuaded her to hold a press conference every month. But she gave up this practice after I left. She treats the press conferences as a necessary evil. Instead of using the press as a forum, she is very evasive in her answers and tries to disclose as little as possible. In the game of journalistic hide and seek, Indira Gandhi is usually the winner. Over the years she perfected a technique which enabled her to ward off inquisitive newsmen. She was always on guard with the press and unlike her father rarely allowed herself to be provoked into emotional outbursts. In the early years of prime ministership she was wont to lose her temper and lash out at pressmen who persisted in asking awkward questions. Since then her style had matured and she fielded questions with calm and good humoured self-confidence, silencing interrogators with humorous and cryptic retorts and sometimes turning inconvenient questions back at them.

"The Indian press and especially those controlled by the Opposition had been critical and even abusive about her. But while supporting suggestions that the newspaper industry should be separated from big business, she consistently rejected proposals for nationalising the press. She believed in a free press though she is not much influenced by it. Press criticism might annoy her temporarily but she soon cooled down."

The worst form of pre-censorship was imposed on the press during the Emergency and a paper of the standing of *The Hindu* had to scrap an editorial on the proclamation of the Emergency as the censor refused to permit editorials on the Emergency. The do's and dont's of unimaginative and authoritarian censorship made it almost impossible for the press to function and even factual news and innocuous comments came under the axe. J.N. Sahni wrote: "In the absence of news, the newspapers filled their columns with such vital topics" as the origin of the Ramayana and Mahabharata, the discovery of skull fossils of the ape man and the relative antiquity of Harappa and Mohenjo Daro."

Defending pre-censorship Indira Gandhi told an interviewer: "To have had to impose regulations on newspapers does not make me happy. But some journals had shed all objectivity and independence and allied themselves totally with the opposition front and done everything to spread doom and defeatism. The press was very much against us even before. Our newspapers are very much class oriented....In today's world, it is absolutely essential to eradicate poverty to the greatest possible extent in order just to keep harmony. It can't be done immediately. It can't be done totally and it should be done as much as possible and yet as soon as we bend ourselves to this task and people see we are serious, the full weight of money, economic power, the press, industry, local and foreign combines. They don't say they are against the policy. Everybody says poverty is bad, nevertheless they want to obstruct our going ahead with programmes to eradicate it. Some of the press-here and abroad-are highlighting baseless charges of corruption. We have always looked into such matters and shall deal them strictly."

The pre-censorship was imposed under Rule 48 of the Defence of India Rules "in order to maintain public order." It prohibited all categories of news, comment and rumour relating to the Emergency, to arrests and detentions unless pre-authorised in writing by an "authorised officer" from the Public Information Bureau in Delhi or by the director of information of a state government. Guidelines for the press which were issued said that "in the manner in which information is printed, published or disseminated, there can be an accretion of enormous strength to those who are posing a threat to internal security." The press was called upon for help "in the fulfilment of the primary taks of ridding the nation of the causes of the Emergency; by suppressing news themselves through moderation, particularly in illustration and headlines; by publishing nothing to excite disaffection towards government established by law in India; nothing to promote feelings of enmity between different classes of persons in India or likely to cause the cessation or slowing down of work in any place, not anything objectionable already published in a foreign newspaper, nothing containing false allegations against leaders or denigrating the institution of prime minister; nothing to subvert the functioning of democratic institutions and nothing relating to agitations."

On July 26, 1975 editors received even more detailed instructions according to which "news was not to be published which contributes to the scare and demoralisation about the general situation or public interest in all respects as determined by the Central Government nothing which will contribute even in a remote way to affect or worsen the law and order situation; nothing which is likely to convey the impression of protest or disapproval of governmental measures." These embargoes were extended to cartoons, letters to the editor and captions.

On December 8, 1975, three ordinances were issued banning the publication of "objectionable matter", abolishing the Press Council, and removing the freedom of the press to report proceedings of Parliament. The ordinance relating to publication of objectionable matter was made into a law on January 28, 1976. Among other things it prohibited "inciting any individual or class to disaffection disharmony or ill-will or causing fear or alarm to any section of the public whereby any person may be induced to commit an offence against the state of public tranquillity." They included anything defamatory (whether by word or sign) of the president, vice-president, Speaker of the Lok Sabha, slate governors, the prime minister and all members of the Cabinet of Central and state governments or deemed to be so by them. The law gave wide powers of search and seizure to the police and other petty officials. It provided for the forfeiture of securities of press deposits as safeguard against "objectionable writing". The Press Council was abolished, it was stated, because it had "failed to curb tendentious and provocative writing."

How did the press react to these draconian laws? According to Sahni: "The year 1976 will be specially remembered for a progressive voluntary blackout by the press and a weakened submission by many editors to proprietors and to the establishment in a conspiracy of suppression. What was painful was that the readers did not show lack of interest in the stuff they read and were least concerned about the adulterated food they were being provided with. While a lot will need to be written to explain the voluntary collapse, one may say that all along money has won and the conscience of the pen has lost Reporters see things but the pen does not see. Editors know things but look ignorant. One cannot remember such transition in the behaviour and attitude of the press anywhere, at any time, so willingly and voluntarily achieved.... There have been in the past repression, suppression and brain washing but never a voluntary collapse of the mind, the desire to do more to suppress or eliminate than even demanded, the refusal to stretch censorship even to the end of the permitted teacher. In the long run, people will say, as of the daily meteorological forecasts, what the press publishes is not in accord with what happens." Sahni was bitter that "today most editors are loyal to the establishment as also to the tycoons who control the purse strings. So what we get as a result is a synthetic form of 'popular' opinion, an amalgam of conformism mixed with self-interest of the controlling tycoons."

However, there was at least one newspaper which fought grimly and with determination the assault on the press and became the special target of persecution, and vindictiveness. The *Indian Express,* with its proprietor Ramnath Goenka and editor, V.K. Narasimham wrote a glorious chapter in the battle for the freedom of the press and when the nightmare ended and the press became free again, they were hailed as heroes. All the restrictions on the press were removed when the Janata Government came to power in 1977 and the Indian press once again breathed freedom, never again to lose it. In the words of Justice Grover, president of the Press Council, "The Indian press today is as free as in any other free country in the world".

The freedom of the press is guaranteed in Article 19 (1) of the Constitution which protects freedom of speech and expression. Although the guarantee is not in the same language as in the First Amendment to the Constitution of the United States where press freedom is specifically mentioned, the Supreme Court of India has held that the freedom of the press is included in the concept of freedom of speech and expression. In 1951, the Constitution Act (First Amendment) Provided for reasonable restrictions being imposed on the exercise of press freedom in the interest of the security of the state, friendly relations with foreign states, public order, decency or morality or in relation to contempt of court, defamation or incitement to an offence. By the Constitution Act of 1963 (16th Amendment), the words "sovereignty and integrity of India" were inserted before the words "security of the state."

In the case *Express* Newspapers Vs Union of India the Supreme Court held that freedom of the press was an essential part of the right of freedom of speech and expression. The court also observed in that case that the fundamental right to freedom of speech and expression enshrined in Article 19 (1) (a) of the Constitution was based on the provisions of the First Amendment to the Constitution of the U.S.A. In another case, Romesh Thapar Vs the State of Madras, the Supreme Court held that the freedom of speech and expression included freedom of propagation of ideas and that freedom was ensured by the freedom of circulation. In Brij Bhushan Vs the State of Delhi the court said that the imposition of pre-censorship on a journal was a restriction on the liberty of the press which was an essential part of the right to freedom of speech and expression declared by Article 19 (1) (a).

The Press Commission said the expression "freedom of the press" carried different meanings to different people. Some people stressed the freedom of the editor to decide what should be published in the paper. Some others emphasised the right of the owners to market their publications. The commission said; "The press as a medium of communication is a modern phenomenon. It has immense power to advance or thwart the progress of civilisation. Its freedom can be used to create a brave new world or to bring about universal catastrophe." The commission pointed out that a citizen was entirely dependent on the press for the quality, proportion and extent of the news supply. In such a situation, the exclusive and continuous advocacy of one point of view through the medium of a newspaper which held a monopolistic position was not conducive to the formation of healthy public opinion. "The assumption in a democratic set up is", the commission said, "that the freedom of the press will produce a sufficiently diverse press not only to satisfy the public interest by throwing up a broad spectrum of views but also to fulfil the individual interest by enabling virtually everyone with a distinctive opinion to find some place to express it."

The commission noted that with the revolution in communication technology on the one hand and the newspapers' development of an antipathy to ideas which were opposed to their commercial interest on the other, the operation of a market place of ideas had ceased to exit. "The constitutional issue generally is whether the expression already uttered should be given the shelter of Article 19 (1) (a)."

Revolution in Communication

But what of those ideas which are unacceptable to the media and which do not find access therein? The usual answer is that Article 19 (1) (a) "guarantees freedom of the owner to do as he chooses with his media. This answer stressed the view that a newspaper is emphatically the private property of the owner who sells a manufactured product at his risk; a newspaper owes nothing to the public which grants it no franchise. Thus, the constitutional imperative of free expression becomes the very instrument for repressing competitive ideas. The freedom guaranteed by Article 19(1) (a) must be reviewed in this light." The commission said a realistic view of Article 19 (1) (a) "has to recognise that the right to expression is somewhat thin if it can be exercised only at the sufferance of the managers of mass communication." "Self-censorship by the press," it said, "is practically as great a menace to the freedom of expression as government censorship. The whole point of a free press is that ideas deserving public hearing and the decision as to which ideas deserve that hearing shall not rest solely within the editors and owners.... The widest possible dissemination of information from as many diverse and antagonistic sources, as could be ensured, alone will secure public welfare and the constitutional guarantee of freedom of speech and expression rests on this postulate. Article 19 (1) (a) does not sanction repression of that freedom by private interests including the press."

9

New Trends

Towards the end of the Raj, the name invented by the print media for British rule in India about which they never tire of writing, many nationalist newspapers had become aware of the need to make a little money, not just keep their heads above water. The activities of two organisations, which came into being around that time, bear this out. The establishment of the Indian and Eastern Newspaper Society, IENS, now rechristened as Indian Newspaper Society, INS, and the All India Newspaper Editors Conference, AINEC, had something to do with the economics of newspaper publication although protecting the freedom of the press was the main objective.

Before independence the press in general had a missionary role and saw itself as a powerful instrument in the struggle for India's freedom, excluding the British owned press, which was generally a supporter of foreign rule. Now the missionary role gave way to its role as a major media industry and this should not surprise anyone. In the days of the British, circulations were limited and advertisement revenue was limited still further, except for the British owned press. There was a constant fear of a hefty security being demanded by the alien rulers, which made no secret of its dislike of expression of opinion favouring India's independence. Often the press itself would be confiscated and the editor would find himself behind bars and sent to prison. Now, although there was continuing confrontation with authority in some parts and the press often disapproved of government policies a and actions, including those which directly affected it, there was no fear of a seizure or the establishment being closed down. The press was an industry and like all industries it had a role to play in the nation's life. What is more, it was recognised as a vital pan of the nation and having a duty and a responsibility to shape the emergence of a new nation.

Changing Hands

The major British owned papers, the *Times of India*, the *Pioneer* and the *Mail* changed hands and the *Statesman* followed a little later. The press as an industry developed a common outlook and now the distinctions were not only gone but a new philosophy of running newspapers as successfully as any private business which did not depend on any largesse replaced the old outlook that newspapers were serving a cause and often they were helped out by all kinds of people. The first Press Commission analysed the economics of starting a newspaper and found that the major problems facing the newspaper industry were ;

(i) heavy initial capital expenditure required for starting a newspaper or periodical ;

(ii) the generally inadequate supply of finance ;

(iii) competition from existing papers with substantial financial backing; and,

(iv) low purchasing power of the people.

The first three have been and are as valid today as when the Press Commission studied the problem during 1952-54 but there has been a substantial rise in the purchasing power in the sense that now many more copies of papers are being brought. Earlier extremely low circulations were recorded even by leading papers as we have seen in the previous chapters. Not only the power of consumers to buy newspapers has increased but so has the advertisement support gone up by leaps and bounds in the past few decades. A newspaper needs it to sustain itself.

In 1993-94, the total advertising expenditure through all media was calculated as Rs. 2,687.5 crores out of which the press share, although it has been declining while the share of electronic media is going up was still substantial. It stood at Rs. 1,773.75 crores.

The first Press Commission had estimated the total revenue of the daily press As it then existed at Rs. 5 crores and of the periodical press at Rs. 2 cores making a total of only Rs. 7 crores for the entire press at that time. The study undertaken on its behalf related to the period of 1951. So we find that between 1951 and 1993-94 the growth of the press advertisement revenue has been nothing short of phenomenal, upwards of 250 times the very modest figure in the early years of independence. Allowing for inflation and for the fact the Commission's figure was arrived at after deducting the agency commission of 15 per cent (it is remarkable how this percentage has endured) the growth has been spectacular.

Otherwise such a large number of newspapers would not have seen the light of the day. The circulation revenue figures are not readily available but if they are definitely below the ad revenue, whereas the circulation revenue of the dailies in 1951 was Rs. 6 crores as against an ad revenue of Rs. 5 cores. In places like Delhi where this is a virtual cut-throat competition and a rate war among the English dailies, which have slashed their subscription to Rs. 1.50 from Rs. 2.50 and above, the circulation revenue ratio can only be even more depressed as against the advertisement revenue.

Advertisement revenue naturally provides the where withals of a successful publication venture but the circulation is the basis on which the advertisement rates are determined. The volume of advertising placed with a particular newspaper is decided by the advertising agencies, through which most of the advertising flows, principally on that basis. Only idealists like Mahatma Gandhi could sustain their papers without taking any advertisements at all. Whether it was the *Indian Opinion* brought out by him in 1904 in South Africa in four languages, English, Hindi, Tamil and Gujarati, or the journals he journals he edited and published in India-the *Navjivan* in Gujarati and *Young India* in English, or later the *Hadjan* in English and its Hindi, Gujarati and other versions, he excluded all advertisements. Yet the papers were bought in thousands and the articles were promptly picked up by the news agencies and newspapers. He even said that he wished there would be only a single agency for advertising. "For each province only one advertising medium, not a newspaper, containing innocent, unvarnished notices of things useful for the public. In other words, he visualised advertisements only as a means of informing the public of things available and their prices, not as a means to 'persuade' people to buy and use the products advertised. Annie Beasant, who often opposed Gandhiji because she could not endorse his advocacy of non-cooperation with the foreign rulers, thought of advertisements as 'coarse' and told a friend she had cleared off all coarse advertisements from a "rag" she had bought in Madras, the *Madras standard*, which she ran as *New India* in 1914 as a daily.

Our newspapers may pay a lot of lip service to Gandhiji but it is the advertising agencies to which they look for their bread and butter. The ad men and women are the virtual new messiahs for the press and the beautiful (women) models sponsored by the ad agencies make front page news in the dailies and are featured prominently in the periodicals which go all out to tell us about what they eat and wear, or what they do not eat and wear since the need for slimness dictates a highly regimented diet and the models would rather discard clothes than wear them. The views of advertising agencies and the "creative" people manning them are conveyed to the readers regularly in special stories and features. Likewise, the models are the subject of many an illustrated feature and if some model is photographed in the nude there are wide coverage, often through a story in which the model would be shown as a helpless victim. The readers have to swallow all that.

This may be an example of the lopsided nature of our

journalism, or an aberration; but the fact remains that the advertisement revenue has grown enormous and yet the press is not satisfied. It is rightly worried that the new and popular medium of television might take away the lion's share. Suffice it to say here that the business and management approach of the press in general, replacing the earlier missionary attitude, determines the deference shown to the advertising agencies and their key figures. The glorification of the models is accounted for by commercial considerations, and perhaps more so, by the fact that glamorous models are rated by the media as greater than sports heroes, not to speak of the discredited politicians. The newspapers are now being taken as a high-tech management affair, designed to maximise revenue, in which the editors are useful allies to the extent they pursue editorial and news coverage policies calculated to boost circulation which, in turn, attracts advertising.

The management factor has risen in the affairs of our newspapers in direct proportion to the decline of the position of the editor. For a considerable time, a leading newspaper did not have an editor; it had only resident editors for its different editions, and of course, a plethora of other editors, not an overall editor. The fact that there are a variety of designations for the editor Edhor-in-charge Editor-in-Chief, Chief Editor, Executive Editor-in addition to a Resident Editor is an index of the changes in the position of the editor. How many people can name one or two good editors today ? In the old days, names like M. Chalapathi Rau, C.Y. Chintamani, Motilal Ghosh, Syed Abdullah Brelvi, B.G. Horniman, and a number of others could be reeled off by anyone knowledgeable about current affairs.

The decline, surprisingly began, soon after independence. The first Press Commission had this to say on this subject :

Decline in Editor's Status : There has been a general decline in the status and independence of the editor and this decline is noticeable particularly in the case of daily newspapers. In the past it was quite usual for the majority of the readers to be both aware and conscious of the role played by the editor in the formulation of the views set out in a paper, and it was quite usual to refer to the paper not merely by its name but by the name of the editor..... The position has changed today and we feel that the bulk of the newspaper readers today may be unaware of who is the editor of there newspaper and indifferent to the name that appears in small print on the last page.

Even in this matter some papers put the management chief before the editor. There were several factors responsible for this situation then and they have only multiplied since then. The major factor, of course, is the ascendance of the management, rather than the ownership, which at one time were a factor and a cause of much controversy in Indian public affairs. The ownership pattern has also undergone a change, a material one. There are no longer many newspapers which are owned by large business houses seeking to project their views as in the days of Seth Ramakrishna Dalmia, who bought the Bennett Coleman company in the early years of independence, rather just before it, and acquired control over the *Times of India,* among others. He not only had large business interests like airways, banking, cement and others, but also definite views on cow protection and on how India should be governed. He did not hesitate to air them through his papers.

The late Edatata Narayanan, who was the editor of the patriot until has death, resigned from the *Indian News Chronicle* founded by *Dalmia* (the paper ceased publication but before that it gave birth to the *Times* Delhi edition). Narayanan was News Editor of the paper and he left it because he did not like the Seth using the paper for letting the people know of his urge to ban cow slaughter among other things. Dalmia continued to use the *Times* as vehicle to express his views until he was removed from his key position by his own kith and kin. He said in the *Times* in July 1950 : "The only right course for saving the country from economic collapse, -ending refugee distress, establishing cordial relations with Pakistan, and assuring complete protection to the Muslims in India is to declare India a liberal religious state which is beyond doubt the wish of an overwhelming majority of India's citizens.

Commercial Projects

All that is behind us. Now newspaper ownership is generally operating from behind the *purdah* and the newspaper is viewed more as an enterprise in itself than as a vehicle to air someone's pet views. Except a few instances, like the ' *Hindustan Times* which is owned by one the branches of the house of Birlas or the *Rashtriya Sahara* Hindi daily and its Urdu periodical which are owned by the Sahara group having finance, airlines and other interests, there are hardly any newspapers which can be said to be belonging to an industrial house having other interests in manufacture or business. Now the papers are rather themselves an industry and the management wants to make a complete success of it as a media venture. The old concept of a major industrial group running a newspaper as a side business is gone. The newspapers are themselves big business, sometimes with T.V. and other media interests, as we will see in a later chapter. Even the two instances we have cited are examples more of business ventures rather than an extension of other business interests.

No wonder, therefore, that in the new scheme of things the editor is seen as a cog in the wheel, as one who enhances the circulation of the paper, which, of course, an editor must do, and not as one who has a definite point of view and a personality of his own. If there are no editors whose names we can recall it is also because the papers do not need them. They want editors who can perform the role assigned to them by the management.

It does not mean the paper does not have a point of view, something which distinguishes a daily or periodical from another industrial product, a consumer product like soap, toothpaste or textiles, consumer durables like radio and T.V. sets or machinery to make any of these or to make other machines. Even the management-run papers of today have a point of view, need a the protection of law for their right to freedom of the press, for which they go to court from lime to time, and launch an agitation as they did in 1988 against the Defamation Bill, or rather the journalists working for them came out in the open to fight the measure and defeat it.

The Disputes

The controversies over issues like diffusion of ownership and the price page schedule which cast a shadow over the media scene for years were stilled when it was recognised that in the context which we had in India and the kind of mixed economy we were operating it was futile to carry them on. Almost the entire American press was lined up against President Franklin D. Roosevelt and his New Deal philosophy. But, he used to say, "Give me the front page and you keep the editorials", and the press had to acknowledge the impact of his personality and his policies by letting him have the front pages or more. Likewise, the press has been recognised as an adjunot, an important adjunct, of the state and society and the old controversies have been stilled. The liberalisation of the economy has its most ardent supporters, among the Indian press, the English media and many of the Indian language papers too. On important occasions, however, the press or large sections of it, have trodden a different path. That the print media have on such occasions been off the mark. It is not the privilege of only the Indian press to voice feelings and sentiments, which may be at variance with the deeply felt emotions of the people.

The role of the press in guiding the people and the government in matters affecting the vital interests of the nation has not diminished. The people in power have acknowledged that role more than once and the fact that the newspapers are now run as a business enterprise has not made much difference to the discharge of that function. As we have seen earlier, the management of the papers is also aware that the papers, the product they sell must be seen by the users, the readers, to air acceptable views and seek to give them guidance. Since this is one of the functions of the press that role must also be performed.

The Constitution has conferred on the citizens the vital freedom of expression. The development of the Indian press has always been in the private sector, unlike the electronic media, which have so far been govemment-owned although autonomy is now sought to be conferred on them. The press has thrived in an atmosphere of private enterprise and right or wrong an elaborate structure has emerged with big and medium as well as small newspapers seeking to give information to the readers and expressing views and opinions which may or may not be palatable to the government of, the day, and with advertising agencies and advertisers who have goods to sell and money to spend on advertisements. All this has got to operate within the framework of the law and the government has also to respect the freedom of the media and the people who service them.

The government has thought it wise not to impose on the press facilities or services, which would impinge on its freedom. The advertisement policy and the allocation of newsprint have to a very limited extent been used to help the small and medium papers but in placing classified advertisements with the papers which have the circulation to reach the type of readers who are the targets of the advertisements ground realities have been recognised. Even display advertisements like those relating to income tax and other taxes have to go to the readership where the tax papers could be approached. There are, of course, display ads like those about family planning or teaching people the ways of good citizenship and health care, which must reach the ordinary people through the papers they may be more likely to read. This realism has governed the policy on release of advertisements. Even though some authorities have at times released large advertisements on their achievements, which are often barely concealed subsidies while glorifying some personality or the other, the day-to-day work has to take into account the actual conditions.

Of course, competition must not lead to the extinction of a set of papers, which are seeking to present a different point of view. Within the four corners of the Constitution the growth of different media has to be encouraged so that a hundered flowers may bloom. That we have, as we have seen, some 5,300 active papers and that the circulation has been rapidly rising would indicate that there are forces at work, which are facilitating the emergence of a wide variety of newspapers although those with bigger clouts manage to get more of the cake. The small ones have a right to exist and their growth must not be hampered but they must also prove that the community needs them. There are any numbers of small papers that have garnered enough support from local businesses, and of course, the local authorities have acknowledged their presence by extending to them whatever advertisement support they could justifiably give. In this process the genuine newspapers have to, stand up and be counted so that the papers, which appear only to pocket advertisements from the various authorities, are weeded out.

It is only through its ability to serve the widest possible cross-sections of the people that a newspaper could succeed. To do it, would need good business management and sound editorial guidance so that the news coverage is varied and accurate as well as comprehensive and objective and different points of view are presented and allowed to be expressed. Good business management ensures that the paper withstands competition and becomes acceptable and accessible to the people. It is well produced and worthy of reading. It would also be the task of the management to ensure its viability. But running a good newspaper calls for many skills and in the process if the fittest survive and the weak fall by the wayside we cannot complain much. All these years the effort has been to help the weak along but that has to be within the framework of the Constitution and the choices are somewhat limited.

10

Growth and Promotion

That there has been a remarkable growth of the press in India, the daily as well as periodical press, is quite apparent and it is also supported by statistical information. The first Press Commission, which reported on the state of the press in India, soon after independence in 1954, noted that "there has been a rapid growth in the number and circulation of daily newspapers in the country both in English and in the Indian languages". The commission in paragraph 47 of its report spoke thus of the daily papers but there had been more or less a similar growth in the case of the weeklies and other periodicals too. The commission had special studies done of the circulation of the dailies according to which 330 dailies had a total circulation of 2.5 million copies. There was no organisation of the Registrar of Newspapers, RNI, then in existence (in fact, one of the concrete recommendations of the commission led to the establishment of that office in 1956), the RNI's figures now show a steady trend in subsequent years, and in fact, a fast growth in the recent years.

Rapid Development

This decadal study, except for the latest period, confirms that the Indian press has advanced at a fast pace, considerably faster than the population which, of course, is growing. It also shows that after 1976 the growth has been all the more remarkable and the importance of monthlies in Indian life has somewhat diminished as the dailies and the weeklies have been gaining ground and even fortnightlies, which had a hesitant start, have maintained a fairly high growth rate.

Significantly, India is rapidly approaching the UNESCO norm of ten newspaper copies for 100 persons for the developing nations. There are now more than eight copies per 100 persons although we have to travel a considerable distance before the figure of 10 copies of dailies can become a reality. Even there, the circulation of the daily papers is upwards of 40 per cent of the total for all categories of newspapers. This rising trend is sure to be maintained although the growth of television has put some brakes on the expansion of the press and could become a problem for the newspaper industry in the years to come.

The changing lifestyle of the people affecting the preference for different periodicity of publications is reflected in the slower growth rate of the circulation of monthlies which, in fact, declined after rising steadily until 1986. Curiously, the number of monthlies has been growing gradually, from 2,352 to 7,857 in 1986 and 9,837 in 1993. This would mean that while the publishers put their faith in the monthlies, the readers could not afford to wait for a whole month and instead chose fortnightlies of which there were quite a few attractive ones in different languages. The dailies have maintained their supremacy while the weeklies, which in 1956 were even ahead of the dailies in terms of circulation, have kept up their second position after the daily papers.

The first Press Commission noted that the English press had the highest circulation 697,000 copies for 41 dailies, and the Hindi dailies had the second highest figure of 379,000 copies, (for the year 1952). It expressed the view that while the growth of the Indian language press would continue, the Commission was pessimistic about the prospects for the English Press. In paragraph 61, it stated, "....... it may be said that the English newspapers do not have any considerable scope of adding largely to their circulation." This forecast has been disproved by events, which have not only helped many newspapers to come up and several to spread out in different cities of India, but also their total circulation has gone up substantially. While Hindi had 41.3 percent of the circulation of all newspapers in the country in 1993 (the latest Year for which the RNI's figures are available), the English dailies had 13.3 per cent. The Hindi papers had an aggregate circulations 27.9 million, the second highest for any language was recorded by English.

The reasons are not far to seek. The literacy levels, rising rapidly in the past few years, have accounted for an upsurge in the demand for the Indian language papers, Hindi as well as other languages. On the other hand, the addition to the population of university graduates, the rise in the purchasing power of the people – there are said to be anywhere around 250 million people in India who can buy consumer durables and fast moving consumer articles advertised day in and day out on the TV and who are targeted by the multinationals operating in the country as a result of liberalisation of the economy - and last but not the least, the continuing importance of English in the government and public life are among the factors for the English Press continuing to occupy statistically and otherwise a position of vantage.

The first Press Commission had good reasons perhaps to come to the conclusion that the English Press's days were numbered or a saturation point had been reached. There was the (largely impractical) fifteen-year limit laid down by the founding fathers for English to be replaced by Hindi and perhaps in the early years after independence that was taken seriously. There could be other factors for the somewhat gloomy prediction that the English Press could not expect to add to its circulation. For example, the leading English daily of the day (which still commands a leading position today), the Times of India's Bombay edition, had not added significantly to its January-June 1952 circulation of 87,002 copies. In fact, by July-December 1953 the circulation had actually come down to 86,088 after rising slightly in the two half yearly periods in between.

The commission argued that 14 lakh people had progressed beyond the matriculation stage to intermediate; graduate or diploma level and they were already buying seven lakh copies of the English dailies. It, therefore, drew the conclusion that there was not much scope for the expansion of the circulation of the English dailies. The others who could read a paper and could afford to buy one were already taking Indian language papers. Anyway, things turned out differently and no one had serious misgivings about the continuation and prosperous existence of the English press, certainly not the people who publish the papers.

Twenty-eight years after the first Press Commission had reported, the second one, under Justice K.K. Mathew, submitted its report. The second body had a chequered history. Appointed by the Janata Government which was formed in the wake of the internal Emergency, under Justice P.K. Goswami (like Justice Mathew, a retired judge of the Supreme Court of India), it was replaced by an entirely new body after the Congress (I), under the late Mrs. Indira Gandhi, returned to power at the Centre. The first body was constituted in May 1978 and the second one in June 1980 after the chairman and members of the commission, under Justice Goswami, had resigned as soon as the new government was formed.

The second Press Commission also made a detailed study of the-state of the Indian Press. It found that India had by then the second largest number of dailies in Asia and the fourth in the world after the United States, (Federal Republic of) Germany, and China. The circulation in 1979, according to the RNI report for 1980, covering the operations in 1979, was as much as four times the figure in 1952, 13-29 million as compared with 2.5 million in the case of the weeklies, the circulation went up from 3 million in 1956 (as in the figures quoted earlier) to 12.9 million by 1979, an increase of more than three times. As for the other periodicals the figure was up from 5 million in 1956 to 20 million.

Smooth Growth

This showed considerable progress and it was tempered by the thought that population and literacy had also gone up. Taking the growth of literacy into account, the actual rise in circulation was seven per cent for 1,000 literate persons in the case of the dailies or 57.4 copies in 1979 from 50.4 in 1960. In respect of the weeklies the increase was from 50 to 56.1 copies for 1,000 persons and in the case of the other periodicals the rise was from 80.6 copies to 88.1 for 1,000 literate Indians. The other limitations that the commission noted for the date collected by the RNI were in respect of the number of newspapers actually in publication, as against the number registered with him, and the claims of circulation which could not be checked from year to year, given the modest machinery at the RNI's disposal for such checks and the untrue claims indulged in by many newspapers while the independent ABC's checks were confined to its membership which was small.

Briefly, the point to be made is that the registration of newspapers is not a true index of the existence of a newspaper. The number of newspapers on the list of DAVP (Directorate of Advertising and Visual Publicity) of the Central government, which places advertisements for most of the ministries except the railways, is more realistic. In 1994 that number was 5,300 while those reporting their circulation to the RNI was about 4,000. This would show that even now the old problem is continuing and the newspapers in actual publication are only a sixth or less of the total number of registered papers. But the fact that there is consistency in the number of newspapers which report their circulations and the RNI is able to check the claims of over a 1,000 papers a year now would show that there is much force in the circulation figures compiled by the RNI. The DAVP list covers 5,000 papers. This would atleast mean that about 5,000 papers are being published as the DAVP figures are based on actual scrutiny of the published issues. Thus about 1,000 or more of the 5,300 papers on the DAVP list do not report the circulation figures to the RNI at all, the total number of copies of the newspaper available to the people may, therefore, be even more than the figure of 67.61 million arrived at by the RNI for 1993.

By 1979 as the second Press Commission analysis shows, the Indian language papers were making more headway than the

English papers. The share of the English dailies came down to 22.5 per cent in 1979 as compared with 27.6 in 1952. For the first time, the Hindi press forged ahead of the its English counterpart, Hindi had a 23 per cent share as against 15 per cent in 1952. But by 1979 the prediction of the first Press Commission about the lack of scope for advancement of the English dailies was already proving way off the mark because the figure of copies of English daily newspapers had gone up from 0.697 million to nearly 3 million. For Hindi the growth was from 0.378 million in 1952 to 3.048 million in 1979. Malayalam, Marathi and Gujarati had each recorded more than a million circulation level for their dailies from under two lakhs in 1952 while other major languages had also made substantial progress. (A lakh is equal to 100,000).

Another indicator of the rise of the Indian language press was the number of dailies with individual circulation of above a lakh. In 1960, there were just two dailies to have that distinction and both were English dailies. Now in 1979 of the 30 dailies in that category, as many as 20 were Indian language dailies. The highest circulated daily was also an Indian language paper, the Bengali daily *Ananda Bazar Patrika* from Calcutta, which had a total circulation of 4,03,047 for a single edition daily newspaper. Remarkably the daily enjoys the same position today also (in 1993) but its circulation has been almost unchanged 4,58,104. It occupied the eleventh position among all the dailies but the lack of any significant progress in circulation since 1979 perhaps shows that the new arrivals on the scene, the *Aajkaal* and the *Bartaman* have prevented the *Ananda Bazar* from getting a significant share of the new readership.

The number of English dailies with a circulation of over a lakh had gone up by 1979 to 10 from two in 1960 while there were five each in Hindi and Malayalam with that circulation, three each in Marathi and Gujarati, two in Bengali and one each in Kannada and Tamil.

New Patterns

The RNI reports shows that there are 992 dailies in the country, including a few tribal weeklies, for which circulation data was available. Of them, 73 came in the big category, or those having a circulation of 75,000 or more, 27 mediums, or those with a circulation of more than 25,000 but less than 75,000 and the remaining 682 were small, or those with a circulation of 25,000 of less. Again, the 73 big ones were further sub-divided into those with a circulation of a lakh of copies or more and those between 75,000 and a lakh. Thus there were 45 dailies with a daily circulation of a lakh or more. These along with the other 28 falling between a lakh and the lower limit had a share of 34.5 per cent of the total circulation of all dailies. The medium had a share of 32.9 per cent and the small papers the balance 32.6 per cent.

The figures, quoted above are for 1993, the latest year for which the RNI report of 1994 is available. It showed a growth of 6.2 per cent in the circulation of Indian newspapers over the level registered for 1992 from 63,667,000 to 67,611,000 copies. The number of dailies had declined but their circulations had gone up by 6.84 per cent, perhaps indicating that the rule of survival of the fittest was operating. Between 1984 and 1993, however, the number of dailies had also risen, as much as 132.5 per cent. Again, we can a guess that the growing presence of television was forcing some of the dailies, as between 1992 and 1993, to close down.

No daily paper, not even those with multiple editions, had crossed the million mark, although the *Malayala Manorama weekly* already had achieved that distinction.

Hindi dailies had a 40.9 per cent share of the total circulation of all dailies, with 11,966,000 copies, with English following behind it at a respectable distance. The English dailies had a circulation of 3,849,000 or 13.2 per cent of the total circulation of dailies in all languages. In respect of the number of dailies published, Hindi was in the lead, followed by Urdu, Tamil, English, Marathi, Kannada, and Malayalam. The *Ananda Bazar Patrika,* as we have noted before, continued to occupy the leading position among all dailies followed by the *Times of India,* Bombay edition which had a circulation of 3,70,273, incidentally the highest for any single edition of an English newspaper. But the Malayalam daily, the *Malayala Manorama,* published from five centres, Kottayam, Kozhikode, Kochi, Thriuvananthapuram and Palakkat, held the first position among all dailies with its combined circulation of 7,18,876. The *Times of India,* having five different editions at Bombay, Delhi, Ahmedabad, Bangalore, and Patna, was not far behind with a total combine circulation of 6,41,264.

The third position again went to an Indian language daily, the Hindi *Punjab Kesari,* with three editions at Delhi, Jalandhar and Ambala and a total circulation of 6,13,129. With fifteen editions, the *Indian Express* came fourth, its combined circulation being 5,50,165 copies.

A majority of Indian Newspapers are periodicals of which again the weeklies constitute the largest single category, 11,136 out of 29,597 periodicals. There are 4,571 fortnightlies and 9,837 monthlies and 4,053 periodicals of higher periodicity mainly quarterlies and annuals. As we saw at the start of this chapter, weeklies had a high circulation of 21.38 million, or 31.6 per cent of the total circulations of all newspapers, monthlies accounted for 14.6, fortnightlies 8.6 per cent and the remaining periodicals had 1.6 per cent among them.

The linguistic diversity of India is fairly well known but even the knowledgeable may be surprised to learn that Indian papers are being published in 96 languages, including the eighteen languages listed in the Eighth Schedule of the Constitution and English. The remaining 77 include a large number of tribal languages. The largest populated state of India, Uttar Pradesh, which has a population bigger than that of most of the countries in the world, (139,112,287), naturally accounted for the largest number of newspapers, 5,131 followed by Delhi, with 4,435, Maharashtra 3,614 and West Bengal 2,896. Of the total circulation of all papers published from India, which is 67.61 million, UP claimed 10,355 million. Maharashtra was second with 8,215 and Delhi third with 7,262 million.

There is thus a virtual boom in newspapers and the boom is not only in respect of the number of papers published but also in terms of the readership they enjoy. It is justified by the high circulations achieved by a number of papers and the wide dispersal of the readership. Newspapers coming out of the metropolitan cities have naturally high circulations as they have better access to news at comparatively less cost (a newspaper from Solapur to Maharashtra would have to incur substantial expenditure to station more than one correspondent in Bombay, the state capital and at least one in Delhi, the national capital), more financial resources, better trained staff and other facilities. It is not surprising that the papers coming out of Delhi, Bombay, Calcutta and Madras, had between them a circulation of 20.6 million, or about 30.5 per cent of the total in India. But the point which has been made later in the book would show that much of this circulation is accounted for by sales in the vast hinterland of the neighbouring states and even a few which are somewhat remote. For example, Delhi dailies have either their own vans or those belonging to their contractors which enable them to reach their early morning editions to cities and towns at a distance of 300 to 400 kilometres by these vans or by a relay of the vans. They, of course, compete unequally with the local or regional papers, but then their circulation is not meant entirely, or even substantially for the citizens of the metropolitan cities only.

More Facilities

Transport by road has played a major part in the propagation of the dailies and periodicals. In the early years of the twentieth century and until soon after independence, railway and postal deliveries were the major means of propagation. Gradually the road vans took over and now you have a Delhi, Bombay, Madras or Calcutta paper, or from some state capitals, at your breakfast table, later if you were living 200 km away from there, and a little later if you were 300-400 km away. What the contractors do is to arrange for relays of the vans at a central point where not only the copies meant for that town would be off-loaded for further distribution by bicycle hawkers but a fresh van would cover the areas which thus constitute the hinterland of that town while the van from the metro goes back with some other fare or parcels.

The state capitals (India has 28 states and seven Union

Territories, UT) excluding the four metros, which are also State or UT Capitals, account for 18.6 per cent of the circulation as they have their own papers. Other cities, outsides the state capitals with a population of a lakh or more, have between them 33.5 per cent of the circulation, the highest for any of the four groups of cities. The fourth group covering towns with a population of less than a lakh, had 16.39 per cent of the circulation. The circulation is thus urban oriented but, as we have seen in the case of the four metros, the papers reach out to the far flung areas of the country and the spread of the newspapers can be said to have achieved a fair level of propagation, although the urban bias would still persist. Some of the cities in this third group, that is cities which are over a lakh in population other than the state capitals and from which prominent papers are coming out are :

> Jalandhar in Punjab; Ambala in Haryana; Agra, Meerut, Kanpur, Bareilly, Varanasi and Allahabad in Uttar Pradesh; Ranchi, Jamshedpur; and Dhanbad in Bihar; Siliguri in West Bengal; Jorhat in Assam; Cuttack in Orissa; Vijayawada, Visakhapatnam and Tirupati in Andhra Pradesh; Kottayam, Kochi, Kozikode and Palakkat in Kerala; Coimbatore, Madurai, Salem, Thiruchirapalli and Tirunelveli in Tamil Nadu; Pune, Nasik, Solapur, Kolhapur, Nagpur and Aurangabad in Maharashtra; Baroda, Ahmedabad, Rajkot, Surat and Bhavnagar in Gujarat; and Indore, Gwalior, Raipur and Jabalpur in Madhya Pradesh.

As we will see later in this chapter, the newspaper have spread out far into the interior and there are now district and even tehsil towns from where dailies and other papers are being published.

We have seen earlier the language-wise pattern of the number and circulation of newspapers in the years-1952, 1960, 1970 and 1979.

The spread of the, dailies and other papers to the interior of the country has been noticeable in the past two decades. The factors which contributed to it have been the gradual spread of literacy (the figure for the 1991 census is 52 per cent but since then literacy has spread further in a big way), the gradual rise in the people's purchasing power and the rise in the level of political and general awareness among the population. Combined with those factors was the fact that the papers were now available in district towns and even places like tehsil or taluka headquarters and reaching many of the bigger villages, fairly early in the day in the case of the dailies.

In the late seventies the number of newspapers on the DAVP's list we around 2,300. This has grown almost by leaps and bounds and stands, as we have seen, at 5,300. Once more we have to emphasise that the DAVP list is a good index of the number of papers in actual publication and in need of advertisements. For the small and medium papers which are not getting sufficient private advertising the DAVP advertisements are extremely important. DAVP empanelment also acts as a stepping stone for getting state government and district administration ads and those of the Panchayati Raj institutions. The DAVP is a kind of measuring yard for these other authorities. In several states like Maharashtra it is even laid down that tender notices and other advertisements pertaining to a district must be placed with the district papers or those being published in the district (even as multiple editions). All this has acted as an incentive to the growth of the district papers, dailies as well as weeklies. A few of them could be papers in name only, with no regularity and coming out occasionally to gobble up advertisements, but the large majority are genuine. In the case of the DAVP, of which the author has personal knowledge having been director of the organisation, rigid tests are applied before a paper is empanelled even in the case of the big English dailies.

What to talk of the small and medium papers even many of the big dailies care for DAVP empanelment both as a source of revenue and because DAVP advertisements like recruitment through the Union Public Service Commission (UPSC) and other

Central government agencies are important for attracting readers. These advertisements are released by the DAVP. The weekly appearance of the advertisements is looked forward to by many young men and women and their parents and guardians. Of course, DAVP has its own rates and these are generally lower than the newspapers' own commercial rates. But no discrimination is practised by the organisation in determining the rates according to a set formula. Fairness is generally observed in placement. Some newspapers still prefer to do without these ads because they would not like to practise a double rate system. The *Hindu, Eenadu and India Today* are among them.

Now we come to the publication of dailies and others being undertaken from district towns and those below that category, although the challenge and competition from the chain and multiple edition papers is a powerful disincentive.

Every district town has a newspaper and sometime more than one. This is in addition to the district editions of the big Papers and the circulation, as we have seen, of the leading dailies in the districts from their publication centres in the metropolitan cities, state capitals or major publication centres outside the state capitals which we have noted earlier. For example, in Andhra Pradesh, apart from the Hyderabad or Vijayawada-based papers, like the *Eenadu*, the, *Andhra Jyoti, Udayam, Andhra Prabha,* and the *Andhra Bhoomi,* which also cover the district towns, or have district-specific editions, there are papers like *State Times (T), Gopi Krishna* and the *Eluru Times,* (Telugu) from Eluru, Poddu from Nizamabad, which also appears from Hyderabad, *Praja Por* and *Praja Portam* from Nalgonda, *Warangal Vani* from Warangal, and *Guntur Express* from Guntur.

The major publishing centres in the state, obviously have scope for not only the leading papers coming out from there but also smaller ones. Besides the Telugu papers listed above there are English dailies like the *Hindu, Indian Express,* the indigenous *Deccan Chronicle* and the equally indigenous but slow-moving *Newstime of* the *Eenadu* group, and Urdu dailies like the *Siasat, Munsiff, Rehnuma-e-Deccan* and *Angarey.* The competition from such powerful papers notwithstanding, there are a number of Telugu papers like the *Krishna Patrika* from the twin city of Secunderabad and *Sayamkalam Patrika,* Telugu evening paper, from the capital. The city of Vijayawada, home to most leading Telugu papers, has room for smaller dailies like *Janatha* and *Praiasakthi.* Visakhapatnam, another major newspaper centre in the state, has place for smaller dailies like Vijayabhanu and *Visakha Samacharam* and Vizianagaram is home to *Grameen Vedica.*

Hyderabad has continued to be one of the major publishing centres of Urdu papers. Besides those we have referred to there are smaller ones like the *Aina-e-Hyderabad, Bhagyanagar Observer, Bhagyanagar Times, Haq Baat, Khateeb, Kamander Maheshar, Naveed-e-Deccan, Rehnuma-e-Hind, Saz-e-Deccan, Shan-e-Hind, Siasi Mahaz, Takeed, Tulway Sahir, Voice of Hyderabad,* and *Watan ki Pukar.* Hyderabad also has, an evening English daily like the *Skyline* and a Hindi daily, the *Hindi Milap.* It goes without saying that the district and smaller papers have come up and been appearing over a number of years.

In another major state, Bihar, there are more than 70 dailies including, of course, the major ones like the *Hindustan Times,* the Aj, the *Times of India, Navbharat Times, Sangam, Sada-e-Aam, Azimabad Express* and *Tanzeem* (all urdu), the *Ranchi Express* from Ranchi, *Awaz* from Dhanbad and *Udit Vani* from Jamshedpur in Hindi. There are a number of papers from Muzaffarpur, Samastipur, Bhagalpur, Khagaria, Vaishali and Saharsha and other district towns. In the state there is a tendency for the newspapers to concentrate in the capital city of Patna, although there is good dispersal also. The old established papers like the *Aryavarta* and *Indian Nation* had been left behind in the race by papers coming in from Uttar Pradesh, like the *Aaj, The Times of India, The Navbharat Times* from Delhi and the *Hindustan Times* and its Hindi stablemate the *Hindustan.* They have lately managed to surface again. Bihar has also the distinction of having in Patna a number of important Urdu papers. Besides those there are quite a few published from the state capital and, what is more, there are some Urdu papers coming out of Bhagalpur *(Desh Bidesh),* Muzaffarpur *(Garam Hawa),* Samastipur *(Halate-Bihar)* and others.

In Gujarat, *Bhoomi* has established itself in Jamnagar, besides the *Nohat, Prasaran* has come up in Dohad, *Saurashtra Bhoomi* in Junagadh, *Valsad Times* (Gujarati) from Valsad, and *Naya Padkar* from Anand and *Navnirman* from Surat. These are in addition to the leading papers Iike the *Gujarat Samachar* and *Sandesh* with their editions from Ahmedabad, Baroda, Raikot, Surat and Bombay (in the case of Gujarat Samachar), the *Times of India* and the *Indian Express* along with its Gujarati counterpart, the *Loksatta* and *Jansatta* from Ahmedabad, Baroda and Rajkot, which are now said to have been sold out by the *Express* group to a local concern, the *Gujarati* of Surat, the *Jai Hind* with editions from Rajkot and Ahmedabad and the *Phulchhab* from Rajkot and its sister publication Kutch *Mitra* from Bhuj.

In Karnataka, the main publication centres are Bangalore, Manipal, Dharwar (Hubli), and Belgaum. Apart from major dailies like the *Deccan Herald* and its Kannada counterpart, the *Prajavani*, the *Hindu, Indian Express* and *Times of India* from Bangalore, the *Sanyukta Karnataka* from Hubli as well as Bangalore *Udayavani* from Manipal, and Tarun *Bharat* (Marathi) and *Kannadama* (Kannada) from Belgaum, there are papers coming out from Chitradurga, Betgiri, Mysore, Mangalore, Hassan, Davangere, Bidar and similar places. Bangalore is home to some Urdu papers like the *Pasban* and some Urdu dailies also come out of other places in the state.

In terms of newspaper publication there is nothing to beat Kerala state where both the numbers and circulations of dailies and even weeklies are high. This is largely because of the high literacy rate and the high degree of political awareness among its people and of course, love of the mother tongue Malayalam. We will have occasion to speak of the prominent papers in different languages and states in a later chapter and Kerala's Malayalam papers will have an important place there. Here it would suffice to say that because of the strong identity of leading dailies the *Malayala Manorama, Mathrubhoomi, Kerala, Kaumudi*, and group papers like the *Chandrika, Deshabhimani, Janayugam* and *Deepika*, the growth of smaller papers in the districts has not been noticable.

The additional reason, an important one, for this is that road and water transport in Kerala being widespread most of the towns and villages are accessible from the main publishing centres-Kozhikode, Kottayam, Thiruvananthapuram, Kochi and Palakkat.

But when you come to the Hindi speaking states of Madhya Pradesh, Rajasthan and Uttar Pradesh, you find that the growth of district papers is almost of phenomenal proportions. There are a number of major publishing centres for dailies in MP like the state capital Bhopal, Gwalior, Jabalpur, Raipur, Indore and Bilaspur, from where the Nai *Duniya, Navabharat, Bhaskar, Deshbandhu, Swadesh* and similar papers are being published. The district towns which have their own papers include Ujjain, Sagar, Katni, Korba, Morena, Balaghat, Neemuch, Datia, Ratiam, Satna, Shahdol, Sidhi, Shivpur, Chhatarpur, Ambikapur, Raigarh, Raisen, Guna, Rewa and Mandsaur. Needless to, add that some of these are more than mere district towns, some are not even district headquarters.

In Rajasthan, Jaipur, the state capital, is of course, a major centre of newspaper publication but there is much publishing activity in Jodhpur, Ajmer, Kota, Bikaner and Udaipur also. From here the leading papers of the state, like the *Rajasthan Patrika, Navjyoti, Rashtradoot,* and those which have come from other states to Rajasthan like the *Navbharat Times,* are published. But newspapers have also gradually been coming out of almost all parts of Rajasthan like the towns of Sriganganagar, Sikar, Alwar, Bharatpur, Churu, Bhilwara, Udaipur, Jalore, Bundi, Sawai Madhopur, Dholpur , Nagaur, Banswara, Jhunjhunu, Chittorgarh, Pali, Tonk, Beawar, Hindon, Gangapur, Sirohi, Dungarpur, Hanurnangarh, Jaiselmer and Barmer. What we are talking here is about dailies only which means daily papers are being published from these far flung centres of Rajasthan. Even the major cities of Jaipur, Ajmer, Kota, Jodhpur and Bikaner are home to any number of dailies other than the big ones referred to above. It goes without saying that, as in other states most of these dailies are small in circulation and find the competition with the well established papers an arduous task.

In the country's largest populated state of Uttar Pradesh, Lucknow the state capital, Varanasi, Agra, Kanpur, Bareilly, Allahabad, Gorakhpur and Meerut, are among the main centre of newspaper publication. These are the places from which the leading dailies—*Aaj, Jagran, Amar Ujala, Pioneer, National Herald, Navbharat Times, Northern India Patrika,* Amrit Prabhat and *Swantantra Bharat,* are being brought out. But many more places, including district towns, and even smaller centres, are home to a number of Hindi dailies. These include Sultanpur, Lakhimpur, Kheri, Etawah, Bijnor, Moradabad, Orai, Deoria, Aligarh, Rai Bareilly, Hardwar, Rishikesh, Ghaziabad, Noida (near Delhi), Unnao, Badaun, Ballia, Gonda, Mathura, Hardoi, Azamgarh, Fatehpur, Dehradun, Saharanpur, Jhansi, Basti, Faizabad, Pilibhit, Mirzapur, Mainpuri, Garhwal, Pauri Garhwal, Jaunpur, Muzaffarnagar, Hamirpur, Maharajganj, Azamgarh, Rampur, Mau, Bulandshaher, Banda, Bahraich, Haldwani, Nainital, and Sitapur. Several of these centres have more than one paper and the major centres like Lucknow, Agra and Varanasi have besides the mainline dailies a number of other dailies. UP has several Urdu dailies too and apart from the leading ones like the *Quami Awaz, Siasat, Paigham* from Lucknow and Kanpur, there are a number of Urdu dailies from these and other centres too.

In Punjab, a number of Punjabi papers have come up in different centres and places like Phillaur, Sangrur, Bhatinda, Rajpura, apart from the old established papers like *Ajit* and *Akali Patrika,* Published from Jalandhar, and the *Charhdikala* from Patiala. Punjab is one of the highly developed states in the country and has a network of roads which facilitates the supply of papers from the main centres at Jalandhar, Ludhiana and Patiala apart from Chandigarh. The *Tribune,* which had moved to Ambala after partition from its base at Lahore in Pakistan, ultimately found a permanent home in Chandigarh serving not only the Union Territory but also Punjab as well as Haryana and Himachal Pradesh and to some extent Jammu and Kashmir also. Jalandhar is also the home of the *Hind Samachar* group which branched out from Urdu Journalism into Hindi through its highly successful *Punjab Kesari* and a Punjabi paper, the *Jagbani.*

In Tamil Nadu, the leading Tamil papers, the *Thanthi,* the *Dinakaran, Dinamalar, Dinamani* as well as the comparatively recent ones like the *Malai Malar* and *Malai Murasu,* have spread out in almost all parts of the state from their bases in Madras city. So their network serves the readers throughout the state, apart from some other papers being published from places like Nagarcoil. Madras is of course, the home of the *Hindu* and the *Indian Express* and there is an Urdu paper, the *Musalman,* being published from there which is one of the old dailies in the Urdu language. The first Tamil paper, the *Swadesamitran,* which had a glorious past but had to close down, has recently been revived but it has yet to make its presence felt.

Calcutta was at once time equal to the whole of West Bengal, in terms of newspaper publication at least. Apart from the *Statesman* and the *Telegraph,* it is home to the *Ananda Bazar Patrika* and the late entrants to the field, the successful *Bartaman* and *Aajkaal,* and noted Urdu dailies like the *Azad Hind, Rozana Hind* and *Akkas, Hindi* dailies -like the *Sanmarg* and *Vishwamitra.* There was practically nothing in the rest of the state. But now the situation is somewhat different and papers have come up in towns like Siliguri, Midnapore, Burdwan and Asansol.

In Maharashtra, Bombay has been dominating the life of the state but unlike Calcutta, not to the exclusion of enterprise in the vast hinterland. Major centres like Pune, Nagpur, Nashik, Kolhapur, Aurangabad, Solapur and some others have provided enough support and sustenance to a number of dailies. The *Times of India,* group has in Bombay its flagship, the Bombay edition of the *Times of India,* and there are other important dailies from Bombay, like the *Free Press Journal.* The *Indian Express,* two good eveningers the *Midday* and the *Afternoon Despatch* and *Courier,* leading Marathi papers the *Loksatta, Maharashtra Times, Samna* and the *Navakal,* Gujarati papers like the *Mumbai Samachar,* the *Janmabhoomi* of the Saurashtra Trust, and the *Urdu Times* and *Inqulab* The *Sakai* of Pune has branched out in other centres. The *Kesari* has done, likewise from its Pune base and the *Lokmat* of Nagpur has also expanded.

But journalism has spread far and wise in the state and besides the major centres referred to above new ones have come up in Satara, Dhule, Chandrapur, Alibag, Ahmednagar, Nanded, Malegaon, Amravati, Jalgaon, Akola, Ratnagiri, Latur, Srirampur and Parbhani.

It goes without saying that the dailies which have come up in the smaller centres, other than the metros, state capitals and the bigger cities outsides the capital cities, are mostly in the small category. But their appearance itself is a sign of the growing expansion of newspapers in India, although for them the competition from the newspapers with larger resources and better financial and other management advantages, is too strong to make out a living. What we have talked about here is only the growth of dailies. The list of periodicals, weeklies and others which have come up in the smaller towns is indeed large, larger than the list of dailies.

The Correlationship

The year 1988 proved to be a landmark in the history of Indian journalism. This was the year in which Indian journalism stood up and fought valiantly when it saw the freedom of expression guaranteed under the Constitution under grave threat through the Defamation Bill introduced in Parliament by the Rajiv Gandhi Government. It led to a confrontation with the government which lasted nearly a month and ultimately the press emerged victorious and the government suffered a humiliating defeat, being forced to withdraw the bill.

It all began when the government introduced in the Lok Sabha on August 29, 1988, the Defamation Bill, 1988, said to have been in the making for over a year. It was clear that it was aimed at drastically curtailing the tendency of a section of the press to indulge in defamatory journalism through insinuations and innuendos and in the name of investigative journalism, fling unsubstantiated corruption charges against individuals in the corridors of power or supposedly close to the decision makers in government. After the Bofors, West German submarine and Fairfax scandals broke out there was a rash of so-called investigative stories all pointing the accusing finger at someone or other case to the prime minister having received bribes in the deals. The prime minister himself was not spared and was the target of suspicion and collusion. Two newspapers in the forefront of the exposure of alleged corrupt deals by the government were the *Indian Express* and *The Hindu, The Statesman* joined them later with the story of kickbacks paid to an Indian by a Japanese firm in a deal with the Oil and Natural Gas Commission. Day after day, these papers unearthed new material relating to the deals and put the government and the prime minister in an embarrassing position. A Parliamentary committee was appointed to go into the Bofors deal and find out the truth about the allegations of kickbacks but its report which cleared the government of any malpractice was ridiculed and characterised as partisan by the newspapers and Opposition parties. And the credibility of the government continued to be questioned. There were demands that Rajiv Gandhi should resign and Opposition parties who were vociferous in this were supported by a section of the press. The phenomenon of trial by the press was witnessed in Indian journalism for the first time on a large scale.

Defamation Bill

It was at this stage that the government introduced the Defamation Bill in the Lok Sabha. It seemed strange and inexplicable that it did not occur to the government that leading representatives of the press, journalists associations and other organisations connected with civil liberties should be consulted and their views taken into consideration before legislation on such an important matter was undertaken. Thereby, the government gave room for the accusation that the "draconian" measure was rushed through the Lok Sabha and would have been similarly got through the Rajya Sabha and made into law if an alert press had not risen in a mighty wave of unanimous protest only too gladly supported by the opposition parties.

It was stated in the objects and reasons of the bill that the aim was to make publication of imputations falsely alleging commission of offences by a person as an offence. It was said that those who made such imputations "often have no intention of pursuing the matter any further with the appropriate authorities.

Their only intention appears to be to bring a person's reputation into question." The government felt it necessary to check this tendency "so that freedom of speech which is the very essence of democracy does not degenerate into mere licence." It was, therefore, considered advisable to have a self-contained law on defamation covering both substantive and procedural aspects. The government also claimed that the recommendations of the Law Commission for amendments to sections of the IPC. dealing with defamation and punishment and also of the second Press Commission which suggested amendments to the law of defamation in certain respects had been incorporated in the Bill.

The Bill (a) incorporated the existing provisions of chapter XXI of the I.P.C. with certain amendments thereto recommended by the Law Commission; (b) provided for the punishment for publication in any newspapers or periodical of grossly indecent or scurrilous matter or matter intended for blackmail on the lines of the proposed section 292A in the Indian Penal Code Amendment Bill of 1978 which after having been passed by the Rajya Sabha lapsed on the dissolution of the Lok Sabha; (c) gave effect to certain recommendations of the second Press Commission for protecting unintentional defamation, fair comment and certain types of privileged statements; (d) provided for punishment of imputation falsely alleging commission by any person of an offence under any law for the time being in force and to provide for the trial of such offence by a court of sessions.

The bill defined defamation thus: "Whoever by words either spoken or intended to be read or by signs or by visible representations makes or publishes any imputation concerning any person intending to harm or knowing or having reason to believe that such imputation will harm the reputation of such person is said, except in the cases hereinafter excepted, to defame that person." It was explained that it might amount to defamation to impute anything to a deceased person if the imputation would harm the reputation of that person if living and was intended to be hurtful to the feelings of his family or other near relatives. It might amount to defamation to make an imputation concerning a company or an association or collection of persons as such. An imputation in the form of alternative or expressed ironically might amount to defamation. No imputation is said to harm a person's reputation unless (a) that imputation directly or indirectly in the estimation of others lowers the moral or intellectual character of that person in respect of his caste or his catling or lowers the credit of that person or causes it to be believed that the body of that person is in a loathsome state or in a state generally considered as disgraceful or (b) that imputation exposes directly or indirectly such person to hatred, contempt or ridicule or disparages or causes injury to such person in his trade, business, profession, calling or office.

The Bill provided that the offence of defamation would not be attracted to the imputation of anything which is true concerning any person if it be for the public good that the imputation should be made or published and it is a question of fact as to whether it is for the public good. The expression in good faith of any opinion whatever respecting the conduct of a public servant in the discharge of his public functions or respecting his character so far as his character appears in that conduct and no further also will not attract defamation. Similarly, defamation will not be attracted by any expression in good faith of any opinion whatever respecting the conduct of any person touching any public question and respecting his character so far as his character so appears in that conduct and no further. Also exempted is the publication of a substantially true report of the proceedings of a court or tribune or the result of any such proceedings. Another exception is the expression in good faith of any opinion whatever respecting the merit of any case, civil or criminal, which has been decided by a court or respecting the conduct of any person as a party, witness, or agent in any such case or respecting the character of such person so far as the character appears in that conduct and no further. Other exceptions are: (a) the passing in good faith any censure on the conduct of a person by a person having authority over that other person either conferred by law or arising out of a lawful contract made with that other person in matters to which lawful authority relates; (b) the preferring in good faith of an accusation against any person or against any of those who have lawful authority over that person with respect to the subject matter of the accusation; (c) the imputation on the character of another provided that the imputation is made in good faith for the protection of the interest of the person making it or of any other person or for the public good; (d) the conveying of a caution in good faith to one person against another provided that such caution is intended for the good of the person to whom it is conveyed or of some person in whom the person is interested or for the public good.

The Bill provided punishment in the case of a first offence with imprisonment for a term up to two years or a fine which may extend to Rs. 2,000 or both and in the case of a second or subsequent offence with imprisonment up to five years or with fine which may extend up to Rs. 5,000 or both.

Where the offence has been committed by publishing an imputation in a newspaper, the court convicting the offender may further order that its judgement shall be published in whole or in part in such newspaper and in such manner as it may specify. The cost of such publication shall be recovered from the convicted person as if it were a fine. The Bill provided that where any matter and which is grossly indecent or scurrilous or is intended for blackmail is published in any newspaper or periodical or circular, the author of such matter the printer, publisher and editor of such newspaper, periodical or circular shall, in the case of first offence, be punishable with imprisonment for a term which may extend up to two years or with fine which may go up to Rs. 2000 or with both and in the case of a second or subsequent offence, with imprisonment which may extend up to five years and fine which may go up to Rs. 5,000 or both.

When a person pleads unintentional defamation claiming that the objectionable matter was published innocently and makes an offer of amends, the Bill provided that the offer of amends shall be (a) in writing; (b) expressed to be made for the purposes of the section under which he is charged; (c) affirm that the person who has published the matter in question published the matter innocently in relation to the party aggrieved; (d) include an offer to publish or join in the publication of a suitable correction of matter complained of and a sufficient apology. The correction and apology shall be published in the same manner and with the same prominence as the matter alleged to be defamatory was published.

In action for defamation in respect of any matter consisting partly of allegations of fact and partly of expression of opinion, a defence of fair comment shall not fail by reason only that the truth of every allegation of fact is not proved if having regard to such of the facts alleged or referred in the matter complained of, as are proved, the expression of opinion is fair comment.

Summary Trial

The bill provided for summary trial of offence in a sessions court which could take cognisance of such offence without the case being committed to it upon a complaint in writing by such person, the sessions court shall try the case in accordance with the procedure for trial of a summons case specified in the code and if the court thinks fit the case may be tried in a summary way and the provision of sections 262 to 264 (both inclusive) of the code shall apply to such trial. Every trial shall, as far as possible, be on a day-to-day basis and concluded within a period of three months from the date specified in the notice calling upon the accused to appear before the court

Notwithstanding anything contained in the Act, a person accused of an offence shall not be guilty of the offence if and only if, it is established the imputation made or published by him is true and if it be for the public good that the imputation shall be made or published and it is a question of fact as to whether it is for the public good. The onus of establishing that the imputation is true and it is for the public good shall be on the accused and the prosecution shall have the right to lead evidence in rebuttal. There was provision for appeal to the High Court for a convicted person.

An important provision in the Bill was that "where the accused being the editor, publisher or printer of a newspaper or periodical is prosecuted for an offence under the Defamation Act, 1988, the court shall not dispense with his personal attendance if it is proved that he has refused within a reasonable time to publish any reply of the person against whom any imputation relatable to such offence was made in the same manner and with the same prominence as the imputation was published in that newspaper or periodical. This proviso was to be inserted in modification of sub-section (I) of section 205 of the code in its application to any proceedings in relation to an offence under the Act.

Section 13 in chapter III of the Bill laid down: "Notwithstanding anything contained in chapter II of this Act, whoever by words, either spoken or intended to be read or by sign or by visible representations makes or publishes any imputation falsely alleging that any person has committed an offence or has done or omitted to do any act which amounts to an offence under any law for the time being in force shall, in the case of the first offence, be punishable with imprisonment for a term which shall not be less than one month but which may extend to one year and with fine which may extend up to Rs. 2,000 and, in the case of a second or subsequent offence, with imprisonment for a term which shall not be less than three months but which may extend to two years and with fine which may extend up to Rs. 5,000."

The second Press Commission in its report in 1984 made some recommendations with regard to defamation. The committee suggested that section 4 of the British Defamation Act of 1952 be introduced in India. This section provides that in a case where a publisher establishes that he unintentionally published words complained of and that he exercised all reasonable care in relation to the publication, he may make an offer to the claimant which would include an offer to publish a suitable correction and an apology. If the offer is accepted, proceedings in respect of the publication are barred. If the offer is rejected, the publisher can plead the rejection of the offer as a defence provided he established in addition to his innocence that the offer was made as soon as practicable after the defendant received notice that the words were defamatory of the plaintiff.

Section 6 of the British Defamation Act, 1952 says: "In an action for libel or slander in respect of words consisting partly of allegations of fact and partly of expressions of opinion, a defence of fair comment shall not fail by reason only that the truth of every allegation of fact is not proved if the expression of opinion is fair comment having regard to such of the facts or alleged or referred to in the words complained or as are proved." The commission recommended the adoption of the principle underlying this section in the law of defamation by the enactment of suitable legislation.

The commission also recommended that section 8 of the British Defamation Act be enacted in India after dropping the proviso regarding "any blasphemous or indecent matter". This section provides that a fair and accurate report in any newspaper of proceedings of cases publicly heard before any court exercising judicial authority within the United Kingdom, "shall, if published contemporaneously with such proceedings, be privileged provided that nothing in this section shall authorise the publication of any blasphemous or indecent matter."

Section 500 of the I.P.C. provides that whoever defames another shall be punished with simple imprisonment for a term which may extend to two years or with fine or with both. The commission approved the recommendation of the Law Commission which in its 42nd report suggested the amendment of this provision as follows; (1) Whoever defames another shall be punished with imprisonment of either description for a term which may extend to two years or with fine or with both; (2) where the offence has been committed by publishing an imputation in a newspaper, the court convicting the offender may further order that the judgment shall be published in whole or in part in such newspaper as it may specify, (3) the costs of such publication shall be recoverable from the convicted person as a fine.

The commission recommended that the schedule of the British Defamation Act, 1952, be adopted in India with certain modifications. Part I of the schedule gives statements having qualified privilege without explanation or contradiction and Part II gives statements privileged subject to explanation or contradiction. The entries in the schedule which are privileged without explanation or contradiction relate to fair and accurate report of any proceedings in public of the legislature of any foreign country, of an international organisation of which India is a member or of organisations recognised by the United Nations or of any international conference to which the Government of India sends a representative; of an international court; any court of a foreign country.

The commission discussed the question whether the defendant should prove not only the truth of the allegation but also that the publication was in public interest. In India today, truth is a complete defence to a civil action against defamation. It was represented to the commission that truth should not be a complete defence unless it is accompanied by public interest. The commission, however, saw no reason for any departure from the present position. "Truth alone should continue to be a complete defence."

The commission said unless "there is *a prima facie* case of malice, the magistrate trying a defamation case should dispense with the personal attendance of the accused. It suggested that clause (1) section 205 of Cr. P.C. 1973 be suitably amended to provide that in criminal complaints for defamation, unless there is a *prima facie* case of malice, the magistrate shall dispense with the personal attendance of the accused whenever summons is issued and permit him to appear through a pleader; but the magistrate may not dispense with the personal attendance of the accused where the accused is an editor, publisher or proprietor of a newspaper or periodical if he is satisfied that the accused has unreasonably refused to publish, within a reasonable time, a reply of the complainant to the alleged defamatory publication. The commission added: "We are not, however, proposing any interference with the wide discretion of the magistrate conferred by section 205 (2) to direct personal attendance of the accused at any subsequent stage of the proceedings."

Right of Reply

With regard to the right of reply, the commission recognised the right of a person whose conduct or views have received adverse notice in the contents of a newspaper to defend or explain his position through the columns of that newspaper. In some West European countries, this right has received recognition in the area of defamation. The commission thought it very desirable to provide for a right of reply "as in our country, it is very difficult and cumbersome at present to pursue a case of defamation." It, however, thought "it is not appropriate to lay down that the reply should get the same prominence or display or the same amount of space as the original report. It should be left to the good sense and discretion of the editor as it depends, among other things, on the news fall at a given time." "The purpose of providing a right of reply is that the public should not be misled and should know the real position. Non-publication of a reply may be indicative of malice on the part of the newspaper and the plaintiff can attribute it in defamation proceedings while its publication will be a mitigating factor in the matter of awarding damages for defamation." The commission concluded: "We are of the view that for the present, a right of reply, should be recognised by convention as a part of professional ethics and-complaints alleging denial of the right should be looked into by the Press Council, as it is already doing."

It will be seen that the government had incorporated the commission's proposals in the bill only partially and in two important cases they had gone against the proposals of the commission. These relate to (1) truth alone as defence against defamation charge; and (2) the right of the newspaper accused of defamation to publish the reply of the complainant subject to consideration of space and importance of matter and in the way he deemed fit and it should be recognised by convention as a part of professional ethics.

The Lok Sabha passed the Defamation Bill on August 30, 1988, by a voice vote after the Opposition parties had staged a walk-out protesting against the Bill. The Opposition opposed the imputation of criminal offence in a defamation case calling it aggravated defamation and said-the Bill had been introduced by the government which was under "the shadow of scandals". The Minister of State for Home, P. Chidambaram, who piloted the Bill, refuted the Opposition charges and said the Bill had been brought forward after careful consideration and would, in fact, advance the freedom of the press instead of muzzling it, as claimed by the Opposition. He said the Bill aimed at liberalising the law of defamation, protecting the reputation of individuals and raising the standard of political debate. "I will defend until my death the right of newspapers to publish what is truth", the minister said. Investigation by journalists must lead to facts and not to insinuations and innuendos, he added. Under the country's law and Constitution, he said, the press enjoyed the same kind of rights as the ordinary citizen. Therefore, it should exercise the same restraints as a citizen.

"Publishing matters which are *per se* defamatory is one thing but defaming a person by charging him with a crime is quite another and there must be a law in the country to deal with such offences", Chidambaram said while defending clause 13 in chapter III of the Bill. Referring to the provision in the Bill throwing the onus of proof on the accused, he said that under section 105 of the Indian Evidence Act, the accused claiming "exception" had the onus of providing the exception. He said those who defamed persons by charging them with crimes must stand by their statements and prove them. "Those who take up the sword must be prepared to die by the sword," he said.

The Bill evoked a storm of protest from journalists and leaders of public opinion. *The Hindu* which along with the *Indian Express* led the frontal attack on the Bill, wrote: "Rather than investigate vigorously the instances of wrong doing brought out in the Fairfax, HDW, Bofors and other controversies it (government) has, first by branding the disclosures as the result of a 'destabilisation' plot and then by launching a whitewash of an enquiry by a Parliamentary committee, strengthened the suspicion that there is a great deal to hide. If the Defamation Bill passed in a raging hurry by the Lok Sabha is meant to be a political counter-attack to stem the tide of disclosures, it is an affront to the nation's democratic conscience". *The Hindu* said that despite the government's claim that the Bill was modern and liberal "it is clear that the law of criminal defamation that emerges from it would be much more rigorous than what exists now." The Bill, the paper said, created a special class of offence—the imputation of criminal conduct "that carries the 'exemplary' deterrent of a mandatory minimum punishment of one month's imprisonment for the first offence and a three-month term for subsequent offences. The paper pointed out that under the Bill an editor, publisher or printer would be entitled to exemption from personal appearance in court only if he published the complainant's reply with equal prominence as the original allegation. "It could well be that the editor, considering the reply to be patently false and not meriting publication, may establish that ultimately in court. Yet in the immediate context of seeking exemption from personal appearance he or she would have no option but to publish even a false or frivolous reply". *The Hindu* said: "At a time where there is a rising tide of press, intellectual and in general public opinion in favour of expanding the freedom of information, reducing the role of official secrecy and dismantling archaic provisions in the legal framework relating to the people's right to know, the government has done the nation and the press a major disservice in pushing through a restrictive and backward looking Bill that every section of democratic opinion must oppose and condemn".

The *Indian Express* listed five major objections to the bill (1) it greatly enlarged the definition of what was to be regarded as a defamatory statement. This was now to include any 'imputation (which) exposes directly or indirectly such persons to hatred, contempt or ridicule or disparages or causes injury to such person in his trade business, profession, calling or office; (2) it greatly raised the penalties for the offence... (3) it incorporated into a central law the provision about "grossly indecent or scurrilous" writing which had been universally condemned when it was sought to be introduced in the Bihar Press Bill of 1982; (4) it provided that the trial should begin at the level of sessions court and the court might not only conduct the proceedings in camera, it might try the charges in a "summary way"; (5) it overturned the very principle on which our jurisprudence rests, namely, that the accused is presumed innocent till he is proved guilty. It decreed that the accused shall have to prove that he is innocent.

Arun Shourie wrote: "So extreme is section 13 of the Bill that even if you reproduce what has been said in the legislature of a foreign country, an international organisation, a court in any foreign country, a commission, tribunal or committee, even if you do no more than reproduce accurately an averment in any of these fora to the effect that X or Y has violated a law or failed to do what the law required him to do, you are liable for prosecution. For instance, if you merely reproduce the report of Amnesty International to the effect that the police in Punjab had tortured, someone you would be putting up yourself for prosecution. And you will put yourself just as certainly for prosecution if you report a statement made in, say, the Swedish, German or British Parliament, a Swiss court that such and such Indian had collected money from Bofors, HDW and Westland."

A statement issued by leading editors and senior journalists from all over the country described the Bill "as a gigantic, many-faceted fraud on the public. It is a fraud which has bent Parliamentary procedures and it is a fraud on the support it claims from the reports of the Law Commission and the second Press Commission. It is a desperate measure and only a desperate government weighted under its own guilt could be in need of the protective cover of secrecy it offers." The statement said: "The Bill is intended to close all avenues to the press and the public to point their finger of condemnation at people known to be guilty of corruption and other forms of malfeasance. Such a diabolical measure has no place in a free and democratic society and it must be withdrawn."

An Appeal

In an appeal to the members of the Rajya Sabha which was to pass the Bill to make it law, the Editors Guild of India said that the Bill had "provoked nation-wide protests from all sections of democratic opinion unheard of in the case of any measure brought before Parliament in its entire history." "The demand for its withdrawal has been voiced by journalists of all shades of opinion, including those who are supporters of the ruling party."

All sections of the newspaper industry, journalists, press workers, and proprietors voiced their protest against the Bill in a massive rally on September 5 at the Boat Club in New Delhi. They took a pledge to fight until the Bill was withdrawn. "Let the word go out from here", the pledge said, "to all corners of the country that we cannot and shall not compromise or be cowed down when the freedom of the press is threatened. None however high in the land can take liberties with our fundamental right. And let it be known that we shall fight with all our might if there is any onslaught on our freedom of expression now or later."

As part of their campaign against the Bill the press and news agencies observed a one-day token strike throughout the country on September 7.

The prime minister's reaction to the volley of protests was to express surprise. "We will like them (press) to read the Bill", he said "We are totally convinced that we are proceeding on the right line." On another occasion he said: "The press will have to convince me that the Bill is rubbish. The press should give suggestions."

However, on September 4, Rajiv Gandhi announced that the government would defer introduction of the bill in the Rajya Sabha and would invite suggestions for modifications and improvements to the Bill from the press and the public. For this purpose, a ministerial committee consisting of five Cabinet ministers had been constituted to receive and hear representations. The reply of the Coordination Committee of the press which was leading the agitation against the Bill was to demand total withdrawal of the Bill before there could be a dialogue.

Arun Shourie wrote in the *Indian Express:* "The government doesn't want a dialogue. It wants to break the momentum that is building up against its idiotic Bill. Once it can put out that sections of journalists have already begun talking to it about possible amendments in the Bill, it will be that much more difficult tc sustain the momentum of the protest. So the answer to a man must be as it has been: there is nothing to talk about. Withdraw the Bill."

The prime minister continued to defend the Bill and to insist that he believed in the freedom of the press. Speaking at the golden jubilee celebrations of the *National Herald* in New Delhi on September 9, he said: "Something has broken down in our system of protecting the individual from libellous or defamatory comment. There are serious allegations of moral misconduct against people in high positions. The judicial process takes an inordinately long time. In the meantime, the moral authority of the person suffers damaging public interest. Matters must be resolved quickly one way or another. Either the allegation is proved and the person involved takes the consequences or the man who has made the false allegation suffers punishment under the law. Names and individuals are not important. What is important is the adequacy of the law and of the procedures to deliver justice."

The prime minister said: "Much of the press is today upset with us. We believe the annoyance is caused by a gross misunderstanding of, and misapprehensions about, our motives and intentions." People who believed they had been victimised or defamed, he said, were hardly able to find justice through the medium of the Press Council or the courts. He referred to one case where the court judgement came after 10 years. "But while the judgement was published, the cause of the complaint found no place in the news reports". Rajiv Gandhi said: "But none of this points to any crisis of confidence on our part. Nor is there any cover up going on as alleged. All we have to note is that while much is right with the press, there are some things which are wrong owing to infirmities in our law and in the functioning of the legal system." He said that "something needs to be done to restore the balance between the freedom of the press and the freedom of the individual to seek protection under the law from defamation." He pointed out that the government, the bureaucracy and the judiciary must all strive to be healthy "even if the reality is that there are lapses and sometimes grave lapses at that. Even so, the press should strive for higher standards and self-correcting mechanism. Members of the press are, like the rest of us, only human and subject to the same kind of failings as the rest of us. There is little room for self-righteousness on anyone's part in those matters. Inaccuracies and errors abound in government as in the press. Mistakes are made by the government. Mistakes are made by the press. There is no denying that dishonesty and deceit can sometimes afflict the government. They can also sometimes afflict the press. When the self-correcting mechanisms of the government do not succeed, the press has to sometimes come in to correct the waywardness of the government. Sometimes, when the self-correcting mechanisms of the press do not succeed, the law has to come in to correct the waywardness of the press."

The prime minister renewed his call for dialogue and said he was open to argument and persuasion. "We are ready to listen to those who will talk to us", he said. "We are ready to talk to those who will listen to us". He reaffirmed "our undying conviction on the need for a free press. We are not afraid of criticism. We welcome it, we are not afraid of unfavourable comment, we welcome it We are not afraid of exposures. We welcome exposures that reveal wrong-doing. We welcome investigation that leads to the truth. We welcome criticism and comment, investigation and exposure because a healthy democracy needs a mechanism other than the government itself to act as the rudder which keeps the ship of state on course, to show up programmes and policies which have gone wrong and to unveil any turpitude and malfeasance of individuals or organisations."

"We look upon the freedom of the press," Rajiv Gandhi said, "as essential to the building of our modern nationhood. The freedom of the press for us it an article of faith sanctified by our Constitution, validated by four decades of freedom and indispensable to our future as a nation."

There was, however, no positive response from the journalists to the prime minister's appeal and the agitation for withdrawal of the Bill continued unabated. Journalists wore black badges and walked out of press conferences if the ministers or Congressmen did not give a categorical answer on the question of the withdrawal of the Bill. The All India Newspaper Editors

Conference and the All India Small and Medium Newspapers Federation whose representatives met the ministerial committee set up to receive representations on the Bill, urged the government to withdraw the Bill before starting a dialogue with the press. C.R. Irani, convenor of the National Coordination Committee of the Press and managing director of the *Statesman,* said the prime minister's offer of dialogue was meaningless as he was not taking note of innumerable writings against the Bill. A dialogue in a democratic manner should have taken place before drafting the Bill, he added. The Editors Guild of India said while it would welcome any move for genuine dialogue aimed at strengthening and improving the law with regard to defamation, it felt the "unprincipled-Defamation Bill cannot be a basis for a purposeful dialogue."

Seeing the intensity of feeling against the Bill from all quarters of the country and the arguments marshalled against it by eminent jurists including former Supreme Court judges and, more especially, the rising tide of criticism in the ruling party itself, the government began to have second thoughts on proceeding with the Bill. According to one columnist, the timing of the Bill made the government's motives doubly suspect that "its introduction closely followed exposures in the press of the sordid details of kickbacks in defence and other deals with footprints leading to persons close to the seat of power. The suspicion that the law was intended to be tightened to check further investigation by the press was, therefore, bound to be strong."

On September 22, the prime minister announced the withdrawal of the Bill in view of the misapprehensions and misgivings it had aroused and in view of the concerns expressed by the press and public. The prime minister said in his statement: "The Defamation Bill, 1988, was brought forward to protect the individual from defamatory speeches, writings and actions and to provide adequate and timely redress to the aggrieved. The Bill seeks to codify the existing law on the subject and to take it forward in some areas. Defamation, as defined in the Bill, is not an issue between government and the press, but an issue between individual and individual, between a person aggrieved and a person accused. The Bill attempts to reconcile the rights of an individual with the right to freedom of expression of another. A free press is an integral part of the inner strength and dynamism of our democracy. Without a free press there can be no democracy. The imperishable values of our freedom struggle have gone into the making of the press in India. We uphold this legacy. We shall continue to do so. Our commitment to the freedom of the press is total. We have no intention of curbing, in any way, the freedom of the press. The freedom and rights of the individual are equally sacred. It is this that makes the issue of defamation a serious issue.

The Bill seeks to resolve the issue in accordance with the basic principles of our Constitution and the laws. It has, however, aroused misapprehensions and misgivings. The press and sections of the public have expressed their concern. We are alive to these concerns. We draw inspiration from Mahatma Gandhi, Jawaharlal Nehru and Indira Gandhi who always responded to democratic expression of opinion. We, therefore, offered an unconditional dialogue on the subject. Some organisations and individuals have responded to this offer. We feel, however, that there should be a wider and fuller national debate. In order to facilitate such a debate and in keeping with our heritage and traditions, we have decided not to make the Defamation Bill, 1988, into law. The issue of defamation remains. It is our earnest hope that concerned citizens, jurists and the media will participate in the national debate on the issue of defamation. In course of time, government may, if necessary, create a suitable forum to carry forward the dialogue in a spirit of understanding and cooperation. A solution based on a national consensus will strengthen the institutions of our republic."

Long Battle

With that a month long battle ended in an undoubted victory for the press which despite the government's best efforts had stubbornly and manfully stuck to the stand that they would settle for nothing short of total withdrawal of the Bill. H.K. Dua, editor of the *Hindustan Times,* a normally pro-Establishment daily that had taken a tough line against the Bill, commented: "The government must have realised the folly of making an attempt to steal through Parliament a piece of legislation that sought to deny 80 crore people of this land the right of expression, forgetting that the laws not accepted by the people are not worth the paper they are written on."

The Confrontation

The confrontation between the government and the press, was unprecedented in the annals of Indian journalism alike in its magnitude and in the unparalleled unity displayed by journalists of all hues and shades and opinion. But it was a truce not a peace for the vital issue raised by the government remained unanswered and the press was nowhere near agreeing to look at it and go along with the government in solving it. The deep suspicions of the press about the government's motives and action remained. The government's alienation of the press had gone too far and taken strong roots and it had irretrievably lost the sympathy which it had in abundance when Rajiv Gandhi took over as prime minister three years earlier.

Rajiv Gandhi became the victim of vicious press attacks and calumny when his name was dragged in the controversy over corruption in the Bofors gun deal by "exposures" made by N. Ram and Mrs Chitra Subramanyam of the *Hindu* who published in their paper secret documents which clearly proved that kickbacks had been paid to Indian agents or middlemen and some names were mentioned. What they allegedly disclosed was supplemented by Arun Shourie and his investigators of the Indian Express who sought to establish that the enquiry and findings of the joint Parliamentary Committee (which incidentally was boycotted by the opposition parties in both houses) were an eyewash and the truth had not been told. The Indian Express led the attack on Rajiv Gandhi and its tirade against the Prime Minister reached such a pitch that epithets like "cheat" and "liar" and "corrupt" were freely used. What the press wrote and its disclosures became fodder for the opposition in Parliament who went hammer and tongs at the Rajiv Gandhi Government and in a desperate show of protest resigned in a body from the Lok Sabha. When elections were held for the Lok Sabha in November, 1989 the combined Opposition front which included the National Front, the Bharatiya Janatha Party and the two communist parties used the Bofors deal and Rajiv Gandhi's part in it as their main weapon against the Congress (I).

Election analysts are not agreed on the degree of impact it had on the electorate which while totally rejecting Rajiv Gandhi and the Congress (I) in the Hindi states of the north and in Orissa and West Bengal returned the party with substantial majority in the four southern states. Although the largest single party the Congress (I) did not stake its claim to form a government as it could not gather support from other parties and it was left to the National Front (formed out of five constituent parties, the Janatha Dal, Telugu Desam, Dravida Munnetra Kazhagam, Assam Gana Parishad and Congress (S) which had barely 141 seats to form a minority government with the support of the BJP (which had emerged as the third largest party) and the Leftist Front (including the two communist parties and subsidiary groups) who said they would not join the government. The new Prime Minister, Vishwanath Pratap Singh, who was Finance Minister and then Defence Minister in the Rajiv Gandhi government and had been expelled, from the party for anti-party activities along with two other former ministers, had a cordial reception from the press and became in its eyes the new "Mr Clean". But very soon the press came to see him as weak» indecisive and not competent to tackle problems of such magnitude as those posed by Punjab, Kashmir, Assam and the Ramajanmabhoomi-Babri Masjid controversy. What finally disillusioned the press was the way he handled the Haryana crisis and the state's strong man and also Deputy Prime Minister, Devi Lal. Trouble began when the Chief Minister of Haryana, Om Prakash Chautala, son of Devi Lal, who was contesting a bye-election to the state Assembly from Meham constituency, was accused of being involved in booth capturing and other irregularities and it was widely publicised in the press, which called for his resignation. The matter was raised in Parliament and was the subject of heated exchanges between the treasury benches and the Opposition who were joined by the two allies of the government. At one slage Devi Lal, who defended his son, submitted his resignation from the Cabinet but was persuaded by the Prime Minister to withdraw it Finally on the directive of his party, the Janatha Dal, Chautala resigned as Chief Minister and he was replaced by a nominee of his. Within a month after he was elected to the Assembly in a bye-election from another constituency, Mr Chautala was quietly sworn in as Chief Minister after the incumbent obliged him by resigning his office. This created another furore both in the press and in parliament for the understanding was that Chautala should be cleared of the charges against him in connection with the Meham bye-election before he could take up office again. V.P. Singh's name was brought into the controversy and there were reports in the press of a deal between him and Devi Lal.

Thirteen Ministers of the Union Cabinet resigned in protest against the reinduction of Chautala as Chief Minister and in a dramatic gesture V.P. Singh himself sent in his resignation to the party president since he felt he had lost the confidence of his party and cabinet colleagues. Leaders of the National Front met in New Delhi and persuaded V.P. Singh to withdraw his resignation and Chautala also agreed to step down. The incident had a sequel which led to dramatic developments in which the press played a big part. It all started with Devi Lal writing to the Prime Minister making allegations against two Union Ministers and following it up by sending him a forged letter in V.P. Singh's name written to the President and mentioning a Cabinet Minister's involvement in the Bofors gun deal. Devl Lal also gave an interview to the Illustrated Weekly of India in which he made derogatory remarks about the Prime Minister and some of his Cabinet colleagues. Devi Lal's actions caused widespared resentment and anger in the press and Arun Shourie led the campaign in the *Indian Express* for his dismissal from the cabinet. After many days of cogitation and consultation V.P. Singh decided to sack Devl Lal. The press applauded his action and said he had after all shown he could take firm action when the situation demanded it. But the changed attitude of the press towards V.P. Singh did not however last long. Early in August, 1990 V P. Singh. announced in Parliament that the Government had decided to accept the Mandal

Committee's recommendations on reservation of jobs for backward classes and that 27 per cent of the jobs in the central government and public undertakings would be reserved for the backward classes as specified in the commission's report. The press as a body criticised the decision and against it was also Arun Shourie who led the fight in the *Indian Express*. Day after day he wrote to prove that the Government had committed a blunder in accepting the Mandal proposals and he also published opinions of experts who were associated with the Mandal committee and who had differed with it on its recommendations. The students agitated against the government's decision all over the country except in two or three southern states and at least in one state the army was called out to control violent mobs. There was an epidemic of student suicides by self-immolation. There appeared to be no change in the attitude of V.P. Singh who said he was determined to carry out the reservations. The press was not happy with V. P. Singh but its hostility to him was still not very visible. However it did not expect him to last his full term considering the problems he faced and his growing unpopularity and opposition from his ally, the BJP.

Matters came to a head when the BJP President, L.K. Advani, started on a Rath Yatra from Gujarat, planned to cover North Indian States and ending in Ayodhya in Uttar Pradesh which had been in the centre of the storm surrounding the Ramjanmabhoomi-Babri Masjid controversy. Advani received tumultuous reception in his campaign which also produced communal tension. All efforts of the V.P. Singh Government to persuade Advani to drop the Rath Yatra failed and the climax was reached when the Bihar Government arrested Advani when he entered the state in the course of the Rath Yatra. This was the signal for the BJP to announce withdrawal of its support to the V. P. Singh Government and the fate of the Government was thus sealed. Singh told President Venkataraman he would prove his majority in the Lok Sabha. The Government was, however, defeated on a motion of confidence moved by the Prime Minister on November 7, 1990. The ruling Janata Dal split with 61 members of the party voting against the Government. The breakaway group announced the formation of the Janata Dal (S) under Chandra Sekhar who had been a thorn in the flesh of V.P. Singh.

The President invited leaders of other parties to try to form an alternative Government but all of them, including the Congress (I) which was the largest and main Opposition party, regretted their inability to do so. The Congress (I) however said it would support from outside a Government formed by the breakaway group of the Janata Dal, under the leadership of Chandra Sekhar. This was accepted by the President who appointed Chandra Sekhar as Prime Minister. The press was sceptical about the chances of the survival of the Chandra Sekhar Government and it was said that the Congress leader Rajiv Gandhi would pull the rug from under the feet of Chandra Sekhar any time it suited him. Chandra Sekhar was described as "Prime Minister on daily wages", "Night watchman Prime Minister" and "Prime Minister by proxy". Chandra Sekhar had hardly enough members in his group to take care of all the portfolios of the Government and many of the Cabinet posts remained unfilled. He had to face a multitude of problems, most of them inherited from the previous Government. His position became precarious when the Speaker of the Lok Sabha disqualified eight members of his party including five Ministers under the Anti-Defection law. The Ministers disqualified included the Minister for External Affairs, V.C. Shukla. The Congress (I) insisted that the disqualified Ministers should be relieved of their posts but Chandra Sekhar was unwilling to do so, and thus began the rift between the Government and its principal ally on whose sufferance the Government was being run. The rift widened with the outbreak of the Gulf war and the Congress (I) vehemently criticised the Government's policy with regard to the happenings in the Gulf. The growing differences between the Government and the Congress (I) reached boiling point when US military aircraft operating in the Gulf were given refuelling facilities at Indian airports. The Congress (I) as also other Opposition parties demanded that refuelling facilities should be stopped at once. Chandra Sekhar was forced to request the US Government not to seek refuelling facilities. The climax to the deteriorating relations between Chandra Sekhar and the Congress (I) came when it was disclosed that the Congress President's house was under surveillance by intelligence men of Haryana Government. Enraged Congress (I) members of Parliament boycotted the proceedings of the two Houses of Parliament, placing the life of the Government in jeopardy. The Congress (I) demanded that Chandra Sekhar should dismiss the Haryana Government or at least the Home Minister and also sack Om Prakash Chautala, General Secretary of his party, who was said to be involved in the affair. Chandra Sekhar refused to oblige the Congress (I) and in a dramatic announcement on March 6 1991 in the course of his reply in the Lok Sabha to the motion for vote of thanks to the President said that he was resigning and would recommend to the President to dissolve the Lok Sabha. Chandra Sekhar criticised the Congress (I)'s attempts to pressurise him on various issues and said he was not prepared to put up with it any longer Thus came to an end the four-month-old Government of Chandra Sekhar, who, surprisingly enough, earned the plaudits of the press as a courageous, outspoken man of sincerity who created a good impression as a Prime Minister in the short time he occupied that office. One press comment was: "Chandra Sekhar who began his entry into the South Block as the most hated man ended his tenure astonishing both his friends and foes". The President dissolved the Lok Sabha after it passed without division the vote on account and a constitutional Bill for extension of President's rule in Punjab and ordered elections with the Lok Sabha to be reconstituted by June 5, 1991.

In the elections, the Congress (I) returned to power as the largest single party, but very much short of absolute majority. It was able to secure 226 seats out of 543 for which elections were held. As in the previous election, the party lost heavily in Uttar Pradesh, Bihar and Gujarat, while it did well in the four southern states of Andhra Pradesh, Karnataka, Tamil Nadu and Kerala. While the elections were in progress, the party lost its leader. Rajiv Gandhi, who was brutally assassinated by a woman suicide bomber in May 1991 at Sriperumbadur near Madras in a bomb blast, masterminded by the Liberation Tigers of Tamil Eelam (LTTE), the ethnic militant outfit of Sri Lanka. The nation was stunned and there was a wave of sympathy for the Congress (I), reflected in the improved showing of the Party in states where polling was held later. Opinion polls by leading newspapers and news magazines earlier gave a very gloomy picture about the prospects for Congress (I). It was widely speculated that the election would produce a hung parliament and it proved to be so, but the Congress (I) was in much better shape than the predictions of press soothsayers.

The Bharatiya Janatha Party (BJP) which improved its strength in the Lok Sabha with 117 members emerged as the main Opposition party. The National Front consisting of the Janata Dal, the Left Front and some regional parties accounted for 137 seats. Speculation was on in the press on what President R. Venkataraman would do and which party he would invite to form the government. At that stage the Congress (I) Parliamentary Party had not yet elected its leader and this led to wild rumours and fanciful stones in the press with much space and energy devoted in highlighting the power struggle within the party for leadership. Sonia Gandhi, wife of the slain leader, occupied the centre stage for some time and the question that went out in bold headlines from the front page of every newspaper was "Will She? or Will She Not?" i.e., Will Sonia Gandhi accept the mantle of leadership left tragically vacant by her husband? This issue became a non-starter when the lady declined to accept the leadership offered to her on a silver platter by the highest policy making body of the party, the Congress (I) Working Committee. The print media later turned its guns on the battle royal for the leadership among three contenders, viz., P.V. Narasimha Rao, Arjun Singh and Sharad Pawar. It was a field day for the press with soaring circulations following the publication of stories of intrigues, manoeuvrings and compromises in the party ranks to gain the upper hand. When it became certain that Narasimha Rao had won the battle with the retirement of the two candidates from the contest (temporarily some papers said), the print media began to evaluate his plus and minus points. It wondered how long he would last with Arjun Singh sulking in the wings and Pawar ever posing a threat.

It was in these circumstances that the President invited Narasimha Rao, who had been unanimously elected leader of the

Congress (I) Parliamentary Party to form the government which he accepted. The President asked him to prove his majority in the Parliament and Narasimha Rao was able to do so with the help of the party ally, the All India Anna Dravida Munnetra Kazhagam (AIADMK) and splinter groups. Unfortunately, his government remained in minority with the majority opposition in good strength to exploit every opportunity to embarrass and topple it. Its guide and friend was the *Indian Express* which timed its expose stories to coincide with the sessions of Parliament, and the opposition parties did not fail to respond.

The Narasimha Rao government opened its innings with an economic liberalisation programme that saved the country from its dire economic straits. The policy was implemented in stages and the ultimate aim was to reduce government's economic activity and throw it open to the private sector. Foreign investment was encouraged on a massive scale and the gates were thrown open in select sectors to the multinationals. While the press generally welcomed the liberalisation policy, a section fought against it, alleging that the country had been sold to the international financial institutions. The Finance Minister, Dr. Manmohan Singh, was the target of attack for his pro-Westem policies and capitalist tilt to the economy. When there were inflationary pressures and a mounting budget deficit, the anti-Manmohan Singh papers cried: "We told you so".

Plethora of Problems

Narasimha Rao faced a plethora of problems, most of which seemed insoluble; he became the butt of ridicule. Uncomplimentary epithets were hurled at him in the dailies and periodicals. He was described as indecisive, incompetent and unsuited to the job. They said he might not last long and his days were numbered. At the same time, they overplayed the dissidence activities in the party by exaggerated accounts of trivial incidents. They even claimed that Arjun Singh was on the warpath to usurp power from Narasimha Rao.

Whether it was the Ramjanmabhoomi issue (which led to the demolition of the 400-year-old Babri Masjid in Ayodhya in Uttar

Pradesh), the security scandal and the aftermath of the Joint Parliamentary Committee's report and the Kashmir and Punjab issues, Narasimha Rao remained unperturbed. He worked slowly and methodically to deal with them, achieving a measure of success in Punjab where terrorism was finally wiped out and peace and security was restored. The economy was looking up and the country was saved from the brink of disaster, but the press was slow or dead set not to recognise his no mean achievements. When Harshad Mehta, the prime accused in the security scandal, dropped his bombshell at a press conference in Bombay, flanked on either side by the eminent lawyer Ram Jetmalani and his son Mahesh Jetmalani, that he had presented a suitcase stuffed with wads of currency notes running into a crore to the Prime Minister Narasimha Rao at his residence in New Delhi, most newspapers carried the news with banner headlines. Some of them called for a commission of inquiry, asking the Prime Minister to clear himself of the accusation. By equating the man holding the highest office in the land with a stock broker, accused of swindling banks of crores of rupees and whose statements should be suspect the press was less than just and fair to Narasimha Rao. The very next day Narasimha Rao issued a denial, but the press joining the opposition outcry was not convinced that the Prime Minister was speaking the truth. The news magazines sent their investigative reporters to find out whether the Prime Minister was at his residence during the time when Mehta handed the suitcase to him and analyse the engagements for the day on duty charts of the security men, to discover if there were any loopholes that might cast a shadow on the denial from the P.M. One columnist even wrote in a well known news magazine that public at large were convinced of some shady deal. It was a sordid business and did not bring credit to the sobriety and maturity of the print media. The matter finally fizzled out with the CBI saying that there was nothing to investigate since no case was registered. The Harshad Mehta affair was soon forgotten and the story of the alleged bribe remained a mystery uncovered.

The press had soon to revise its views on the Prime Minister. The success of Congress (I) in the mid-term elections to state assemblies and the party's unwavering faith in the leadership of Narasimha Rao as demonstrated at the meetings of the All India Congress (I) Committee; besides the respect and regard he had in international capitals brought a remarkable change in the image of the Prime Minister Narasimha Rao presented to its readers. There was grudging respect for his ability and judgement to tackle difficult situations and even his so called indecisiveness and procrastination were seen as virtues. That Narasimha Rao was able to convert his minority government into one enjoying comfortable majority due to accretions to his party was another feather in his cap and improved his standing with the press. But one had the impression that he was indifferent to what the press thought or wrote about him. That he did not go out of his way to cultivate the press was evident from the fact that he did not hold a single press conference in the capital after his assumption of office. He was supremely confident about his full term in office and the press, rather belatedly came to believe that fact.

In the latter part of 1994, the print media found two new heroes a suspended Bombay municipal corporation official, G.R. Khaimar, who hurled charges of corruption and collusion with the underworld dons against the Maharashtra Chief Minister, Sharad Pawar and the other the Chief Election Commissioner, T.N. Seshan, who posed problems for central and state governments with his crusade against electoral malpractices. The press lionised Khairnar and his speeches were lead stories in Bombay newspapers. It was again a case of pandering to sensationalism without concern for ethics and morality. Khairnar achieved the maximum publicity and some of the elites of Bombay even pledged their support to him. But Khairnar who said at a meeting that Sharad Pawar incited the communal riots of 1993 in Bombay could not substantiate his accusations against the Chief Minister when asked to do so. He lost credibility and the press too had lost interest in him.

But T.N. Seshan still survives as a hero and he continues to be good "copy" wherever he speaks and whatever he does. There is no doubt that Seshan has put the fear of God in the minds of politicians and his efforts to cleanse the electoral arena are bound to yield results. He has the full support of the print media which revels in highlighting his sermons and homilies to governments and the politicians alike.

Narasihma Rao served his full five-year term in office, a remarkable feat for a government which started its reign without a majority and ended up in full possession of the Lok Sabha. As the decks were being cleared for elections to the 11th Lok Sabha the press while giving him credit for the economic reforms and the restoration of peace in Punjab painted a gloomy picture for him and the Congress (I) in the elections. Opinion polls conducted by newspapers and news magazines predicted a hung Parliament with the Congress (I) being the worst sufferer. And so it proved.

Even otherwise the Congress (1) was not in good shape and on the eve of elections several leading Congress politicians were involved in corruption scandals and as tainted members of the party they were denied ticket to contest the elections. Many of them left the party and formed rival groups.

What began as one scandal, the Jain Hawala multi-crore scandal in which politicians of major political parties were alleged to have received bribes from a Hawala dealer, soon blossomed into many more scandals involving leading politicians. In fact 1996 became a year of scandals with an all time record.

Narasihma Rao did not escape this avalanche of wrong doing. He was the main accused in three of them. One of them, St. Kitts forgery case which began in the late eighties and lost its way was reactivated through a public litigation petition in the Supreme Court. In another the JMM (Jharkand Mukti Morcha) bribery case Narasihma Rao was accused along with some of his partymen of having conspired to bribe four members of Parliament belonging to the Jharkand Mukti Morcha to vote against the no confidence motion against the government in the Lok Sabha and save the Narasihma Rao government. In the third case Narasihma Rao was accused of cheating a London based Indian in collusion with one Chandra Swami after promising to get him a government contract in India and being paid a big sum for the favour. Narasihma Rao's relatives were involved in another scandal, the urea import case in which several crores of rupees were lost by the government.

Another major scandal was the Bihar fodder scam in which Animal Husbandry department officials swindled the government of vast sums of money. Leading politicians were also allegedly involved in this and one of the persons interrogated by the Central Bureau of Investigation was the state's Chief Minister, Laloo Prasad Yadav.

Judiciary, the Hero

The hero in all these cases and investigations was not the press as one might have expected but unbelievably the judiciary, the Supreme Court, High Court and the subordinate courts. It is they who goaded the CBI to investigate and show results and they were monitoring the cases all the time. The press was robbed of its investigative role by this judicial activism and remained a spectator and recorder of events and proceedings in court. The magistrates in the Delhi courts became its heroes and one of them created history by launching a vitriolic attack on politics and politicians which were later expunged by the Delhi High Court. But the press which loves sensationalism had much to write about the political scene. It revelled in gossip and speculative reports on the power struggle in the Congress (I) which lost the 1996 general election yielding place to the Bharatiya Janta Party as the largest single party in the Lok Sabha. Its cup was overflowing when Narasihma Rao was up to the neck in criminal cases and was forced to give up the presidentship of the party and later of the leadership of the Congress Parliamentary Party. Narasihma Rao vanished from the front pages and was given a paragraph or two in the inside pages when he struggled hard to get bail and not be thrown into prison. But not before as Congress President he lent support to the United Front government from outside.

The United Front government was a coalition of 13 parties-some of them one-man and two-man parties-mainly consisting of regional parties and the four leftist parties. Its total strength in the

Lok Sabha was less than 180 and it was given the chance to form a government after the BJP government with Atal Behari Vajpayee as Prime Minister failed to get a vote of confidence in the Lok Sabha and resigned after being in office for less than two weeks. H.D. Deve Gowda, who headed the U.F. government succeeded in getting a vote of confidence, as required by the President, with the support of the Congress (I) which had 140 members in the house.

Prime Minister Deve Gowda, who called himself a "humble farmer" and who had been catapulted to the top post of government through sheer accident, was allergic to the press which returned the compliment. In the succeeding 10 months of his being in office the relations between the Prime Minister and the Fourth Estate were anything but smooth. The press lampooned him and published pictures showing him dozing in Parliament and at important public functions. They called him "Prime Minister of Karnataka", "Chief Minister of India", ridiculing his frequent trips to his home state of Karnataka (where he was Chief Minister before he came to the Centre) and highlighting his frailties and lapses. In their unexplained and unjustified prejudice against him they lost sight of some of his achievements in foreign policy and in the economic sphere during the very short period he held the reign of government. When he resigned on April 11,1997 after the rejection by the Lok Sabha of his motion of confidence which became inevitable following the withdrawal of support by the Congress (I) the Press did not shed a tear on his exit.

However it turned its guns on the Congress President, Sitaram Kesri who with the full support of his Working Committee, had written to the President withdrawing his party's support to the Deve Gowda government. In an unprecedented unanimity it accused him of bringing down the government to further his personal ambition to grab power. It wanted to know what were the reasons, the provocation, which led to his precipitate action. There was no response from the Congress President who had the solid backing of his party in Parliament but from the sequence of events later it became clear that it was personal antagonism to Deve Gowda that was responsible for what was widely described as "a hasty step".

The Debate

Even as the debate on the fall of the United Front government was going on the Congress (I) announced it would support another U.F. government if it changed its present leader, Deve Gowda and elected another. At first there was resistance to this demand from the U.F. constituents and the Left parties but the universal fear of a mid term poll ultimately forced the U.F. partners to agree to drop Deve Gowda. The Congress President, true to the party's pledge, wrote to the President offering to support the U.F. to form a government with a new leader. The U.F. leaders plunged into the task of finding a new leader. This was not easy as the claimants to .the post were many and threw the field open to the press to indulge in speculative reports on who will be the winner.

Meanwhile in the deep south, in the state of Tamil Nadu a whole host of former ministers, including the former Chief Minister, Jayalalitha were put behind bars on charges of corruption or for offences under the Foreign Exchange Regulation Act by M. Karunanidhi's D.M.K. government and central agencies. Jayalalitha spent nearly a month in prison before she was released on bail and many of her former colleagues could not secure bail. The variety of offences with which leading lights of the previous AIADMK government and prominent officials were charged and the money which changed hands were staggering and the press was clearly taken unawares by the magnitude of the crimes alleged although the undesirable activities of Jayalalitha's associate, Sasikala, had been exposed by some newspapers and magazines.

The press however was not too unkind to Jayalalitha. It continued to give ample space in its columns to her statements and speeches on the policies and actions of the DMK government and its Chief Minister and gave the impression that it thought that Jayalalitha was still a force to reckon with in the state and national politics. This was seen when she created a storm of protest at the publication of a group photograph by the Indian Express, its sister Tamil daily, Dinamani and a Tamil news magazine allegedly showing Jayalalitha with Dhanu, the assassin of Rajiv Gandhi and Sivarasan the mastermind behind the assassination. It later turned out that the photograph was taken in 1989 and the persons identified as Dhanu and Sivarasan were in fact AIADMK functionaries living in Hosur in Dharmapuri district. Jayalalitha showed them to pressmen at a press conference and demanded a CBI inquiry into the incident. The Indian Express published her denial prominently but did not offer any explanation or apology beyond saying it meant no offence to anyone. But the question remained. Who supplied the photograph to the press and what was the provocation? It was clear beyond doubt that whoever gave the eight year old photograph intended to embarrass the AIADMK leader and the Indian Express fell into the trap. It is a matter for the Press Council to decide if its conduct was ethical and it did not violate the canons of decency and fair play.

The emergence of Inder Kumar Gujral as India's 12th Prime Minister on April 21,1997 after two weeks of political crisis which followed the exit of the Deve Gowda government was widely welcomed by the media. Gujral, who was External Affairs Minister in the out-going government is a non-controversial politician who has achieved an international stature as a diplomat and statesman with whom it was a pleasure to do business. He has rich administrative talent and experience having served in various governments going back to the days of Indira Gandhi. But whether he could handle a conglomerate of 13 parties with pulls and pressures and with the supporting Congress party breathing down his neck all the time from outside is a question which has no easy answer and time alone will provide it.

The interaction between the Press and the politicians is something unique to India. Nowhere in the world does the press devote so much of its space, time and energy to the indoings and outpourings, their plots, intrigues, frauds and manipulations as in India. The politicians do not resent it and in fact most of them use the press to serve their own ends, the press becomes a sort of post office for them which is only too willing to act as a forum to put up their show. It has been so in the years following independence and one fears so it will be in the foreseeable future. The press must get rid of its obsession with politicians and realise that there are many more important, vital issues and challenges to be faced for the country's economic and cultural progress and freedom from poverty and illiteracy.

The years between 1997 and 2000 were a period of political instability and economic recession. Two governments fell and there were two general elections. In between India exploded a nuclear bomb conducting two tests and proclaiming to the world that it had joined the nuclear club of the world and that it was now a nuclear weapon state. The country also went through a minor war on the Kargil front in Kashmir involving the Pakistan Army. The media had its hands full with speculative stories about political happenings and international reaction to India's emergence as a nuclear power and of Pakistan following suit.

In the political field it found a new dominant charismatic leader from the South, a woman called Jayalalitha who had been Chief Minister of Tamil Nadu for five years and was in the opposition fighting a grim battle against the corruption charges framed against her by the ruling D.M.K. Government. The Bharatiya Janata Party which was the single largest party after the general election which followed the fall of the United Front Government headed by I.K. Gujral was forced to seek the support of Jayalalitha's AIADMK Party in the Lok Sabha. The BJP formed a coalition government of more than 14 parties and Jayalalitha was at its throat from day one like Damocles Sword keeping it on tenterhooks all the time. Newspapers reported in detail and with sadistic pleasure about the BJP leaders going to her on bended knees to please her and crave for her continued support. The press speculated that Jayalalitha's demand was that the Centre should dismiss the DMK Government and also have the cases against her withdrawn. They said that the Vajpayee Government was firm in refusing to accede to the demand and this led to threats by Jayalalitha to withdraw her party's support to the government. The media ran stories envisaging the fall of the BJP Government any moment. But Jayalalitha was not in a hurry and she prolonged the agony as long as she could. And when the announcement of withdrawal of support came at last no one was surprised. The press now turned to find out what Jayalalitha would do next. A tea party given by a party leader in her front in her honour to which Opposition leaders, including the Congress (I) President, Mrs Sonia Gandhi, were invited assumed political significance and the press and the electronic media went crazy talking about it.

There were all kinds of stories connecting Jayalalitha and Sonia Gandhi. It turned out that the Congress President was attempting to form a government with the support of the AIADMK and other Opposition groups. Sonia Gandhi met the President and handed over a list of her supporters which, however, later turned out to be based on false expectations. The whole move fizzled out and resulted in the Lok Sabha being dissolved and another general election ordered. This time the BJP had a new partner from the South, the DMK which had been the cause for the resignation of the Gujral Government of which it was a constituent. The BJP managed to cobble together 24 parties including the DMK to fight the elections under the label of the National Democratic Alliance (NDA). The NDA in the elections held in 1999 secured a comfortable majority and formed the government. The media was sceptical about the longevity of the new coalition government and the crises faced by the Vajpayee Government in less than a year of its coming into office seemed to justify their fears. In forming a coalition with its allies the BJP had to put in cold storage its declared objectives like *Hindutva* and opt for a common minimum programme which its allies could accept. The Opposition, however, was not convinced that the BJP had really abandoned its programme and this misgiving was shared by the media.

Opposition and Media

The Opposition and the media saw their apprehensions coming true when the RSS and its sister organisations launched a campaign against Christian missionaries and churches in Gujarat and later the murder of an Australian missionary and his two sons in Orissa. And then came the Gujaraṭ Government's order lifting the ban on Government employees taking part in RSS activities. The Opposition parties and the media saw this as the BJP's hidden agenda coming into the open and this led to the

Opposition parties stalling proceedings of Parliament to bring pressure on the government to have the Gujarat Government withdraw the offending order. The government was forced to take action.

The BJP gave rise to another controversy when the Government decided to appoint a high-powered commission to review the Constitution. The pages of the newspapers and magazines and the electronic media were full of arguments for and against tampering with the Constitution but the government unmindful of the protests stuck to its decision. The BJP coalition government had also its moments of glory and appreciation in the press. This happened in two occasions once early in 1999 when Prime Minister Vajpayee went to Lahore in a bus to symbolise friendship with Pakistan and later signed the historic Lahore Declaration along with his Pakistani counterpart, Nawaz Sharif, assuring peace and security in bilateral relations. Vajpayee was hailed as the harbinger of peace in relations with Pakistan and he was applauded in the Indian and international press. But the euphoria turned into shock and surprise a few months later when it was discovered that the Pakistan Army and militants aided by it had crossed the Line of Control (LOC) and occupied several strategic heights on the Kargil front in Jammu and Kashmir. Pakistan had clearly practised deceit and deception on the Indian Prime Minister, for the incursions had taken place even while the Pakistan Prime Minister was talking of peace and friendship with India at Lahore with his Indian counterpart.

As the Army launched a major offensive to dislodge the intruders from the snow-capped heights in Indian territory the nation as one man stood by them and the government and the media mobilised public opinion to support the armed forces. Every victory on the battle front was hailed in banner headlines and descriptive stories and every soldier who sacrificed his life in the cause of the country was treated as a hero and extensive coverage was given to the military honours at their funeral. Funds were collected by various newspapers for the defence fund and for the welfare of the families of the soldiers who had laid down their lives. The military operation was long and loss of human life was heavy but the armed forces triumphed in the end and the entire area was cleared of Pakistani intruders. The brave soldiers were the heroes of the day and they stole the limelight in the press and the electronic media.

Even as the nation and the media celebrated the victory in Kargil awkward questions were beginning to be asked. How did the government fail to notice or be warned of the Pakistani intrusions which should have been going on long before it became aware of them. This was the question which was posed to the government. Reports in the media said there had been a woeful failure of the intelligence services and the demand was made by the Opposition parties for an inquiry commission to find out how it all happened. Responding to this widespread demand the Vajpayee Government appointed a high-powered commission to probe the whole affair.

Hardly had the country recovered from the shock of the Kargil war when an Indian Airlines plane was hijacked on its flight from Kathmandu in Nepal to New Delhi by Pakistanis. After a tortuous journey during which it halted at Amritsar, Lahore and Dubai it finally landed in Khandakar in Afghanistan which was controlled by the Taliban. The hijackers who numbered five killed one passenger and threatened to kill more if militants held captive in Kashmir were not released. After protracted negotiations the government was forced to agree to release three militant leaders in exchange for the passengers' lives. The action of the government in surrendering to the hijackers provoked a bitter debate in the media and the government was accused of mismanaging the affair. One question for which the government had no convincing answer was why did the government fail to take action against the hijackers when the hijacked plane landed in Amritsar before it flew on to Lahore? The plane was forced to land in Amritsar for refuelling and there was time enough, it was argued, for commando action to rescue the besieged passengers and crew.

A political figure who claimed the attention of the media to a considerable extent was Sonia Gandhi, wife of Prime Minister Rajiv Gandhi who was assassinated in 1991. Mrs Gandhi had been requested by the Congress Working Committee, the highest policy making body of the Congress (I), to assume the mantle of leadership, but she refused saying she will not enter politics. Ultimately she had to bow to intense pressure and agreed to take over the leadership of the party. She was appointed Congress (I) President and canvassed vigorously for the party in the two general elections and in the elections to state legislatures. A crucial moment in her political career came when after the fall of the first Vajpayee Government in 1999 Opposition parties mustered strength to form an alternative government and Sonia Gandhi was in the forefront as the prospective Prime Minister. The move, however, fizzled out at the last minute as one Opposition party said it would not join the government if Sonia Gandhi was the Prime Minister. The objection was to her foreign origin and thus began a heated controversy which was taken up by a section of the Congress (I) itself and finally led to a split. A leading member of the party and Leader of the Opposition in the dissolved Lok Sabha, Sharad Pawar who led the campaign against her, said the country could not have a Prime Minister who was not born in India. He was expelled from the party with two others and they formed a new party called the Nationalist Congress Party. The party was able to prove its strength in Maharashtra and the North-East in the general election. The controversy raged in the press and the electronic media and at one time it was even suggested that the Constitution should be amended to bar a citizen of foreign origin from holding the high offices of President, Vice-President and Prime Minister. However the issue lost its urgency and died down when Sonia Gandhi got elected to the Lok Sabha from two constituencies from North and South in the 1999 general election, proving that the people were behind her.

Period of Trial

The collapse of the country's news agencies under government pressure during the 1975-76 emergency betrayed their financial fragility and consequent vulnerability. There were four wire agencies at that time: PTI, UNI, and the Indian language agencies Hindustan Samachar and Samachar Bharati using Devanagari teleprinters for the Hindi service. The threat of discontinuance of subscription by All India Radio was enough to bring the news agencies, divided and weak, to their knees. They agreed to amalgamate into a single government-sponsored agency called Samachar.

Fight for Survival

In contrast to the meek surrender of the news agencies was the resistance to thought control put up by a few brave spirits among newspaper publishers and journalists.

L.K. Advani, as Information Minister in the post-emergency Janata government headed by Morarji Desai, made the celebrated remark that journalists had been asked during the emergency to bend but some of them had chosen to crawl. Among publishers who would not bend, let alone crawl, was Ramnath Goenka of

Indian Express. When Goenka died in October 1992, C. Subramaniam, Governor of Maharashtra, recalled in an article in *Bhavan's journal* how, during the Quit India struggle, Goenka had helped to print clandestine literature in his press and befriended underground workers like Aruna Asaf Ali, Achyut Patwardhan and R.R. Diwakar. He displayed the same courage in defying the emergency regime. Kuldip Nayar, one of Goenka's editors, recalls: "RNG went on urging us to convey a message of defiance which the people could read between the lines. He often said that he did not mind losing everything--he was a self-made man--but he did not want to see the day when there would be no voice to challenge Mrs. Gandhi's authoritarianism."

Another intrepid publisher, Cushrow R. Irani of the *Statesman*, successfully fought, through a writ petition filed in the Calcutta High Court, a notice issued by the Company Law Board in December 1975 at the instance of the Ministry of Information &-Broadcasting asking the *Statesman* to show cause why government directors should not be appointed on the company's board. After failing to establish the charges made against the management of the *Statesman*, and fearing an adverse verdict, the Government of India-after wasting a good deal of public money withdrew the notice served by the Company Law Board. It is noteworthy that C.R. Irani was against government interference with newspaper publishing irrespective of the political complexion of the government. He recalled in the course of the first Gora Sastry Memorial Lecture delivered by him at Hyderabad on 12th June 1983 how the Janata government had sponsored an amendment to the Industries (Development & Regulation) Act bringing, additional industries, including printing, within its purview: "Within four days of this amendment an attempt was made to attack Mrs. Gandhi's newspaper, the *National Herald*. The Indian & Eastern Newspaper Society had to go to George Fernandes, the then Minister for Industry, and argue him to a standstill, and no further steps were taken against the *National Herald*. The blatant abuse of power was checked."

Among editors who showed grit was Nikhil Chakravartty of

Mainstream. The first issue of the weekly that came out after the declaration of emergency failed to carry the "Editor's Notebook". In its place was the announcement: "Somewhere in the excitement of national emergency, the editor has lost his notebook. However, Rabindranath Tagore has, in the abundance of his generosity, lent him his own notebook." There followed a Tagore poem beginning with the words, "Freedom from fear is the freedom I claim for you, my Motherland."

Edatata Narayanan of *Patriot* ruled out of the columns of the newspaper any mention of the sayings and doings of Sanjay Gandhi, second son of the Prime Minister who was virtually functioning as deputy prime minister following the declaration of emergency. Narayanan would take no notice of the extra constitutional authority, though this led to a diminution of such meagre advertising revenue as the newspaper had.

Integrated Effort

A variety of pressures were applied by the emergency regime to get all the four teleprinter news services to merge in a single agency which, it was hoped, would remain pliant even after the emergency. Among the signals sent out to K.S. Ramachandran, general manager of PTI who was opposed to the merger proposal, was the cutting off of electric supply to the PTI building. This was followed by the New Delhi Municipal Committee's move to attach the building for alleged arrears of municipal taxes. During these displays of the government's muscle power, senior officials of the Delhi Electric Supply Undertaking and of the NDMC remained inaccessible on telephone to the general manager and the Delhi manager of PTI. Finally, hints were conveyed to Ramachandran that he would be arrested. The decisive form of pressure applied on both PTI and UNI was financial. All India Radio served notice on both the agencies that its subscription would cease with effect from 1st February 1976.

Soon after the declaration ration of emergency and the imposition of censorship, P.C. Gupta of *Dainik Jagran*, Kanpur, became Chairman of PTI on 29th July 1975 in place of C.R. Irani.

Gupta and the heads of the other news agencies eventually succumbed to pressure and agreed to merger in Samachar, which began to function as India's sole news agency from 1st February 1976 (the exact date from which All India Radio had threatened to discontinue subscription to PTI and UNI). W. Lazarus was appointed Acting General Manager following resignation of K.S. Ramachandran.

The day following, on 2nd February 1976, there was a debate in the Rajya Sabha on the Bill to replace the Presidential ordinance repealing the Press Council Act Krishna Kant, independent member, referred in the course of the debate to the forced amalgamation of the news agencies: "The Prime Minister rejected the idea of a government news agency because, she said, she did not want a 'Tass in India'. The Ministry (of Information Broadcasting) went ahead with speed for a ,voluntary Tass'. I would not like to use the words 'at the point of a gun or on the threat of a dagger': it can safely be described as the American method of squeeze, which Moynihan and Kissinger are using, for Third World countries." Pointing out that several members of the U.S. Congress were criticising the Administration for resorting to this method of squeeze, Krishna Kant said: "One feels depressed when no resentment at such pressure is shown in this country." His remarks were duly censored out of newspaper columns at the time.

Samachar functioned as trumpeter of the emergency regime's achievements. It complied unquestioningly with the instructions of the Chief Censor who started issuing orders orally on the telephone since conveying them in writing took some time. A sample of such orders is given in a book on the Press during the emergency brought out in 1979: "One item in October 1975 reads, 'No reports on today's disturbances in Tihar Central jail, Delhi'. And no wonder: for how could the world be allowed to know that innocent people had been arrested and taken away from the Rajghat prayer meeting on Mahatma Gandhi's birthday and then beaten up in the Tihar jail? Another banned item was 'Justice Khanna's judgement on the Bombay appeal case'. Yet another--after

J.P.'s release (because of ill health) from detention in Chandigarh'J.P.'s visit to Bombay is subject to precensorship. No photograph to be used. Those days when Delhi was being beautified and the poor mercilessly thrown out of their *jhuggies,* the then Prime Minister had no tears to shed for them; it was necessary to keep the news back from the rest of the country and from the world. So, 'no report, no photos, no features on demolished *jhuggies*' and 'no reports or pictures of DDA demolitions around Jama Masjid'."

The 1950 Constitution had provided in Article 83 that "the House of the People, unless sooner dissolved, shall continue for five years from the date appointed for its first meeting and no longer". There was a proviso that the period of five years "may, while a Proclamation of Emergency is in operation, be extended by Parliament by law for a period not exceeding one year at a time, and not extending in any case beyond a period of six months after the Proclamation has ceased to operate." This Article was amended during the emergency to make the term of the House six years instead of five. The last elections to the Lok Sabha having been held in 1971, they were due, in terms of the amended Article 83, early in 1977. Samachar set a record of sorts by reporting on 16th November 1976, on the basis of a nation-wide survey of public opinion claimed to have been conducted by its correspondents, that the people, were against the holding of fresh elections. They were, according to Samachar, happy with the emergency and wanted no change. This was presumably to prepare the ground for a law to be passed by parliament to postpone elections by a year, till 1978. (As it happened, Prime Minister Indira Gandhi, acting in this instance against the advice of her son Sanjay, decided to hold elections in March 1977-and lost.)

Samachar continued to act as a lapdog of the political party in power at the Centre even after Press censorship was relaxed in January 1977 following the announcement of elections. There was a largely attended public meeting at the Ramlila Grounds in Delhi on 6th February 1977, addressed among others by Jagjivan

Ram who had left the Congress led by Indira Gandhi to form a Congress for Democracy, and by H.N. Bahuguna, Left-leaning Congress leader of Uttar Pradesh. A report in the Delhi Statesman of 8th February quoted Bahuguna as complaining that the Ramlila Grounds meeting had been dismissed by Samachar in 540 words. Jagjivan Ram had been allowed 240 words in all, and he himself 40 words. Bahuguna said: "We can understand it because the government is sitting on the neck of the agency which the people of this poor country are paying to run". During 19.76, the Government made grants totalling Rs. 50 lakhs from the public exchequer to Samachar: Rs. 25 lakhs towards increased pay and allowances to employees, all of whom were given scales applicable under a wage board award to a Class I news agency; Rs 10 lakhs towards discharge of previous liabilities of the amalgamated agencies and Rs. 15 lakhs for meeting the current deficit.

When elections were held in March 1977 to the sixth Lok Sabha, within two months of the relaxation of censorship, the reportage was more vivid and based more on legwork than on previous occasions. It was as if, far from the faculties of journalists having atrophied during the 19 months of rigorous censorship, the Press found a new zest in exercising the freedom it had lost and regained. Similar enterprise in conveying information from the constituencies was evident in the coverage of the elections held to the Assemblies of ten States in June 1977.

The Lok Sabha elections brought into power the Janata Party, a conglomerate consisting mainly of the Congress (Organisation), the Bharatiya Lok Dal, Jana Sangh and Socialists. Before the combination broke up in mid-1989 due to internal stresses related to power sharing as well as ideology, the Janata Government headed by Morarji Desai took a series of steps to restore freedom of the Press. Censorship was dismantled, the Press Act of 1976 was repealed, the Press Council revived, and protection for truthful reporting of legislative proceedings restored through an amendment of the Constitution. Whereas the Feroze Gandhi Act, repealed during the emergency, protected the reporting only of the proceedings of parliament, Article 361-A, newly inserted by the

Constitution (44th Amendment) Act of 1978, extends protection to publication of the proceedings of State legislatures also.

It remained to decide about Samachar. A committee on news agencies appointed by the new government in April 1977, with Kuldip Nayar as chairman and eleven other members, recommended by a majority in the report submitted by it in August 1977:

(i) "Samachar should be dissolved and in its place there should be two news agencies, Varta and Sandesh. They in turn should set up jointly an organisation for international services which may be called News India. The whole setup should be created under an Act of Parliament, which should be reviewed after ten years."

(ii) Varta would provide its service in Indian languages and concentrate on gathering regional news, and provide a service in English too for newspapers which desire it.

(iii) Sandesh would work in the English language and strive to expand coverage in terms of areas and subjects. It would have the stimulus of a certain amount of competition from the English service provided by Varta.

Two members of the committee on news agencies C.R. Irani and A.K. Sarkar--submitted a dissenting note strongly opposing the creation of monopolistic agencies for Indian language or international services, and urging instead the restoration of PTI and UNI as fully competing news agencies "primarily in the English language, for the simple reason that this is the language in which the service is demanded, but with the provision for both to branch into regional languages depending on the demand."

The Janata Government finally decided on restoration of the pre-emergency position. The four news agencies that had been amalgamated under pressure resumed their identity and separate operations in April 1978.

The Repercussions

It is understandable that, in the flush of the reaction against the Indira Gandhi government's misuse of power during the emergency, the successor government should have rejected the recommendation made by the majority of the Kuldip Nayar Committee. News agencies in the public sector, established by parliamentary statute, would in the last analysis be under the thumb of the political party for the time being in power at the Centre.

The decision to restore the pre-emergency status of the news agencies did credit to the liberal instincts of the Morarji Desai government. But the publishers of India's, leading newspapers, who own the two major news agencies, could have reflected seriously on the future of PTI and UNI. Should they duplicate each other's work in the name of competition, as they had done hitherto, or develop on complementary lines so that the services of both would be indispensable for major newspapers as well as for radio and television? Alternatively, should the two merge so as to cover more centres within the country and abroad and begin to offer services in the Indian languages too? Was it conceivable that the Indian-language Press, not as strong financially as its English-language counterpart, could support two rival agencies aiming eventually at providing services in each Indian language?

The concept of a single news agency had been brought into bad odour by the circumstances of the formation and the manner of running of Samachar. But the U.K., France and Germany are examples of democratic countries whose Press has been served adequately by a single news agency. The Kuldip Nayar Committee said on this subject: "There is a section of opinion which holds that the country should have only one major news agency. Such evidence was laid before us by several eminent journalists, including some who had themselves suffered during the emergency as a result of the creation of Samachar. The employees union of the UNI, in its resolution dated 21st January 1976, welcomed the proposal for I a good, independent, viable and autonomous national news agency'. It would not, therefore, be right to view the idea of a single agency as something diabolical. The difference lies in the motivation with which the Government carried out this operation." A single domestic agency, not statutory but run in the private sector by newspaper publishers, would be very different from the Samachar of India's brief experience of fascism.

The First Press Commission's recommendation regarding the ownership and management of news agencies were naively socialistic, but the roles which the Commission envisaged for' PTI and UPI (as UNI then was) were complementary and not duplicatory. The Rajadhyaksha Commission said: "We do not propose to deal in detail with the allegations of improper management and nepotism that have been brought to our notice... We are convinced that it is essential, especially in the present international and national circumstances, that the news agency (Press Trust of India) should work at the maximum of efficiency and integrity and for this purpose we recommend the setting up of a public corporation... The United Press of India is a_ public limited company. Some of the proprietors of newspapers are directors of the company. In our opinion this form of management is not desirable in the case of a news agency of national importance... We do not however recommend for it the same form of ownership as recommended for Press Trust of India. We would suggest a trust form of management for United Press of India wherein the management is entrusted to a board of trustees in which there should be representation for subscribing newspapers and the staff of the United Press of India."

On the respective roles of the two agencies, the Rajadhyaksha Commission said: "We have referred to the regional service that the UPI has developed in Bengal. We believe it will be possible and also desirable for the UPI to develop similar regional services in the areas around Delhi, Bombay and Madras. Such regional services can form a special feature of UPI and would improve the value and utility of the service. We suggest that the United Press of India undertake this because we feel that the expansion of overseas coverage by the appointment of correspondents at different world centres which we have recommended in the case of Press Trust of India would fully absorb the manpower and financial resources of that organisation. We would therefore prefer the development of regional services to be undertaken by the United Press of India."

What the Kuldip Nayar Committee recommended as the roles of Varta and Sandesh was substantially the same. But newspaper publishers paid no heed to the suggestion, with the result that PTI and UNI have continued, in the name of competition, to duplicate each other's work. The Second Press Commission noted the extent of duplication in its report (1982): "All the four agencies compete in 19 centres (the national and State a capitals). Three news agencies (i.e., other than either Hindustan Samachar or Samachar Bharati) compete in 12 centres. Two news agencies compete in 16 centres. Only eight centres are served by a single agency... There are now 405 district headquarters in the country. Three hundred and fifty of these are not covered by any full-time agency correspondent. Nor are there full-time correspondents of any agency in four Union Territories: Andaman & Nicobar Islands; Dadra & Nagar Haveli; Lakshadweep; and Mizoram. All the four agencies have the largest number of correspondents posted in Delhi: PTI has 58, UNI 65, Hindustan Samachar 28 and Samachar Bharati 27.

Since the two agencies that have survived PTI and UNI largely duplicate each other's coverage, competition between them has sometimes taken unhealthy forms including enticement of newspapers heavily in arrears to the other news agency, undercutting of subscription rates and making innuendos against the rival agency. Ground rules to govern competition were worked out early in 1986 as the result of discussions held by the general managers of PTI and UNI under the auspices of Ramnath Goenka, then Chairman of PTI. The principles, embodied in an exchange of letters between the two general managers in February 1986, include the following:

(i) Subscribers in arrears should not be allowed to move from one agency to another in order to evade clearance of arrears. The service of one agency should not be made available if a subscriber is in arrears to the other. Any accommodation to be shown to a newspaper which is in difficulties will be by mutual consultation between the two agencies.

(ii) There will be no undercutting of subscription rates. Each agency will adhere to the declared tariff as approved by the respective Board of Directors.

(iii) In the issue of denials, no attempt will be made by the agencies to run down one another.

(iv) No personal or institutional attacks will be made in public, or in private dealings with government, clients and others concerned.

(v) Any points of difference in the implementation of this code of ethics in competition will be sorted out by mutual consultation and discussion.

New Pattern

The two agencies, divided and weak, have been at the mercy of the Central Government which owns and runs All India Radio and Doordarshan. These media together constitute the largest single source of subscription revenue for both the agencies. Though government leaders have from time to time inveighed against concentration and monopoly in the Press, they have themselves used their muscle power as monopolist owners of the electronic media to dictate the terms on which AIR and Doordarshan will buy news from PTI and UNI.

The First Press Commission as well as the Second noted that the news agencies received less than what was their due for the news supplied to the government-run media. The Rajadhyaksha Commission recommended in 1954 that the fixed charge payable by AIR to PTI should be as for the agency's 'A' class service to newspapers published in English, with royalty at the rate of ten annas per annum per broadcast receiver licence. The Commission said that in proposing payment by AIR on this scale, it took into account "the fact that all newspapers accept paid advertisements while the radio does not." The position with regard to commercial advertisements on All India Radio and Doordarshan, and therefore their ability to pay, has changed vastly since then. Commercial advertising was introduced in All India Radio on lst November

1967, when Indira Gandhi was Prime Minister (Jawaharlal Nehru in his time did not countenance commercials on radio). From a little over Rs. 12 crores in 1980-81 AIR's income from commercials rose to Rs. 24 crores in 1986-87 and stood at nearly Rs. 53 crores in 1991-92. Doordarshan went commercial on 1st January 1976, during the internal emergency. From Rs. 2 crores in 1977-78, income from TV commercials rose to Rs. 136 crores in 1987-88 and stood at more than Rs. 300 crores in 1991-92.

The Second Press Commission was informed by All India Radio that payment to the news agencies was governed by a formula suggested by a committee of officials in 1978. The formula is based on the conversion of radio and television receivers in the country into an equivalent number of newspaper copies, the conversion being done on the basis of the news component, in the broadcast time of AIR and Doordarshan. The total amount payable to all the four news agencies, after applying numerous special provisions, has been distributed between PTI and UNI in a ratio determined by the government after taking into account the revenue derived from daily newspapers in India as reported by the agencies. The government has thus assumed the role of the monkey, in the fable, which arbitrates to its own advantage between two quarrelling cats.

The determination of the rates payable to PTI and UNI, after the closure of Hindustan Samachar and Samachar Bharathi, has continued to be unilateral. The rates are recommended by committees of officials whose reports are treated as secret documents. The situation is comparable to that described in the Supreme Court's judgment, in April 1986, *in Central Inland Water Transport Corporation v. B . N. Ganguly:* "When the weaker party is in a position in which he can obtain the means of livelihood only on the terms imposed by the stronger party, the alternative being to do without, the contract would be such as to shock the conscience of the Court."

In order to get over the controversy on the apportionment of payment as between PTI and UNI, the general managers of the two news agencies addressed a joint letter on 30th October .1989 to the Secretary, Ministry of I & B, proposing that payment be made on the basis of the respective newspaper tariffs of the agencies:

"We suggest that the payment to each agency should be on the basis of its tariff for newspapers, applied to the number of radio and TV sets converted into their equivalent of newspaper copies. While doing this, it is necessary to take into account the actual number of radio and TV receiving sets in the counting, and not the gross underestimates which have been employed so far. Besides simplifying the entire process and resolving some of the existing problems of subscription sharing between the two agencies, a new system such as proposed here will provide to news agencies a long-term perspective of the revenue yield from the electronic media."

The letter was signed by P. Unnikrishanan, then General Manager of PTI, and by K.P.S. Kutty, General Manager of UNI.

With the population of radio sets in the country already above 100 million in 1992, and of TV sets about 33 million, payment on the basis suggested by the news agencies would be several times what they now receive, and help them to expand and improve both domestic and international news coverage. The agencies can set their own terms if they present a united front. Till the time of this writing, however India's newspaper publishers have acquiesced in the news agencies currying favours from the Government, whether it be UNI securing a grant of Rs. 25 lakhs for starting a service in Urdu or PTI being funded for functioning as the Indian partner in the News Pool of professedly Non-Aligned Countries.

It is arguable that merger of PTI and UNI is a pre-condition for securing fair payment from the government media of radio and television, as well as for the development of an adequate flow of objective news from and to India. No arrangement can be satisfactory that relies on subsidy from the government. It is therefore a pity that the historical precedents of Reuters being funded, sometimes openly and sometimes secretly, by the British government in the days of empire, and of the Associated Press of

America and the United Press Association being backed by the U.S. Administration in the first half of the 20th century, should be cited by some who want to see established an India-based international news agency. No subsidised newspaper or news agency, domestic or international, can exercise professional autonomy or command credibility. The ringing words written by Maulana Azad in 1912 are still relevant: "We believe that any newspaper which asks an individual or jamaat (the community) for any contribution other than its retail price, is not a newspaper, but a blot and disgrace heaped on journalism Gandhiji threatened at one point to discontinue the publication of Young *India* (1919-32), a weekly which eschewed advertisements and was brought out in English primarily for readers in South India who could not follow Gujarati or Hindi, if the number of subscribers did not pick up.

Experiments like the Organisation of Asian News Agencies (OANA) and the Non-Aligned News Pool (NANP) have been undertaken in order to supplement and improve the quality of international news flow which has been dominated during the 20th century by transnational news agencies based in industrially advanced countries. If these efforts have yielded very limited results, the reason is primarily that many of the participating news agencies are under heavy governmental influence or control and lack of professional freedom; inadequacy of resources is another reason.

OANA was formed in December 1961 at the conclusion of a UNESCO-sponsored conference of Asian news agencies in Bangkok. The organisation was enlarged in 1981 to include the entire Asia-Pacific region. Since 1982, the member agencies of OANA numbering more than two dozen, in some 20 countries, have been exchanging a small volume of news through an Asia-Pacific News Network (ANN) that links the member agencies.

Though limited in its geographical spread, OANA is a forum for interaction of news agency professionals, unlike NANP which is under the control of governments of non-aligned countries spanning the continents of Asia, Africa and Latin America. The rulers of most of these countries would like newspaper readers, radio listeners and television viewers not only at home but around the world to be exposed to their own versions of truth, and to be prevented from exposure to other versions. Even the Government of India, largest of the newly free countries distinguished from most other Third World regimes by its democratic political system and freedom of expression, ordered in August 1970 the closure of the British Broadcasting Corporation's offices in India because BBC-TV screened a series of films made by Louis Malle that were held to show India in a poor light.

By a coincidence, the constitution of NANP was adopted at a conference of Information Ministers of non-aligned countries held in New Delhi in July 1976, when India was under a temporary dictatorship with the Press and news agencies under censorship. The heavy governmental bias of NANP is illustrated by the following extract from the constitution of the Pool drawn up at the New Delhi conference: "Countries participating in the Pool should meet at the level of governments and national news agencies at the beginning of each year in which a conference of heads of State or Government of non-aligned countries is to be held. At each such meeting a coordinating committee will be elected (on the basis of equitable geographic representation) by the participants to facilitate mutual cooperation... The chairman and other office-bearers of the coordinating committee will hold office until the next coordination committee is elected as mentioned above."

The role to be played by, NANP was reflected in the action plan drawn up on the same occasion. It noted that "the communication network, including the transnational press agencies, was created by and in the interests of the colonial powers." This is historically accurate. And there is basis for the complaint that even in the post-colonial period the western transnational news agencies have tended to notice only such happenings in the Third World as coups, earthquakes and civil wars, and to ignore their efforts at economic development and social betterment. On the other hand, it is necessary for Third

World news agencies and communication media not to fall into the error of treating as news only good tidings, or the sayings and doings of those in power, and to sweep under the carpet negative developments whether they concern social evils, group conflicts or corruption in public life.

Presentation of a rounded picture of both the positive and negative elements in a given situation is desirable. In the words of the non-official U.S. Commission on Freedom of the Press headed by Robert Hutchins, "The account of an isolated fact, however accurate in itself, may be misleading and, in effect, untrue. The greatest danger here is in the communication of information internationally. The press now bears a responsibility in all countries, and particularly in democratic countries where foreign policies are responsive to popular majorities, to report international events in such a way that they can be understood. It is no longer enough to report the fact truthfully. It is now necessary to report the truth about the fact." Three decades after the Hutchins Commission, an International Commission for the Study of Communication Problems was formed by UNESCO in 1977. The chairman was Sean MacBride who had the distinction of being honoured with both the Nobel Prize and the Lenin Peace Prize. The MacBride Commission called for "democratisation of communication within and between countries". The two are inter-dependent, and can strengthen each other when they proceed hand in hand.

A fair and rounded presentation of problems is necessary for promoting mutual understanding among newly free and developing countries as well as between them and the industrially developed countries. These latter are not free of racial conflicts and financial scandals. There was a candid admission of this by Dr. David Owen, Britain's Foreign and Commonwealth Secretary, when he addressed the Indian journalists' Association in London on 14th March 1979. This was in the wake of the bad Press which Britain received in India following the virginity tests conducted on Indian women seeking entry into the U.K. as wives of Indian males already resident there. David owen said:

"I will not attempt to avoid the story that has commanded so many headlines in the last few weeks: the recent medical examination at Heathrow. I fully understand the feelings that have been expressed. I share them. What happened was wrong, and that was why it was stopped the moment it was brought to light by the *Guardian*. The government did not hesitate...

"I think it is fair for me ask you to keep a fair balance in your reporting bad stories. Try and ensure that your editors give space for some of the good stories too. Tell the people back home of the thousands from India and elsewhere in the sub-continent who have settled in this country and are fully accepted here, enjoy themselves, are respected, and are doing well for themselves... Tell them how every sort of religion flourishes here; how everybody is able to speak his, mind. Much of this will not command headlines, but it can form a positive background against which to set the inevitable stories about immigration, prejudice and racial tension."

Here was an acknowledgement, somewhat rare from the other side of the fence, of the need for two-sided or multisided presentation of social and political reality rather than the oversimplification to which journalists in a hurry are prone.

It is through background information or soft news that understanding abroad of a given problem in a country can be promoted. And such feature material, including photographic illustrations, does not need expensive modes of instant communication like wireless or satellite but can be conveyed through air mail. Mutual understanding through appreciation of each other's problems needs to be promoted specially between those developing countries which have bilateral disputes that result in the diversion of scarce resources to defence from development. This calls for the lowering of barriers, erected by governments, that impede the flow of information across State boundaries. There has also to be willingness on the part of newspapers and other communication media in one country to expose their audience to a rounded presentation of the other country's-and of third countries-perception of problems between the two.

Of interest in this connection is the following candid comment by an eminent Indian on the need to rise above the 'my country right or wrong' tendency, 'country' in this context often meaning the government for the time being in power: "The citizens of a country are prone to unquestioning support of the government of the day on issues of foreign relations. Each Nation State evokes the veneration of its citizens, even though Nation States are but products of history and are as liable to error as the human beings who govern them at a given time. When the governments of two countries are locked in conflict, each will tend to claim that it is wholly in the right and the other wholly in the wrong. Despite these constraints, non-governmental associations like those of intellectuals and artists, trade unions, and women's organisations can help to keep the lines of communication between a country and its neighbours open, stem the tide of chauvinism, and promote understanding of each other's viewpoint. This will help to create a climate of tolerance in which problems between countries can be resolved peacefully through negotiations."

Universalisation Process

Advances in communication technology now enable Indian television viewers to watch in their homes BBC's and other foreign news programmes telecast via satellite. This technological revolution has rendered somewhat obsolete two decisions relating to news flow that were taken by the Indian government in the mid-1950's. One was that foreign-owned newspapers or periodicals would not be allowed to be published in India, nor Indian editions of foreign publications that deal mainly with news and current affairs. The other decision, taken a year later, in 1956, was that the services of foreign news agencies should be made available to communication media in India only through an Indian news agency and not directly.

The latter decision was in effect departed from early in 1992 when the Indian authorities allowed Reuters to distribute the Money Report directly to financial and commercial institutions in India, instead of through PTI which had been earning a substantial revenue as the distributing agency. This was followed by a reference by the Ministry of Information Broadcasting to the Press Council of India inviting its views on a proposal to review and modify the policy regulating the inflow of foreign media formulated by the government in the 1950's., The majority view, in the Press Council was that the throwing open of the Indian news market to foreign investment and enterprise should be deferred pending fuller consideration of the implications. The question of allowing foreign news agencies to circulate news copy directly to their subscribers in India could be reviewed, the Council's resolution said, after three to five years,

The other viewpoint was expressed in an editorial comment in *Indian Express* of 27th June 1992: "While suspecting the judgment of Indian newspapers, it (the Council) seems to have complete faith in that of the Indian news agencies. This is totally unwarranted and arbitrary. The Council is either unaware of, or has ignored, the occasions on which these agencies, heavily dependent on government revenue, have acted as instruments of the government's disinformation." The newspaper went on to say that the publication of foreign papers in India should be allowed subject to the laws of the land, and that foreign television companies should be able to telecast their programmes to Indian viewers.

There is a view that there is little choose between the sex and violence purveyed by Doordarshan in its compilations of song-and-dance sequences and many of the films telecast by it, and the soft pornography offered by MTV or other transnationals via satellite. Early in 1984, a Working Group on Software for Doordarshan said in its report: "It is ironical that television should be claimed-as it has been by a widely quoted American writer-as a medium which retribalises humankind. If Doordarshan, with its foreign social comedy serials and Indian feature films projecting the aping of Western life styles, is promoting a process of universal tribalisation, it is by inducting sons and daughters of TV viewers and the moneyed Indian upper crust rust comprising businessmen and politicians, civil servants and academics, and every other category of the privileged, into the international fraternity of rock and roll, live and disco. The elite of the developed and developing countries do indeed constitute one tribe, irrespective of their skin colour and geographical distributional.

On the other hand, the news programmes from abroad may do some good by shaking up Doordarshan's controllers, bureaucratic, and political. They have not only been sitting on the back of the news wing and making it put out illustrated official gazettes, but subjecting the video news magazines compiled by independent producers to censorship.

A danger from globalisation lies in the possibility of a further diversion of commercial advertising from the relatively free Indian Press. A good chunk of advertising outlay in the country has already been claimed by Doordarshan. If the programmes beamed to India via satellite by TV multinationals should attract a further slice of the advertising outlay, it is likely to be at the cost of Indian newspapers. Apparently as a hedge against a decline in advertising revenue, some leading Indian newspaper publishers have diversified into the production of radio and television programmes (laced with commercial advertisements), not only of news and current affairs but entertainment of the pop variety. There has been a vigorous public debate on the lowering of standards of popular taste by the programmes both of Doordarshan and of other television agencies whose signals are telecast via satellite and are disseminated in India by cable operators using dish antennae.

13

JP's Role

"This struggle in Bihar is not just a flash in the pan of history," wrote Jayaprakash Narayan in the front-page story of the December 1, 1974 issue of his weekly *Everyman's*, "but a continuing process of revolutionary changes." Jayaprakash Narayan was referring to the struggle between *"Chatra Shakti"* (student power) and *'Jan Shakti"* (people's power) on the one hand and *"Rajya Shakti"* (state power) on the other. He further wrote in the same article titled 'Direct Action of Youth and People': "In this revolutionary process governments and political parties will certainly play a role but the main moving force will be the direct action of the youths and the people."

It is this direct action of the youth and the masses that Jayaprakash Narayan harnessed to launch one of the most eventful, memorable and effective mass movements in post-colonial India. Often termed as the 'Second Liberation' after Gandhi's freedom struggle, the JP movement in the 1970s with its wide appeal is perhaps the best example of effective political mobilisation in the democratic set-up of independent India.

It may be relevant here to point out one of the theoretical issues that we discussed in the chapter on political mobilisation. It was postulated that the student community in developing countries is among the most sensitive groups in becoming aware of and asserting allegedly deprived rights. The student groups have played an important role both in providing successful support for mobilisation regimes, as well as in opposing and often overthrowing unsuccessful ones. They perceive the value system of national development, which is articulated through symbols, as right. Their access to information probably helps them to scan and evaluate performance more accurately than any other single group of society, except perhaps the ruling elite. It has been found that students are less willing to accept information dissonance and they require a greater level of information constraint than that at which the ruling elite are accustomed to operate for the benefit of the peripherally mobilised population. Jayaprakash Narayan understood this well. He also believed that political mobilisation is focused on national perspectives in developing countries. "Mobilisation is a functional process for the attainment of the goal of national integration; the regained saliency and level of commitment are high."

Additionally, much like Gandhi before him, Jayaprakash Narayan was conscious of the power of the press and continuously used this potent medium for communicating his ideas on political, social and international issues. "His ability to express political theories and sentiments in comprehensible terms provided a model for anyone involved in mass communication. Like Gandhi, he believed in placing his views before as wide a section of the people as possible, not confine them to ideological journals." It is pertinent here to point out an observation by Lucian Pye. He notes that "a direct relationship exists in all societies between the structure and organisation of communications and the character, tone, and even to a degree, content of political expression."

The politician's role both as articulator of the collective identity and as champion of specific interests, is invariably conditioned and limited by the media of communications available to him. No leader can rise above the restrictions posed by the specific communications networks to which he has access, and at the same time none can escape the consequences of being surrounded by a communications system.

Jayaprakash Narayan realised this best and made full use of the print media. He wrote political pamphlets, besides writing for his own journal *Everyman's* that was being run by a group of professionals appointed by him. He also used to give interviews to a number of mainstream newspapers and magazines, besides relying a good deal on speeches. On the whole, his was quite a sensitive mind and "he could react spontaneously to events. In the days of his retirement from politics, where there was a brutal police firing on students in Bihar, JP came out denouncing the government, and in the campaign that followed he did not hesitate to join hands with the Communists. At the same time, during the Hungarian crisis in 1956 he wrote an open letter to the CPI journal raising basic issues about democracy and socialism—which brought forth an equally frank response from the then leader of CPI, Ajoy Ghosh. This correspondence between JP and Ajoy, now forgotten, is one of the landmarks in socialist thinking in India, while the second landmark came when the CPI two years later at its Congress under Ajoy Ghosh's leadership laid down in its constitution that under the Socialism of its model in India, there would be room for pluralism of political parties."

A survey of the most momentous times of JP Movement vis-a-vis Jayaprakash Narayan's use of the press for mobilising the youth and masses (he did use other techniques like rallies and signature campaigns also) will help us establish the relevance of our question.

Effective Communicator

Jayaprakash Narayan was an effective communicator who put across his point of view systematically and convincingly. His communication strategy, much like Gandhi's, included the use of both oral and written media. In an active political career spanning over five decades, JP constantly made use of speeches and writings to put forth his ideas on a wide-ranging national and international issues. He relied on this technique from his youthful days of the Quit India Movement when he wrote three monumental letters known as 'Letters to the Freedom Fighters', through the days of the post and telegraph trade union movement when he wrote an article 'Incentives for Goodness', to the simmering seventies when he started his own weekly "with a view to communicating his ideas regularly and systematically to the educated elite and the students."

In addition to his writings, Jayaprakash Narayan used speeches and even undertook fasts to communicate his ideas. For instance, in 1952, during the strike of post and telegraph employees, he carried on negotiations with the then minister of communications, Rafi Ahmad Kidwai. After the negotiations, he announced that wages for the strike would be paid. But when the minister contradicted him, he made himself responsible for the arising situation and said, "I led the trade union movement and after the negotiations gave an assurance to my colleagues and comrades in the struggle that your strike wages would be paid. But I find that my understanding with the Minister was wrong and it was my failure as a trade unionist. Now it is my moral duty to repent and purify myself." Thereafter, he undertook a 21-day fast at Pune. This was not a protest but an effective communication strategy. He said, "I ought to have taken assurance in writing. It's my failure.

Why should I blame the Minister?" This was a good example of his communication skills. No wonder he was liked by all, across parties and ideologies.

'Jayapraksh Narayan has carried with him fulsome tributes from all political circles—his adherents and admirers, his adversaries and detractors. A life of ups and downs, of heroic times and despairing moments, living beyond the Psalmist's assigned, span, JP had not only witnessed mighty deeds but participated in them in the company of the great and was often acclaimed as one of them. Where history will place him in the pantheon of the architect of a freedom, it will be known only to posterity. For us, who have lived in his life-time, the millions who bade him a tearful farewell on the banks of the Ganga testify to his eminence, and the regard and the affection in which he was held by his countrymen and women."

Jayaprakash Narayan exhorted the masses and especially the

youth to action through his speeches. "While college and University students have every right to participate in politics," he said, "and political parties may have their student branches or sections, the latter should not interfere with purely student affairs. Students should have only one organisation, the college or university students union, which alone should deal with their problems and represent the students where necessary."

On another occasion he urged the students and teachers "to establish mass contact with voters in order to enlighten them." For he believed that "voters are arbiters of destiny in a democracy, but in practice vote-catchers have become the arbiters of destiny of the people. Widespread illiteracy is certainly an obstacle to enlightenment, but let us not presume that they cannot cast their votes widely until they become educated. India has a tradition of knowledge being acquired through audition so that the illiterate people of India possess unexpected intellectual maturity. What is needed is that they are awakened and told how to use properly their invaluable right to vote. This social education is far more important than propaganda in favour of a party or candidate. If we do not enlighten our voters in this decade, the future of our democracy will become dark."

Jayaprakash Narayan's use of the media for political ends is also reflected in his use of his journals for monitoring his movement. The journals *Everyman's* and *Prajaniti* were effectively used to inform the course and direction of JP Movement. Jayaprakash Narayan followed Gandhi in this model. Not only proforma of membership forms were printed in the journals but developments from various states on the progress of the movement were also reported. Ajit Bhattacharjee informs that a good deal of *Everyman's* was devoted to various aspects of growing discontent against the Indira Gandhi regime in different states. This acted as a morale booster for the revolting students in Bihar and Gujarat. Another important section of the English journal, *Everyman's* was on international issues. It was aimed at educating the readers with, at times, examples of revolutionaries from abroad. The journal also carried profiles of leaders of national and international stature to motivate the adherents of the JP Movement.

Much like Gandhi, Jayaprakash Narayan used cultural channels of communication during the movement. The cultural symbolism as expressed in poetry and street theatres added to the effectiveness of the movement led by him. "A lot of reputed poets like Baba Nagarjuna, Satyanarayan and Ravindra Rajhans hold forte in Patna and read out satirical poems against the Congress regime."

In fact, a whole lot of poets, writers, theatre artists and painters had joined Jayaprakash Narayan during the JP Movement. "For the first time in the history of mass movements in India these cultural messengers had come out on the streets." This speaks of his success in formulating a communications strategy where the creative strata of the society joined a mass struggle. This aspect of JP Movement was widely reported in the mainstream media and was duly appreciated. It also became a model for others to follow. This element was missing in Gandhi's communication strategy.

The leader posed a mighty challenge to the Indira Gandhi regime through the scientific use of the press. No wonder it forced the government to apply censorship across the board. Many veteran journalists resisted courageously and some of them were imprisoned. Several others participated in underground resistance. C.R. Irani's *The Statesman* and Ramnath Goenka's *The Indian Express* refused to bow to the pressures. Nikhil Chakravarthy preferred to stop the publication of his weekly *Mainstream* rather than conform. Jayaprakash Narayan's journal *Everyman's,* needless to say, too was banned.

The press as a whole, however, was unable to offer resistance during the Emergency which took it by surprise. It was effectively muzzled and it regained its voice only after the defeat of the Congress in the Lok Sabha Elections of March 1977 and the establishment of the Janata Party government— the first ever non-Congress government at the centre.

Such was the effect of Jayaprakash Narayan's use of the press during the movement that "even the people in villages had realised the government's motive behind censoring the press." It is significant to note that while his communication channels were choked by the government when it suspended press freedom and banned newspapers, he found expression in the international media. For instance, *The Times*, London brought out the following advertisement by Free JP Society on 15 August, 1975: "Today is Indian independence day. Don't let the light go out in Indian democracy. Free JP, Jayaprakash Narayan, follower of Mahatma Gandhi, fighter for the independence of India, leader of the non-violent campaign against corruption, unjustly imprisoned by the Indian Government on 26 June 1975, now reported to be seriously ill."

The Solution

The solution to overcome administrative corruption and other ills of society, felt Jayaprakash Narayan, lay in social revolution, which according to him meant "a fundamental change in the socio-economic-political structure of power." This, in turn, implied that "all power, social, economic and political, is seized and wielded directly by the people, who in this context include petty farmers, rural and urban labourers, low-income groups in offices, shops and schools, artisans and even such petty traders as hawkers and street vendors. The people in this sense perhaps constitute eighty per cent of the population of this country."

Jayaprakash Narayan conceived of the concept of total revolution for bringing about an all-round change in the society. "While unfolding his plan of struggle on behalf of the Student's Struggle Committee of Bihar at a mammoth public meeting in Patna on June 5, 1974, he declared that the struggle was not going to be limited to securing the demands of the students, including the resignation of the ministry and the dissolution of the Assembly in Bihar, but would aim at bringing about a total revolution or *sampoorna kranti* which alone could solve the urgent problems of the country and usher in a new society." This concept of total revolution, that has been called a descriptive label of his last phase, was essentially his version of the sarvodaya non-violent revolution. In terms of their social content and broad objectives, the two are the same: both involve a comprehensive transformation of man and society in accordance with Gandhi's original vision.

One should not be surprised, therefore, to learn, as the leader himself pointed out, that Vinoba Bhave had earlier used the phrase and that it gained currency in India in the title of a book dealing with the campaign from *gramdan*.

Without using the term total revolution, Jayaprakash Narayan himself had been emphasising the need for a social revolution since the mid-1940s. This revolution, he thought, would not merely bring about a change in the structure of society, but also an improvement in the character of individuals that constitute it. He laid particular emphasis on it after joining the Bhoodan Movement in the 1950s.

In an article published in 1969, he also used the term 'Total Revolution' to describe the objective of the Sarvodaya movement in India. Referring to the Bhoodan and Gramdan programmes, he observed: "Gandhi's non-violence was not just a plea for law and order, or a cover for the status quo, but a revolutionary philosophy. It is indeed a philosophy of a total revolution, because it embraces personal and social ethics and values of life as much as economic, political and social institutions and processes."

What led Jayaprakash Narayan to give a call for total revolution in 1974? Some of the issues we have already mentioned earlier. In addition, "more than a quarter of a century of experience of public life in independent India, first as a socialist and later as a sarvodaya leader" had convinced him "that piecemeal reforms of the socio-economic and political system operating in India since the achievement of independence would not be able to bring about any significant change in the lives of mass of the people and that what was required was a radical transformation of the entire social system." That system, according to him, had hardly undergone any change since independence.

He recognised that *zamindari* had been ended, land reforms measures had been adopted by the various legislations and untouchability had been abolished by law. But most of the Indian villages still continued under the grip of the bigger and medium landowners, who mostly belonged to the upper castes. The majority of villages in almost all parts of India consisted of small and marginal farmers and landless labourers, comprising harijans and others belonging to the backward castes. Their condition remained miserable. Adivasis and harijans continued to be exploited.

The condition of the urban poor was hardly better. Jayaprakash Narayan found no improvement in the educational system as well. He discovered that despite several committees and commissions, the educational system had remained basically what it was under the British rule: "class education designed as an escalator to reach the top." Population was growing at a fast pace, so was poverty. More than 40 per cent of the population lived below the poverty line.

The pertinent question of the time was: could a drastic change be brought about in this gloomy picture by merely changing the government or the enactment of some laws by the legislature concerned? Jayaprakash Narayan's emphatic answer was based on his understanding of India's economic and social development since the country's independence. Several progressive measures had been enacted by the legislatures in the socio-economic field, but they had remained largely on paper. "A radical change in the situation, therefore, could come only through a systemic change in the society or a revolution in every sphere and aspect of society. In other words, a Total Revolution."

Jayaprakash Narayan had clear ideas about the form his kind of revolution had to take. He worked within the parameters that he had set for himself. While referring to total revolution in his writings and speeches in 1974-75, he continued to lay stress on the fact that such a revolution had to be brought about through non-violent methods and care needed to be taken to see that the democratic structure of the state was maintained intact.

Indeed, one of the objectives of total revolution was to strengthen democracy by ensuring direct participation by the people in the work of government as much as possible. As Jayaprakash Narayan put it in his notes while in prison on 23 August 1975, "Total revolution has to be peacefully brought about without impairing the democratic structure of society and affecting the democratic way of life of the people." He was conscious, though, that this would prevent radical changes from being introduced at one go, as may be possible through a violent revolution, and would delay the process of social change. He, however, preferred this slower process to prevent violence and ensure a more permanent result. He also felt that in such revolutionary times the period of transition can be shortened, though not to the same extent as in a violent revolution. As he put it in his prison notes in 1975: "The revolution being peaceful, it was not to happen suddenly and swiftly. It would take time, but the times being revolutionary, not too much time—perhaps a space of a decade or two." This is, on the whole, not very different from the ideas of Gandhi, who also looked forward to a social revolution through non-violent means. Change, he believed, had to be brought about by a non-violent, popular upsurge against misgovern-ment rooted in man's inherent desire for justice and freedom, in moral and social values, not by an imposed ideology. He appealed especially to the student community to fight social and political corruption.

When there was a response in Gujarat in early 1974, he supported the movement. When there was a much bigger response in Bihar, he agreed to lead. 'JP tried to infuse the movement with wider social and educational objectives." He invited educationists like Ivan Illitch of *Deschooling Society* and other proponents of non-violent social change for this. "He also invited journalists." To expand a student campaign into a national movement required widespread popular awareness, for which the press was needed.

The weekly journal *Everyman's* was started precisely because Jayaprakash Narayan, like Gandhi, understood the role media could play in an open society. Like Gandhi, he wrote prolifically. And like Gandhi's *Harijan* and *Young India*, *Everyman's* too was banned when the threat it represented to the status quo were sought to be extinguished by Indira Gandhi's Emergency.

Like a seasoned journalist, Jayaprakash Narayan followed all the ethics of the press. *Everyman's* was published at the facilities provided by Ramnath Goenka's *Indian Express*. Ajit Bhattacharjee, editor of the journal, recalls, "Though it was JP's journal, I do not remember ever receiving any instructions from him. I felt free even to criticise him on occasions, once for expanding the movement beyond Bihar before it seemed to be firmly established there."

Historic Movement

Jayaprakash Narayan was equally forthright in criticising the journalists when he felt the need for it. Thus he commented during the Emergency. "Most of our journalist friends have not even used the margins of freedom that the press has in the present circumstances. Is it because the press in India is in the hands of big industrialists who have submitted to the dictatorship out of fear?"

Besides writing for *Everyman's*, Jayaprakash Narayan wrote a large number of pamphlets and books. All contributed in great measure to the propagation of many of his ideas and were quite effective in arousing people against the autocratic rule of Indira Gandhi. The pamphlets too contributed to political mobilisation.

It was this power of the people that Jayaprakash Narayan relied most on while waging his struggle in Bihar, popularly known as JP movement. The genesis of JP movement can be traced to Musahari, a small block in Muzaffarpur district of Bihar. Recalling how naxalites had become suddenly active in Musahari block and "had committed four murders," JP wrote in a popular pamphlet titled 'Face to Face' in 1970 that naxalite threat posed "an urgent call to demonstrate through positive action how the challenge of violence could be used to speed up the process of non-violent social change and reconstruction." And this, felt he, set the stage "for a new turn to be given to the movement" of *gramdan*, "from being extensive and widespread to becoming intensive and deep-going."

JP's encounter, "face to face", with the socio-economic reality of rural India and the "utter poverty, misery, inequality, exploitation, backwardness, stagnation, frustration and loss of hope," led him to his quest for a mass movement based on 'people's action'. "It was in this spirit of quest," he said while referring to his stay in Musahari, "and with a modest programme of action that I came to this area determined either to succeed or perish in this effort."

In the Musahari block, it was found that a large proportion of the villages had been improperly declared *gramdan;* they were 'bogus *gramdan,*' in which the work had to begin again from scratch. Similar findings were reported in other areas and, although some progress was made in implementing *gramdan* and, beyond that, in engaging a few hundred villages in the task of development, the overall results of all the efforts were extremely disappointing. "There was certainly no evidence that the Sarvodaya movement had reached the take off point at which 'movement of workers' was being transformed into 'a movement of the people', signifying the revolutionary elite's success in generating 'people's power'. In this situation, the natural response of many Sarvodaya workers was to question the movement's strategy."

In 'Face to Face', JP provided a clear hint of what was to be one element in a revised strategy.

After reflecting on the failure of the government's land reforms and the futility of the Naxalite movement, Jayaprakash Narayan wrote: "If democracy is found wanting and violence offers no solution, what then is the way out? To find the ways we will have to go back to Gandhiji... conditions seem to be ripening in the context of our present programme that may necessitate large scale Satyagraha." Besides following the model of Satyagraha, there were many new elements in the revised strategy for his non-violent revolution. "A study of the movement's publications, recording what amounts to a prolonged strategy debate, reveals that by the end of December 1973—that is, before the Gujarat agitation erupted in January 1974, Sarvodaya's new thinking had embraced several additional points."

Firstly, it was felt that it was necessary to enlarge the existing cadre of revolutionaries. The main source of new recruits was identified as rebellious students and idealistic youth, the group that in recent years had constituted the 'revolutionary vanguard' not only in many advanced industrial countries of the West but also in developing countries such as Thailand. Hence, he issued 'Appeal to Youth Power' in December 1973.

It was equally important to enlist the active support of concerned but politically uncommitted citizens, especially middle class professional people and intellectuals. Plans for a new weekly paper directed to this group and for an appropriate organisation, were laid in the summer of 1972—plans which led to the publication, beginning in July 1973, of *Everyman's Weekly* and the setting up of Citizens for Democracy in April 1974. By setting up a weekly, Jayaprakash Narayan created a 'newspaper's newspaper'. The main focus of the weekly was to cater to the intellectual class and answer their questions pertaining to the ideological stand taken by him during the course of his struggle in Gujarat and Bihar. In the reports of the mainstream press, many of his views were distorted. It was *Everyman's* which did the damage building exercise. "*Everyman's* would immediately counter any such distortion of JP's views." In order to mobilise wider popular support that the programme of *gramdan* had achieved, it was necessary for Sarvodaya workers to take up, articulate, and seek to resolve the problem then affecting the masses, such as rising prices, unemployment, endemic corruption and the eviction of tenant farmers. The movement hitherto centred on the villages had to extend to towns and cities, developing a programme and organisational forms that would be appropriate to both rural and urban areas. In this connection Jayaprakash Narayan, in December 1973, put forward "a programme of immediate socio-political action" to build a structure of direct 'people's democracy' as an alternative to the existing 'people's democracy'.

Jayaprakash Narayan realised that his reconstruction of Indian polity was possible only if it emerged from the democratic, if faulty, processes of India's existing system of government. By December 1973, he felt the situation was conducive for a revolution as it had been in 1942, and he "felt an inner urge to give a call to youth" to enter the political scene. He had set the tone for revolution through his writings in *Everyman's* and other publications. He wrote a series of three articles in *Everyman's* to arouse the intelligentsia and the youth and inform them about the "complete collapse of the moral authority of the country's political leadership." By focusing on the literate and politically active class, JP, much like Gandhi, realised the way his journal could make an impact. He fell in line with the 'two-step flow' hypothesis of Lazarsfeld that postulated that media messages are first received by the "opinion leaders" in society; they are then passed in a somewhat changed form to the "opinion followers", who are thus influenced by the media only indirectly.

According to Jayaprakash Narayan, "the common people.... have come to believe that most, if not all, ministers including chief ministers, most of their representatives from *gram panchayat* presidents to members of Parliament, most, if not all, officers of the government, high or low, have become corrupt.... Ministers of the Union government are not exempt from this common belief. The Prime Minister's own image has become clouded." He went on to argue that "in the minds of the urban intelligentsia—the unattached and non-partisan—the picture is darker still. Is it any wonder then that the moral authority of the political leadership, including that of the opposition, with more exceptions, should have collapsed so completely?"

The revolt that this leader predicted broke out in 1974 against growing unemployment, 30 per cent annual inflation, rampant profiteering, inadequate supplies of essential goods, and food rationing queues for rice, wheat and sugar. Bitterness was mounting as thousands of students were jailed without trial for protesting against price rise. Gujarat was convulsed by mass demonstrations largely led by students against the corruption of the legislative assembly. The Congress Government retaliated with police and military firings. More than a hundred people were killed and disorder increased.

Jayaprakash Narayan rushed to Gujarat to ensure that the protest was non-violent. He knew that non-violent protest did not necessarily ensure a non-violent response, but in time it might ensure that the conscience of the community was aroused. "In non-violent militancy you face all attacks without flinching," he said. "I do not know if I can face immediate death without flinching but that is the militancy of nonviolence." Jayaprakash Narayan appealed to the young dissenters to give up a year of their studies to do constructive work to restore democracy. He felt that the Gujarat movement launched by the youth should be an example for the youth in other parts of the country.

By March 1974, public outrage forced Indira Gandhi to

dissolve the Gujarat Legislative Assembly. But she imposed President's rule, delaying the election her party might have lost. "The revolt spilled into Bihar which had been worse hit by rising food prices and students mess charges. Students put up fourteen demands to the Bihar government including the resignation of Chief Minister Abdul Ghafoor and the dissolution of the Assembly."

The following events were outlined by Jayaprakash Narayan in his booklet *Total Revolution.* On March 18, the students picketed the Assembly to prevent the governor from entering it. The police tear-gassed, baton-charged and fired on them. Over 10 days, thousands were jailed without trial, hundreds were wounded, and 27 were killed. After the army was ordered back to barracks, the 'security forces' were deployed and a curfew continued.

Out of despair the students sought Jayaprakash Narayan's advice and he agreed to lead them if they would use non-violent methods. He was soon in action. Declaring that police firings in Bihar had "surpassed the brutalities of the British regime," he demanded dissolution of the legislative assembly, judicial inquiries into the firings, and expulsion of 12 Congress ministers who were continuing in office although they had been found guilty of corruption by commissions of inquiry. "If Indira refused their demands, his Bihar Citizens for Democracy Movement would launch a Satyagraha and paralyze the government," he said. He announced in *Everyman's,* "I have decided to fight corruption and misgovernment and black-marketing, profiteering and hoarding.... for.... a real people's democracy."

Jeering Attack

Indira Gandhi launched a jeering attack on Jayaprakash Narayan's character, calling him corrupt, a traitor, a fascist and a believer in violence. The Bihar Government continued to rule through ordinances and attacked Jayaprakash Narayan for threatening democracy with mob rule. He responded on 9th April, riding on a jeep as the head of Gandhian Peace Workers for ten kilometres through the Patna streets. The marchers had cotton pads tied over their mouths, emphasising the silence of their protest against police cruelty. At the Patna *Gandhi Maidan*, to a gathering of over two hundred thousand, he declared: "The gravity of the people's problems has crossed its limits. Many are starving, the problem of unemployment is acquiring disastrous proportions and those who are launching an agitation to protest against the government's failures are being dubbed as fascist and reactionary forces. Nothing short of a fundamental change in the system can cure the chronic disease. I will not any more remain a silent spectator of the suffering of the masses."

He announced his determination to lead a five-week people's struggle for the resignation of the Bihar Congress Government "which has compelled almost everybody to go corrupt." He was then admitted to Vellore hospital and released again on 13 April when in Delhi, he presided over a Citizen for Democracy conference. He urged the leaders of the opposition parties to engage in a mass national movement to force the Congress Government to reform the electoral laws.

Jayaprakash Narayan led a procession on 5th June 1974 which delivered a petition to the Governor asking him to dissolve the Assembly. He declared, "Friends, this is a revolution, a total revolution. This is not a movement merely for the dissolution of the Assembly. We have to go far, very far... you will have to make sacrifices, undergo suffering... The people are being crushed under all sorts of injustices... countless children in Bihar go to sleep without food..." And he made his intentions clear through his journal *Everyman's:* "My interest is not in the capture of power but control of power by the people."

Jayaprakash Narayan invited the wrath of Indira Gandhi's Government in no time. On his return to Patna on 22nd July, the Bihar police, under a prohibitory order, bashed and jailed anyone who tried to go to the airport to meet him. Intelligence bugged his telephone connection. Despite his physical frailty his efforts to correct political immorality went on for the next six months. In the colleges he called for continuing revolution, challenging students, as Gandhi had once challenged him, to boycott their studies for a year to devote themselves to the people's struggle. He declared in *Everyman's:* "This movement is of the youth, of students, of the people." Colleges became empty, prominent artists gave up government honours they had received. Villagers resisted payment of taxes.

As a result of the assistance of most opposition parties in his no tax without elections campaign, by September JP claimed that the administration had been paralysed throughout the rural areas of Bihar. "The JP Movement reached its height in October when during a three-day *bandh* all shops, businesses and schools were closed, trains were halted by people squatting on the tracks and citizens turned out for the huge meeting that Jayaprakash addressed. "I rely on the power of the masses... a peaceful, organised expression in democratic ways, of the will and wish of the people."

Jayaprakash Narayan, like Gandhi, relied on a multi-pronged approach in his mobilisation efforts. He would constantly air his views in speeches; his *Everyman's* would come out with all the details and ideological arguments of his movement and he would time and again resort to delegation and processions. He kept the momentum of his movement alive both in Delhi and Patna. Thus even while the campuses of Delhi University and Delhi's Indian Institute of Technology rang with wild cheers of 'Long Live Jayaprakash, the People's Hero,' he led a historic march on 4th November to "paralyse functioning of Bihar's ministers by a sit in in front of their houses."

This was followed by another historic march on 6th March 1975 in Delhi when he led a procession of an estimated one million, who had pledged themselves to his total revolution, to present the people's charter to the speaker of the Lok Sabha and the chairman of the Rajya Sabha. "The charter demanded free elections in Gujarat and the dismissal and re-election of the Bihar government, with supervision by an electoral commission, and elections free of the influence of violence, money or use of public servants. An end to political corruption was demanded through public declaration of their assets by politicians and the establishment of judicial tribunals to inquire into allegations against politicians and prosecute dishonest ones. Stating that sixty per cent of the population were living in semi-starvation, the charter requested practical policies to boost the stagnant economy, halt inflation, control prices, create full employment, guarantee minimum wages, distribute land and reduce economic inequality to the ratio 1:10."

Prior to this, Jayaprakash Narayan had already indicated that he wanted to give a real mass colour to his movement. "The Bihar struggle is no longer a state issue. It has acquired an all-India importance and country's fate has come to be bound up with its success or failure."

The situation started worsening and he appealed to the government to reverse the vast expansion of state use of police and army under emergency ordinances. "Aware of how limited the checks on government power were in India with her elite so permeated with caste arrogance and the majority of her people poverty-stricken, illiterate and powerless, he appealed to the police and army to uphold the Constitution against totalitarian threats; to refuse to shoot on peaceful demonstrators; to refuse to obey order from superiors to commit illegal acts; to refuse to act against their conscience. It was a sensitive man's practical response to the habitual cruelty of police firings and assaults and the use of torture in jails. Total revolution was his moral response to total brazenness. Significantly, Indira's propaganda against him became frantic."

The movement got a shot in the arm when on June 12, 1975, the Allahabad High Court ruled that Indira Gandhi had been guilty of corrupt electoral practices. Added to Indira Gandhi's woes was the loss of the Congress in Gujarat elections. On 25th June Morarji Desai and Jayaprakash Narayan demanded her resignation at a mammoth rally at the *Ram Lila* Grounds in Delhi. The latter proposed that protesters offer Satyagraha outside Indira Gandhi's residence. This remained in the air as "at 11.00 p.m. without consulting party or parliament, she had President Fakhruddin Ali Ahmed sign a proclamation of emergency." The same night at 3.00 a.m. Jayaprakash Narayan was arrested at the Gandhi Peace Foundation in Delhi.

A reign of terror and violation of all democratic means was unleashed during the period of Emergency. It came as a crushing blow to Jayaprakash Narayan's dreams, as expressed in his journal

Everyman's, of the "fulfillment of the people's desires and needs, their freedom from exploitation, oppression, poverty and a host of similar injustices."

But then Jayaprakash Narayan's revolution did not go waste as Indira Gandhi faced a crushing defeat and the first ever non-Congress Government came to power after the 1977 general elections. He went on to become one of the greatest heroes of modern India who fought valiantly against corruption. Just after Emergency, a citation for Jayaprakash Narayan in Delhi rightly read: "We venerate you as the messiah who led us to freedom from native dictatorship through a unique ballot-box revolution in 1977, as we do the Mahatma who led us to freedom from foreign rule through a historically unique non-violent revolution in 1947." And according to M.C. Chagla, who read the citation, "While Gandhi created the nation, Jayaprakash taught the nation how it should live." However, there was some critical soul-searching immediately after Jayaprakash Narayan passed away. His abilities and contributions have come under some serious evaluation and a number of opinions have emerged. According to one view, his shortcomings in organising resistance played an important part in determining the course of his total revolution. Nikhil Chakravarthy summarises the post-1975 scenario thus: "What happened from 1975 onwards is recent history. More than what JP could do, Indira Gandhi by her folly, power-hunger and attachment to her son's mafia forced the pace and brought upon the nation the curse of Emergency. Inevitably, JP in prison became the symbol of resistance. But significantly, no organised resistance could be discerned, because JP was never a man of organisation. This absence of resistance led Indira further astray into more misdeeds. By the time the election was announced on January 18, 1977, many of the Janata heroes had already, from prison, compromised themselves by almost beseeching overtures to the Indira Government." Janata Party registered a landslide victory "not because JP had welded it into a party but because of the anger of the electorate against the Emergency Raj. The dismal history of the Janata Raj must have come as a matter of utter distress for Jayaprakash Narayan. From the sick bed, there was nothing that he could do to stem the riot. However, one wonders, with due deference to his memory, how much more he could have done had he been in a better state of health, except occasional admonitions which power hungry politicians would have ignored without qualms of conscience. The very manner of choosing the new

Innate Drawbacks

Janata Prime Minister gave an inkling of the innate drawbacks that has always afflicted JP in handling of organisational matters at the best of times. His Total Revolution was at best an emotional urge without the contours of a well-framed idea. This was indeed a career bereft of consummation."

Jayaprakash Narayan is no more today but has "left this world of sordid politics with an abundance of tributes and gratitude from his countrymen and women. If one has taken a critical view of his life-work, it is with the fullest knowledge that JP belonged to the generation wherein leaders could listen to criticism and were not scared at nor insensitive to the slightest murmur of dissent as do those who strut about the political stage today. Under different aegis and in different times Jayaprakash Narayan would have had a better epitaph than the crumbing edifice of the discredited Janata Party."

In his whole exercise, Jayaprakash Narayan made good use of the press. He used to write regularly and express his ideas on various issues. In fact, he made the press a partner in his campaign during the JP movement. This was so because he was aware of the power of the press in political mobilisation. He regularly used this potent medium for communicating his ideas on political, social and international issues. His speeches, much like Gandhi's, were equally powerful and he used them to propagate his political philosophy. In conjunction with his writings, his speeches left a long-lasting imprint on the masses. His prowess as a communicator resembled that of Gandhi's.

14

Perspectives and Prospects

The Indian press today is in the throes of a revolution. A revolution, not in content or thinking but a revolution in production technique and commercialisation. A whole new genre has been added to it with the magazine explosion which began after 1976. The Emergency declared in 1975 was a turning point in the history of Indian journalism. It saw the emergence of the news magazine in a big way and of the investigative reporter. According to one writer: 'The last decade undoubtedly had cut a swath of excitement and vitality through the quagmire of staid punditry in which Indian journalism had bogged down. With the end of the Emergency, the Indian press came back on a rebound perhaps unmatched anywhere else in the world. It was as if Prometheus had been unchained. A revolution was under way not only of style and substance but also in variety, management, circulation, technology, professionalism, marketing and design."

Arun Shourie, described as the father of Indian investigative reporting, noted: "The Emergency affected the politicisation of the Indian middle class with the result that they wanted to know more and more about the people ruling them." And in the words of another noted journalist: "The job these readers and consumers wanted the new breed of eagerly responding reporters and editors to do for them was to take the cobwebs out of reporting."

The Emergency left in its wake a plethora of scandal, gossip and unpleasant stories which were like manna from heaven to the news-hungry magazines which exploited them to their best advantage and circulations soared to unheard of heights bringing in more and more magazines which flooded the market. Two of them which have managed to forge ahead and establish themselves with unprecedented circulations are *India Today* and *Sunday*. *India Today*, a fortnightly, first came out in late 1975. It was intended to be a news magazine for Indians living abroad. Madhu Trehan, its founder editor, was an Indian resident abroad with a journalism diploma from an American university. Seeing that the first issue had evoked a good response from the domestic market it was decided to cater to Indian readers and Arun Purie, brother of Madhu Trehan, took over as editor. An accountant by training, Arun Purie proved an able editor and he put *India Today* firmly on its feet. According to one writer: "With skilful editing and slick production, *India Today* captured two kinds of readers: one, the existing newspaper reader who wanted access to well-written stories; second, the kind of reader who did not read the newspapers too carefully and wanted the news delivered to him once a fortnight in a glossy, easy to digest package."

India Today is the largest circulated fortnightly and besides English has also two other editions, one in Hindi and the other in Tamil both of which are said to be popular commanding good circulation. A Telugu edition was also under preparation.

Sunday, a weekly, from the *Anand Bazar Patrika* group, was launched in 1970 under the editorship of M.J. Akbar and it was an instant success. The same group started the English daily, *Telegraph*, in Calcutta in 1982 with Akbar as editor. The *Week*, published by the *Malayalam Manorma* group from Kottayam and *Frontline*, a fortnightly from the publishers of *The Hindu*, were other news magazines which have made good. Also making a determined bid to capture the front rank was the *Illustrated Weekly of India* of the *Times of India* group which under its energetic and enterprising editor, Pritish Nandy, had a face-lift with interesting articles and features.

Pritish Nandy soon captured the imagination of the newspaper reading public with his startling interviews with the most important politicians, ministers and VIPs in all walks of life which cost many of them their jobs or reputation because of the statements made by them or the views they expressed. Nandy had a way of extracting information from the most hesitant and unwilling person he interviewed and literally made them incriminate themselves. This was seen in the interview he got from Devi Lal, Deputy Prime Minister, in which he described the Prime Minister as "spineless" and cast disparaging remarks on other ministers. The interview was one of the reasons for V.P. Singh sacking Devi Lai from the Cabinet. In the same way Chandrasekhar, a prominent leader of the ruling Janata Dal, told Nandy in an interview that his telephone was being tapped and his drawing room bugged and this became a question of privilege and was referred to the Privileges Committee of the Lok Sabha.

Unfortunately the centurian *Illustrated Weekly of India* ceased publication early in 1993, as its circulation fell steeply and it became a total loss. The investigative scoop, the personality profiles, the arresting photo feature and the no-hold-barred interviews, not to mention the scandals and gossip of the film world which the news magazines provided in profusion, were lapped up by a sensation-starved readership. There was a dramatic jump in circulation of periodicals and newspapers. In 1975, there were 225 publications—newspapers and magazines—with a combined circulation of just over 14 million. In 1985, there were 300 publications with a combined circulation of more than 26 million.

Great Impact

The journalist who made the greatest impact on his readers was Arun Shourie, who first wrote for *India Today* and later became executive editor of the *Indian Express* which published his investigative stories day after day, and week after week. He exposed Emergency excesses and abuse of authority and his particular target was Indira Gandhi. He successfully uncovered the misuse of official position by a chief minister to collect funds and his story created a storm in Parliament and in the country, and finally resulted in the ouster of the chief minister and in his prosecution. An admirer has said: "Shourie had an impact on Indian journalism that few will be able to equal. Firstly, he proved the power of newspapers. If you have a story on the front page of every one of your editions when Parliament is in session, then the government has to take notice. Secondly, he showed journalists how to push themselves, how always to investigate further and to document everything. And thirdly, he was the first Indian journalist to become a nationally respected figure and thereby altered the entire perception of journalism as a profession." Another journalist described Shourie as a man of "phenomenal intelligence, passionate intolerance of injustice and unerring grasp of how best to break a story."

As a campaign journalist and also as an investigative reporter Arun Shourie has many scoops to his credit. A cartoon published in the Indian Express on August 27 1990, claimed that the newspaper had successfully captured the scalps of two former Prime Ministers, a former Home Minister, a former Lok Sabha Speaker and most recently of a Deputy Prime Minister. The man responsible for this achievement is Arun Shourie. His anti-Devi Lai stories in the Indian Express almost every day became the staple diet of its readers and the climax came when he disclosed that the Deputy Prime Minister had sent a forged letter to the Prime Minister which V.P. Singh is said to have written to the President in 1986 making allegations against Arun Nehru now a member of his Cabinet. This revelation was largely responsible for the subsequent Ouster of Devi Lai from the Union Cabinet. Arun Shourie then turned his attention to the 27 per cent reservation for the Backward classes under the Mandal Commission report for jobs in central government and public undertakings announced by V.P. Singh early in September 1990. He carried on a campaign against it and wrote columns of articles about the Mandal Commission's report tearing it to pieces. He even supported the students agitation against the announcement which spread like wild fire throughout the country except in the south. Earlier Arun Shourie was a recipient of Padma Bhushan in the Republic Day awards in January, 1990. Arun Shourie was sacked again by Indian Express proprietor Ramnath Goenka early in 1991 as he did not agree with his writings. That was his third dismissal from the paper which he did so much to popularise as a guardian of the people's rights and protection of freedom of the press.

Arun Shourie later retired from active journalism and concentrated on writing books. His latest book on the work of missionaries during the British rule was widely reviewed in the print media.

Another investigative journalist to be honoured by the Government with Padma Bhushan in the Republic Day awards was N. Ram Associate Editor of *The Hindu* who distinguished himself by his investigative stories on the Bofors deal. The documents which he published in his paper in association with the paper's Geneva correspondent, Mrs. Chitra Subramaniam created a sensation and made it beyond doubt that something shady had taken place in concluding the deal and some highly placed individuals had received kickbacks. But unfortunately before he could complete his work he got into trouble with his Editor and the controversy came into the open with both parties accusing each other in public. The dispute between Ram and Editor G. Kasturi went to court but was finally settled outside the court Not long after G. Kasturi resigned as editor, which post he had held with distinction for over four decades and N. Ravi, Ram's younger brother succeeded him.

There were some editorial changes in the major newspapers. Girilal Jain retired as Editor of the *Times of India* after a distinguished record of service, and passed away after a few years. He was succeeded by Dilip Padgaonkar, who resigned following differences with the management. Gautam Adhikari was appointed Editor. *The Hindustan Times* got a new Editor, V.N. Narayanan with H. K. Dua joining the *Indian Express* as Editor-in-Chief. With the passing away of Girilal Jain, the era of the great editors came to an end. Today, there is no editor comparable in stature and influence with the giants of the past in India.

The Arun Shourie expose stories set off a chain of other investigative stories, some of them gruesome and revolting. The *Indian Express* took the credit for most of these. One of the reporters, Ashwin Sarin, heard that women were being bought and sold like cattle in Madhya Pradesh and he pursued the story in spite of government denials. He went out to that state and disguising himself 'bought' a woman and brought her to Delhi, proving that women were being sold in Madhya Pradesh. The same reporter got himself arrested on a drunken charge and went to Tihar Jail of Delhi to expose the abominable conditions there. Another reporter, Arun Sinha, created a sensation when he reported the blinding of undertrial prisoners by the police in Bihar. In Bombay, Sheela Barse, a free-lance journalist, who wrote a series of articles on child prostitution followed it by moving the court to release children languishing in a remand home. Praful Bidwai of the *Times of India* in a series of articles exposed the inefficient administration of the nuclear establishment.

In recent days, some women journalists have entered the field of investigative journalism with outstanding ability and performance. They include Anita Pratap, *Time* correspondent in New Delhi, Rasheeda Bhagat, Chief of News Bureau, *Indian Express,* Madras and Sucheta Dalal of the *Times of India.* Anita Pratap, who was in the *Sunday Weekly* and the daily *Telegraph* before joining the international periodical *Time* has a number of investigative stories to her credit including an exclusive interview she got from the LTTE leader Prabhakaran at his hideout in Jaffna. Rasheeda Bhagat, entering the *Express* as a reporter, quickly became Chief Reporter and then Chief of Bureau. She has exposed many scandals of official misconduct of bureaucrats reflecting poor administration. Her investigative stories are invariably foolproof and incontrovertible. Sucheta Dalai was responsible for exposing the security scandal that rocked the country, convulsing the stock markets and the Indian Parliament.

An observer of the scene today writes: "Editors in the new magazines get five-figure incomes and even the sub-editors of yester-years now begin jobs in progressive organisations with four-figure packets. With so much money beckoning, several senior journalists have quit cradle-to-grave secure positions to strike out on their own as syndicated columnists. And they are getting rich quick." According to one writer: "Whereas earlier journalists had been underpaid hacks, eager for subsidised accommodation and government handouts, the new type of journalist was irreverent, iconoclastic and had a healthy contempt for politicians."

In the first flush of success, the news magazines went all out to provide a diet of sensationalism and in the words of a writer they specialised in "stripping bodies and reputations". As one observer wrote: "News had the same meaning in the developing countries as in the West—placing a premium on the sensational violence, crime, wars, dacoity and dirty politics. The trend was in giving more importance to what was wrong than what was right, to conflicts rather than to resolving them." This observer noted that the stories published by the magazines "had no relation to the typical lives of rural people or people in general. The result of this was that at times reportable incidents were crowded out by stories of murders, race and communal riots, strikes, violence, *gheraos* and quarrels among public functionaries." The Second Press Commission referring to this aspect of journalism said that the objection was not to reporting these incidents, which in any case formed a part of the news flow, but to the preoccupation with them to such an extent that the readers were not supplied the information they needed to "discharge their responsibilities to society."

Many of the reports and features carried in the news magazines bordered on defamation and libel and it could be said of them what was said about American newspapers by a commentator: "Most present day newspapers knowingly print potentially libellous statements. They do so because otherwise they would have a dull paper. Consequently, some of the best stories in the paper would run a chance of being adjudged libellous if examined in court. But the newspaper, in its attempt to present interesting material, is willing to take the risk. It also prints potentially libellous material because many of the people libelled are not in a position to sue the paper or because the paper can often secure a small out-of-court settlement if the probable outcome appears dark. The wisdom of the newspaper's course is evidenced by the small number of cases won by the plaintiffs as compared with the abundance of material which is potentially libellous."

The Reflection

The news magazines are also a reflection of the state of mind of the people today. In the words of Norman Cousins: "What is happening today is that the natural reactions of the individual against violence are being blunted. The individual is being desensitised by living history. We are developing new reflexes and new responses that tend to slow down the moral imagination and relieve us of essential indignation over impersonal hurt. We are becoming casual about brutality. We have made our peace with violence."

There is a brighter side to the news magazines. Of them, M.V. Kamath, the well-known journalist wrote: "I envy them, their style, their elan, their self-assuredness—even their arrogance.... I admire all the new writers and commentators. There is a certain freshness about them like that of newly laundered sheets. The commentators, the critics, the reviewers and the reporters sound knowledgeable. There is so much educated writing.... Perhaps their sentences lack the natural flow of thought. I often notice the absence of harmony and grace in the new writing. But what they do not have in these departments they make up by the vigour of their style and the force of their argument. They are very provocative and persistent and if I may say so, irreverent." Kamath noted: "There is a sharp and happy emphasis on design and layout in the new journalism; the lay-out man and the artist are coming into their own. And another welcome development is the respect given to columnists and commentators."

What one writer calls the "aggressive spirit of the decade"

has been confined to the news magazines and the newspapers, by and large, have been unaffected by it. While they have made considerable progress in updating techniques of production and management, there has been no appreciable change in their contents and thinking. What V.S. Naipaul wrote of the Indian press some years ago still holds good in the large majority of cases. "Indian newspapers", he said, "have a limited vision and there is an absence of enquiry, the absence of what may be called human interest. The liveliness of the Indian press is confined to the editorial pages. Elsewhere, there are mainly communiques, handouts, reports of speeches and functions. Indian journalism developed no reporting tradition; it often reported India as a foreign country." Naipaul said: 'The Indian press has interpreted its function in an Indian way. It has not sought to put India in touch with itself; it doesn't really know how and it hasn't felt the need.... Away from the political inferno of its editorial pages, it saw few causes for concern.... With its restricted view of its functions, it matched the triviality of the politics; it became part of the Indian anarchy. It reported speeches and more speeches; it reduced India to its various legislative chambers. It turned into national figures those politicians who were the least predictable." Another foreign observer has noted that a feature of the Indian press was that its reporting lacked initiative. "Well-known writers," he said, "were philosophical in outlook; their criticisms were pitched at a high level of generality.... It was perhaps little wonder that faced with India's problems, India's newspapers sometimes seemed to be preaching."

James Cameron, the veteran journalist, wrote that it was uncommonly difficult to find out what was going on anywhere if one depended on an Indian newspaper. "It had not", he wrote, "the purposeful stubbornness of the communist press nor the meretricious stupidity of the pop press of the West it was just semi-literate, ill-argued, imitative; when it was not boring it was exasperating. The newspapers occasionally professed to be combating pressures from government which was quixotic since the Indian press was a processing plant for government handouts and for convoluted obfuscation Indian Government handouts have to be read to be believed or otherwise as the case may be."

Arun Shourie has remarked that a "distressingly large" number in the profession today were not even "good professionals". "Many of them", he said, "have incestuous relations with their subjects—in particular with government authorities. Many have the most cavalier attitude to facts, many are too lazy to inform themselves of the laws that impinge on their work—and the laws are just a few pages each; so many are too lazy to examine the allegations they purvey; they are so cynical and casual as not to have even an author's concern about whether what they write is used at all, whether it is mutilated or not, the limit of their concern being to file their 750-word dispatch. A distressingly large proportion among them spend more time on petty intrigues and back-biting than on their work."

"Modern Indian journalism", wrote another journalist, "is doubtless producing specialists, investigators, unearthing interesting potential but much of the talent is insecurely based because of a certain disregard for precision in the use of language and rigour in reasoning. This arguably is true of far too many recent knight errants in the profession, though there are obvious and distinguished exceptions. Actually, some of the older 'new' columnists too are not free of this disability which prompts them to rush into areas of rhetoric where the more circumspect would fear to tread."

The Second Press Commission said in its report: "Many foreign observers have commented on the preoccupation of the Indian press with politics and politicians. There would be nothing wrong if it were preoccupation with politics in the large Aristotelian sense of concern with the building of a society which shall make the good life possible. The preoccupation, however, is largely with the petty politics of conflict between and within political parties and with the sayings and doings of ministers and other prominent politicians." The commission cited the example of newspapers giving prominence to what the home minister said while inaugurating the World Religious Conference held in Delhi and virtually ignoring what the world religious leaders had to say about the oneness of religion. The commission was only highlighting what is a common failing of Indian newspapers. At all conferences, meetings, and seminars what the professionals or experts or people intimately connected with the topics discussed say does not count and is given minimum space while the amateurish platitudes and generalities of ministers and other dignitaries secure maximum space and headlines.

The Press Commission said: "The role that the press plays in a country is considerably influenced by the news values which prevail among journalists. If conflict is news but not the resolution of conflict, if the unusual and the bizarre is news rather than the normal, if news is what happened just a while ago (even if the event was not significant) and not a significant happening of a week or month earlier which has only now come to light the portrayal of reality in the press is bound to be distorted." The commission found the influence of the news and pictorial values of Western newspapers even in highly reputed daily newspapers and magazines. "It arises", it observed, "from the prevalent news values among editors, news editors, sub-editors and reporters who are collectively referred to as 'gatekeepers of news' because they determine what shall be published." Pran Chopra wrote: "The journalist confronts innumerable events every hour of the day and handles innumerable messages about them. Out of the heap he picks a few by purely his own subjective judgement and he puts them on a paper of whose ultimate destination he has no idea. His audience is varied and largely unknown to him. And lately he has begun to care a little less about what his reader's preferences are and to care a little more about what he thinks they should be."

Most Elementary

Accuracy is the most elementary thing in journalism and yet it has not been completely mastered by Indian newspapers. As one writer put it: "Its lessons may be learnt by heart one day, only to be imperfectly remembered the next. No journalist regards inaccuracy, either inadvertent or deliberate as a good thing but, nevertheless, many journalists condone it as a necessary evil in the attainment of speed and the maximum of news interest, trusting in a higher general average of authenticity to maintain confidence in the paper within the margin of safety."

Distortion of news is another malady of many Indian newspapers. Distortion can happen in the following ways; (1) Highlighting of events that have no real importance by interweaving the anecdotal with the irrelevant and what is considered picturesque with facts of real national significance; (2) Making news by putting together isolated facts and presenting them as a whole or presenting partial truths in such a way that they amount to the whole truth; (3) Misrepresentation by implication characterised by the presentation of facts in such a way that the implicit conclusions are favourable to particular interests; (4) Distortion by "pre-conditioning" of events, specific facts being presented in such a way that unfounded or exaggerated fears and misgivings are created in order to condition later action by individuals, communities and Governments; (5) Distortion by keeping silent on situations presumed to be no longer of interest to the public; (6) Distortion arising from government control of news, from restrictions on the freedom of access to news sources, from censorship and from government authority infringing press freedom.

It seems necessary to broaden the concept of news specially in a developing country like ours. News must include not only "events" but entire "processes"—hunger being a process while a hunger strike is an event; a flood being an event while a long struggle to control floods is a process. Our reporters and journalists must give greater coverage to processes and to long term ends. A new objective in the pursuit of journalism is called for. Good news should be considered just as worthy of interest as bad news. As has been remarked by a writer: "If communication is essential so that development effort receives the support and cooperation of the people at large should not communicators not only objectively report events which constitute 'valid' news but also serve as society's analysts and educators, thus, playing a vital role in the national and international struggle to promote human progress?"

A recent study on the role of the press in the Third World stressed the importance of development journalism, a field much neglected in India. "In addition to the basic task of carrying news stories or reports, it was felt that the press in developing countries should also act as a social monitor, a constructive critic, the stimulator of debates on public issues, a medium of feedback, a watchdog of democracy, a balancing wheel in the governmental structure, a great social vitaliser, a big enemy of tyrants, the right arm of liberty, an exposer of public corruption, an interpreter of public events and a professional forum for investigative and interpretative journalism." There was barely five per cent of development reporting in the Indian press in the sixties and seventies. According to the Press Commission, it was only later that language papers in Telugu, Malayalam, Bengali, Hindi and Marathi started giving appreciable space to coverage of topics such as health, family welfare, industry, science and technology, agriculture, education and public utilities. But the reporting or coverage was poor in quality, largely due to the fact that the reporters depended heavily on official handouts or briefings and did not make field study or personal observations. Reading the reports one hardly got a feel of participation in the programme or social change. According to one writer: "These reports did not provide a glimpse of what the beneficiaries directly felt about the programme or said what they got out of them.... The reporter of big and small newspapers can help to bring dynamism to the process in rural areas by keeping their feet on the rural soil, report as correctly as possible the facts and events and interpret them to the best of their light."

"The free press in a developing country," the Press Commission said, "should be more socially conscious and enterprising." It noted that development reporting should "tell the story of what is going well as well as of what is going wrong. It should investigate the reasons for success as well as failure at different places under different conditions, of various development programmes affecting the lives of common people.... Most of our newspapers merely carry official handouts giving statistics of milch cattle or poultry enabled to be brought under these schemes, the man-hours of work provided or the number of persons made literate. They do not enable the reader to 'meet' the extension workers who are the agents of change or the beneficiaries of the programmes and to hear what they have to say in their own words about their triumph and difficulties. The reporting of non-official initiative in rural development, educational reforms, leprosy relief and other areas is even less extensive than indepth reporting of the implementation of official development programmes." The commission said that lack of followup was a widespread failing of the Indian press. "It is not enough to report," it said, "in depth, a present problem; it is necessary to keep track of the further development of a situation that has been reported, in context and depth."

Following the economic reforms, based on the liberalisation policy of 1991, there has been a spurt in economic journalism with business journalists acquiring high market value, drawing fat salaries. There has been tremendous growth potential for economic newspapers and journals with increasing readership values. Prabhu Chawla, Executive Editor of the *Financial Express* said that economic liberalisation had created a new executive class. "These are the five-figure-plus income-wallahs, who want to read more about how to make money." T.C.A. Srinivasa Raghavan, Associate Editor of the *Business Standard,* echoed this view : "The growth of business journalism is related to economic liberalisation. The reader has a high interest in economic matters today, because with liberalisation the opportunity to make money has increased." According to another leading economic journalist the resurgence of the Indian economy is one of the reasons for the growth of economic journalism. "The main factor is the growth of the capital market to which the growth of financial journalism is directly related," he said. "Business papers have a natural monopoly, since the bulk of the market is institutional. The business reader has to buy the papers because he is dependent on them for information about money matters," according to Srinivasa Raghavan.

Among the economic newspapers the *Economic Times* of the

Bennett and Coleman Ltd continues to lead with 70 per cent share of the total readership. *The Financial Express* of the Indian Express group revamped its format and contents by following its track. New entrants in the field are the *Business Standard* of the Ananda Bazar Patrika group, *Calcutta and Business Line,* published by the owners of The Hindu, Madras. An upcoming fortnightly journal is *Business Today* published by the India Today group, New Delhi.

There was no daily exclusively devoted to economic or financial matters as per the first Press Commission Report of 1954. Today the position is vastly different with more and more economic newspapers and journals coming to the fore, but curiously enough there has been very few economic newspapers or journals in Indian languages so far.

Notable Feature

A notable feature of the Indian press is the prominence they give to astrological predictions. With very few exceptions, all newspapers, dailies, and periodicals, carry them as a regular item every week. The first Press Commission had condemned this practice and said: "The spread of the habit of consultation of, and reliance upon, astrological predictions, particularly of the nature and in the manner they are published at present, is certain to produce an unsettling effect on the minds of readers. We would describe the practice of publishing such predictions are undesirable." The second Press Commission endorsed this and said: "We are of the view that editors of general interest and periodicals who believe in promoting a scientific temper among their readers and in combating superstition and fatalism should discontinue the publication of astrological predictions." But apparently this sane advice has fallen on deaf ears for there has been no diminution in the publication of what the stars forecast in the daily, or periodical press, English or language.

The Indian daily press continues to suffer from a shortage of pictorial coverage of news. The Press Commission observed: "There is still a general lack of understanding of the scope of photographs in journalism among newspaper editors who have a bias for the verbal medium.... To most editors, the photo department in a newspaper is a part of the production department rather than the editorial department,... Photo journalism does not in most cases form a part of journalism training." News magazines in recent years have filled the gap to a certain extent and with the adoption of latest techniques, the reproduction of pictures has vastly improved.

While the freedom of the press has been assured, the freedom of the editor has been left in doubt. In recent years many Indian editors have had to resign their jobs or been dismissed in their bid to assert their independence and protest against proprietorial interference. James Cameron put the problem in a nutshell when he asked: "How is it possible to equate the commercial success that is indispensable to a liberated paper with the business interests that will always encroach upon that liberty?" The Press Commission said: 'The interest of the owner of a newspaper generally lies in its economic success. However, commercial considerations ought not to override editorial considerations. The freedom of the owner is only a part of the freedom of the press. The owner has the basic right to have his point of view expressed through the newspaper. In the case of a large newspaper operating in modern conditions, this right of the owner should not extend beyond laying down the policy of the newspaper and the appointment of an editor of his choice. But the editor chosen ought to be a man of known ability and integrity and should have sufficient authority to conduct the newspaper in public interest while following the policy laid down by the owner."

"Journalistic freedom", the Commission said, "is the heart of the freedom of the press. To maintain a free traffic in ideas for the good of the community and to discharge his social functions, the journalist should have an atmosphere of freedom. But the unity purpose of a newspaper can be ensured only by the development of a spirit of cooperative enterprise whereby everyone realises that he is working towards a common goal. The effective exercise of journalistic freedom depends largely on the editor. The freedom and independence of the editor is the crux of the matter."

The commission found that by and large "the policy of the newspaper is not reduced to writing and if there are differences of opinion between the editor and the proprietor over a matter of policy, the former is obliged to quit. The status of the editor varies from paper to paper and in many cases it is not what it should be. It appears that in many cases editors do not have enough say in the selection and appointment of journalistic staff and assignment of professional duties to them." The commission which held editorial independence to be of the utmost importance, suggested as a safeguard against proprietorial or management interference in editorial independence, the appointment of a Board of Trustees as a buffer between the management and the editor. The Board, it said, would ensure that the policy of the paper is carried out and it would act as an umpire in disputes between the management and the editor. The trustees of the Board would be public men of unquestionable integrity and of eminence in the field of journalism, law, science and other learned professions. This recommendation was not accepted by some members of the commission and it does not seem to have had any positive response from, newspaper owners.

Classic Example

A classic example where the editor was sacked because he would not submit to the dictates of the proprietor was that of B.G. Verghese, editor of the *Hindustan Times,* who was dismissed by G.D. Birla, owner of the paper. Verghese had been press adviser to Prime Minister Indira Gandhi and when he left that job Mrs. Gandhi, it was stated, recommended him to Birla. Birla appointed him editor of the *Hindustan Times* but very soon he found Verghese was pursuing an editorial policy which was at variance with his own intentions and objective. Since Verghese proved not amenable, he sacked him. The working journalists led by the I.F.W.J.. protested against this action and went on a strike. They took the matter to the Press Council and said that Verghese had been penalised because he would not follow a particular editorial policy as a matter of conscience. The Press Council pleaded helplessness in the matter and declined to interfere. Many years later, the noted journalist Khushwant Singh suffered the same fate when he had to quit as editor of the *Hindustan Times* in similar circumstances. For Khushwant Singh it was the second time such a thing had happened. Earlier, after a sucessful term as editor of the *Illustrated Weekly of India* (a *Times of India* publication) he found one morning his chair occupied by another editor and the notice of discharge waiting for him. Arun Shourie had a similar experience when he was Executive editor of the *Indian Express* before he joined the *Times of India* and, curiously enough, he came back to the *Indian Express* early in 1987 and within a few months the editor, Suman Dubey, had to go, leaving the post vacant for Shourie for whom the Express became the biggest and most powerful forum for the anti-Rajiv Gandhi campaign.

J.N. Sahni, the veteran nationalist-newspaper editor, made a caustic comment on the attitude of Indian editors. "Under the British," he wrote, "the fear of iron chains or a whole series of coercive measures threatened press freedom. These also served as a challenge which journalists had to meet. After independence, silver chains made cowards of many a star writer than penal restrictions. To ensure big salaries and expensive comforts, one naturally had to first serve those who controlled the papers and only then the common people. With independence, editorial salaries had spiralled up to impressive figures. Most editors, therefore, struggled between the prudence of self-interest and the abandon of self-expression. The result was higher salaries and controlled opinions. With fabulous investments at stake, 'responsible' editors could not play ducks and drakes with policy. At the same time, high circulations had to be built up to attract maximum advertising at the highest rates. Unless readers felt attracted and interested, high circulations were not possible. Proprietors, therefore, were prepared to pay high salaries to able editors who combined tact with adaptability. Failing that, a few preferred to become editors themselves. Through the process of orientation and adaptation to changed conditions, the Indian press began to attract at its helm as much ability as elevated ignorance....The Indian press could, therefore, be appropriately described as a capably edited institution working under proprietorial control through 'confidence men' where necessary in an atmosphere of legal freedom." Another journalist of standing who found improvement in all branches of journalism added: "It is only in editorial writing that I would hesitate to make that assertion. For the editorial writers of old, especially in the nationalist papers had greater passion and a loftier cause. Gone are the giants."

In an interview to the *Illustrated Weekly of India,* Ramnath Goenka, the press baron, was asked: "Is there any journalist around whose work you like, who you can find is a crusader in the real sense of the word?" "I'm afraid none." Question: Is there any columnist you read regularly whose opinion you respect? Answer: None that 1 can think of right now. In reply to another question, Goenka said: "Where is the talent to hire? Where are the editors you attract? There just are not enough editors around, I mean, good editors, men of courage and integrity."

Major Problem

A major problem of Indian journalism today is the big business ownership of multiple newspapers. The Press Commission noted: "It appears to us that a very significant part of the press in the country in general and a major portion of the important daily press in particular is controlled by persons having strong links with other businesses or industries." According to Press in India, 1985 published by the Registrar of Newspapers there were 108 common ownership units in 1984 (a common ownership unit is one which has two or more news interest newspapers of which at least one is a daily). These units, owned among themselves 374 news interest newspapers (299 dailies, 63 weeklies and 12 other periodicals). Among the big units are Bennett Coleman Company (15 news interest publications) claiming the highest circulation of 17,19,000 copies, and the Express group (33 news interest publications) with a circulation of 14,66,000 copies. The big units dominated not only English journalism but also language journalism. The percentages are English: 85; Bengali; 70.9; Gujarati: 81.4; Hindi: 41.2. Eleven big units published 34 dailies from metropolitan cities. Hindi led all other newspapers in 1982 with 5655 papers (28.4 per cent) with English coming second with 3689 papers (18.5 per cent) and Bengali third with 1537 papers (7.7 per cent).

The Press Commission said: "When newspapers are controlled by other big business they become vehicles of expression of the ideology of their owners and the selection, presentation and display of news in such newspapers would be dictated by that ideology. The newspaper industry in their hands becomes involuntarily the cultural arm of other businesses and industries and takes a vested interest in maintaining the existing socio-economic system. The newspapers controlled by them may be selective in their presentation of news and views in return for benefits conferred in respect of their other business interests... If all major newspapers come to represent a similar if not the same viewpoint as is not unlikely when all of them belong to large private business enterprises, a viewpoint which is against the interest of private big business may not receive a fair deal in their columns. It is enough for our purpose to say that legislative measures needed for achieving the goals of our state run counter to the vested interests of the owners of these big newspapers who have large interests in other business." At one time, delinking and diffusion of newspaper ownership was considered by the government and in 1971 a draft bill was even prepared for the purpose but it was not proceeded with.

Should there be a code of ethics for journalists and newspapers and if so who should frame it? This has been a hotly debated question and an answer has not yet been found. Government spokesmen have made it clear that it is a matter to be decided by the press and they would not take any initiative. Arun Shourie has said that a code is necessary because "standards of the press are indeed very low" and they should be improved. "The prevailing laxity", he said, "harms the community as well as individuals". He thought that a code would be a shield for the pressman, a code that would not be just an ideal but which when worked "will have the virtue of drawing out the best in the journalist and will constitute a protection so that should the authorities attempt to put down a person adhering to the code, they will at once put themselves in the wrong."

The *Indian Express* said in an editorial: "For the press as a whole the path of self-control remains the safest and the most effective. A code imposed by an outside agency, even by the Press Council, could become the thin end of a wedge of governmental intervention. But a journalist's credo, voluntary and gallant, is surety necessary. Such a credo would despise falsehood and indecency, call for accuracy in facts, impartiality in display and swiftness in admitting error. A code of this kind will not make a saint of the all-too-human journalist, but his awareness of its contents can make him a worthier citizen. An unprofessional press hesitating to set its own standards might invite harsher laws. Equally, a press inspired by a professional credo will be the more able, should a test occur, to stand up to opponents of media freedom.

At present, the only body which watches the conduct of the press and entertains complaints against it is the Press Council which, however, has no punitive powers. The utmost it can do is to censure a newspaper if warnings and admonition fail to produce results. The Press Council, supported by the Press Commission, has urged the government to amend the Press Council Act to give it more teeth. The council is against framing a code of ethics. It said it would build up such a code in course of time through precedents established in the process of dealing with specific complaints. The council has held that mere enunciation of certain basic principles in general terms had not proved helpful when it came to applying them to individual cases. In its view, if these principles were to be reduced to a kind of code of conduct or journalistic propriety by the council, they would have a tendency to attain a degree of rigidity which might give rise to difficulties. The Press Commission's conclusion was: "We are of the view that it would not be desirable to draw up a code of ethics for newspapers. As the Press Council has maintained such a code could be built up case by case over a period of time."

An Arrangement

The commission suggested that the Press Council should enter into arrangement with selected university departments of journalism, the Indian Institute of Mass Communication and the Press Institute of India for monitoring the performance of newspapers in respect of important issues from time to time in a given language or languages. The commission observed that the underlying principle that "governs or should govern the press is that the gathering and selling of news and views is essentially a public trust. It is based upon a tacit contract with the public that the news shall be true to the best of the knowledge and belief of those who offer it for sale and that their comment upon it shall be sincere according to their lights. A journalist who sells or is a party to selling news that he knows to be false or only partly true or who trims opinions so as to make them palatable, is more guilty than a tradesman who gives short weight or a manufacturer who offers adulterated goods. The spreading of false statements is more harmful than the sale of material wares under false pretences. The journalist who betrays his trust is more blameworthy than a dishonest tradesman. Journalism as the basis of the newspaper industry, holds a special position because its raw material is really the public mind and it trades chiefly in moral values."

Chanchal Sarkar has advocated that Indian newspapers should employ ombudsmen as watchdogs on the doings of the newspaper and as intermediaries between the newspaper and the public. In the past 18 years, he said, many newspapers in the U.S.A., Japan, Sweden and Canada had appointed ombudsmen with gratifying results. Some ombudsmen wrote a column in their newspaper analysing controversies about news coverage by the newspaper and some confined themselves to sending memos to top brass of the newspaper and negotiating to have readers' grievances redressed. Some put memos on the notice board for all the staff to read. No Indian newspaper has yet decided to have an ombudsman. "Is it arrogance, lack of courage, or an inability to take criticism which is very much a characteristic of Indian public affairs?" Chanchal Sarkar asked.

One of the oft heard complaints against the Indian press is that it does not publish contradictions or refutations promptly and prominently. According to one commentator: "Certain newspapers show a general reluctance to publish contradictions unless the matter is brought before the Press Council. If the right of reply is properly understood and given effect to, the grievances of numerous persons would stand redressed."

The Indian press today is free but it does not have a wide enough reach. It has an urban and middle class base which limits its contribution towards making the development process more widely participatory. Daily newspapers and periodicals published from the metropolitan cities, especially Delhi, have hitherto commanded a degree of attention which is out of all proportion to their share of the total circulation. Today, however, the difference between the metropolitan and provincial papers, between English and language papers is not so great. In fact, some small town papers have gone in for more advanced technology than the big ones. In the words of a commentator: "There is a lack of improvement in the quality of articulation in the language press. There is a tendency to go away from the speech of the common people, from the spoken word." But as the Press Commission has remarked, it is the language press "which is becoming increasingly relevant to the bulk of our people with the growing use of Indian languages as the media of education. Apart from this trend which will continue, the relevance of, and demand for, language newspapers will be enhanced to the extent that they acquire a development orientation." It is the language press which holds the key to the future growth and strength of Indian journalism.

The latter half of Mrs. Indira Gandhi's prime ministership was a period of political unrest, communal eruptions and administrative problems in the north-west and north-east states. Mrs. Gandhi had her hands full tackling Sikh extremist violence in Punjab and the violent agitation in Assam over the nationality question, not to speak of the widespread discontent and corruption in her own Congress (I) party and the deteriorating relations with the non-Congress governments in the states, especially West Bengal and Andhra Pradesh. In Punjab, she ordered the army to enter the Golden Temple and flush out the extremists and that led to the outbreak of terrorism by misguided Sikh youths which assumed monstrous proportions resulting in enormous loss of innocent lives and property and which continues unabated to this day. Her partymen indulged in attempts to topple non-Congress governments in states and with disastrous results in Andhra Pradesh where for a brief period they were able to instal a dissident leader as chief minister with the connivance of the governor. And the country's situation became grave when in October, 1984, Mrs. Gandhi was shot dead by her Sikh security guards. Mrs. Gandhi's eldest son, Rajiv Gandhi, was quickly swom in as prime minister by President Zail Singh. There was a wave of sympathy throughout the country for the youngest prime minister of India and this was reflected in the general elections of 1985 when the Congress (I) was returned to power at the centre with a stupendous majority crushing all opposition parties.

In an effort to stem the tide of terrorism in Punjab, Rajiv Gandhi signed an accord with the Akali leader, Sant Longowal, agreeing to most of the Akali demands but this did not solve the problem as there was delay in the implementation of the accord and Sant Longowal himself was assassinated by the extremists. He also entered into a pact with the agitators in Assam. The Congress (I) lost elections in Punjab and Assam, but Rajiv Gandhi was not worried; his partymen were. Rajiv Gandhi was a great success in the international arena and was acclaimed as a statesman. At home he was called "Mr. Clean" as a tribute to his dynamic leadership and incorruptibility. But within two years Rajiv Gandhi's high ranking popularity took a nose dive and by early 1987 an unprecedented high velocity attack was mounted against him by the print media and at least one newspaper accused him bluntly of accepting bribes and urged the president to dismiss him.

Indian newspapers and news magazines had a field day from the closing years of Mrs. Garlhi's regime and circulations soared and more newspapers and magazines made their appearance, to share in the prosperity. The era of "controversial journalism" began in full blast and politicians of all hues, and glamorous and not so glamorous personalities in other walks of life became willing instruments of polemical and character assassination journalism. Rumour mills and gossip vendors worked overtime and the reputation of no politician, however mighty and powerful he might be, was safe from the devastating pen of the so-called investigative journalists of the news magazines, who, it seemed, vied with one another in destructive criticism. It became, in fact, a competition as to who could dig up more dirt and damage the reputation of the greatest number of people. In this most rewarding type of journalism the device of the "interview" was used with telling effect and a tape recorder was the constant companion of every investigative reporter. These stories were displayed at times without regard to the laws of libel and defamation to get the maximum impact. One prominent weekly carried the report of an interview with a chief minister who stoutly denied he was a sex maniac and did not do anything wrong. But in the main story the writer stuck to his defamatory charges and it was reflected in the lead and heading. In another instance, a chief minister who entertained a well known journalist made some injudicious remarks off the record and when the journalist published them breaking the unwritten understanding, the chief minister got into trouble with his party and ultimately lost his job. In the case of at least two politicians, the interviewing journalist by cleverly drawing them out and allowing them to satisfy their ego and let off steam was able to publish "juicy" interviews which led to their being expelled from the party. A leading national newspaper one day carried this heading in bold type and prominently displayed: UP chief ordered 'massacre' of youths. The heading was based on an interview by a politician and the story began with this lead; "Uttar Pradesh Chief Minister V.P. Singh ordered the massacre of 81 youths belonging to a particular community at Hassimpura area of Meerut on May 22 night in a bid to 'teach them a lesson', Lok Dal (A) Secretary Subramanyam Swamy alleged here today."

Not all news magazines lived by sensation and controversies. Some have matured and proved to be reliable and balanced in their approach to news stories. The fortnightlies, *India Today* and

Frontline and the weekly *Sunday,* may be cited as examples. One noteworthy feature of the news magazines is that every week or fortnight, they almost always carry the same stories or interviews with the same personalities and if you read one you have read them all except that the angle and the emphasis may be different. By covering the same ground, the news magazines, both English and language, have established a wide range of readership in large parts of the country and this has led to the emergence of an educated electorate which is well aware of the political developments in the country and the personalities involved in them.

The newspapers, both English and language, are, with a few exceptions, free from the type of journalism specialised in by the news magazines. In fact, investigative journalism or what passes as such in India, has not percolated to daily newspapers in a big way yet. But there are at least two English dailies, *The Statesman* and *The Indian Express,* who claim investigative reporting as their strong point. The Insight Team of the Statesman has been responsible for many expose stories and the Indian Express has not lagged far behind. With Arun Shourie back at the helm (he resigned his job in the *Times of India* and rejoined the *Indian Express* as editor in 1987) the tempo of investigative journalism has quickened. The *Indian Express* today is in the vanguard of the newspapers campaigning against Rajiv Gandhi and calling for his resignation as prime minister. It has waged a long and relentless battle and it has left no stone unturned to achieve its objective. At the height of the controversy over the relations between the prime minister and the president which was triggered by reports that the prime minister was not keeping the president informed of developments at home and abroad and that he was not meeting him as often as he should, causing unhappiness to the president, it was the *Indian Express* which reproduced the copy of a letter written by President Zail Singh to Rajiv Gandhi contradicting his statement in Parliament about his relations with the president and detailing the wrongs done to him. The publication of the letter opened the floodgates of a political controversy which reached a stage where the president was advised by the *Indian Express* and opposition parties to dismiss Rajiv Gandhi for violating the Constitution.

Even as this battle royal was going on with Rashtrapati Bhawan and its occupant claiming centre stage in the press and the evolution of "peephole journalism" in which some newspapers and magazines indulged to aggravate the crisis, the Fairfax issue exploded and with it the V.P. Singh affair. Fairfax is an American investigating agency which, it was alleged, was employed by V.P. Singh while he was finance minister to detect economic offenders abroad. By the time the story broke out in the course of a raid on the house of a journalist connected with the *Indian. Express,* V.P. Singh had been shifted to the Defence Ministry. There was an outcry that Singh who had wanted to bring within the scope of investigation Amitabh Bachchan, the film star turned politician and close friend of the prime minister, and his brother Ajitabh, had been punished for embarrassing Rajiv Gandhi. The press called Singh "Mr. Cleaner" and Rajiv Gandhi was found to be a little less than clean.

As Rajiv Gandhi tried to ward off this challenge to his authority and reputation by appointing a commission of two Supreme Court judges to conduct an enquiry into the Fairfax affair. V.P. Singh as defence minister dropped a bombshell. He told reporters travelling with him in a plane on official business that in a submarine deal by India with a West German company, an Indian middleman had been paid a huge commission and that he had ordered a departmental enquiry. Rajiv Gandhi had been in charge of defence before V.P. Singh took over and so his name was again brought in. Hardly had the ink dried on this sensational revelation than the Swedish Radio dropped the biggest bombshell. In a broadcast it said that in an arms deal between Bofors, a Swedish company, and India, bribes running into crores of rupees had been paid to Indian officials and politicians. All hell broke loose and the country was in an uproar. The *Indian Express* in an editorial which it carried on its front page said in so many words that Rajiv Gandhi was guilty of corruption and appealed to the president to dismiss him. The cry was taken up by other newspapers and magazines and politicians joined the fray and there was enough and more for the avid newspaper reader to munch and talk about. Rajiv Gandhi was in deep trouble and there were scandals galore which made his position extremely vulnerable. Everyday newspapers and periodicals were publishing interviews with Swedish Radio, Swedish government officials, Bofors company officials and their own interpretations and surmises. But the truth was never established. While it was clear that a huge amount was paid and deposited in a Swiss bank account, it was not known to whom it was paid and why.

The Denial

The government denied that any middleman was employed and asserted that one of the conditions of the deal was that no middleman should be used. Rajiv Gandhi's denials and defence of government failed to carry conviction. Confusion was worse confounded when V.P. Singh resigned from the Cabinet and this was taken by Rajiv's critics as vindictive action against an honest colleague who had exposed shady deals. Even Rajiv's announcement that a Parliamentary Committee would go into the Bofors deal and the charges of corruption did not satisfy the newspaper and opposition critics and they wanted their pound of flesh. A well-known Supreme Court lawyer was given space in the *Indian Express* everyday to put searching questions to the prime minister and charge him with complicity in shady deals of his friends and relatives. This went on for nearly a month and gained wide currency all over the country. This lawyer and another opponent wrote to President Zail Singh asking for permission to prosecute Rajiv Gandhi for corruption. This again brought the president and the prime minister on collision course and the newspapers and journals ran wild with speculation that the president might lake some drastic action against the prime minister. Every day the question was posed: Will he? The situation bristled with graver possibilities when the opposition parties (barring the Communists) and some in the Congress (I) itself pressed Zail Singh to stand for presidentship for a second term. There was a riot of speculation and guessing games in the press on the president's intentions and some overenthusiastic journalists wrote that if Zail Singh contested as an opposition candidate, a sizeable number of Congress (I) members of Parliament would vole for him and ensure his election. Whatever might be the intention of the president, the ground was cut from under his feet by the two Communist parties which rejected his candidature. The other opposition parties were thereupon forced to support the candidate named by the Communists. The Congress (I) members voted solidly for the party candidate and Mr. R. Venkataraman was elected president by an overwhelming majority.

Zail Singh, who had maintained studied silence at the height of the controversy, gave vent to his feelings and emotions a few days before he shed office in frank interviews to three news magazines which made them their cover stories. The future of the Congress (I) and the growing dissidence in the party dominated the news and editorial columns of the Press and when Rajiv Gandhi in his capacity as party president expelled four party MPs including V.P. Singh for "anti-party activities," it was seen by opposition parties and the press as a sign that the party was in shambles and many of them said that the days of the Rajiv Gandhi Government were numbered.

During this exciting drama and bewildering political developments, all in the space of a few months, the press played a major role in gathering, interpreting and presenting the news to a readership hungry for information and to be educated on what was going on. There was partisanship, of course, much disinformation and slanting of news and open accusation of the prime minister without producing evidence, a great deal of speculative reports which passed for hard facts and inviting a credibility gap. But the fact remained that the press was the one source of information for the people (AIR and Doordarshan being tainted as official mouthpieces) and, by and large, this responsibility was discharged by the press with enthusiasm and in a professional manner. Many newspapers and journals conducted Gallup polls with the help of professional marketing research groups in the metropolitan cities on what people thought of the prime minister, his policies, his feud with the president and his party. The results were displayed with great prominence. Columnists, specially those writing for periodicals, came into their own and their analysis and interpretation of current events were read with avidity. Kuldip Nayar, M.V. Kamath, M.J. Akbar and Khushwant Singh have a large circle of readers.

The government's attitude to the press, both at the Centre and in the states has been one of non-interference. There is no sign of open hostility or of benevolence. In at least two states, Bihar and Tamil Nadu, Bills were introduced in the legislature to curb the freedom of the press by the government but they were withdrawn after vehement protests from press and platform by journalist organisations and public bodies. There were sporadic reports of harassment of journalists in some states but what created a sensation and led to countrywide angry protests and demonstrations was the action of the Tamil Nadu Assembly in sentencing the editor of *Ananda Vikatan,* a Tamil weekly, to a term of imprisonment for publishing a cartoon which was considered derogatory of the legislature. The editor's contention was that the cartoon was a humorous drawing and intended to be a joke. It did not cast any aspersion on any particular person or persons. The Speaker of the Assembly sent a warrant for his arrest. The police picked him up as he was returning home from office and drove him to prison where he spent the night as a convict. The entire country seemed to rise in protest at this outrageous action and within 48 hours the Speaker was forced to rescind the decision of the Assembly and order the release of the editor who became a hero overnight.

The Tamil Nadu Assembly's confrontation with the press surfaced again in 1993. A warrant for the arrest of the Madras correspondent of the *Illustrated Weekly of India* was issued by the Speaker of the Assembly on a charge of contempt. It was stayed by a division bench of the Supreme Court. The action was taken against the correspondent for an article he wrote on the proceedings in the Assembly. The press was again involved in a collision with the Assembly early in 1994 when the latter sentenced the News Editor of a Madras Tamil daily, *Dinakaran,* for publishing in his paper the expunged proceedings, but later revoked the sentence. Meanwhile the journalist had gone to the court of law with a writ petition and this provoked the Assembly to reimpose the sentence on the journalist. The High Court, however, quashed the conviction and sentence.

The Indian newspapers and periodicals today are riding the crest of a boom which in the prevailing developing political situation and a new awareness among the rising middle class is likely to persist for a long time. The advantage, as has been noted already, is with language press but the English press is still supreme in many fields and in its resources and respectability. The English newspapers cost more and make a big dent in the domestic budget. But today, the newspaper is a must in the urban areas and the habit is spreading fast to rural areas too. Unlike in the days of colonial rule, the newspaper today is a profitable business and it is being commercialised so fast that the reading public has started complaining that news is being sacrificed for advertisements. The Indian newspaper generally does not carry a full budget of foreign, news not many newspapers have foreign correspondents. Many stop with correspondents in London and Washington and none in Moscow. There is near total reliance on foreign news agencies for what little foreign news is published and there is a virtual blackout of neighbouring countries like Burma and Nepal. With the advent of radio and television which broadcast news bulletins by the hour, newspapers in the West and America have gone in for more indepth and interpretative news presentation and reporting, thus, enabling the reader to understand the background and meaning of news he has already heard on the radio or TV. Not much in this respect has been done by Indian newspapers which repeat the news already purveyed by radio and T.V.

Coveted Profession

Journalism has become a coveted profession in India and the educated youth, men and women, fresh from college are choosing it as a career in larger numbers. Employment opportunities are growing with the expansion of the newspaper industry in diverse fields like film magazines, sports journals and women's periodicals in addition to the regular newspapers and news magazines. The rewards are most satisfying. The emoluments are attractive and the prestige and influence commanded by a working journalist are considerable.

The need to improve it and give dignity and sustenance to journalists who played an important role in the affairs of the nation was realised after freedom was won. M. Chalapati Rau, a great editor (whose profile appears in an earlier chapter) was the moving spirit behind the working journalists movement which took strong roots under his able guidance and stewardship, He founded the Indian Federation of Working Journalists in 1950 and was its president for three terms. He nurtured it and made it strong to fight for the rights of working journalists and for a living wage for them. As a member of the first Press Commission appointed in 1952, he was largely instrumental in the commission recommending the appointment of a wage board for working journalists. The commission found that the emoluments received by journalists were on the whole unsatisfactory. It could not undertake a detailed investigation for fixing scales for different categories of employees. But it recognised the necessity of fixing a minimum wage for journalist employees and made recommendations relating to the minimum wages to be paid to them. The Government of India accepted this recommendation and constituted a Wage Board for working journalists under the chairmanship of H.V. Divatia in 1957. Besides fixing minimum wages for all categories of journalists, the Board brought within the definition of working journalists proof-readers and examiners. This was opposed by some newspaper owners and when the Wage Board's recommendations became law they went to court but failed in their effort to exclude proof-readers and examiners from being treated as working journalists. The Wage Board's decisions came as a boon to working journalists. They were assured of a minimum wage, with suitable grades, to be paid regularly within a specified date every month and their hours of work were fixed and a weekly rest day assured.

A second Wage Board was appointed in 1977 under the chairmanship of Justice Palekar. The Board, however, could not complete its work as representatives of newspaper owners, the Indian and Eastern Newspaper Society and the Indian Language Newspaper Society, resigned from the Board owing to differences. The Government of India through an ordinance in 1979 appointed Justice Palekar as a one-man tribunal to give an award on working journalists wages. Justice Palekar gave his award in 1980 and it provoked opposition from newspaper owners many of whom challenged it in the courts. The Press Commission noted that many small papers had not been able to implement the Palekar award (for journalists and non-journalist employees) and some big newspaper undertakings had also not fully implemented the awards. The commission was told by newspaper owners that the Palekar award would adversely affect the economy of newspapers, especially the small newspapers. Small newspapers told it that with regard to some categories, a small newspaper with a gross revenue of only Rs. 50,000 and a big newspaper with a gross revenue of Rs. 10 lakhs would stand on the same footing. Representatives of the I.F.W.J. told the commission that right from the time of the first Wage Board, newspapers had been saying that they would close down if they had to implement the awards. But, they added, this had not happened and, on the other hand, newspapers were flourishing. There was unrest among working journalists and the I.F.W.J. organised demonstrations and strikes to compel the newspapers to implement the awards.

A third Wage Board was appointed by the Government of India in July, 1985 under the chairmanship of Justice U.N. Bachawat. It presented an interim report in 1986 and recommended interim relief of 7.5 per cent of basic pay. This was considered too low by the I.F.W.J. and other journalist bodies and the matter was raised in Parliament with a demand to increase the quantum of relief. The government announced on May 31,1986, that it had increased the interim relief to 15 per cent of basic pay with effect from June 1 of that year. There were strong protests from newspaper organisations against the government action which was described as arbitrary.

A fourth wage board for working journalists was appointed in August 1994 by the Government of India.

Besides the minimum wages fixed by the various Wage Boards and assured security of service, working journalists enjoy several concessions from the government, both Cenffal and of the States. Correspondents accredited to the Information Bureau in Delhi and to some state governments are allotted government residential accommodation at rents which are very much below the commercial level. In Delhi there is a separate press pool of 110 dwelling units. In many states there is reservation of housing plots for journalists. The Press Commission reported that some state government did not even bother to collect the concessional rent "and the journalists concerned are happy not to pay." The commission expressed its opposition to grant of housing concession to journalists "as we are unable to persuade ourselves that accredited correspondents as a class are more useful to society than teachers or public health staff." Press correspondents are also given travel facilities, free passes on state transport and rail fare concessions. The Tamil Nadu Government has initiated a scheme of pension to old, retired and indigent journalists.

Politicians have sought the favour of journalists in their own way. The *Indian Express* (Madras) carried this item on its front page on July 24,1987, with the heading "Spreading money culture": "Howdoes it cost to get a news item published in a newspaper? According to the Tamil Nadu Congress (I) Committee's Labour Cell it would be Rs. 25. The convenor of the now revived N.C.C. (I) Labour Cell, A.K. Shanmughasundaram, had on Thursday called a press conference at a hotel in Egmore to explain the steps to be taken by the cell to propagate the 'progressive and welfare measures taken by the Congress (I) Government'. At the end of the press conference, as the dozen reporters came out of the hall, two of the cell's low level functionaries were busy trying to distribute plain brown envelopes to the reporters. The contents of the envelope—Rs. 25 in currency notes. The culture of giving 'envelopes' is a recent development in Madras news circles as regards politicians. One has, of course, come across businessmen and film producers distributing such largesse at press conferences."

The working journalists movement in India was unique as it was able to achieve its aims—protection of the rights of working journalists, a minimum wage and security of service—without a struggle, after the country became free. This was largely due to the fact that leaders of the freedom movement and the working journalists had marched hand in hand against a common foe, sharing persecution and suffering for a noble cause. When freedom came, the role played by journalists was readily acknowledged and when the I.F.W.J. was formed by veterans of the freedom battle, there was instant support from the new free India government. Among the early leaders who worked hard to strengthen the movement, besides the founder, Chalapati Rau, were J.P. Chathurvedi and T.R. Ramaswami. The Working Journalists Act of 1955 which they were able to see through on the statute book was unique as there is no similar legislation anywhere in the world for the protection of working journalists. The working journalists movement split in 1971 and a rival organisation called the National Union of Journalists (India) was formed with L. Meenakshisundaram and Pritish Chakravarthi as its chief sponsors. Both the I.F.W.J. and N.U.J. are recognised by the Government of India.

Before independence, there were no institutions to train journalists and journalism was not a course of study in universities. There was no prescribed qualification for a journalist. Anyone could become a journalist who had the during, courage and enterprise. Most newspapers worked with raw hands who learnt as they worked. The great journalists of the past were the products of training in the newspaper by trial and error. The position today is vastly different. Almost every university has a degree or diploma course in journalism (also called mass communication) and many private institutions like the Bharatiya Vidya Bhavan, have sprung up which, with government approval, teach journalism. These universities and institutions send out from their portals hundreds of boys and girls every year as fully qualified journalists. For practical training in journalistic skills, laboratory journals are brought out by the students in universities and other teaching institutions. The Indian Institute of Mass Communication, established in 1965 is a premier institution offering training in journalism and mass communication. Situated in Delhi and administered by an autonomous society and funded by grants by the Ministry of Information and Broadcasting, the IIMC offers courses which comprehend all means of communication, traditional and modern, with emphasis on communication for development. There is also the Press Institute of India which was started in 1963 by some leading newspapers and is affiliated to the International Press Institute. It organises seminars, workshops and courses of study for journalists and those connected with the mass media at different levels. In its own words, its aim is "to provide a professional institute for the training of Indian journalists, for the dissemination of knowledge about better techniques of production and of gathering and distributing news, for elevating the standards of Indian journalism and for training Indian journalists to a high awareness of their responsibility."

At present, facilities for training of journalists in English journalism are more than for language journalism. In many states, reporters and sub-editors of language papers lack training and there is no place where they can be trained. The Press Commission noted that large numbers of female students were joining journalism courses in universities and private institutions and it wanted that "ways should be found to attract trained women journalists in larger numbers to the press, particularly, Indian language newspapers, by providing facilities such as transport to their homes after late duty or night shifts." It suggested the establishment of a National Council for Journalism Training, preferably to be sponsored by the Press Council. It should comprise not only journalism teachers but also newspaper publishers and editors and distinguished men of letters. It said such a body could institute fellowship for training and research, and awards for meritorious performance in journalism on the lines of the Pulitzer Awards in the U.S.A.

Indian journalism is today 200 years old. It has come a long way from the two-page scandal sheet of James Augustus Hicky which passed for a newspaper in 1780 and which introduced an essentially Western media into India. It passed through many stages in its evolution and there were many occasions and periods in its long, chequered career when it was very nearly crushed out of existence. From the very beginning, the alien rulers hated newspapers and journalists but their hatred and contempt for Indian newspapers was more and the fact that Indian journalism survived their concentrated and sadistic onslaught on the press, especially during the freedom struggle beginning from the 1920s, must be considered a miracle and a tribute to the spirit of sacrifice and patriotism of those pioneers who stood shoulder to shoulder with the freedom fighters. With hardly any resources or equipment and with the Damocles's sword of government suppression hanging over their heads, brave men and women came out to spread the message of freedom and to educate their countrymen on what was happening in the country in improvised and badly printed newspapers and journals. Considering the perils and suffering they went through, their achievement was great and noble. Without them, the clarion call for freedom would not have reached the remote comers of the motherland and roused the masses.

Rich Inheritors

The Indian journalists of today are the rich inheritors of a glorious tradition of dedicated journalism, a saga of undaunted courage and determination to fight for a cause, of a noble band of men and women who took Indian journalism to the pinnacle of fame and achievement. We are on the threshold of a new revolution, a revolution in technique and production of the most modern newspaper or news magazine. Great changes have come about in the gathering, style, presentation and interpretation of news. Vast strides have been made in reaching out to the people even in remote areas, informing and educating them on the day-to-day developments in the political, economic and social fields. There is a new breed of journalists, educated and trained, with uninhibited style and curiosity and perseverance who have made today's journalism vibrant and active. The Indian press is now a powerful organ of public opinion and it has come to occupy a position of influence in the body politic. There is greater recognition of its potentialities for good and also for evil. The task before it is immense; it has to serve as a watchdog of the interests of the country and the people and it must expose misdeeds, maladministration, official lapses and social evils without fear or favour and it must present the news with accuracy and impartiality, leaving opinion free. There is a great future for Indian journalism.

As 1994 was coming to a close a matter, agitating the pint media, was the question of entry of foreign publications into the country and its likely impact on the Indian press. Acting on the recommendations Of the first Press Commission, the Government of India had decided in 1955 that no foreign owned newspaper should be allowed to publish in India and those newspapers and periodicals dealing mainly with news and current affairs should not be allowed to bring out any Indian editions. A year later, the Union Cabinet decided that foreign news agencies could avail communication facilities, if they served within India through an Indian news agency. The latter would decide the selection of foreign news and exchange Indian news to them on a working arrangement. For some years, several prestigious foreign publications have been seeking to publish their papers in India with local financiers. The demand has grown especially with the announcement of the liberalisation policy in 1991. A cabinet sub-committee in 1994 is reported to have recom-mended that foreign print media be permitted to bring out their Indian editions while safeguarding national interests. A nation-wide debate has been on since then whether it is in the national interests to allow the entry of foreign print media into the country. On the whole there seems to be greater opposition than support to the issue.

Conclusion

Journalism is both an art and a profession which records events and opinions and seeks to interpret and mould them for the benefit of the educated public. Its history is the story, in the words of an American writer, "of humanity's long struggle to communicate freely with each other, to dig out and interpret news and to offer intelligent opinion in the market place of ideas. Part of the story has, as its theme, the continuing efforts by men and women to break down barriers that have been erected to prevent the flow of information and ideas upon which public opinion is so largely dependent."

Is journalism an art or a profession? This has been the subject of a controversy and the last word has not been said on it. C. Rajagopalachari, the last Governor-General of India, believed it was an art. Himself an outstanding journalist in his later years, he told a gathering of journalists: "I want you to look upon journalism as an art and not as an industry. Journalists are like painters and poets rather than factory workers. They are really creating works of art. When you journalists write an article or a leading article or even when you present an item of news, you are creating a work of art." Rajaji said: "Whatever may be your difficulties, whatever your internal pains and travails, you must look upon what you produce as productive and creative art."

It is, however, safe to conclude that journalism is both an art and a profession. The trend in modern journalism, at any rate in India, is to emphasise the professional aspect more than the artistic side.

Man from times immemorial has been curious to know about the what, why and how of events and objects in places far and near. This lack of information and knowledge, because of a communication gap, he tried to overcome in various ways and the continuous striving and experimentation over a period of centuries produced the journal (recorder of events and views) and the newspaper.

In the olden days, news travelled by word of mouth. Kings and nobles spread news through messengers and through proclamations which were read out in public places. Hindu mythology records the exploits of a one-man oral newspaper who supplied news to both heaven and earth, to gods, demons and humans alike. He was Narada, a *rishi,* who by modern standards must be considered an ace reporter, who was welcomed everywhere, who was a friend of all and enemy of none. He was called a "lover of trouble" *(Kalaha Priya)* and he was the cause of conflict and quarrel in high places which ultimately ended in peace and amity. He was a lover of music and always carried a veena with him. With it he announced his arrival to the victims of his pranks. He had no transport problem. He walked on the clouds and descended from heaven like a glider with the sweet fragrance of his own music. Wherever, he went, the first question asked of him was; "What is the news, Narada?" He was a super-journalist who carried on a one-man crusade against injustice and evil and followed a unique method of provoking conflict so that good might result.

In ancient India, as it is very much in the modern world, what the government (or kings) did, its laws and action against citizens and generally its achievements, formed the staple diet of news. News was given in inscriptions on walls of temples and in copper plates and through victory coins and writings on rocks. There were government officials who by the beat of tom-tom gathered the populace and announced the policies and decisions of the king or government. The King who met his ministers and commander-in-chief daily at a durbar gathered news of what was happening in his kingdom and abroad from his counsellors who were expected to be fully informed of events and public opinion. According to tradition, the very first question the king asked of his prime minister at the *durbar* was: "Well, prime minister, what is the news today?"

In Europe also, news was mainly carried by word of mouth. Kings and noblemen had their own sources of news. Town criers made announcements of local interest. Wandering minstrels, acting as "correspondents" moved from the royal court to another, picking up news of battles won or lost. They gathered useful information for courtiers and merchants and also titbits of gossip which enlivened their stories. They, no doubt, embroidered their news to make a good story as reporters today still sometimes do.

The newspaper as we know it today is of European origin and even there it did not take proper shape until the early part of the 18th century.

Wall posters were the forerunners of the newspaper in Europe and they first appeared in Venice, the Italian city, in 1566. They were called *Notize Scriite* (written notices) and were displayed in public places. A token fee of a small coin called gazetta was levied on those who wanted to read them. This supplied the name of gazettes to the wall newspapers and the word has come down to us even today. They became quite popular and a Venetian magistrate had details of a battle being fought in Dalamatia announced in the wall newspaper. Thirty volumes of these "gazettes" have been preserved in a library in Florence.

Paper, which was first made by the Chinese as early as the second century A.D., did not reach Europe till the 16th century. It is recorded that a member of the Chinese emperor's household used bark from the mulberry tree which he pounded and strained through bamboo screens and pressed into flat sheets and dried.

The Chinese discovered the art of printing also. In 868 A.D., Wang Chieh published a book printed from blocks. Copies of it still survive as man's oldest printed book. The first known use of movable types was by another Chinese, Pi Cheng, in 1045 A.D. The oldest evidence of Chinese printing is a Buddhist scripture known as "Diamond Sutra" dated 868 A.D. The printing was done by carving the Chinese characters in relief (and in reverse) on wooden blocks, then spreading the raised surface of the block with ink and pressing the paper on it. The ink was made from a mixture of lamp-black and resin or gum.

In Europe, a German, Johann Gutenberg, built one of the earliest movable cast metal type printing machines in Mainz in the middle of the 15th century. William Caxton of Kent set up the first printing press in England in 1476, but it was nearly two centuries before the country had a genuine newspaper. Caxton, who was a prosperous merchant, brought printing to England from Bruges in Belgium, 21 years after the first book, a bible, had been printed in Mainz. Caxton set up his printing press in London close to Westminster Abbey and he printed a large variety of books and pamphlets. News, however, continued to circulate by word of mouth or by private or semi-private letters. These newsletters in the 16th century were either those which carried foreign news or those written by "scribes" employed by booksellers in London, to collect items of interest to people who bought them. The foreign newsletters came mainly from Italy which was then a news collection centre. Here news came from all over Europe and was categorised under the names of the towns where it originated. Subscribers to these newsletters, who included statesmen and businessmen from all over the continent, had the newsletters sent them personally. The newsletters ran into eight pages, whereas the London letters containing local news were four pages long.

During the same period there were published what were called newsbooks which looked exactly like any other book of the time. The earliest of those was published in 1513. They were quite small and contained a description of just one but very important event. The title of a newsbook released in 1557 was: *Valiant Exploits of Sir Francis Drake.* Another gave a detailed account of the battle of Flodden and its curious title was: "Hereafter ensue the true encounter of battle lately done between England and Scotland in which battle the Scottish king was slain." Newsbooks became very popular in the 16th century.

In the summer of 1621, a very rudimentary prototype of the modern newspaper appeared in the streets of London. It was a primitive news sheet called coranto. The corantos lacked the regularity that marked a newspaper and they were too specialised in content, but they satisfied a long felt need. It was not until 1624 that the corantos began to be identified by name. One of them was called: "The continuation of our weekly news" and the publisher was mentioned as the office of Bourne and Butter. Initially, the corantos carried only foreign news. The first report of domestic news came with the publication of Parliamentary proceedings by the Westminster clerk in 1628. Out of these accounts developed the "Diurnals" daily reports of local events. Says a writer: "The Diurnals" flourished during the struggle between King and Parliament when it was safe to comment on local news because neither side was strong enough to take punitive measures and when both factions were seeking public support." The oldest known "Diurnal" was John Thomas "Diurnal occurrences" which first came out on November 29,1641.

Anthony Smith has mentioned four stages through which publication of news passed in Europe before the regularity and frequency of publication and the diversity of content generally expected of a newspaper was achieved. The first was (as already mentioned) the publication of a single story known in most of the European languages as a "Relation" or "Relacionn", written so long after the occurrence it dealt with that it often sufficed merely to mention the year in which the event took place. The second stage consisted of a series of "Relations" published in the form of a coranto. On May 22, 1622 there appeared a coranto which described itself as "Weekly News from Italy, Germany , Hungary, Bohemia, the Palatinate, France and the Lower countries." This front page title changed from week to week. Very often one week's issue would begin by describing itself as "Continuation of previous week's." The coranto, says Authony Smith, was an invention of primary importance, for it attempted to provide an account of the entire world and to give the reader the feeling of comprehensive periodical knowledge of world affairs. The Dutch printed the greatest number of corantos which they circulated in many countries and in many languages.

The third stage was the emergence of the 'Diurnal'. The 'Diurnal' gave a weekly account of occurrences of successive days. Robert Coles and Samuel Pecke were the most prominent publishers of the 'Diurnal in English. They devoted themselves largely to affairs of Parliament. Diurnals'- came out in profusion in the 1640s as attention shifted from the Thirty Years Wars, which provided the main news for most of the publications in Europe, to the domestic problems in England which were moving to a civil war. Most of them were described as "A perfect Diurnal of the passages in Parliament," followed by the first and last dates when the events described took place.

The fourth and final stage was the Newsbook, also called "Mercury". The "Mercury" was written by a journalist who tried to attract and maintain an audience for the pecuniary advantage it provided or the political returns it commanded. Even so, the underlying concept remained that of a book of news published section by section. The pages were numbered consecutively throughout the series from week to week until the hazards of war or censorship removed the publishers from the scene altogether. Alongside the Newsbook or "Mercury" there developed the "Intelligencer" which had the flavour of being slightly more official than its contemporary. In German it was called the "Intelligenzblatt". With the advent of the "Intelligencer" a wide variety of subjects was covered, indicating an attempt to add new layers of information or entertainment whenever there seemed to be a demand for them and the supply was at hand.

A new era of journalism was ushered in with the publication of the *Oxford Gazette* in 1655, edited by one Muddiman. It was the first periodical to come very close to a true newspaper. It was printed twice a week by Royal authority and after 24 issues it became the *London Gazette.* It continued to be published right up to the 20th century.

The 17th century saw the establishment of the technical and administrative framework for newspapers in Europe, and the 18th century went on to create the newspaper in its complete form with daily publication and miscellaneous content. The progress, of journalism was speeded up by the development of the party system in government. Parties emerged at the very time when the newspapers came to be a force in the political and social affairs of a people interested more and more in government. A noteworthy fact in the early days of news publication was that it began with a description of events across immense geographical areas and did not confine itself to a small local area. As one writer puts it: "In the societies of Europe, it planted in the mind of the individual literate citizen the picture of a world of public events which he could never see or experience for himself. It placed his own society within the context of the continent and the world."

Once the authorities realised the value of printing and publishing news, they kept a firm grip on the press and nothing could be published without a licence. And that was when the battle started between those who claimed that the public had a right to know and say anything and everything it liked and those who wanted to censor and "use" the press for their own purpose. An English writer described the situation in these words: "The 17th century was a world which presented the writer with two possible dictions: truth and lies. One could not know very easily where truth lay and so authority (whether governmental, traditional or spiritual) had to lead the way. The argument against licensing the press when such was offered, was not an argument against censorship, it was directed solely against a process, which prevented truth and lies engaging in open encounter. The classic Miltonic case against licensing in Areo-pagitica is for freeing the contest so that truth could put untruth into flight."

On March 11,1702, the first daily newspaper appeared in London and it was called the *Daily Courant.* It was produced and sold by E. Mallet but it lasted only for a few days. However, it was revived by Samuel Buckley who made it into a remarkable newspaper. He insisted on a standard of journalism unheard of at that time. He did not want paper to be a rumour mill and was determined that it should report factual news rather than opinion. He was impartial in the publication of news and was careful to indicate the place and date for the news he published. He did this, he said, "so that the public seeing from what country a piece of news comes with the allowance of that Government, may be better able to judge of the credibility and fairness of the relations." Buckley practised what he preached. Himself a Whig he did not slant news in favour of the Whigs although they were engaged in a desperate struggle for power. Printing on a single sheet of paper with the reverse devoted to advertising, he had not much space to experiment in make-up. He used maps and tabulated statistics to explain his reports. The 18th century saw the emergence in England of great writers and journalists like Daniel Defoe, author of *Robinson Crusoe*, Jonathan Swift *(Gulliver's Travels)* and Henry Fielding. Defoe was probably the most important English journalist of that time. He printed and edited the weekly, *Review*. The famous essayists Steele and Addison, started, the *Tatler* and *Spectator*. Dr. Samuel Johnson was going strong with his journals, *The Rambler* and *The Idler*. Johnson himself was one of the early Parliamentary reporters. According to one writer, "the literacy set of the early 18th century was not the only one to find journalism both interesting and profitable; many other later novelists, essayists even playwrights and poets have been found to write for newspapers and to call themselves journalists and over the years they helped to raise the standard of writing and reporting often to great heights."

These essayists and journalists never became full-fledged members of a profession. Journalism emerged historically with regularity of publication. Only when the postal service, printing capacity and supply of material were all sufficiently and consistently developed to the point at which the appearance of the journal as a weekly, tri-weekly or daily could be assured, could journalism be said to have recognisably come into existence. There were no means of checking statements made by any writer.

In the words of a writer: "Journalism does not become professionalised or even occupationalised until it acquires the essential tool of double checking. Until then it remains a mere appendage of printing or in its grandeur forms, a sub-branch of diplomacy".

Politics dominated the pages of the London newspapers in the 18th century and they were involved in the intrigues, corruption and factions of the political system. The pre-occupation of the journalist lay quite outside the accurate reporting of facts. As one observer of the scene remarked: "There were no facts more important, nor more urgent than the fate of factions; it was these that provided the revenue, the market and the intellectual compulsion behind the product. The journalist as a so-distant professional processor of information did not yet exist .....Money could be made by running a weekly journal partly for profit, partly for payment by a group of politicians. Parliament had become a place within which the affairs of the nation were discussed; the power lay outside the chamber as well as in it and Parliamentary discussions required to be spread through the new political world. Ministers might rail against this paper or that and might prosecute for trivial infringements of the complex laws of sedition and libel but political life had come in large part to depend upon its dissemination and extension into the medium of print."

The demarcation of the various functions or jobs inside a journal or newspaper had not yet taken shape. The printer was the chief man although he might not be the sole or even part owner of the enterprise. The editor was no more than a processor of materials. There was as yet no organised or professional group that could provide an accurate and truthful version of events. The technique of reporting fashioned within the newspaper office was still absent. Accounts of events were taken from foreign journals, private newsletters, hospitals, prisons, markets, and courts. Most material which reached the periodical or the newspaper was sent direct by the source. The printer acknowledged the writer's right to express his views by suppressing his identity.

"The press, throughout the 18th century," says a writer, "was at pains to provide a variety of versions of unproven material for the benefit of ideological factions. The very titles of the papers expressed their function as carriers of observations and 'freshest advices' rather than original material. The journalist was not yet a man who went to look, though occasionally he might by chance see."

By the end of the 18th century, England was flooded with newspaper reading rooms, each subscribing up to four score papers. John Doherty, a radical reformer, ran a 'coffee and Newsroom' in Manchester which opened at six in the morning and remained open till late at night with the "most able and popular publications of the day, whether political, literary or scientific, available in a comfortable and genteel apartment" which was "brilliantly lit with gas" in the evening. The ale houses purchased newspapers to attract customers where earlier an inn would have charged for the right to read them. The number of readers of newspapers far exceeded the number of purchasers. In 1878, the *Anti-Jacobin* had 2,500 subscribers but claimed a readership of between 17,500 and 50,000. The press was a more active instrument of propaganda than the platform. William Coblett was among the earliest to exploit the medium of print to build up a radical mass opinion dedicated to dismantling the oligarchic political machinery surviving from the previous century.

According to one historian, the 18th century newspaper had been synonymous with political bribery and journalistic scurrility. It was normal for editors to charge "insertion and contradiction" fees, "a polite euphemism for a system by which anyone could print attacks on his enemies at the price of an advertisement and his enemy pay the editor for the opportunity to return them in kind. Even John Walter I, founder of the *Daily Universal Register* (later *The Times*) made money by this means."

Despite the unsavoury milieu in which the late 18th century press was conducted, by the beginning of the 19th century, important advances were made in the technique of journalism and the production of newspapers. A notable advance was the systematic reporting of speeches and debates. The advent of shorthand transformed the art of reporting into a science. "Shorthand", as one writer has remarked, "was the first of that long series of journalistic techniques which at first seemed to promise the reader the complete recovery of some semblance of reality. A fully competent shorthand reporter seemed to have acquired an almost supernatural power and shorthand was invested with the same kind of social optimism as the microphone and television camera in later times. The acquisition of various systems of shorthand leading up eventually to the universally applicable system perfected by Pitman gave reporters their true mystery. It separated the correspondent from the reporter. It meant that a man could specialise in observing or hearing and recording with precision. It was the promised ability to recover the dimension of reality in reporting that turned it into an occupation. One of the most important divisions of labour within the business of newspaper making had taken place—important because it appeared to satisfy a reader's demand. It gave the reporter an aura of neutrality as he stood between event and reader, it gave him the chance to feel that he represented the interests of the newspaper's clients; it connected the task of reporting to the perspective of experimental science and it gave the writer a tool which enabled him to rise to the status of an engineer and the philosopher."

The newspapers of the mid to late 19th century consisted in very large measure of shorthand reports of speeches—political, religious, scientific or educational. "The basic image which emerges", as one writer puts it, "from the newspaper of the period is of a man on a platform speaking to rows of listeners and reaching a wider public via the shorthand reporter. The reporter became as it were, the principal broker for the substantial discourse of society. In the mid century, the reporter and his notebook bore something of the magic of the new television teams of the 1960s, moving from riot to battlefield, demonstration to sit-in, widely accused of causing the scenes which they recorded and reproduced. In the 1840s and 1850s, the new generation of reporters was credited with having helped to cool the tempers of politics and enabled as it were a national village to develop within which social change could proceed through argument and debate."

The reporter serviced a medium; unlike the author or the printer he was not and could not by his nature be his own boss. The boss was the editor who put him on the job, who commissioned him to report this event or that. The evolution of the editor is a key development in the shaping of journalism as a tool for gathering and interpreting news. It was not until 1802 that the term editor was used to describe the man in charge of a periodical or newspaper. If the word was occasionally used it was only to indicate a subordinate employee working under the printer. He was supposed to collect paid material from the public and he would often stand in for the printer when facing outraged members of the public.

The man who led the way to modern editorship was James Perry, editor of the *Morning Chronicle.* Together with Daniel Stuart and Johan Walter II of the *Times* he professionalised the job of the editor. With him the demarcated role of the editor as the supreme arbiter, short of the owner, was established. The newspaper became an organisation presided over by a man skilled in delegation, arrangement and judgements of various kinds about the world. With the roles of the editor and the reporter becoming distinct entities, the newspaper took on a new shape and form.

The discovery of the telegraph and telegram created further divisions and demarcations in the newspaper. Reporting from more than one place became easier though much more expensive. As one writer remarks: "The telegraph created most certainly a global village but it raised more issues than it resolved when readers troubled to ask themselves whether they were being given a complete and balanced account. The telegraph created a pressure world within journalism. It made possible the idea that a daily newspaper should encompass the events of a day. Henceforward, daily journalism operated within a new tense, as it were, of the instantaneous present."

News agencies helped to speed up the process of supply of

news from all parts of the world. The first Englishman to run a news agency was Thomas Phelippes in the Elizabethan era. Among the first to work on a large commercial scale was Charles Havas, a rich Portuguese merchant who ran a news bureau in France in the first half of the 19th century. His contemporary, Bernhard Wolff, a German Jewish physician, with a strong interest in the money market, started a news service in Berlin. Another competitor, who beat them all to stay in the field was Paul Julius Reuter. Reuter, born in Hesse, Germany, set up his news agency in a small room in Paris with only his wife to assist him. The invention of the telegraph provided Reuter with a splendid opportunity and he opened a small telegraph office at Achen in Holland to supply bankers and merchants with financial information. As more and more telegraph lines opened, his business expanded. When there were gaps between telegraph services, he used carrier pigeons to transmit news. Reuter moved to London in 1850, the year of the Great Exhibition. By 1860, he had established himself as one of the chief suppliers of foreign news to almost every newspaper and periodical in Britain and of news from Britain to continental papers. One of his most famous scoops was the news of the assassination of President Abraham Lincoln of the United States in 1865. The American mailboat was leaving New York as the news broke out. Reuter's representative in the city rushed to the docks as the mailboat was moving away. He took aim carefully at the transatlantic ship buffeted by the waves and hurled his despatch packed in a waterproof canister and it landed on the deck safely.

As the news agencies supplied the newspapers all the news they required of a routine character, shorthand became less and less necessary to the London journalist. Lobby correspondents took over in Parliament and talked to members freely in the lobbies and extracted the news behind the news. Their role has been described by a writer in these words: "The idea was born that beneath the straight reliable account of what was happening in the formal affairs of Parliament, there lay a half-secret, half-conscious world consisting of what was really going on behind the scenes. Reporters who once felt that with shorthand you could capture the essence of the real, now slipped slowly downwards through the professional scale of status, their places at the pinnacle being taken by those who extracted truth from a cloud of obfuscations put up by politicians. Thus, it was in other areas of life. The story lay behind the account of an event. It lay somewhere in the minds of men, however. It could be found and recorded in print, given tenacity and space."

In the newspaper office, the "story" became the basic molecular element of journalistic effort—-a structured nugget of information, the basic unit, through which the reader was to be presented with events. As one writer puts it: "The technique of journalism became analogous to that of fiction and lay partly in the ability to discern those elements which could be made into a transmittable artifact. There was the clear underlying recognition of the audience as a market. The specialism of the journalist and especially of the editor lay in knowing what the market required. News was categorised and pages provided under headings as "Home", "Overseas", "City", "Sports", etc. The "New Journalism" of the 1880s building on the experience of the Sunday press of the mid-century was the first step along the road to the Northcliffe revolution. I recognised that journalism took place within an ever-burgeoning market. The interests of the reader were an unplumbed well which could be explored and re-explored for ever. "Journalism became the art of structuring reality rather than recording it" as has been remarked by one writer.

Journalism now provided, it was claimed, "scope for every type of brain; there was writing for the well-read man, sub-editing for the man of detail, and management for the man of business. The age of specialising left its mark firmly upon the world of journalism. The specialist correspondent closed in on his sources and became an expert in his own right within a given field. His colleague, the non-specialist general reporter was free to pounce upon his subject and extract news."

The greatest newspaper of England, *The Times*, was born in 1784. It was then called the *Daily Universal Register* and it was started by John Walter. The name was changed to its present appellation *Times,* in 1788. It was John Walter II, son of John Walter I who installed the first steam printing press and took the *Times* towards greatness. John Walter I described the function of the newspaper thus: "It would seem that every newspaper published in London is calculated for a particular set of readers only. A newspaper conducted in the true and natural principles of such a publication ought to be the register of the times and faithful recorder of every species of intelligence ... .the general object will be to facilitate the commercial intercourse between the parts of the community through the channel of advertisement; to record the principal occurrences of the times and to abridge the account of debates during the sitting of Parliament."

William Hazlitt, who served on the *Times,* wrote: "The *Times* was the greatest engine of contemporary opinion in the world. It is the witness of the British metropolis; the mouthpiece, oracle and echo of the stock exchange, the origin of the mercantile interest....It takes up no falling causes; fights no uphill battle, advocates no strong principle.... It is ever strong upon the stronger side." Another wrote: "*The Times* took its position just behind the frontline of the middle-class and this became the customary seal from which the political engine of the 19th century paper was driven. It tried to marshal its readers, not goad them. The newspaper, during the era of Revolution, had ceased to be the simple hand-maiden of Parliamentary faction and taken on the mature role of an independent actor in the political world." The *Times* was the first to have its own foreign correspondent in 1807, in Germany. About this correspondent it has been written: "He composed beautifully written, rather leisurely essays, believing that a foreign correspondent's job was to give 'the tone and spirit of his time and place rather than to convey hot news. When he was sent to cover the battle of Corunna in 1808, he based his dispatches mainly on translations from the local papers, then put them on board whichever ship happened to be leaving harbour before amusing himself by associating with the grand ladies and gentlemen of the city. 'However, the times scored with its first and greatest ever special correspondent in 1850, William Howard Russell, who covered many historic events of his day. "His dispatches were read like instant history," wrote an admirer, "and there is no doubt that they influenced and even changed events."

The 1880s and 1890s were the golden age of journalism according to writers and owners of newspapers in England, Europe and the U.S.A. Public opinion appeared to have become the primary force by which society moved and its miraculous dynamism was the end product of the newspaper. W.T. Stead who as editor of *Tall Mall Gazette* and later of the *Times,* pioneered the "New Journalism" of England in the 1880s and prepared the way for the mass newspaper of the 20th century, wrote that the telegraph and printing press together "had converted Britain into a vast Agora or Assembly of the whole community in which the discussion of the affairs of the state is carried on from day-to-day in the hearing of the whole people." The combined operations of a broad electorate, a free platform and a cheap newspaper were widely deemed to have created a perfect mechanism for the governance of society. In the words of W.T. Stead again; "The newspaper is the great court in which all grievances are heard and all abuses brought to the light of open criticism."

Another great editor of that period, C.P.Scott who founded the *Manchester Guardian,* proclaimed the credo of the press: "Comment is free but facts are sacred." He said, "Fundamentally, journalism implies honesty, cleanness, courage, fairness and a sense of duty to the reader and the community. The newspaper is of necessity something of a monopoly and its first duty is to shun the temptations of a monopoly. Its primary office is the gathering of news. At the peril of its soul it must see that the supply is not tainted. Neither in what it gives nor in what it does not give, nor in the mode of presentation must be unclouded face of truth suffer wrong."

In 1815 press freedom in Europe was an idea, a dream, an experiment, a fearful dread; by 1881, it had become an enduring institution, its most admired text enshrined in the French Press Law passed in July of that year. In 1881, Britain also abolished the compulsory deposit required to be made by newspaper publishers and a new libel law was passed which freed newspapers from the fear of prosecution for criminal libel. In the course of six decades the basic pattern of the press was established which has survived into the late 20th century. Everywhere in Europe and America, the mechanical and organisational basis was being laid for the popular newspaper of the 20th century. A much greater range and variety of newspapers was developing than had been ever known before—Sunday, evening, regional, financial, and women's papers—aided by a proliferation of experiments with new techniques and new methods of organising the flow of material through the telegraph, news agencies, syndication and serialisation of fiction.

Across the Atlantic in the United States in the early 18th century, the American colonies presented all the preconditions for the rapid growth of a newspaper industry. They consisted of communities of craftsmen and tradesmen serving rapidly rising populations settling in new areas connected by roads and postal services. Postmasters played a key role in the early development of the American newspaper. They collected news and published them in news-sheets. They occupied a strategic position since they had access to most of the news of interest to the community. They broke the seals of official pouches and were able to publish important official information. They heard much of the local gossip, were in the know of much that happened in the community and were in an advantageous position to make use of their knowledge.

The first American newspaper was printed in Boston on April 24, 1704, and the editor and publisher was Postmaster John Campbell. It was called the *Boston Newsletter.* It was followed in 1721 by the Franklin Brothers' *New England Courant* and Andrew Bradford's *American Weekly Mercury.* The *Boston Newsletter* was printed on both sides of a sheet and consisted of items taken from incoming London newspapers, already weeks old. Since Editor-Publisher Campbell did not have space for all the news from Europe, he put aside left over items for use in a future issue. This meant that some of the news which the reader read was more than a month old. However, Campbell was able to publish local news more promptly. He cleared all his items with the state governor or his secretary before publication and that made his paper libel-proof, censor-proof and well-nigh reader-proof. Although it was the only newspaper in the colonies for many years, Campbell did not have enough subscribers to make the paper profitable. His circulation seldom exceeded 300. But he had a strong sense of responsibility to the readers and he continued to bring out his newspaper in spite of public apathy and financial strain. In one issue he apologised for misplacing a comma in a previous issue although this was only a drop in the sea of errors.

The first daily newspaper was started by Benjamin Towne in Philadelphia, in 1783. Called the *Pennsylvania Evening Post,* it had a brief existence of 17 months. By 1800, most big ports and commercial centres in America had daily newspapers. In 1820, of the 512 papers that were being brought out, 24 were dailies, 66 were semi-weeklies or tri-weeklies and 422 weeklies. They were patronised by the more prosperous citizens and the price was more than the average citizen could afford.

A new era in American journalism began on September 3, 1833, with the publication of the New York *Sun* by Benjamin H. Day. It was printed on four pages, each about two-thirds of the area of the modern tabloid page. The front page was three columns wide and devoid of any display. The stories featured were local happenings with the emphasis on news of violence. Most of what was published was trivial, flippant but it was highly readable and it was priced just a cent (penny). Within six months, the *Sun* had a circulation of 8,000, nearly twice that of its nearest rival. Human interest stories were a speciality of the *Sun*. It became the newspaper of the common man, especially the labour class which was coming into its own during this period. While the penny newspapers reached out to the common people as no other medium could, they were not of a high standard. In the words of an observer: "The student of journalism will look in vain for any profound expression of political philosophy in the early editions of the penny press but after the first wave of sensationalism, these publications began to offer information of a more significant type and readers began to show a little more interest in the Government they had the power to control."

It was during this period that the worlds's greatest newspaper, the *New York Times* was born. Its first issue which came out in New York on September 18, 1851, was called the *New York Daily Times.* Its publishers were Henry J. Raymond and George Jones. Its price was a cent (penny) and it was a paper of the masses from the beginning, but it eschewed the sensationalism of the *Sun* and other contemporaries. Its editor wrote: "We do not mean to write as if we were in a pension unless that shall really be the case and we shall make it a point to get into a pension as rarely as possible." The *Times* specialised in foreign news and Raymond, its editor, gained a reputation as a reasonable and objective editor. He developed what was called "reasonable decency" in public reporting. The *Times* was invariably fair in its writing and it avoided personal invective. It gained the confidence of its readers by its technique of careful reporting and it was wedded to accuracy. It soon came under financial strain and the man who rescued it from the verge of bankruptcy in 1896 was Adolph's. Ochs who bought it and guided its destinies until his death in 1935. Under his stewardship the *Times* became a great newspaper with an international reputation,

Ochs, who started life as a worker in a press in Tennessee, came up the hard way. In a declaration of his principles, he said, "It will be my earnest aim that the *New York Times* gives the news, all the news, in concise and attractive form, in language that is Parliamentary in good society and give it as early, if not earlier, than it can be learned through any other reliable medium, to give the news impartially, without fear or favour, regardless of any party, sect or interest involved; to make the columns of the *New York Times* a forum for the consideration of all questions of public importance and to that end to invite intelligent discussion from all shades of opinion. On the death of Ochs in 1935, his son-in-law, Arthur Hays Sulzberger, took over. The *Times* ranked first in public opinion polls on newspapers and has continued to hold its place in the forefront of American journalism by maintaining its tradition of giving the news with completeness and integrity.

Another great newspaper publisher of this period was Joseph Pulitzer, who has been called the leading American editor of modern times. He published the *Post Dispatch* of St. Louis in 1878 and in a statement of policy, said: "The *Post Dispatch* will serve no party but the people, be no organ of Republicanism but the organ of truth; will follow no causes but its conclusions; will not support the administration but criticise it; will oppose all frauds and scams wherever and whatever they are; will advocate principles and ideals rather than prejudices and partisanship." When he was nearing retirement in 1907, he wrote in his paper: "I know that my retirement will make no difference in its cardinal principles, that it will always fight for progress and reform, never tolerate injustice or corruption, always fight demogogues of all parties, never belong to any party, always oppose privileged classes and public plunderers, never lack sympathy with the poor, always remain devoted to the public welfare, never be satisfied with merely printing news, always be drastically independent, never be afraid to attack wrong, whether by predatory plutocracy or predatory poverty."

Pulitzer's immense energy and his highly developed journalistic sense enabled hint to adopt and to develop in his own way the publishing concepts and techniques of his time and to satisfy his passionate desire to win unquestioned recognition as the builder of the brilliant staff and the complex mechanism of a great modern newspaper. His true greatness lay in his high-minded conception of a newspaper's role, particularly in exercising editorial leadership and in the way in which he made that conception live in the newspaper. Not content with reporting the surface news, Pulitzer told his staff: "Never drop a thing until you have gone to the bottom of it." His watchwords were: "Continuity, continuity, continuity until the subject is really finished." This resulted in the paper's determined crusading in the public interest with an intensity heightened by Pulitzer's personal involvement.

Pulitzer considered the day a loss if his paper did not have one distinctive feature—a crusade, public service or big exclusive story. He wrote once in the *New York World* which he bought in 1883 and made into America's largest circulated newspaper: "A newspaper should seek what is original, distinctive, dramatic, romantic, thrilling, unique, curious, quaint, humorous, odd, apt to be talked about without shocking good taste or lowering the general good tone and, above all, without impairing the confidence of the people in the truth of the stories or the character of the paper for reliability and scrupulous cleanness."

At the turn of the present century, American newspapers were able to produce well over 100 pages in some of their issues. From 1910, off colour printing became possible and colour was extensively used in display advertising.

Today, in America, the traditional definitions of a newspaper are being modified and expanded to accommodate changes in society, reader demands and new technology. But the traditional roles remain too. In the words of an American writer: 'The newspaper is historian, reporter, analyst, communicator, salesman and advocate. Information is the staple of any good newspaper. But most hope to influence their readers as well as inform them. Newspapers influence through their total presentations and their image in the community and not through their advocacies alone."

Modern technology in newspaper printing and publishing has reached stupendous proportions with the advent of the electronic era but in 1820 printing a newspaper was a hazardous job and posed many problems. Before 1860, newspapers were being produced through single stamped sheets and in that year rolls of paper were used successfully to make the printing of newspapers easier. Four thousand copies reeled off the machine without interruption from rolls of paper three and a half miles in length.

The American inventor, Richard Hoe, in 1840 developed the first version of the rotary press which he sold to a Paris newspaper. He found a way to fit the printed type round a cylinder which was then inked by automatic rollers, while four smaller cylinders brought the sheets of paper into contact with it. More cylinders were added later meant a greater number of copies could roll down the rotary. The lino-type machine which set up type and which revolutionised printing was not in the market until 1892. It was originally made by Ottman Mergenthaler, a German emigrant to America. The problem of printing continuously and simultaneously was solved by Hippolyte Marinioni who demonstrated his advanced rotary press in the Paris Exhibition in 1869. This model turned the roll of paper back on its path enabling successive sheets of large or small size to be printed on both sides and then cut and folded into piles of completed newspapers, all at great speed.

Bibliography

Almond, Gabriel A. and Coleman, James S. : *The Politics of the Developing Areas,* Princeton University Press, Princeton, 1960.

Almond, Gabriel A. and Verba, S. : *The Civic Culture: Political Attitudes and Democracy in Five Nations,* Princeton University Press, New Jersey, 1963.

Baehr, H.: *Women and Media,* Pergamon, London, 1980.

Bailey, Thomas: *The Man in Street,* Macmillan, New York, 1948.

Bell, D.: *The Coming of Post-Industrial Society,* Basic Books, New York, 1973.

Bell, D.V.J.: *Power, Influence and Authority,* Oxford University Press, London, 1975.

Bell, Daniel: *The End of Ideology: On the Exhaustion of Political Ideas in the Fifties* (Rev. Ed.), Macmillan, New York, 1962.

Blumer, J.G.: 'The Political Effect of Television' in Halloran, J.D., *The Effect of Mass Communication,* Leicester University Press, Leicester, 1970.

Chaffee, S.H. and Berger, C.R. : *Handbook of Communication Science,* Sage Publications, Beverly Hills, London, 1987.

Cohen, B.C.: *The Press and Foreign Policy,* Princeton University Press, Princeton, N.J., 1963.

Cohen, S. and Young, J. : *The Manufacture of News,* Constable, London, 1973.

Czitrom, Daniel J.: *Media and the American Mind: From Morse to McLuhan,* University of North Corolina Press, Chapel Hill.

Davis, Dennis K. and Baran, Stanley J.: *Mass Communication and Every Day Life—A Perspective on Theory and Effects*, Woodworth, California, 1981.

Davis, Howard and Walton, Paul : *Language, Image, Media*, Basil Blackwell, Oxford, 1983.

Davison, W.P.: *Mass Communication and Conflict Resolution*, Praeger, New York, 1974.

De Fleur, M.: *Theories of Mass Communication*, David Mckay, New York, 1970.

Deutsch, K.V.: *Nationalism and Social Communication*, MIT Press, Cambridge, 1966.

Dexter, L. A. and White, D.M. : *People, Society and Mass Communication*, Free Press, New York, 1964.

Dube, S.C.: *Communication, Innovation and Planned Change in India*, International Development Institute, East-West Center Press, Honolulu, 1964.

Eaman, Ross A.: *The Media Society: Basic Issues and Controversies*, Butterworths, Toronto and Vancouver, 1987.

Eisenstein, E.: *The Printing Press as an Agent of Change*, Cambridge University Press, New York, 1978.

Febvre, L. and Martin, H.J.: *The Coming of the Book*, Verso Edition, London, 1984.

Feliciano, G.D.: *An Overview of Mass Communication Research in Asia*, Papers of the East-West Communication Institute, East-West Center, Honolulu, 1973.

Fiske, J.: *Introduction to Communication Studies*, Methuen, London, 1982.

Gaulding, Peter, Murdock, Graham and Schlesinger, Philip : *Communicating Politics: Mass Communications and the Political Process*, Leicester University Press, New York, 1986.

Gerbner, G. : *Mass Media Policies in Changing Cultures*, Wiley, New York, 1977.

Gurvitch, M., Bennet, T. and Woollacott, J. (eds.): *Culture, Society and Mass Media*, Methuen, London, 1982.

Hagen, E.: *On the Theory of Social Change,* Dorsey Press, Homewood, Illinois, 1962.

Hopkins, M. W.: *Mass Media in the Soviet Union,* Pegasus, 1970.

Katz, E. and Szecsko, T. : *Mass Media and Social Change,* Sage Publications, Beverly Hills and London, 1981.

Kelley, H. H.: *Prime Time—The Life of Edward R. Murrow,* Little Brown, Boston, 1958.

Kraus, S., and Davis, D.K.: *The Effect of Mass Communication on Political Behaviour,* Pennsylvania State University Press, University Park, 1976.

Lakshmana Rao, Y.V.: *Communication and Development: A Study of Two Indian Villages,* University of Minnesota Press, Minneapolis, 1966.

Lucian W. Pye : *Communication and Political Development,* Princeton University Press, Princeton, New Jersey, 1963.

McQuail, D.: *Towards a Sociology of Mass Communication,* Collier Macmillan, London, 1969.

Mendelbaum, S.J.: *Community and Communicating,* Norton, New York, 1972.

Nimmo, D.D. and Sanders, D. : *Handbook of Political Communication,* Sage Publications, Beverly Hills and London, 1978.

Paletz, D.L. and Entman, R.: *Media, Power and Politics,* Free Press, New York, 1981.

Peterson, R.C. et al.: *The Mass Media and Modern Society,* Holt, Rnehart and Winston, New York, 1965.

Pye, L.W.: *Communication and Political Development,* Princeton University Press, Princeton, 1963.

Schramm, W: *Mass Media and National Development,* Stanford University Press, Stanford, 1964.

Voos, H.: *Organizational Communication: A Bibliography,* Rutgers University Press, New Brunswick, N.J., 1967.

Williams, R.: *Television, Technology and Cultural Forms,* Fontana, London, 1975.